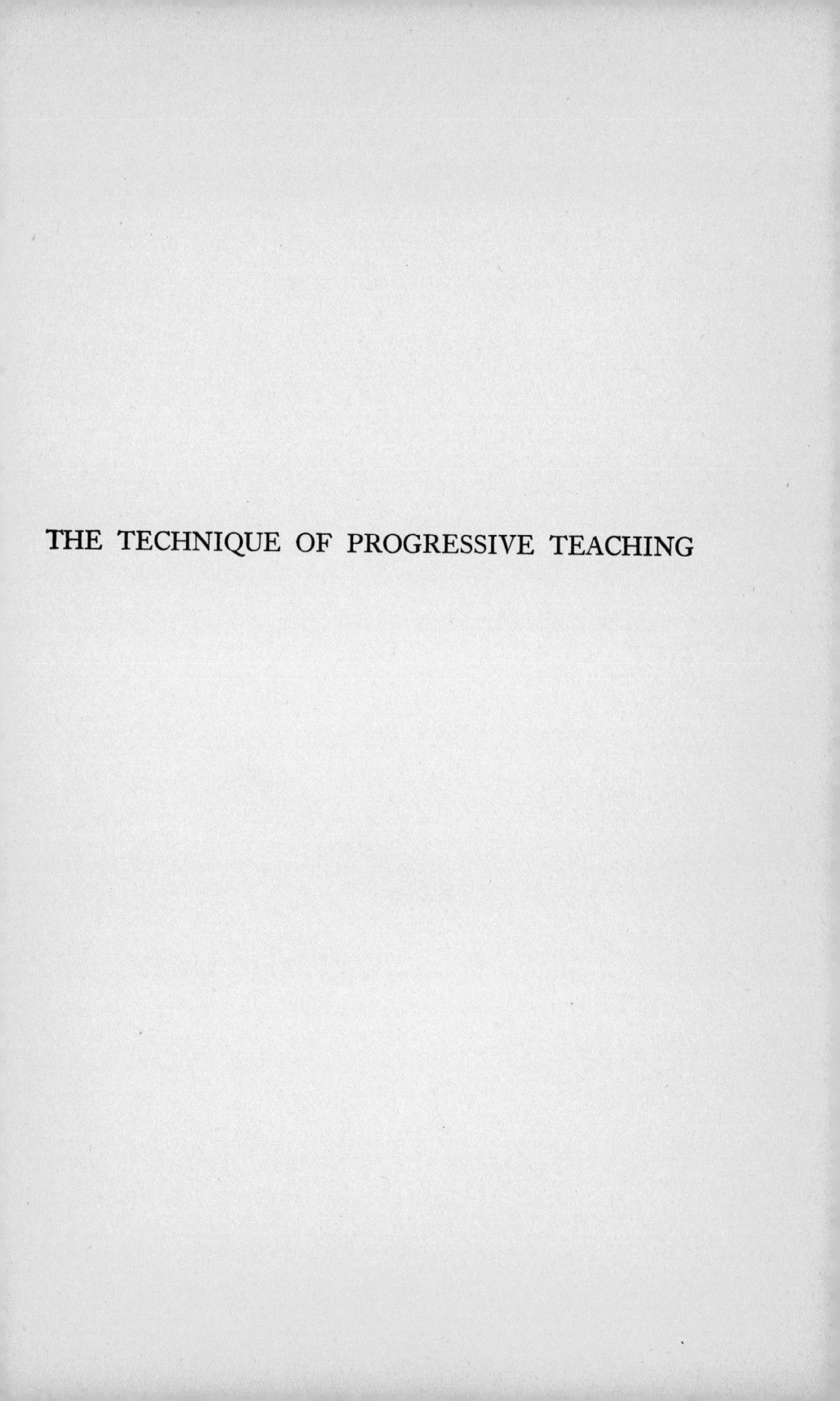

THE TECHNIQUE OF PROGRESSIVE TEACHING

The imaginative play of these grade one children developed into a little community. First came the home, then the grocery store, and the theatre, and finally in the Spring the flower shop. It is the class of Mrs. Cowan in the Public Schools of Englewood Cliffs, New Jersey.

THE TECHNIQUE OF PROGRESSIVE TEACHING

by

A. GORDON MELVIN

SCHOOL OF EDUCATION, THE COLLEGE OF THE
CITY OF NEW YORK

AUTHOR OF "PROGRESSIVE TEACHING"

THE JOHN DAY COMPANY

NEW YORK

COPYRIGHT, 1932, BY A. GORDON MELVIN

SECOND PRINTING, NOVEMBER 1933
THIRD PRINTING, OCTOBER 1934

MANUFACTURED IN THE UNITED STATES OF AMERICA
FOR THE JOHN DAY COMPANY, INC., NEW YORK
BY J. J. LITTLE & IVES COMPANY, NEW YORK

TO A PROGRESSIVE TEACHER

MY MOTHER

FOREWORD

So rapid is the spread of the progressive movement in the schools of the United States that everywhere supervisors are urging their teachers to adopt newer ways of doing things. In many cases, however, the teachers concerned are at loss where to turn for assistance. In the meanwhile there is danger lest urged on by eager supervisors teachers may blindly adopt mechanical and formal methods—"projects" which are teacher-dictated and "activity programs" which are a mere succession of artificial prescribed "units."

This book has been written as an attempt to be of help in this situation. It is hoped that both teachers in training and teachers in service will find here a description of the newer teaching which will meet their practical needs. It attempts to set forth the philosophy and the technique which will enable them to develop and administer an activity program which is no formal array of imitative procedures but which is organically developed, new and ever changing.

To the very many classroom teachers from whom the writer has sought guidance he is deeply indebted. Their advice and the activities of their classrooms have contributed more to this book than the words of philosophers. Particular thanks are due to Miss Emily Ann Barnes of the Lincoln School, Columbia University, Miss Margaret Batten of the Bronxville Public Schools and Mrs. Lucy Sprague Mitchell, formerly of Public School 41, New York City. Many others have helped in the improvement of the manuscript. More than to any one else the writer is indebted to his friend and Dean Dr. Paul Klapper for numerous and invaluable suggestions. Special thanks are also due to Professors W. C. Bagley and Thomas Alexander of Teachers College, Columbia University, Professor W. H. Burton of the School of Education of the University of Chicago and to the writer's colleagues, Professors Samuel B. Heckman and Egbert Turner and Dr. Harold Abelson.

A. G. M.

CONTENTS

CHAPTER		PAGE
I.	Perils of the Educative Process	3
II.	Changing Schools in a Changing World	6

PART I
BASIC THEORIES OF TEACHING

III.	The School as a Place for Living	19
IV.	The Significance of Differing Points of View of the Newer Schools	37
V.	The Unit of Living	45

PART II
THE FUNDAMENTALS OF TECHNIQUE

VI.	The Technique of Teaching	61
VII.	The Fundamental Bases of Technique	68
VIII.	The Nature and Function of Interest	73
IX.	The Technique of Environment and Equipment	83
X.	Interest Centers in the School Environment	94
XI.	The Selection of Units of Conduct Suitable for School Life	98
XII.	The Nature of Curriculum	110
XIII.	The Teacher's Use of the Curriculum	124

PART III
THE TECHNIQUE OF CLASS MANAGEMENT

XIV.	Problems and Techniques of Class Administration	137
XV.	Further Problems and Techniques of Class Administration	158

x   CONTENTS

CHAPTER   PAGE
XVI.   CLASS DISCIPLINE AND ORDER 177
XVII.   BUILDING ORDER IN THE SCHOOL 189
XVIII. SOME SPECIAL PROBLEMS OF THE TEACHER 210

PART IV

TECHNIQUES FOR DIRECTING LEARNING

XIX.   TECHNIQUES FOR DIRECTING LEARNING 223
XX.   FURTHER TECHNIQUES FOR DIRECTING LEARNING . . . 240

PART V

THE TECHNIQUE OF CLASS TEACHING

1. TYPICAL FORMS OF ENTERPRISE AND THEIR GUIDANCE

XXI.   TYPICAL FORMS OF PUPIL ENTERPRISE AND THEIR
        GUIDANCE 257
XXII.   GUIDING INDIVIDUAL CONSTRUCTION AND EXPRESSION . . 263
XXIII. GUIDANCE FOR INDIVIDUAL MASTERY 283
XXIV.   THE DIRECTION OF PLAY 303
XXV.   GUIDING GROUP CONSTRUCTION AND EXPRESSION . . . 310
XXVI.   GUIDING THE GROUP SEARCH FOR KNOWLEDGE . . . 323

2. TEACHING PATTERNS

XXVII. TEACHING PATTERNS 334
XXVIII. TEACHING PATTERNS (*continued*) 353
XXIX.   TEACHING PATTERNS (*continued*) 362
XXX.   THE RECORDING AND REPORTING OF TEACHING PATTERNS . 377

3. WIDER IMPLICATIONS OF TEACHING

XXXI.   THE LIFE OF THE WHOLE SCHOOL 382

LIST OF ILLUSTRATIONS

A CLASSROOM COMMUNITY . . . . *Frontispiece*

                                                                                                   PAGE

THE SHADY HILL SCHOOL 86

JAPANESE LIFE IN A THIRD GRADE 112

A FIRST GRADE IS A HOME FOR THE THREE BEARS 194

AT THE FIRE HOUSE 340

THE TECHNIQUE OF PROGRESSIVE TEACHING

CHAPTER I

PERILS OF THE EDUCATIVE PROCESS

WHAT is more discouraging in history than the way in which, again and again, the human spirit is freed from its shackles only to be more tightly bound by its very liberators? So the glorious burst of freedom which heralded the Renaissance in the voice of Petrarch died away in the pretentious artificialities of decadent Humanism, and the Reformation's zeal for educational development dwindled to the pettiness and narrowness of the classical gymnasium. Even before any movement for the rebirth of a new spirit in the educative process is well under way, forces seem to develop which tend to formalize and mechanize. The forces which tend toward such a hardening of the teaching process seem to be numerous and inevitable in their action. It therefore behooves teachers and those concerned with the development of the new teaching to be more than usually careful to avoid any situations which will make of the new teaching an artificial thing, and rob it of the flexibility and fluidity which is vital.

Nor is this any plea for lack of system and order in the organization of curricula or of schools. These matters must not be confused with class teaching. With all the system and order of a well-organized school system behind her, the teacher must yet avoid mechanical teaching. Teachers who carry on in new ways cannot be too clear upon the fact that their teaching, if it is to be genuinely progressive, must not be imitative in any gross sense, nor mechanically patterned upon that of other teachers. Rather must it be the result of an intelligent and carefully developed personal philosophy of teaching, which interprets actual teaching situations in the light of previous knowledge and experience. The essence of the new teaching is often its ephemeralness, its merely temporary validity, its actual dependence upon its own transitory characteristics. The new teacher must realize that she cannot do artistic teaching if she is hampered by the numerous forces which make for the stereotyping and mechanizing of teaching. It is not enough for the teacher to value her freedom. She must fight for it.

The Web

Public school systems in many places today are bound in a net of tradition and established ways of doing things. The teacher finds herself caught in a web of time-tables and systematic groupings, of statistical reports of administrators who don't use them, of supervision, of regulations, and of academic prejudice. The new teacher longs for freedom. She is anxious to teach well, she is able to teach well, but her wings are caught and damaged in the web of an antiquated system of school administration. Let us as teachers come out frankly and claim our freedom. We have no longer any faith in a blustering form of supervision which places the clerical and fiscal aspects of school life above the art of teaching. There is rising a new type of administrator for the new schools—no longer a boss who dispenses jobs and whips his teachers to work by making their positions dependent upon his favor. He is rather a helper, an inspirer, one to whom teaching is really an art, one who is in awe of the good teacher, and ever ready to respect and serve her. He is ever willing to allow teachers freedom even to make mistakes, and is willing and eager to help detect and correct them without signs of rebuke. It is such men who are needed to fight the battles of the new teacher and the new school, because they, too, are teachers at heart, and are fired with a true zeal for their community, its children, and the teachers of them.

The Development of New Modes of Teaching

The good school administrator, like the good teacher, realizes that the good school must ever be, to a certain extent, an experiment. If society were static and the world unchanging, the problems of school keeping might be solved and systematized. In a changing world, however, school life must also be ever changing. There must be a flux of school and community life. So the teacher must ever be making new efforts and interpretations, must ever be considering new plans and fresh ways of doing things. As school life develops, and as her own thinking changes, she must continually be developing new modes and working out new techniques.

It would be a serious mistake to think that the present modes of the new teaching are anything more than the earlier attempts to develop new ways of teaching. The progressive movement is but now taking shape and form, and many of the problems involved in its development are only now becoming clear. Teachers need not fear that there is no further opportunity to contribute in the interpretation of the new philosophy in the schools. On the contrary, such active development is only beginning, and the rapid spread of the new movement will stimulate thinking and practice to such an extent that many new modes and techniques will appear. As thinking proceeds, and new progress is made in the science of education, new developments are sure to follow.

The Teacher's Faith

Through it all thousands of new teachers will find in teaching the thrill of real adventure. Beginning with an unfaltering faith in children, faith which is not a sentimental belief that children are naturally right, but rather a deep-seated realization of their unfailing eagerness and power to learn, many a teacher will set forth not knowing the way clearly or fully, knowing only the journey's end. The way would be blind indeed, however, were it not for one other great faith: faith in our human experience and heritage, cultural, ethical and spiritual. To be without this second faith is to be immature, and cynical, and unstable. Without this faith, one had better not become a teacher. With it, the adventure becomes more thrilling and more precious as it develops in surprising and exciting fashion. So the teaching process moves forward in its breathless way until the teacher's faith is reborn in the lives of children.

CHAPTER II

CHANGING SCHOOLS IN A CHANGING WORLD

It is beyond doubt that we are entering a new era in the art of teaching. So distinct is the new teaching from the old that differentiation becomes contrast rather than comparison. This new teaching takes its widest issue from the old in the matter of the child's attitude toward the learning process. The old school proceeded upon the supposition that children do not like to learn, and that learning is both unpleasant and unnatural to them. To this point of view the new teacher gives no quarter, for the new teacher is firmly convinced that children are not merely willing, but actually eager to learn, and furthermore, that learning is easy and natural for them. So the teacher's function is no longer that of a task-master, but that of a catalytic in the learning process. The old teacher's greatest problem was to compel children to learn. The new teacher has no such problem; instead there are new problems of allowing children to learn best things in best ways.

How Old Is the New Teaching?

"There is no new thing under the sun." By the same token there is nothing old but lethargy and decay. It is when we stand still that we begin to die. The new and the old have existed side by side since the world began. This is well illustrated by one real glimpse into the past. On one occasion I was traveling in a small fisher boat through the canal from Kingchow to Kingmen in the interior of Hupeh. The sun was setting over the Chinese farmlands, with their blossoming peach trees, and the light was reflected from the ancient city wall and from the glassy waters of the canal. Silently the boats of the fisher folk pushed off from the shore, and a net shot out with a splash. All was centuries old. It was a world of a thousand years ago, and yet it was today. Certainly the newest things are not the most recent in time. To be old is to stand still; to be new is to grow, to be a changing thing in a changing world.

It is in this sense that we speak of the "new" teaching. So it is that there were new teachers long ago; as long ago as Socrates and Aristotle. But for the roots of the so-called new teaching, we look back to the days, perhaps of Rousseau, certainly of Pestalozzi, the inspired teacher who taught first and theorized afterward, the radical who discovered how to teach without books by means of activities. Once he had discovered the new path others might follow if they would. But there were few to follow. For Pestalozzi wrought better than he knew; too well for his own time, and too well for our time, when many play lip-service to his ideals but draw back from putting them into practice.

Continuing through the last part of the eighteenth century, Herbart, Froebel and their followers learned from the master, and interpreted, enriched and amplified the earlier work. Particularly did the mystic Froebel, perhaps because he was a mystic, see deep into the life of children. Timidly school men followed the lead. A kindergarten was set up here and there, by way of a sop to the idealists. But the great majority either failed to understand or could not be convinced. It remained for Dewey to interpret, clarify and modify for our own times the teachings of the great reformers, and to become the inspirer of a host of teachers.

These teachers sometimes style themselves "progressive." The term deserves passing notice. It is not an especially good term, but what term would be? It is not fully descriptive, and is therefore subject to the misuse that falls upon terms which need technical definition. It has been used in educational literature for years, and was chosen by the founders of the Progressive Education Association in 1918 as a word suitable to indicate the best things in modern education. It is in this sense that it is intended to signify continuous change and adaptation. It implies the active attitude toward teaching. It indicates not merely that teaching of today should be different from and better than that of yesterday, but that the teaching of tomorrow should be different from and better than that of today. It denies the validity of fixed formulæ in teaching. It is intended to provide for years to come, for continuous revision and improvement.

The term "progressive" is never intended here to indicate alliance with any particular unchanging creed or cult. The history of creeds and labels gives ample reason to fear that the term "progressive" may become limited in its meaning to describe a movement local in time and fixed in characteristics. The greatest care needs to be taken lest any such congealing process vitiate the meaning of the word. There is already evidence that certain so-called progressive teachers are making distinctions among themselves in terms of "more progressive," "less

8 THE TECHNIQUE OF PROGRESSIVE TEACHING

progressive," "rather conservative," and "reactionary," the standards of judging being those of their particular cult. Such teachers are static and merely propagandist. They are beginning to make their own modes the norm for judging others, that is to say they are non-progressive. If the word "progressive" means anything that is worthwhile, it means truly scientific in the sense of being willing to face truth, long known or newly discovered, and acting upon it. It is used in no other sense in this book. It is not intended to indicate any narrow, fanatical or unchanging point of view. It may include those who move slowly because they carry heavy responsibility and cannot wisely risk an untested program, others who dare a little more, and most daring of all, those who are not afraid of danger in the search for ways that are new and valuable. Such teachers are in direct line of descent from Pestalozzi, Herbart, Froebel and Dewey. Let those who would cast stones at these men cast them at the new teacher, but let those who reverence the great reformers hold their peace.

POVERTY IN PUBLIC EDUCATION

There is a group of educators who respect and admire the work of reformers, old and new, but who feel that the ideals of such zealots must be toned down to meet the practical situation. The practical situation is to these men dollars and cents. They are in historic line with figures and costs, a trend far different from that of progressive teachers. Public education was conceived and brought up in poverty under economic stress. In New York, for instance, public schools were early sponsored by the Free School Society and made possible by the invention of Lancaster, which enabled one teacher to handle a thousand children. Education became so cheap that public education became feasible. Educational administration became the savior of public education. The systematizer, the fund raiser, the foreman became the controlling agent in these earliest days and to some extent remains so today. Traditionally the system has needed a man of ability to help raise money which the public has reluctantly supplied, and to arrange a system to operate within the budget. The growth of public education was a continual battle against poverty.

But the days of pioneer poverty are over in the United States, and with them passes the glory of the systematizer and the mechanizer. The real problem is no longer merely that of finding an energetic leader to draw a large salary because he bosses a large gang, but a new and far more complex problem, first of securing the best young people of the country for teachers, and second of training them fully and richly.[1] The teacher must become the true servant of the child, and the administrator the servant of the teacher.

THE NEW TEACHER

The new teacher is no longer the type so ignorant, untrained, and inexperienced that a foreman-supervisor is necessary to control her and keep her in order. The new teacher is an artist. In calling her so we need make neither reservations nor apologies. It is only necessary to enter her schoolroom, to watch her artistry.

Take a glimpse of the new teacher in her classroom. This classroom with its colors, its curtains and its vital living atmosphere, is a veritable studio. The teacher herself is a woman of wide experience and culture. If there be such a thing as the artistic temperament she is more than likely to have it. Talk to her about teaching and watch the animation in her face as she converses. Hear what she says about her school. She loves her work and is absorbed in it. To her it is an adventure. "Teaching is so exciting," she says.

THE NEW CLASSROOM "LESSONS"

Perhaps you wish to see this teacher teaching. You want to see "a lesson." Probably you expect to find the children in her classroom sitting listening to her, while she stands before them and talks, or tells them what to do. Possibly it is your notion that if she carries on this way for a half an hour, busying herself and her class with problems in addition, she is "teaching," the children are "learning their lessons," and the lessons are the customary "arithmetic" or possibly "spelling." If such are your preconceptions, you will be little prepared for what you do see; little prepared to see the children active and moving about engaged in different tasks, and the teacher sitting still, talking to a child who has come to her. There is no "lesson," there is no "teaching"; and in these lower grades you cannot label what it learned during some given half hour and call it smugly "arithmetic," "geography" or "music."

In fact it is most difficult to describe what you will see in terms which will be familiar and easily understood. A major difficulty in

[1] To W. C. Bagley, more than to any other contemporary educator, must go the credit of realizing and emphasizing the fundamental nature of this problem.

doing so arises from the fact that whole class "lessons"[2] do not begin and end with regular time periods as they do in the orthodox formal school. If you must have "lessons," then you must conceive of them in terms not of what the teacher teaches, but of what the child learns. He learns to do what he does. If you must observe "teaching" you must observe it not in terms of what the teacher makes the child do, but in terms of what the child is being assisted in by the teacher.

You may observe a group of fifteen seven-year-olds who are this morning particularly interested in preparing a birthday luncheon for one of their members. One cannot fail to be enthusiastic about a birthday celebration, and any one who knows anything about preparations knows how much work they involve. It is a time for special effort and the laying aside of more regular routine tasks. The luncheon has to be prepared—red tomatoes stuffed with salad, and various other things to eat. They have to be set in readiness for lunch hour, for today the children will lunch together in the classroom and not as usual in the lunchroom. Plans must be made, so, of course, the children talk things over together with the teacher. Doilies must be cut and favors arranged for. Decorations also have to be prepared. Water color pictures will be useful, and some boys set about making them; the girls are more inclined to make dolls of colored yarn for favors.

They are particularly interested in dolls just now. They have been interested in dolls for some days, and in the dolls' costumes. They have made a trip to the museum and collected some information about the way the people of different countries dress. Most of the children are going to make dolls and dress them in various native costumes. Thus it becomes fascinating for them to learn how people who dress in these different costumes actually live. Soon it will be Christmas time and surely any one would want to know how these children in other lands keep Christmas, if they keep it at all. Then there are stories about peoples of other lands and a hundred and one things which might prove of interest in days to come.

You may see what the children are doing today, but if you want to see what they are doing tomorrow, you will have to come back again to find out. Such things cannot be clearly foretold before they hap-

---

[2] Burton points out that "the European use of the word *lesson* has usually indicated the treatment of a whole topic as differentiated from the American usage indicating a daily recitation." See BURTON, W. H., "The Nature and Direction of Learning," D. Appleton & Co., New York, 1929, p. 270.

CHANGING SCHOOLS IN A CHANGING WORLD 11

pen but only carefully reported when they are over. If you insist on knowing with any degree of completeness what kind of things the children do, it will not be possible to find out from a mere examination of classwork for twenty minutes or an hour at a time. Twenty minutes chosen at random from living do not give a cross-section of the life of any individual or group. It will be necessary to study full length reports of class activities extending through periods of days or weeks. Such teaching patterns are presented at length in Chapters XXVII, XXVIII, XXIX of this book. They may be consulted at this point if the reader feels that a more concrete account of procedure in the new schools is essential for a clear understanding of what follows. Otherwise they may be left until they are presented in logical sequence in the chapters which follow.

THE NEW SCHOOL

The new teacher is the maker of the new school. And the new school, which is so different from the old, actually looks different. It is a walking-about school rather than a sitting-down one. The children in it may be doing anything that it is good for children to do. It is not an institution run by regulation and rule, but a community of self-determining children busying themselves about dozens of things. It is not a room with rows of seats where children stay still by the hour; it is, on the contrary, a social organism in which the individual has great freedom to develop in and about buildings, around town, and, best of all, often outdoors in the country.

In order to provide a more complete notion of the kind of thing which children in such schools are likely to do, the following account is given of part of the work which has been done from time to time in the Ojai Valley School, at Ojai, California. The quotation taken from the school announcement is prefixed with a warning that the account is not a fixed program, nor should it be supposed that all the topics or types of work enumerated would be taken up in the course of a year, nor that other topics not mentioned would not arise as school life develops. The account given is a compilation of records of past work rather than an account of work which will be taken up in succeeding terms. Suffice it to say that in the course of a year the children of the school will be sure to have some such rich series of experiences which cannot be forecast in detail, but which will be worked out as the days go by to fit the particular situations and conditions which arise from the children's living.

GROUP I (*Ages 5 and 6*)

The children in Group I are the youngest in the school, five and six years of age.

Their daily life is an active, informal one. They sing, dance, work in a garden, take care of pets, build houses, churn, weave, draw, paint and model in clay. They listen to stories, learn poems, dramatize and make up their own songs, stories, poems and plays. They keep store, buy and sell the necessary school materials. They take walks, and bring back interesting material for observation and study.

These children come to school with many experiences and interests. The school utilizes these, organizes them and builds further on them.

Following the play instinct of "keeping house" the children furnish a large playhouse. A rough shelter against sun and rain, large enough for the group to occupy, is constructed. Fires are built and a feast prepared.

The Indians who occupied this valley only a hundred years ago have left their implements behind, so that a newly plowed field may yield treasures of stone arrow-heads, mortars, stone-axe heads, etc. Such material fires the imagination and the children ask pertinent questions and learn about these people. Many visit the pueblos of New Mexico and Arizona, and come back and play Indians in song and dance.

Out of their garden activities, care of pets, and walks in the hills and fields, grows an intimate acquaintance with earth, plants, animals and their relationships, habits and adaptations of life.

Many stories and poems are learned and dramatized.

The techniques of reading, writing and arithmetic are not emphasized during this year, but introduced incidentally.

GROUP II (*Average Age 7*)

The school-day of the children in this group continues, as in their first year, to be filled with activities important to them.

They spend considerable time in the textile room. The weaving of small mats and rugs on simple looms and of a larger rug for the first grade playhouse, arouses an interest in textile materials, including clothing. Then follows the shearing of a fleece and the washing, carding, spinning, dyeing and weaving of wool to make a tiny wool blanket for the doll-bed in the same playhouse.

The children take excursions to visit goats on near-by ranches, and, in the spring, to see the goats and sheep sheared. They read together descriptions of shepherds and shepherd peoples and their geographical environment;

they listen to poems and stories which lend greater significance and charm to their own experiences. The many pictures which they paint, and the scenes, with clay-modeled figures, which they set up, are largely inspired by these excursions, and by this particular literary material.

This group also assumes the care of a small flock of chickens. This year they were fortunate in having presented to them one laying hen for each child. There is a feeling of individual ownership, but, since the hens are kept together and cared for by committees appointed by the group, the social motive is strong. Each child who acts on a committee (and every child in the group is at some time appointed) is responsible to the others. This care of chickens demands the keeping of records, the making of reports to the group by committee members, the study of the best living and feeding conditions for the hens, the buying of their food supplies, and the marketing of eggs. Of still greater importance, it stimulates in a most natural and effective way a feeling of responsibility toward animals. No excuse, no matter how plausible it sounds, is a vindication of failure to care for them, once that responsibility is assumed. Yet, their care, under these school conditions, is seldom an irksome responsibility.

For these seven-year-olds, even reading has assumed almost the natural importance it has for the grown-up. "Will you teach me to read?" is not an unusual request at this age, provided children have already been filled with a love for that which books contain for them. And so mature is their understanding of what reading means, that the teacher may present all the phases of learning to read, including phonics, with perfect confidence that the child understands and can immediately use such learning to further his own reading ability. At the age of seven, learning to read seems a pleasant thing. Almost no use of charts or other learning-to-read devices is necessary; hours of drill are eliminated. Children read for content almost at once.

Writing, too, when begun with seven-year-old children is a means of expression almost from the first. Our school-made books relating to the activities of the room, contain labeled pictures, simple records, even original poetical expressions, inspired by the experiences of the group. "This is a sheep farm," "A man driving goats," "This tent you see is Abraham's tent" —are the titles under pictures in some children's "Weaving Books."

As for arithmetic, it, too, has importance for the children themselves. The actual demand made by the care of chickens; paying for feed, selling eggs (which includes knowing current prices), making change—in a word caring for our real business affairs—makes necessary from the children's own point of view, the learning of much arithmetic. Their own business dealings with the school-store makes similar demands for the learning of number facts and of the simple processes of adding and subtracting.

In general these children as well as the six-year children investigate and study their own world; but in this second year of school they begin to acquire those tools of learning—reading, writing and arithmetic—which will make possible a continued, wider, and more independent investigation as they grow older.[3]

A Visit to a Modern School

Go to such a school some morning and see what is going on. If you get there early enough you may find some of the children in assembly, holding a meeting which belongs to them, where they entertain one another and make their own announcements. Assembly being over, remain in the auditorium a while to see the stage being used by a class rehearsing for a play they intend to give. "When the other children come back from the mumps we are going to play it for the higher assembly," one of the children reports. The stage, set between walls of wainscotted oak, is hung with a curtain in lieu of scenery, and is suffused with colored light. In its center a Viking boat, in which three boys are sitting, is being pushed across the stage. This is the last act of a play which the children have written, based on their study in a book of Viking tales.

Ask a question or two if you can find a pupil who is not too busy to talk.

"What do you do here in school? Play all day?"

"Oh, no. It's not all play. There's music and we have Viking tales, and the Days of the Giants. On Thursdays we have this [dramatics], and we have art in the afternoon and we have arithmetic, reading, map work and diary and poems."

"Do you like your arithmetic?"

"Fine, yes."

"Do you have any English?"

"Sometimes—write stories and things like that."

Perhaps these words about the orthodox school subjects may be reassuring. When you pass on to the classrooms, you will have the promise fulfilled by seeing some children working problems at their wooden tables, while others may be engaged in making things—a sword, a shield, a great map on which several coöperate. Passing from classroom to classroom, you may find the little ones dancing or playing with their big blocks and materials, resting, having lunch, or washing their hands. In other rooms children may be engaged with saws, hammers and planes on some precious objects they are anxious to make, a bird perch or a toy wooden engine. Here a little girl may be copying

[3] This quotation is from the announcement of the Ojai Valley School, Ojai, California, April, 1928.

a poem she has written, while others may be painting or sewing. It is a busy world and a happy one both for the teacher and the children.

WHAT THE NEW SCHOOL IS NOT

But with all its activity and all its motion and bustle, it may be somewhat of a mystery. Visitors to such active schools often carry away with them numerous wrong impressions. It may therefore be well to mention briefly some of the things which the new school is not, and some of the things which it does not stand for. Thus the ground may be cleared for the later discussion of what it is, and how it is maintained and carried on.

In the first place, in spite of careless statements sometimes made, it is not a place where children do whatever they like. Children may be given great freedom of choice as to the time and manner in which they shall learn certain things, and some degree of choice, the amount of which varies with different schools and different teachers, as to what they shall learn in certain fields of activity. But there is no school in the land where a child with destructive tendencies is allowed to develop them nor any in which in the course of their elementary school life children are not expected to learn to read, to spell and to add. And there is never likely to be any such school.

In the second place, it is not a school in which there is no discipline. Grown-ups who are used to lock-step schools sometimes gain the impression that because children are moving about, talking, and active, they are therefore disorderly. It does sometimes happen that there is disorder in any school, but there is likely to be less in the new schools than in others. Nor is the discipline which the children undergo less rigid or less potent because it is self-imposed. In a school which is well conducted the children actually behave *themselves*. Furthermore, they willingly take up tasks which impose upon them the severest discipline.

Nor is the new school a school which is all play. It is true, especially for the small children, that there is a great deal of play, and there is some play for large and small. But for children play is often one of the best means of learning. In the properly organized school there are many other activities in addition to play activities. What play goes on exists not because of any idea of sugar-coating the learning process, but because of its real educational value. The justification of play is not that it is pleasant but that, under certain circumstances, it is the best and most natural way of learning.

The New Teaching Technique

Having given this brief description of what the new school is and what it is not, these pages will attempt to offer a fuller and more concrete account of the nature of the new teaching and of its technique. For ten years or more teachers have been working out new ways of teaching, and little time, comparatively speaking, has been found by any one to examine what they have been doing, or to make their findings and their modes of teaching known to hundreds of teachers who are eager to learn what has been discovered. The new teaching has only now reached the point where it may be regarded objectively and called good. It has but recently passed through its initial stages of experimentation and emerged with anything like distinctness, even to the most watchful observers. Little has been written in a form which would make available to teachers in training the results of the new developments. Consequently an attempt is made in these pages to present an analysis and interpretation of what has been going on.

It is imperative that in these changing days teachers should make every effort to keep up with the rapid progress which is taking place on every hand. It is the teacher's duty to help mankind to win the "race between education and catastrophe." To do so is but to keep faith with generations of progressive teachers who have given us of their best.

Part I
BASIC THEORY OF TEACHING

CHAPTER III

THE SCHOOL AS A PLACE FOR LIVING

IT SEEMS advisable, before going on with the more concrete matters with which it is the purpose of this book to deal, to present some account of the general theory which governs the development of the progressive movement. This is difficult for several reasons. In the first place the matter must be briefly presented. Furthermore, the case is one in which Philosophy has outsped her lingering handmaiden, the Science of Education. For years scientific educators have concerned themselves chiefly with school problems which have arisen under a very different régime. Such investigators are only now beginning to be conscious of the challenge of the new teaching, so that the dicta of scientific authorities in this realm are comparatively few, and objective definitive judgments in the form of the results of experiment are far from copious. Nor should it be supposed that the problems of interpreting in school practice the ideas here set forth are by any means settled or solved. They are merely in process of solution, of fuller, wider and more understanding application in the development of superior teaching. In the meanwhile much for which glib scientific justification may be sought must be taken on the testimony of teachers and those who have actually been engaged in working with children.

We should not be too ready to admit that the professor's lecture room and the scientist's laboratory are the only places from which valid educational judgments may be issued. We have, perhaps, tended to rely too much on academic interpretations of professional educators whose work sometimes smacks more of statistical processes than of contact with schools and children. We have too often neglected the judgments of teachers themselves, persons who are actually engaged in teaching children. We should not underrate or underestimate the cogency of the positions set forth in this chapter because they have been formulated not merely on scientific evidence but, where this was inadequate, on wide and careful study of class practice and consultation with many teachers. In spite of these various difficulties involved in setting forth the progressive position, it is nevertheless presented in this chapter because it seems essential to a clear and logical development of the material of the whole book.

A Fundamental Point of View in Education

We are tempted, by the simplicity of the phraseology, to choose as the fundamental statement of the educational philosophy of the modern school the well-known aphorism, "education is life." If we must confine ourselves to three words in setting forth a fundamental point of view in education, in all probability this is the best we can do.

Like all catch phrases, however, this one depends for its validity upon the interpretation we place upon it. If we are to force it to logical extremities we may simply invert it and say, with syllogistic precision, "therefore, life is education." Thus is revealed the inadequacy of any mechanical or narrow interpretation of the original phrase as a basic concept of school life.

Yet the limitations of this phrase are only partial. If we do not force it to a logical *argumentum ad absurdum*, but interpret it as any wise writer would intend it to be interpreted when applied to the school, it is most valuable. We might then find ourselves able to say without reservation that the activities of the school should be the living of the children. Consequently we regard a school as a community, in which children are living complete individual lives, yet lives which are harmoniously adjusted to the group with which they mingle. We must be duly cautious in our realization that this is child life, not adult life. Thus we might re-state our original proposition as applied to the elementary school by saying that elementary school education is children's living. This brings home to us the fact that the living which goes on in school is really the beginning of living. It is not merely life but it is in the most obvious and direct sense a preparation for life. Thus we may not say that education is life and not a preparation for life. Rather we must say that education is life which is a preparation for life.

Definition of Education

The process of defining education is a popular and an ancient one. In spite of this fact it is really impossible to define education. It is one of those vast, living, great things which are beyond definition. The

THE SCHOOL AS A PLACE FOR LIVING

meaning of education has been misrepresented by every definition which has ever been devised. And yet we can define it with reservation. If we are willing to recognize in our definition an attempt to guide and not to stultify our thinking, we may formulate a tentative definition. It is really in this sense of agreement upon terms to be used in discussion that writers have defined education.

The historic definitions of education are numerous. Each writer has formulated his definition in his own way. Klapper provides a very satisfactory and adequate analysis of historic definitions and conceptions of education. He classifies them thus: (1) Education as harmonious development, a conception which we associate with ancient Greece; (2) Education as the acquisition of the spiritual inheritance of the race, a notion of education which is a result of the vast accumulations of knowledge which have come down to us from the ancient world, from medieval scholasticism, and from modern science; (3) Education as economic preparation, a point of view which is associated with the rise of democracy and the new emphasis placed upon the individual by the Renaissance and the Reformation; (4) Education as habit formation, the contribution of our present-day school of physiological psychology; and finally (5) Education as complete socialization, the most modern of these five ideas of education, one which is associated with the social outlook which has been characteristic of modern peoples during the fifty years preceding the war.

It is clear that while all these definitions have a real contribution to make toward our total conception of education, today they are all outmoded. The newer world in which we live is one that is characterized by ultra-modernization, increasing consciousness of world-unity, unprecedented complexity. These characteristics of modern society are all directed to the production of incessant change. The morning paper, once a luxury for the town gossip, the medium for the leisurely essays of a "Spectator" or a "Tattler," is today a rapid and drastic necessity. In this kaleidoscopic society we need a daily check-up on the doings of the world. But this is merely indicative of the changes which occur in our ways of doing things. The problem of today is no longer merely that of learning a few specific skills, habits and attitudes which will equip us for life. It is in addition the problem of securing the power to continually change and adapt our skills, habits and attitudes in the light of newly discovered knowledge and invention. We must learn to change ourselves to meet the world's changing complexities.

Education as Adjustment

Where, then, shall we find a conception of education which will cut across all the others, a notion which will not commit itself to any, and yet provide for all? Some have sought this notion by defining education as adjustment. Education is the adjustment of the individual to social life. If in this notion of adjustment we include the attainment of the power of *readjustment* we have a fairly workable definition of education, workable chiefly because it is so noncommittal, so meaningless, and so flexible. It gives little idea of a definite aim, end, or method of education.

Education a Process, Not a Result

This flexibility of the notion of education as adjustment and its refusal to set up a definite end or aim are among its virtues. It is important to avoid any tendency to regard education as a result. The idea of an education as a concrete residuum which is left over when the process is completed is a common misconception of the man in the street. It is associated with his opinions of what his son should get in school, and explains why in country districts the school house is sometimes referred to as the "knowledge box." There a child is expected to get something definite—knowledge, earning power, learning. An education is something to be secured much as one purchases a bar of soap in a shop. But education is not such an objective, concrete, material and static result. It is a process. The educated man is one in whom something is going on, because a process which has been begun is continuing. Thus, to define education as adjustment, while it is comparatively meaningless, is in this respect true to the nature of education.

The Aim of Education

This conception of education as a result rather than a process is connected with discussions which are frequently held concerning the aim of education. The figure of speech which is inherent in the use of the term "aim," does considerable violence to the actual nature of education. It is a figure derived from archery, from the custom of shooting at a target. Now it is clear that the target is something very concrete and real. Furthermore, it is not merely the target that is aimed at, but a point at its center. This is the utmost in definition.

THE SCHOOL AS A PLACE FOR LIVING

The whole process of shooting is to culminate at one point, the center of the target, and that objective defines with clarity the whole process of shooting. Such a conception is false to the nature of education. There is no single definite end point to the educative process. What we desire to secure by means of education is much more like a talking picture than a point on a target. Yet even this figure misrepresents the meaning of education. Certainly the careless use of the word "aim" in educational discussion is most disorganizing and disturbing to our educational thinking. The use of the term "adjustment" to describe education by recognizing that education is a process rather than a result has the additional virtue of avoiding this fallacy.

Education as Magic

Another misconception of education which is altogether too common, even among those of considerable schooling and ability, is that education is a form of magic. To send a person to school is thus a substitute for consulting a palmist or phrenologist, or listening to an astrologer on the radio. The teacher is a magician who is in possession of certain cabalistic secrets which he will reveal to initiates. Education is esoteric. The elementary school teacher can equip a child to earn a living by delivering to him the "open sesame" of the business world. The high school teacher will reveal to the boy the formula by which he may secure a white collar job, while the college professor is a master of the inner secrets, those mystic and possibly diabolical devices which give man mastery in a hostile world. The term "adjustment" helps thinkers to avoid any such shallow point of view. It emphasizes the fact that mastery of the environment comes not by the potency of hidden magic but by the slow and natural process of gradual changes in personality.

Adjustment Through Living

Unfortunately, however, the term "adjustment" gives no light on the method by which it is to be attained. Thus we are reënforced in our belief that what is needed is not a definition but a conception of education. We must interpret and amplify the meaning of any definition until it provides us with some notion of method and procedure. Consequently we must place some interpretation upon the word "adjustment."

The term "adjustment" takes on its fullest and richest meaning when we regard living itself as a process of securing adjustment. It is only by adopting such a complex notion of adjustment that we are able to derive a sufficiently fluid yet obviously definite notion of what should go on in school. In other words, the process of adjusting in school should be a foreshadowing of the process of adjustment in our great society. School life and life in the world should be made continuous. The school should be a group of children generating and carrying on a well-balanced program of living. It is only thus that children may secure a preparation for well-balanced living in the community. A school which is the living of the children may be affected by that same ultra-modernization, that consciousness of world unity, that complexity, that same incessant change which characterizes the world in which the children are living now and will live in the future. By a complex program of well-balanced living, adjustment is made to the present world and preparation is at the same time made for future adjustment. Thus the least common denominator between the school and the world is no longer a seriatim compilation of knowledge but a form of conduct. Specific subject-matter objectives become less important, and generalized attitudes, ways of doing things, and the power of ever fresh change and adaptation, become an integral part of the educative process. So if we are forced to conclude with a definition to be used as a basis for interpretation and discussion we may say that *education is a process of adjusting the individual to the world in which he lives by a well-balanced program of living.*

An expansion of the notion of the living of children which leads on to further living is to be gained from the following quotation. Here Miss Pollitzer gives an excellent picture of school life organized on the child's level in terms of conduct in such a way that it grows and contributes to the life of the adult.[1]

"The idea of a school world isolated from the world outside is not to avoid reality, but to give the dawning consciousness of the child a chance to meet reality on its own terms. A world that is real for the child is child size. He can manipulate the materials he finds there. He may indulge in his own curiosity. He may pry and poke, and put together, or take apart. He can work out his imaginative fancies in concrete material, or in games and plays with others who share his interests. The inhabitants of his world are of the same size, and approximately the same level of ability. Within these limits, however,

[1] POLLITZER, MARGARET, "Education for Creative Living," *The World of Tomorrow*, May, 1924.

it is composed of all varieties of human beings, with their varying interests, special abilities and divergent points of view, all asserting themselves.

"In many ways, then, it mirrors the world of adults. But here is what most 'grown ups' are apt to forget—that their world is seen only from the under side by a child. He has no chance to take active part in this life. Rather, he peers up into this strange world of giants, and wonders what it is all about. The ability to meet reality means meeting one's own problems on a realistic basis. Hence, if at each level a child has a chance to propose and solve problems of vital importance to himself, gradually he approaches the point of having adult problems to solve, and of meeting them in a mature way. From year to year, occupations, standards and techniques evolve, quite simply and naturally through different age levels. The individual baby learns to play with a small group, and consciousness gradually widens until first the school, later the community, is included in the individual's concepts and relations. In the same way, the scope of the educational content widens until first the school, later the community, is included in the individual's concepts and relations. In the same way, the scope of the educational content widens from such activities as imitating life at home, and building miniature cities in blocks, to combining chemicals in the laboratory, or inquiring into the origins of human customs and languages."

BASIC PRINCIPLES OF TEACHING

In harmony with the fundamental principle of education through living are a number of other principles and practices which have been variously expressed by different teachers. These ideas have sometimes been loosely formulated and over-enthusiastically set forth. For this reason it seems wise, after careful study, to re-state them in a form which will preserve their fundamental relation to the basic philosophy from which they are derived, but which will not violate the recognized scientific foundations of education. With these principles, as set forth below, most thoughtful teachers would probably find themselves in agreement, although some of them may not be accustomed to expressing themselves in such conservative terms. It has seemed expedient to tone down some of the more extreme statements of writers in this field in the hope that rhetorical values may still be made subject to scientific moderation without the sacrifice of basic educational worth.

Children Learn as They Live

Without going to the extreme of saying that "education is life," we may yet recognize what is too obvious to be gainsaid; namely, that children learn as they live. Consequently, when the living of children is restricted, when it is limited to some one or several phases of their being, there is a corresponding limitation in the development of the whole child. For the child's personality is an organic whole which develops through natural and normal living. It should not be unduly analyzed and divided into separate strands or segments for purposes of separate unrelated training. This position, which has been reënforced by the integrating viewpoint of Gestalt Psychology, is well set forth by Sir Percy Nunn, Principal of the London Day Training School for Teachers: [2]

"For reasons, some historical, others philosophical, the teacher under the old régime was prone to consider that he was concerned only, or mainly, with the 'mind' of his pupil. The distinction between mind and body is, of course, a very ancient, as well as a very important one, but since Europe imbibed the philosophical doctrine of René Descartes there has seemed to be so profound a difference between the two that men have come back to think of them as distinct entities, brought together in an indestructible way in each individual person, but wholly diverse in nature. Thus education, as I have said, became conceived mainly as the business of training the mind, and from that conception the aridity and artificiality of the old education followed inevitably.

"The New Education, in distinction from this philosophy, insists on thinking of the pupil as a whole. While recognizing that his being has, so to speak, its mental or spiritual end and its bodily end, it refuses to accept the Cartesian separation between these. To use a pregnant term of the English philosopher Bosanquet, it regards the young human being as a 'body-mind' which grows as a whole and is to be educated as a whole."

The position set forth above has been violated when schools have attempted to educate children piecemeal by piecemeal living. When, for instance, they have been kept in schools which have cared for their mental development but have regarded it as separated and unrelated to their physical development; when they have taught children arithmetic, reading, and spelling, and have kept them sitting in their seats for hours; when they have given them mental training in the school subjects and neglected to care for their health. Again, children have

[2] NUNN, PERCY, *The New Era*, London, October, 1929, p. 205.

been taught arithmetic which they have had no use for, either because they were too young, or because the arithmetic itself was of little use in life activities. They have been trained to write sentences but not friendly letters, to write compositions isolated from their own ways of thought and from any intention to make use of them. In short, they have been taught in ways which have been segmented and scattered because they have not been unified in life molds or related to life situations.

Children should be allowed to live fully and naturally, to develop and grow by enjoying self-initiated and consequently unified experiences. When, for example, a child makes a small castle of clay to be glazed and sent as a present for a friend to use in his gold fish bowl, the activity has all the implications of life and is unified by the child's original self-initiated drive, the desire for a present to give his friend. The case is similar when a child writes to invite his cousin to a class play, takes the guinea pig home from school to feed and care for during the Christmas holiday, or makes a library study of the Olympic games to present to a class interested in Greece. Such unified experiences may be called whole-activities. They are whole because the child, having enlisted himself in their behalf, executes them with his whole being rather than merely with his mind or his body, or some part of him for which training is, as it were, administered locally. Such whole-activities are to be found in abundance in spheres such as the home, the community and the out of doors. Consequently the school should be first of all like a home, secondly it should be a social group, a community in little, and last it should be as much as possible outdoors in a natural environment.

1. *The School as a Home*

It is useless to suppose that the school can take the place of the home. Nevertheless, it must be regarded as an extension of the home. Children now spend in school many of the hours which once were spent at home under parental care and in simple home duties. Surely it would be a pity if the children from the homes of the best and wisest parents should leave home for school and live in an environment where the culture and refinement of their own homes were absent. And that children, who have not such homes, but whose homes are barren in opportunity or ideals, should not find any home life in school, would be equally tragic. Certainly there is something about the good home which gives to children an invaluable training.

One of the most eminent educators in the United States, who was commenting on the serious situation brought about by the wide use of machine labor and the crowding out of men and women from laboring work into more intellectual occupations, was asked:

"What is the significance of the change for education?"

"It means," he replied, "that we must find a way to make children's minds grow."

"But how are we going to do that? What is there that will do it?"

"Well," he replied, carefully weighing his words, "good homes do it. I'm convinced, for one thing, that good homes do it."

There are many others who share this same conviction. In the first place, in homes children carry out whole-activities: simple tasks, unified bits of living which are so obviously related to their own lives and to living as to be pursued actively and naturally. Here we have no chopped off bits of subject matter, no unrelated chunks of learning, but living, pure and simple. Again, in homes which are worthy of the name, we find high ideals. It is in homes that children learn to talk, to use language that is good or bad, to enunciate clearly and purely or in slovenly fashion. It is from their parents that children learn those fundamental habits of homely and decent living, such as washing their hands before meals and paying their bills, of unselfish helpfulness, of economic integrity. Still further, what the schools have well-nigh forgotten is that in the home the child learns the things of the spirit, the love of beauty and the practical significance of religion. It is these things which explain the statistics that we sometimes see concerning the success in life of children from the homes of clergymen and missionaries, a class of men obviously no better mentally endowed than educated men in the other learned professions.

The home is a powerful factor in the life of the child. But all children do not come from good homes. Consequently, it is all the more necessary that the school should supplement home life and be like a good home. For, in those remarkable words of Dewey, "What the best and wisest parent wants for his own child, that must the community want for all of its children."

2. *The School as a Community*

There is great danger of excessive individualism in any theory of education which lays great stress upon the development of the child. It is necessary therefore to be quite clear upon the fact that the child's personality should grow in modes which are not merely his fullest self-expression, but which also contribute to the welfare of his fellow beings. If he is to live so throughout his life, he should begin to do so during childhood. Consequently, school should be a community similar to the larger community of grown-ups, but on the child's level. For the community is another of those spheres in which men are engaged in whole-activities. Here again is no arbitrary and unrelated conduct. The things men do are related to themselves and their modes of living, to their needs and desires. If school living is like community living, if the school is a real community, we will find children doing such things as keeping the class accounts, making their own toys, and sweeping up the floor when they finish. This is living an integrated life. This is community living.

3. *The School Outdoors*

The school outdoors is a far-away ideal. Can it be farther away in the future than it is in the past? The outdoors is the natural birthright of children which grown-ups took away from them when they put them into school buildings. Of course, there is but a restricted outdoors in a city like New York, which indicates that living in New York is far from natural. Even in that city there will doubtless come a tendency to spread out pan-cake fashion like Toronto or London. In the meantime, while some teachers are holding up their hands and crying "obviously impossible," teachers in other parts of the country are actually holding school out of doors a large part of the time, and even in sections of New York City children spend some part of their school hours out of doors.

It is out of doors that we find people, especially children, engaged in whole-activities. Children who are free in the country pick flowers and climb trees, search for wild strawberries, swim, and build. It is experiences such as these which should make up a great part of living in and out of schools.

Children Learn Best by Their Own Self-sustained Efforts

This is no new doctrine. It is based on Froebel's conception of the self-activity of the learner which has been widely accepted and expounded by educational authorities.[3]

---
[3] For excellent treatments of this subject see KLAPPER, P., "Contemporary Education," D. Appleton & Co., New York, 1929, Ch. XV, p. 323, and BURTON, W. H., "The Nature and Direction of Learning," D. Appleton & Co., New York, 1929, p. 69.

30   THE TECHNIQUE OF PROGRESSIVE TEACHING

It has been too often supposed that children learn by the efforts of the teacher. The new schools by laying the burden of the learning process on the child challenge him to put forth the effort required for mastery. The old type school was too often a place of idleness. It was replete with opportunities for inattention, day-dreaming and even for disorderly activities. It is responsible for untold hours of wasted time. Some years ago, I sat at the back of a classroom in one of the largest cities in Canada, a city painfully proud of its schools which are distinctly of the old régime, and watched pupils in the back seats eating oranges, passing notes, and reading cheap novels while the teacher was standing in front "explaining" with excellent clarity and splendid diagrams the motions of the moon. The teacher of this class was a man of excellent reputation in a demonstration school. He was unfailing in his effort, and a splendid teacher according to the system in which he taught. But the moon could not have been farther away from the classroom than the minds of a large number of the pupils. Nor was there anything farther from the mind of the teacher than permitting the pupils to carry on such useful activities as writing notes or reading stories.

Children are active beings and there is but one way for them to learn, namely, through activity. Conversely, there is one best way to keep them from learning, namely, to prevent full activity by fastening them into seats and forbidding them to speak, to move or to do. Fortunately teachers cannot stop children's minds from working. Sometimes pupils *do* listen, and to such an adventitious circumstance is due much of the success of teacher-effort schools.

When a child is engaged in a whole-activity, such as making a garden, writing a letter, or thinking out the answer to a problem in physics, an activity which he himself has initiated because of a need which he himself has felt, then he will carry out that activity more whole-heartedly than under any other circumstances, and with the maximum of effort.[4]

Children Work Hard When the Work Is Significant to Them

Modern teachers are easily convinced that children like to play, but some of them do not realize that children also like to work. A small boy of ten, who attended a famous progressive school, said

[4] It should be noted that this categorical statement, while it seems to be in harmony with modern educational philosophy and psychology, has never been scientifically proved. A scientific study of this matter is urgently needed.

to his mother recently, "I'm tired of that school. There's too much play. We have to play all day." Evidently his teachers were making a mistake in underestimating the child's desire to work. It should be carefully noted, however, that in one respect a child is just like any grown-up. The work on which he puts his effort must be significant to what he regards as his needs. The grown-up saws wood when he realizes the necessity of keeping his stove burning in winter, and writes stories when he expects to get paid for them. Fortunately a child is made to recognize his needs much more easily than a grown-up. A child is full of faith. Explanation from a grown-up that he needs to add and to spell is often sufficient to enable him to work hard, particularly when his accomplishment is observed by himself and recognized by others as work done. In fact, Mrs. Wallace, of the Dawson School, claims that such an explanation by a trusted adult is quite adequate to make children conscious of their need for a great deal of school work, that it is not imperative that simple arithmetic, for instance, be motivated by finding the immediate need for its use arising in the progress of constructive activities. On the contrary, however, this does not mean that the need for measurement in the construction of a toy garage or of a wooden engine may not often be the means of helping children to realize their need for numbers. At any rate, whatever be the means of awakening in the child the consciousness of his need for some particular piece of work, when the child actually feels the need and remains conscious of his progress, he willingly works because he loves to learn.

Children Are Disciplined by Responsibility

We live in a world of unprecedented freedom in which the only safe guide is self-control. In an older society where men recognized the right of one man to make a bond-slave of another, the force of extra-personal compulsions was recognized. The development of democracy has given a greater dignity to the individual and has laid upon him a greater responsibility. It has made the development of self-control of paramount importance. The development of restraint and personal assent in matters of law and order are absolutely necessary if the individual is to stand by the force of his own personality. Bagley stresses the importance of discipline in present-day American society in no uncertain words.

"During the past generation the forces that have operated to expand the reach and holding power of education have operated also to weaken the educational fiber, and consequently to prevent education from exerting its full potential influence against debilitating tendencies that almost certainly go with increased material prosperity. . . .

"But we now face the very serious problem of correcting the tendency of looseness and softness that our policy so easily involves. Here, I believe, is the crucial problem of the next decade in American education. . . .

"For the motto of an educational theory meet for the needs of democracy in an increasingly industrialized civilization, I suggest the phrase, 'Through Discipline to Freedom.' " [5]

Discipline which is imposed from without and in which the will of the individual does not concur has no educational value. When in the progress of his school life a child accepts the responsibility for carrying through some activity to completion and finishes it successfully he has disciplined himself. When he is engaged in some cooperative enterprise, such as producing a class play, he is engaged in an activity in which any failure in responsibility will immediately be obvious and suffer the rebuke of social disapproval. In soundly organized schools children undergo the rigid discipline of accepted responsibility for every kind of task.

Under Certain Circumstances Children Learn by Unrestricted Expression of Their Imaginative Tendencies

Children are imaginative, original, and sensitive to esthetic values, but always on their own level. A child is full of fancies and dreamings which, if allowed to develop, and if properly directed, may become the basis of literary activities. Furthermore, children are conscious of simple beauty in nature, art and music. They are original because unhampered by knowledge of convention. But in matters of esthetic self-expression children are extremely sensitive and lack a realization of their own powers. If they are permitted to live in a rich environment, and given the tools and materials for self-expression, they will develop along these lines simply and naturally. Witness the interesting art products in clay or in painting which are to be found in such schools as the City and Country School, where such matters are clearly understood. These products are seen best by visiting the classrooms, but an excellent idea of them may be gained by examining

[5] BAGLEY, WILLIAM C., "Some Handicaps of Character Education in the United States," *Educational Administration and Supervision*, April, 1929, pp. 245 and 249.

the reproductions given in the early issues of *Progressive Education*. Such products are not haphazard. Development of this sort only takes place in an atmosphere of understanding, sympathy and encouragement. Techniques need not be taught the child, for simple techniques will be developed naturally with accompanying development in the child's ability to call on the full resources of his personality in problem solving. The original and esthetic in the child is such a delicate plant that it withers in any but the most favorable environment. In the traditional school it soon perished in the stultifying atmosphere of formal tasks.

It may be well to call attention, at this point, to a matter to which we will return in a later chapter. While it is true that children, given an opportunity to express themselves in the fields of music, art and literature, will make considerable progress in such forms of living, nevertheless, all learning does not partake of the same characteristics. It is not here suggested that the "creative act" be made the model, as some teachers have attempted to do, for every kind of school experience. It is not here advocated that children be given an opportunity to "express themselves" in arithmetic or geography. Any such wholesale application of theory is bound to be absurd. In the realms, however, in which human beings are prone to express their imagination, free self-expression is the most desirable form of activity for children. By such artistic self-expression children learn.

Good Health Affects the Learning of Children and Successful Learning Improves Their Health

In matters of health the schools have again failed to realize the organic unity of the whole child. There has been a tendency to break him up into compartments and sections, to regard his health as one aspect of his personality, and his learning as another. The two are, however, intimately connected and interrelated. It is not enough to look after the child's health so that he will be well, and to teach him so that he will learn. Health is the health of the whole child; he should be healthy in mind and body so that he may live well.

The health of the body is intimately related to the health of the mind and the whole life. When the body is not healthy, the mind does not take a healthy or active attitude toward work. The normal vitality of the child is decreased so that the active desire to learn which is so intimately connected with his dynamic life is no longer so powerful.

Again, a fact recognized even less than the former is that the health of the mind reacts directly upon that of the body. Failure to learn is seriously detrimental to health. The sense of thwarted action, of failure, is so direct in its action upon the general vitality that the whole being is rapidly and fundamentally affected. A healthy, happy atmosphere of achievement and progress is absolutely essential for the good health of children.

"The close parallel existing between physical and mental development was recognized by Bowditch as early as 1891, and the work of later investigators has served to emphasize his conclusions."

"[Baldwin reports that:] 'Dull children are shorter than precocious children of the same age, or average children.'

" 'Successful pupils are taller than unsuccessful, and the rate of growth is quicker than in the unsuccessful.'

" 'Dull children are lighter than precocious children.'

" 'The lung capacity was found to be much greater in children whose standing in school is high, and distinctly inferior in a school for laggards.'

" 'The tall, heavy boys and girls, with good lung capacity are older physiologically, and further along in their stages toward mental maturity, as evidenced by school progress, than are the short, light boys and girls.' "

"Clinically, the physical changes that take place in the malnourished infant or older child as he returns to a normal physical condition are often remarkable, so great that the child can hardly be recognized. The mental transformation that accompanies physical recovery is frequently as great, so that it is a customary comment of parents and teachers,—'He is a different boy. His whole mental attitude is changed. You would not know him.' " [6]

Still another aspect of the child's life which may affect the mental and physical well-being is the emotional life. Fortunately, for the normal, healthy child brought up in a well-balanced home this problem may be a minor one. But children who come from homes in which the emotional balance is upset are apt to suffer from emotional maladjustment. A boy of nine whose parents were divorced, prayed nightly that his mother would return to the home. "If she doesn't come back, I will never believe in God," he said. Another child of six, after the crisis which caused his separation from his mother screamed at the very mention of the word "school," fearing that it might mean the loss of his father also. Even in normal children coming from normal homes there may be found many minor fears and complexes which injure living and learning. Mateer relates a case

[6] EMERSON, R. P., in *The Child,* The Children's Foundation, New York, pp. 176 *ff.*

of a child whose whole school learning process was inhibited by a slap from the teacher for a spoiled task.[7] Children frequently suffer from odd beliefs, such as that they are dull or stupid, that they have some deficiency in a particular type of learning, that they are weaker, more cowardly, or more wicked than other children. Any of these strange irrational obsessions common even to normal children may prove most injurious in the child's learning process. Strictly speaking, this may be regarded as the field of the school psychologist. Few teachers have any well-developed technique for dealing with the minor emotional or mental ailments of children. Others, however, by natural sympathy which meets the child on his own level and by experience and knowledge of children, are frequently able to remove such causes of disability.

Children's Minds Grow as They Learn.[8]

A most unfortunate pall has been cast over the educational faith of many by the injurious and shallow doctrines of the determinists to the effect that the mind does not grow in learning. These teachings are so manifestly absurd that one wonders how teachers, even in the entanglements and obscurities of statistics and technical terminology, could have wandered so far from the path of the obvious.

It seems clear that learning cannot be anything less than mental growth. To deny that children's minds grow is to deny that they learn. Undue analysis of the child's personality and the theoretical separation of his life into the effects of heredity and environment, into maturity and immaturity, may cause confusion. At any given moment in the real situation the effect of inherited and learned responses in the child's conduct are indistinguishable. Division and analysis of educational problems in terms of abstract categories are most useful in the discussion of educational problems. Such procedure, however, should never blind the teacher to what she beholds going on before her in the classroom. There are thousands who watch with

---

[7] MATEER, F., "Just Normal Children," D. Appleton & Co., New York, 1929, Ch. 13.
[8] FREEMAN, F. N., and others, "The Influence of Environment on the Intelligence, School Achievement, and Conduct of Foster Children," The Twenty-Seventh Yearbook of the National Society for the Study of Education, Pt. I, Bloomington, The Public School Publishing Co., 1928, Ch. IX.

BURKS, B. S., "The Relative Influence of Nature and Nurture upon Mental Development; A Comparative Study of Foster-Parent Foster-Child Resemblance, and True-Parent, True-Child Resemblance," *Ibid.*, Ch. X.

FREEMAN, F. N., "The Effect of Environment on Intelligence," *School and Society*, March 10, 1930, pp. 623-32.

delight the unfolding of blossoms in their garden. It is infinitely more fascinating for teachers to watch the expanding abilities of children and their growth from month to month as they gain a newer grasp on the ways of life.

In her teaching the new teacher is earnestly trying to govern her class teaching by the principles here set forth. Consequently she is ever alert to see that learning begins with the child's own eager desire to learn. She is ever watchful to see that during the progress of his learning in school, the lessons which form his experiences are moving forward on his initiative while she guides them in desirable channels. There is no question of imposing a certain fixed curriculum or a certain few pages of a geography or history text upon the child. One does not whip a galloping horse or impose food on a hungry boy. So the teacher does not begin with a fixed, arbitrary, dry-as-dust curriculum and compel the learning process to move backward. Rather, she allows the child to initiate and maintain his own learning process while she guides it toward a curriculum which, provided it is a good one, is the normal child's dearest goal.

CHAPTER IV

THE SIGNIFICANCE OF DIFFERING POINTS OF VIEW IN
THE NEWER SCHOOLS

IN MOST of the new schools the general principles set forth in the last chapter are operative. It must not be supposed, however, that the organization, the modes of attack, and the procedure of all modern schools are exactly the same. Most of the experiments which are going on in various parts of the country have had independent origins. They have risen here and there in response to a general feeling for the inadequacy of traditional schooling, and their sponsors have proceeded on their own course, unaware that the same kind of problems were being attacked elsewhere. It is only in recent years that these pioneer schools have begun to realize that they are not alone in this movement, but that in many centers others are carrying on similar work. It is, therefore, not surprising to find among modern teachers that, while basically their ideas are similar, yet there are some differences among them. The schemes and plans evolved for the realization of ideals are not exactly the same in each case. There are differences, not merely in opinion, but in the degree of thoroughness and devotion which different teachers have shown to the principles they have embraced. This may be realized better by a consideration of several differing points of view and the type of school organization which is associated with each.

It is not to be supposed that various schools or points of view may be classified in any absolute fashion, or that any given school is exactly described by any of the following groups of characteristics. Good schools have an individuality all their own. It may be possible, nevertheless, for purposes of convenience, to distinguish three general types to one of which any given school might show more resemblance than to the others. These types may be distinguished as the experimentalists, the practical idealists, and the newer public schools.

The Experimentalists [1]

The most extreme and radical are the thoroughgoing experimentalists. These teachers number among them those who have thrown over everything that pertained to the old type of school and have attempted to start afresh. They have aimed to free themselves from every prejudice against any mode of procedure, to begin at the bottom and feel their way, to allow their schools to grow in original fashion as they developed from the lower grades. They have usually begun with small children, carrying them on and up and solving their problems, not according to preconceived ideas of pedagogy, but naturally as they arose. Always, as they proceeded, they have attempted to fit their schools and their modes to the development of the particular children and the special type of group which they were caring for. Such schools are sometimes found among the most famous privately sponsored schools in the large centers of population.

The teachers in these schools are the true radicals of the teaching profession, eager, original people who tend to be "advanced" in their social attitudes, in their esthetic, social and religious thinking. In many cases they have desired to approach the task of teaching without any careful or thoroughgoing study of education in order that they might be the less hindered in their outlook. For that reason they have often stepped in where angels fear to tread. They have sometimes discarded the fruit of educational experience and have failed to avoid procedures and attitudes which a thorough acquaintance with previous social and educational efforts might have enabled them to avoid. Nevertheless, in so doing, they have thrown into relief the rigid practices of self-satisfied systems of teaching. They have discovered by practical experience much of what they must discard, and have by their fearless and fresh approach led the way in discovering and applying new techniques and new methods. It is scarcely conceivable that any system of public schools could ever become dominated by such an advanced and courageous spirit. It is always for such pioneer workers to keep well ahead of the general social development, and to be continually blazing the trail which the later highways are to follow. Their function is to discover and carry on in new ways, prove all things

---

[1] Experimental schools are usually called so because they adopt or try out some procedure on a chance of its succeeding. Bagley says: "None of these schools has been experimental in the scientific sense; that is, none of them has provided for the testing of different procedures under rigidly controlled conditions. They are not true experimentalists in such cases, because they are strongly prejudiced."

THE SIGNIFICANCE OF DIFFERING POINTS OF VIEW

and hold fast that which is good, so that others may learn from them and follow on.

In the organization and conduct of school life these teachers in their fearless attempts to work out the problems of teaching in our present-day world are very insistent on a "hands off" policy. We are very definitely reminded by this attitude of Rousseau's "negative education." The similarity is to be seen by comparing his point of view with that expressed in the following statement made by a well-known proponent of progressive education who says, "A program of 'watchful waiting' is to be advocated." "No one knows," says the same writer, "what children could do if adult ideas of what they should do were not imposed upon them from almost the moment they are born." This point of attack is obviously much influenced by a great faith in the possibilities of child development. In schools governed in accordance with such a philosophy, the child reigns almost, if not quite, supreme. The children are given the greatest possible freedom of choice as to what they shall do so long as they do something. If possible to avoid it, adult standards are not used in judging children. Just what standards of judgment are used and how they are arrived at does not seem to be obvious. Nor has the validity of children's judgments, if operative, been clearly established. At any rate, the burden of finding out what is good and what is bad conduct is often laid upon the children under environmental circumstances which, it is expected, will reveal to them sound values. Thus it is hoped that the children may become their own prophets.

The curriculum in schools of this general type is described as a fluid curriculum. More than in any other type of progressive school it is adventitious and not predetermined. It is presupposed that if children keep on learning in an environment which is normal for them, and normal for the society in which they are to live, that they will ultimately learn what they need to know. When such schools were first started they began to build from the bottom. The teachers watched the children to see what they did and how they progressed. A great deal of what went on in these schools seems to have been governed by the principle:—try it, and see if it works. Just what criteria and method were then used to determine whether it worked or not is not very clear. Schools of this type would doubtless have the sympathetic attention of many if they could be somewhat clearer in these matters.

By the study of what actually has taken place in school and the experimental working out of a program, teachers have a norm of reference for future work. They are thus able to forecast within certain wide limits what children will be likely to do in school hours. This provides them beforehand with a more or less clear notion of what may go on in school during the year—a tentative notion which is thus based on their past experience with similar conditions. In other words, the teachers use what has been referred to as a "fluid curriculum." It is assumed that the chief goals of the curriculum will be reached some time or other, but just when or by means of what activities cannot be definitely prophesied. The material is thus so presented that "the children themselves assist to a certain extent in sifting and selection of the year's work." [2]

This lack of a definite predetermined subject matter for children to learn, and even in some cases, it is to be feared, of definite curriculum goals, has led some extremists among these teachers, when asked what subject matter they teach, to claim that they teach no fixed subject matter. The implication sometimes intended is that nothing definite is taught. Similarly there are some who claim that in their school there is no fixed curriculum. The implication made, and sometimes directly spoken, is that there is no curriculum. This is manifestly absurd. Such teachers are using terms inaccurately and expressing themselves badly. By so doing they encourage criticism and lack of sympathy from critics who might otherwise lose their hostility. The teacher who has no curriculum teaches nothing. A teacher may not be able to forecast just what her children will learn in some given period of time, but the teacher who has no notion of what she wants to teach invalidates her own existence. Teachers who use a fluid curriculum have actually very definite notions of what children will learn. Their unique characteristic is that they are attempting to reform the school by experimenting in the organic growth of school life.

This type of development through the experimental or empirical determination of a new curriculum in terms of children's adaptations is one type of the educational reform which is having wide vogue in America. Certain of the reform movements are characterized by emphasis on improvement through new curricula, while others emphasize improvement in method. The two are intimately connected and should not be prosecuted separately. In the new schools the matter of curriculum and the matter of method are unavoidably interrelated.

[2] NAUMBERG, MARGARET, "The Walden School," Twenty-Sixth Yearbook of the National Society for the Study of Education.

THE SIGNIFICANCE OF DIFFERING POINTS OF VIEW 41

The Practical Idealists

A second group of teachers among those known as "progressives" might be called the practical idealists. It is in the schools of such teachers that we are apt to find the soundest and most desirable models for public school practice. They are usually directed by educators of wide training and experience. In certain cases these individuals have been unable to content themselves with the restrictions of service in traditional systems and have consequently entered private school work where they would receive adequate financial backing and have a free hand to develop their own schools. In other cases the teachers in charge have received appointments in schools sponsored by some university or foundation in the interests of educational research. Because the teachers are well trained and are fitted to carry out a well-conceived and balanced program, they set up schools which are the envy of all who see them. These schools may, however, awaken antagonism on account of their undemocratic nature in a country which is founded and lives by democratic ideals, and has committed itself to free state-supported education.

Certain of these private schools are day schools, supported largely by fees. Others are residential schools for the rich and are sometimes appointed and operated with a degree of luxury which may be neither salutary for the pupils nor satisfactory to public school teachers who look to them to see what results they obtain. If such schools could content themselves with being more democratic, it might be easier for public school men to see through the haze of expenditure and discover the practical and sound nature of the organization without being alarmed at its cost. It is to such schools that we may well look for examples of desirable educational practice.

This type of established pioneer school usually has a well-worked-out year program for each group of children, but great freedom is allowed the teachers in organizing this program. Such schools are characterized by a more thoroughgoing organization of the work in terms of conduct than is to be found in schools which carry on under a more restrictive administration. A great deal in the way of definite accomplishment is expected of the teacher and class during the year, but the limits of accomplishment are not always rigidly defined. Great freedom is taken by each teacher and each class in organizing the year's work. There is no division of the school program into two halves, one for activities, such as the making of Christmas gifts, operating a store, or writing stories, and the other for certain subjects such as arithmetic, spelling, and reading. The whole work of the school is regarded as organically one. The school is a community of children in which living goes on, and because living is going on in the school community, various units of conduct arise. These units of conduct may be as diverse as singing a song, devoting an hour to practice in arithmetic, or building a train. They arise and are governed not mechanically, but in accordance with the situation from which they develop. The complexity of this state of affairs is so great that no simple example can be given.

In such a school the children carry on their work according to their own needs under the guidance of the teacher in units of conduct which, under skillful direction, branch forth and lead on into subject matter. For example, the necessity for keeping class accounts may lead to arithmetic, and the tracing of an air journey may involve the use of geography. Units of conduct carry the children forward through the materials of the curriculum in steps which are in accordance with their maturity and needs, but not necessarily in a rigid, predetermined sequence. It is true that this program is not always perfectly administered in certain schools which attempt to carry on in this fashion. There are times when the units of conduct seem cumbersome, overlong, and artificial. In other schools there is a certain haziness, not merely concerning the sequence of curriculum goals, which may be of little importance, but concerning the goals themselves. Many things are sometimes regarded as satisfactory goals, which are of very doubtful value as such. But the general program of these schools makes for healthy, happy, normal growth. When it is properly lived up to, it is the most balanced and the least influenced by fads and fancies of any to be seen in the newer schools.

Newer Public Schools

The third group referred to is composed of those who are introducing and carrying on newer methods in public schools. These are public school teachers of training and experience who are so fortunate as to find a place in a community which gives them, or from which they have won, an adequate backing.

The newer methods of teaching are, in fact, beginning to influence the public school life of the whole country. In certain centers this influence is very much stronger than in others. In such places, for instance, as Winnetka, Illinois; Bronxville and Scarsdale, New York, the communities have definitely committed themselves to a system of modernized public schools. It is, of course, much easier to set up a

THE SIGNIFICANCE OF DIFFERING POINTS OF VIEW

new school system along new lines than it is to remodel a system of long standing. Consequently, it is in such new and comparatively opulent communities that the finest examples of the new public school are to be found. In older cities, with years of custom behind them, where there are many teachers brought up under the old régime, things naturally evolve more slowly. Yet even in the most reactionary systems there are educators of vision and enterprise who are making changes.

The program of the new public schools, while it is infinitely superior to that of the old school, nevertheless, uses a tested program for which the confidence of the public may be secured. Such schools insist upon the maintenance of the old subject-matter standards and of sound returns in this direction for public expenditure. From the point of view of educational administration they are smoothly running machines. They are shining examples of what can actually be done in a public system at the present time. They must be particularly careful to avoid any tendency to crystallize into such a fixed system as that of their forerunners. If this is to be avoided their guardians and sponsors must be continually willing and eager to change for the better. They must be ever watchful and continually observant of those institutions which may be just ahead. They must follow the example of the Winnetka schools which, in spite of their high standards, are by no means self-satisfied but are seeking to improve an excellent program by salutary changes which will provide an ever more flexible plan, and one better adapted to children's needs.

Unfortunately this type of progressive public school usually tends to organize its work in two halves, one of which is looked after in half of the school day, say the morning, and the other half of which is taken care of in the afternoon. Such activities as outdoor play, dramatics, art, and music are regarded as one part of the program, while the various skills involved in the mastery of the tools of knowledge, such as reading and spelling, form the other. By skillful teachers the two are related and integrated. The orderliness of the children in good schools of this type, and their devotion to school tasks, carries with it a most prepossessing air of conviction. One seems to see in such schools the promise of a new social order.

In addition to these schools, which have been able to put into practice an entirely new program, there are public school systems all over the United States which are struggling with the problem of improving and remodeling school life. Numerous smaller communities, such as West Hartford, Connecticut; Raleigh, South Carolina; Kensington, Michigan; Norristown, Pennsylvania; and Norfolk, Virginia, are introducing new methods throughout the system or as each new elementary school is built. In the larger cities, also, there have been important developments. In these cities changes generally begin with a program of curriculum revision, such as that which instituted reform in Denver in 1922-23. A similar movement is under way in Seattle. Los Angeles has made sweeping changes by developing an activity program, by issuing through the supervisors information and bibliographies, and by the opening of a demonstration school. This school is administered by the Board of Education and supervised by the University of California. In other cities, like New York, improvements are being made *en bloc*. In this city improved curricula are being worked out. Again, there has been a recent ban on home work for the lower grades. In many of the New York public schools principals of vision are allowing their teachers considerable freedom, and in such schools the approach to the curriculum is increasingly made by means of such activities as the keeping of news bulletins, the making of news reports, the keeping of current event books, and the planning and execution of posters. Furthermore, the Board of Superintendents has authorized an experiment in curriculum making for young children which is being conducted by the Public Education Association in Public School 41, on Greenwich Avenue. So it is that teachers even in well-established school systems are being called upon to familiarize themselves with the new point of view and with methods which are current in the newer schools.

Differences in Practice Less than Differences in Theory

It has been difficult to make the distinctions in theory and school organization which have been set forth in this chapter. It is still more difficult to make distinctions between classroom practices as they may be observed in these various types of schools. In spite of their secondary differences in theory, teachers in the new schools are alike in their fundamental philosophy. Consequently wherever one goes in the new schools one may find teachers solving their problems in similar ways, and carrying on their work by techniques which are very much alike. The children themselves will be found engaged in activities which resemble one another. In each of these schools one will scarcely fail to find children painting original pictures, writing stories, solving problems of measurement and making useful things of wood or clay. Consequently, it is possible to ignore unimportant differences and present an account of the way in which such teachers carry on, and to give some analysis of their technique of teaching.

CHAPTER V

THE UNIT OF LIVING

VALUABLE as the concept may be of the school as the living of children, it nevertheless requires analysis if it is to prove a guide to the teaching process. To deal with life unanalyzed in the mass, with its intricacies and interrelations, is a task so complex that it is wellnigh impossible. Thus if living is to be the basis of schooling, it will be necessary to discover some unit of living, some unit of life, which may serve as a philosophic basis for the guidance of teaching.

Let us pause to consider the meaning of the word "unit." It implies, first of all, the notion of separation which enables us to consider it as a part of something larger than itself, and secondly it indicates a certain wholeness within itself which depends upon some binding principle. For instance, we may regard each stone in a granite wall as a unit. Its unity depends first upon the fact that it is a separate though integral part of the wall, and secondly upon the fact that each stone is in itself a whole and is held together by some binding force or principle. In this case, the binding or unifying principle is the force of cohesion.

In a similar fashion we may regard school life as composed of certain units. We are already sufficiently familiar with the nature of the unit of traditional schooling. So far from being a unit of life, it was rather a unit of subject matter. It was devitalized rather than vital. The least common denominator between the school and the world was found in a chapter, a paragraph, a sentence. It was subject matter extracted from life by a process of induction and generalization. It was regarded as the concentrated essence of life in the form of facts and principles. In reality it was the structure and skeleton, but it lacked the energy and spirit of life. The binding principle by which it cohered was the principle of logic. Consequently, school life was organized into subjects and the logical organization of subject matter became the guide to the teaching process.

The unit of living has been variously called an activity, a complete act, and a unit of work. It seems more logical to use the term "unit of conduct," or "unit of life." Such a conception makes it possible to find in conduct that least common denominator between the school and the world which the teacher must find if the life of the school is to be the living of the children. It further provides a philosophic basis for an analysis of school life. The unit of life or the unit of conduct, while it suggests that separateness of a part from its whole, at the same time provides for the notion of wholeness and coherence which is suggested by the term "unit."

It is very important to consider just what is the binding principle which provides for this idea of wholeness or coherence within the unit of conduct. I have dealt with this matter at length in another book.[1] Using Kilpatrick's analysis of the complete act as the basis of description, I have suggested a radical difference in this analysis which, coming at the very root and origin of the unit of conduct, is of fundamental importance. I have suggested that the root and origin of the unit of life is not to be found in the *purpose*, but rather in the *need*. Consequently, the unit of conduct is to be regarded as an act which may be analyzed into the five processes of needing, purposing, planning, executing, and using or evaluating. More important than this analysis, however, is the fact that each of these processes throughout the progress of the whole unit is dominated, directed and governed by the original need. It is the need which is the unifying principle within the unit of conduct. It is the binding force which is analogous to the force of cohesion in the granite unit of the stone wall. Thus when an individual feels the need of a window box to brighten up the front of his house, he plans for it, goes through the necessary steps to secure it, puts it in place on the house, and passes judgment upon it, all in terms of his original need. It is the original need which is the rise and the cohesive principle of a unit of living. So when the child in school feels the need of a window box for the school, he may carry out in school a unit of conduct which is analogous to a unit of conduct in the world outside the school, an act which is a real unit of living because it is unified by a fundamental need.

Thus it is that the unit of life or the unit of conduct provides a basic concept for the analysis of school living. It lies at the basis of the treatment of teaching which is discussed in this book. So we may develop a plan of school living which will involve the children in a series of units of conduct which interweave and intermingle in the very texture of life itself. In the school we may find children

[1] MELVIN, A. GORDON, "Progressive Teaching," D. Appleton & Co., New York, 1929, Ch. VI, The Unit of Conduct.

discovering their needs, choosing from among them those which are most pressing and genuine, and carrying them through in coöperation with their companions, eating and drinking and reading and acting and singing and playing and talking and writing poetry and sawing and hammering and weaving and praying; all these things and many more. Thus by fulfilling their best needs, children will be learning.

Types of Life Units

For fear that we may make the mistake of attempting to force all learning into one mold, it is necessary to make a further analysis of living in and out of school by attempting some classification of life activities. This is most necessary if we are to proceed further in the application of our thinking to the actual process of teaching. It has already been pointed out that if the learning process is to assume the form which is given to it by the child, it must assume the form of conduct. Such conduct, moving forward toward its goals, may adapt and organize whatever subject matter is suitable to its modes of expression. Children, in fulfilling their needs, may live through such units of conduct as going for a swim, estimating the cost of a Hallowe'en party, or investigating local rock formations. They carry on such activities as writing stories, printing them in books, and binding the books. They engage in such separate and complete acts as furnishing a doll's house, giving a shadow play, or building a fish pond to improve the school pet park. They perform such simple duties as taking a rest after meals, putting away the tools they have been using, and washing their hands. When the things which children do are wisely organized into these units of conduct, the learning process takes on the semblance of life itself. We have still to attempt some additional analysis which may assist us in understanding the process involved in such diverse activities.

Before proceeding to this analysis, it should be made very clear that this discussion is philosophical and theoretical rather than practical or technical. In this connection it is important to note the distinctive function of educational philosophy, which is to become a guide, not a pattern to the teaching process. Its significance for teaching lies less in itself than in the educational corollaries which may be derived from it. The philosophy of education should be a touchstone, a norm of reference for technique and method. It may ever serve as a standard which may be used in a thoughtful checking of technique and method. So in the succeeding paragraphs, the analysis of units of conduct into varying types is intended in a philosophical rather than a practical sense. It is in terms of theory rather than in terms of practice. It is intended to form a philosophic basis for the formulation of technique, but is in no sense intended to be an analysis of technique or method.

It is doubly necessary to be clear on this distinction if confusion is to be avoided in the study of the succeeding parts of this book, which are devoted to a discussion of the practical aspects of method, rather than to a consideration of theory. In the later sections further analyses will be offered in the form of teaching procedures. These procedures will present a practical account of the way in which teachers in school may actually, in the practical situation, secure the bridging of the gap between the child and the curriculum. They will indicate ways of doing things which are not patterned after the philosophic analyses of units of conduct given in the present section of this book, but they will be in harmony with these philosophic concepts.

The attempts which have been made to classify activities have been largely arbitrary. Numerous writers have indicated classifications, but they have not been made on any intrinsic principles. The result is often a mixture of two philosophic points of view; the one based on subject matter, the other on a conduct theory of teaching. One writer, for example, distinguishes curricular, social, constructive, English, artistic, recreational, supplementary activities. Other groupings are equally unsatisfactory.

There is need, however, for further classification of activities in terms which will be of assistance in evolving method which is in accordance with the nature of a conduct organization of school life. Several classifications have been suggested to this end. One writer, in dealing with the matter, discusses problems, projects, motives and interests. Kilpatrick uses the word "project" as a blanket term for all activities suitable for school life, and classifies them as enjoyment projects, constructive projects, problem projects, and learning projects.

The teaching set forth in these pages is teaching in schools in which the organization of school life is in terms of units of conduct. This form of organization has been elsewhere described.[2] The unit of conduct differs in certain respects from other concepts which have been used to interpret the learning process. It provides a unitary basic concept of school organization but, nevertheless, allows a diverse interpretation of the learning process for various types of learning. While it recognizes various types of learning, all these types may

[2] MELVIN, A. GORDON, *opus cit.*, Chs. 5, 6, 7.

proceed without any violation of the fundamental organization of school life in terms of conduct. The conduct unit is, therefore, *a basic concept of organization,* not a blanket term for the guidance of the learning process. It does not result in an attempt to squeeze all learning into a single mold, to interpret all learning in terms of a single formula. It does not describe learning in terms of a single "psychological rubric."

The origin of a unit of conduct, in the need of the individual initiating it, provides an intrinsic basis for the classification of units of conduct into three types, each distinguished by characteristics which indicate a different type of learning. Basing the distinction between them upon the origin of the need [3] giving them rise, constructive units, play units and work units have been differentiated. To this classification was added a fourth group of mixed units,[4] partaking of the mixed characteristics of the other groups. As this is the classification in mind here, it may be well, even at the risk of some repetition of what has been written elsewhere, to make clear the distinction between the various types of conduct units.

Types of Conduct Units

The distinction between types of units of conduct may be made in two ways. It may, figuratively speaking, be made latitudinally or longitudinally. That is to say, one form of classification runs across the other. This might be represented by a diagram as follows:

	Constructive	*Play*	*Work*
Physical	Making a Table	Swimming	Sawing Wood
Mental	Writing a Poem	Reading a Story	Balancing Accounts

It has already been pointed out that the distinction between these various types may be made on the basis of the origin of the need.

---

[3] Attention is called to the fact that this analysis is not arbitrary, but is based on a philosophic distinction.

[4] The use of the term "mixed units" in no way invalidates the original classification. It merely recognizes the fact that there are no categories in the social sciences which do not overlap. We classify here on the basis of distinguishable processes, rather than on the basis of objective acts. The fact that a large unit of conduct is usually divisible into numbers of subsidiary units which are again often divisible makes it obvious that large units must often be mixed in the sense that they are composed of diverse subsidiary units.

(1) The *constructive or creative* unit has its rise in the need for some object which is to remain subsequent to the action involved in carrying on the unit of conduct concerned. Such an object might be a table on which to keep one's books, a house in which to live, or a picture to beautify the living-room. In each case something tangible is wanted because there is a need for it.

(2) The unit of *play or recreation* arises under very different circumstances. In such a case there is no need for any objective residuum or for any palpable reality which is to remain when the activity is over. On the contrary, the need is for some simple expression of the personality, for some release of the energy called life in a fashion unrestricted by conditions outside the personality of the individual. When boys wrestle aimlessly with one another on the lawn, they do so in response to a felt but possibly unrecognized need for the expression of energy. This drive is not interfered with in any way. There are no restrictions placed upon it by time or circumstance. The boys have nothing else to do with that portion of time. There is no formal restriction involved. Furthermore, when they are finished, there will be nothing remaining to show for the energy expended.

(3) There is a third way, however, in which a need may arise to result in a unit of *work or duty*. In such a case it arises not from a desire for any objective result, which may be set aside when the unit of conduct is completed, nor from the need for a mere unloosing or expression of energy. It takes its origin from the necessity for the accomplishment of some activity which is made imperative by a set of conditions which preëxist in the environment when the unit of conduct is undertaken. Thus an individual may find himself surrounded by a family which must be supported. He works, obtains money and alleviates the strain resulting from the existing conditions. His energy results in making a satisfactory adjustment of conditions in the environment. A man may be hungry and he must cut somebody's lawn or shovel somebody's snow in order to get food to eat and satisfy his hunger. A man who is anxious to play golf may give up his game under the moral compulsion of visiting a sick friend. Units of work or duty are such activities, undertaken, not for some objective result remaining after the activity is over, nor for the freeing of energy without the restrictions resulting from the need of an end product or restrictions imposed by circumstances, but for the meeting of some moral or physical obligation due to a set of circumstances which govern the situation when the activity begins.

It is obvious, of course, that all units of conduct are not easily classified correctly by being placed under any one of the three heads mentioned. (4) Provision must be made for units of conduct which partake of the characteristics of two, or even of all three of the types referred to. Such units may be called *mixed units*. Such a unit might be one in which a man spends his morning, which on this particular occasion he would prefer to spend in entertaining some friends, in what is to him a pleasant occupation, writing a chapter in his new novel, the money from the sale of which is necessary to support his family. When the conduct concerned arises from such complex needs, it partakes of complex characteristics.

Again it should be pointed out that objective activities, that is activities aside from the personality who carries them on, do not really exist and therefore cannot be finally classified. For instance, sawing wood may, under certain circumstances, be either an aspect of a constructive unit, pure play, or hard work. If one is sawing a board to build a cabin, one may be engaged in the step of executing involved in a unit of construction. A child who sees a saw and some wood often saws in play for the fun of sawing. The hungry man who saws for food is at work. On the other hand, there are certain typical circumstances under which certain activities take place which make a tentative classification possible. For example, one usually saws wood under conditions which are those of work.

Besides this longitudinal classification into units of construction, units of play and units of work, there is the further latitudinal classification already referred to. The fact that any one of these three types of unit may be undertaken on the physical, mental, or possibly spiritual level is not without its significance. It is to be feared that the general tendency of current philosophy and school practice is to attack the problems of teaching on the low levels of physical conduct. We are today very much inclined to base our whole educational psychology on physiological psychology, and to make our findings in this field the analogy for procedures in the higher realms of mental conduct. Thus we tend to assume that an individual learns to fill out his tax returns honestly, and learns to sacrifice his own convenience in his daily tasks for the comfort of others, by a habit process identical with that by which he learns to tie his necktie or hold his pen. In the same fashion in the realm of method of teaching we seem inclined to find the key for the understanding of all activities of body, mind and spirit in the realm of physical conduct. Thus some individuals use such gross physical acts as the making of a sailboat as the analogy for acts undertaken on higher levels. Fortunately there must be a certain amount of validity in such a procedure, or the science of education would have been much less successful in modifying and improving teaching than it has been in recent years.

The Conduct Unit in School Life

1. *Units of Construction or Creation*

When a child in school is engaged in weaving a rug for a doll's house, or making an engine for his steamboat, he is engaged in a unit of construction. When he is composing a theme or writing a poem, he is engaged in a unit of creation. It is most unfortunate that the progressive movement has largely taken its direction from units of conduct of this nature. In an attempt to develop and guide the whole of the learning process by analogy with these types of activity, teaching has frequently fallen into serious error. This bias, which has governed certain proponents of the progressive movement, has resulted in the nauseous insistence upon the "creative" tendencies of the child. It seems that the unguarded use of the word "creative" is but another example of excess in the use of language. In such a sense as that of the creation of a flower or a raindrop, not even the most sophisticated scientist in the land, let alone an ignorant and untrained child, is a creator. The word smacks somewhat of sentimentality. It may be an indication of a tendency to child worship of which the new schools need to be more than usually cautious. The word has come into use, however, to indicate those activities of the imagination and of the higher functions of the mind and spirit which are involved in original work in the arts, and for want of a better word may be judiciously used.

It is these original, imaginative expressions of the personality against which the traditional school has been the greatest sinner. They demand for their early development a freeing of the personality, and such an opportunity for freeing development has often been denied to children in the older type of school. The extent to which adolescents brought up in the old type of school may suffer is pitiful. A high school boy of sixteen, after some encouragement, showed the writer a story which he had outlined but had not the courage or training to write. When told that it was interesting and should be written out completely, he timidly replied, "Do you really think it's all right? I was afraid to show it to any one for fear it might be foolish." Contrast the assurance of a bright child of ten who chattered merrily,

THE UNIT OF LIVING

"I wrote three plays this year, and I produced them and acted in them all myself." This ten-year-old, brought up in a modern school, showed his notebook in which he had "written" the three plays. In no case had the writing been carried beyond the first act. This youngster had a well-developed "bump of creation" but he knew very little about the meaning of work.

a. The Project.—The new schools have made a magnificent contribution by the introduction into school life of copious opportunities to build and construct. Constructive units of conduct have been sadly missing in traditional schools. Opportunities to build houses, make bridges, work in wood and iron, vitalize the work of the whole school. Yet it is to be feared that the unit of construction, sometimes called the "project," has often been made the model for the carrying on of school work of a very different sort.

The word "project" has been so variously defined, and the term so differently described by different writers that considerable confusion has arisen as to its use. According to Burton,[5] who gives an admirable account of the history and numerous definitions and interpretations of the word, it was first used as an educational term by Richards of Teachers College, Columbia University, in 1900, to indicate a practical problem, such as making a rack to hold one's books, in which the pupil participated in the planning and execution. In 1908, the Massachusetts State Board used the term "home project" to indicate a "pupil-planned, practical enterprise which was being carried on at home, as for example, raising an acre of corn, raising a litter of pigs, remodeling a barn, etc." [6] Again, in 1918 the Federal Board for Vocational Education in one of its bulletins says the following: "The term carries with it the idea of a program of importance, of some duration, and an expectation of certain tangible results." [7]

It is obvious that the word, when used in the sense in which it developed historically as an educational term, refers to activities which are of the nature of units of construction. Furthermore, it is only when used in such a sense that it preserves its etymological meaning derived from the Latin *projicio*, to cast, or throw forth or forward. It is thus correctly applied only to activities which are thrown forward, that is, which have at their completion some objective result,

---

[5] BURTON, W. H., "The Nature and Direction of Learning," D. Appleton & Co., New York, 1929, p. 255.
[6] BURTON, *ibid.*
[7] Agricultural Series, No. 3, Bulletin 21, 1918, p. 7.
The term "project," it seems, has been used for a long time in the *École des Beaux Arts*, and also in American schools of architecture.

namely, units of construction or creation. Certain writers, however, have used the word indiscriminately to indicate far more than its historical educational use or its etymological meaning really warrant. The total result of such a broadening of the meaning of the word seems to have been a distortion of the life of the school, which has precipitated considerable confusion in the practice of the new schools.

This use of a lower form of activity such as the making of a table as an analogy for the interpretation of all the activities of the mind and spirit is unfortunate. There can be little doubt that such procedure from the lower to the higher is fraught with danger to the development of the finer values of life. Such an outlook has doubtless caused an undue stress upon the importance of outward physical acts in the development of the child, irrespective of accompanying mental development. Undirected physical play has thus sometimes been given a place in the kindergarten and lower elementary school out of proportion to the child's educational gains for the time spent. There has been a great deal of aimless doing and making of this, that and the other, carried on by children whose teachers have been fashionable rather than astute.

Overemphasis on the importance of mere physical acts has been accompanied by a corresponding underemphasis upon mental acts, by a minimizing of the higher values involved in units of work and duty, which involve the development of inner controls and the building of moral habits. It is to be feared that some of the new schools have failed to realize the waning value of undirected physical play and the rising value of mental work as the child progresses from the lower to the higher grades of the elementary school. The neglect, furthermore, of spiritual values in recent years has been so marked that reference to them has practically passed out of educational literature. Is not our vast ignorance and neglect of higher values a great challenge to teachers?

The use of the project as a basal analogy for all learning has been unfortunate. Such an interpretation of the whole learning process in terms of lower values may be, to a certain extent, avoided if consideration be given to all the various types of conduct suitable for school life. It is hoped that this chapter may contribute to lessen the confusion resulting from the use of a single psychological formula to describe all learning. Such a procedure has seriously injured the growth of progressive schools by producing a persistent and deliberate attempt to treat all types of school activity as if they were alike in their origin, direction and development. If the modern school is to become a thorough educational instrument to equal and rival the school of the past, it must discard all wholesale formulæ, no matter how compact and intriguing they may appear. Simple explanations of learning must by their very nature fail to illuminate so complex a problem.

2. Units of Play

Thanks very largely to the influence of Froebel, units of play have found practically universal acceptance on their own merits in all schools everywhere. But teachers should be extremely clear that play holds its position in the school only to the extent to which it has educative value in proportion to the time spent upon it. Play is not soft pedagogy unless it holds an undue or false place in the school. While play is educative, it competes with other activities for its position in the school on the basis of equivalent educational values.

a. Educative Values of Play.—A full discussion of the educative value of play will not be given here, as the matter has been so often and so thoroughly treated elsewhere.[8] A brief reference to the matter, however, will serve to emphasize the fact that play is a valuable medium for teaching. (1) Play is educative in itself. As children mingle with one another, and carry on their various games involving running and throwing various kinds of balls, and their quieter aimless chatting and story telling, they are developing in various ways. They are learning to use language, to control muscles, and also endless things concerning personal relationships and social intercourse.

(2) Play provides basic experiences which are invaluable for the support and enrichment of other school activities. Children who have been farther afield, playing in woods or meadows, living on a farm or watching the Punch and Judy show in the Jardin du Luxembourg have more to say, more to write about, and are consequently better developed personalities than children whose life has been spent in tenements and on sidewalks. Myra Kelly relates the story of a child in the east side of New York who when asked to make a picture to illustrate the line, "Flowers in their little garden beds," drew several flower sprigs reclining at length on cots. It is difficult for grown-ups with their wide sensory experience to understand how limited a child

---

[8] Cook, H. C., "The Play Way," Frederick A. Stokes Co., New York, 1910, Ch. I et seq.
Klapper, Paul, "Contemporary Education," D. Appleton & Co., New York, 1929, Ch. V.
Merriam, J. L., "Child Life and the Curriculum," World Book Co., Yonkers-on-the-Hudson, 1920, Ch. 14.

is by his brief and narrow experience. By providing him with an opportunity to play in a rich and natural environment, we may assist him to become a better and more useful member of the school community. Given wider interests through wider contact with the world through play, the child is more easily awakened to activities which lead on to learning.

(3) Play is not merely valuable in and for itself, but because it leads on to units of construction and units of work. This is well illustrated by the activities which a group of children have been carrying on in the Francis W. Parker School of the University of Chicago in "a much littered and properly segregated slice of one end of the playground" called "Investigation Lane." [9] Given this place to play, the children casually began by digging an occasional cave. As time went on the caves were succeeded by huts, spades giving way to hammers and saws. The huts grew in size and decency of appearance, shaky and leaky structures gradually being replaced by less unsightly dwellings, one of which was supplied with homemade furniture, brightened with blue paper cambric and equipped with a little wood stove for cooking. As the days went by, the life of clubs and societies grew out of this home base, to the infinite enrichment of the life of the school and the life of the children. Construction and work done under such circumstances closely following on from what was in the beginning pure play partook of the free forward-moving dynamic nature of play. So play leads on to other activities which are closely related to it.

(4) Finally, good play trains children to make sound use of leisure time. One of the great problems of our schools today should be the training of children to a wise use of leisure. The increasing amount of free time which is falling to the lot of men today, through the invention of machines, is being wasted on every hand. Our present-day untrained generation is amusing itself by buying commercialized pleasures. People must pay to be entertained because they cannot entertain themselves. The schools should see to it that the rising generation shall not succeed to this social inheritance of inertia. If children are trained to find satisfaction in outdoor play, in appreciation of the beauties of nature, in the finding of mental recreation in good literature and in the appreciation of art and music, then they will understand how to use leisure time as children and also for the remainder of their lives. The leading-on character of such activities will give them

[9] For the full account of this work see Francis W. Parker School Yearbook, Vol. 1, June, 1912, p. 33.

increasing joy in whatever realms they have developed adequate techniques and appreciations.

3. Units of Work or Duty

When children spend laborious moments painstakingly editing the school paper, or tediously working over the materials for a play, or energetically working on tests in arithmetic, they are engaged on units of work. "Is it possible," said a recent visitor to the Dalton School in New York, "that children will work hard on their assignments just in order to get more work to do?" Those who have worked with children in a school where work holds its natural place in the school day know for a certainty that that is just what children will do. The need to work is quite as important as the need to play. It is just as valuable for a child to recognize his need to work as to recognize his need to play. It frequently happens, however, that human beings are slower to feel and recognize the need to work than other needs. Especially is this true of those who have not been trained to do so. Because work imposes limitations upon the ego, it demands effort. To live in accordance with imposed conditions requires moral stamina. Only children who are trained to be interested in work are willing to put forth the required effort. Such interests are based on the recognition and evaluation of needs in terms of respect, obedience, and social sanctions, quite as much, and perhaps more so, than in terms of results, objective success, or happiness.

The new schools have been accused, and not without some warrant, of producing children wrapped up in themselves and in their own interests and success. If we are to avoid this, children must learn to do things in school to please others, to give up their own wishes for the sake of their companions, to obey directions without being given the reasons for them. Thus a child who forfeits his right to compete for a prize in order to help a friend to win it, a child who visits a sick friend instead of going to see a moving picture, is living well. There is the greatest necessity for children to learn the demands of thoroughness and to recognize the compulsion of the spirit. The community needs persons who are unwilling to fall below the standard of excellence in whatever they do, persons who not merely post-judge, but pre-judge their own conduct. It is only when children are trained in school to carry out units of work or duty that they will attain all the higher values of training. Then only will we develop a generation of men who are trained to love work for work's sake.

The development of a habit of enjoying work, of liking it for itself, is all the more important because much of the work of the world is not done for its own sake but for some other reason. When a man wants a book rack and makes it, the process is motivated by the need. The activity is under his own direction from beginning to end. When he works in a furniture factory to support his family, it is not the furniture he wants but the money. If he is to be happy in such work, he must enjoy the work for its own sake. But if the whole process is taken out of his hands: if the planning is that of another designer, the judgment of the work carried on by an inspector, and only the execution left to the worker, then work becomes drudgery. It is the last straw when the worker is not even permitted to carry out a complete piece of execution. In certain mechanically managed factories he spends the day fastening bolts on something somebody else has made. The human being becomes part of a machine. This is the final dehumanization of living.

If the child is to be trained for the work-a-day world, he should be made conscious of the irrefragable laws of social and natural life which lay their compulsions upon the individual, whether he will or no. Children need to learn to respond to situations which are governed by these inevitable laws. Furthermore, they should learn to find joy in work activities in and for themselves. They should even learn to transfer the interest which they have in such an ulterior reward as money to the work itself. They should recognize in work, activity which satisfies their own needs. Then work proceeding happily and successfully in school may lead on to a happy lifetime of balanced work.

Part II
THE FUNDAMENTALS OF TECHNIQUE

CHAPTER VI

THE TECHNIQUE OF TEACHING

No GOOD teacher is without a technique of teaching. Yet it has been said that "the new teacher shuns technique." The paradox needs explanation. If technique is essential, why this temerity? Why should any teacher try to avoid, or pretend to avoid, the technique of teaching?

In the first place, there are some teachers whose technique is a matter of unconscious habit rather than of deliberate procedure. Such teachers, because they are unaware of their technique, refuse to name it. Their point of view is well expressed by Phelps [1] when he says: "Teaching is an art, not a science: and I may as well confess at the start that I know nothing whatever of the science of pedagogy. I am unable, therefore, to use technical terms, as I am not sure what they mean. I know a great many children, boys and girls, young men and maidens: but I have never studied the 'psychology of the child,' and have never attempted to find the way to a boy's heart through a scientific formula. The science of pedagogy is today a recognized branch of learning, and there are admirable men and women who seem to have achieved distinction in its pursuit; but I have been too busy teaching and studying my own specialty—English Literature—to give any serious or prolonged attention to that or any other science."

But no matter how great the artist, nor how naïve his mode of achieving results, that mode of achieving results is his technique, whether he calls it so or not. In teaching, as in every art, there are some distinguished teachers whose technique is original, and consequently difficult of description in terms of common concepts, not explicit or clearly understood in terms customarily employed in common language. Such teachers have a tinge of genius. They are the "born teachers" of whom we hear so much and see so little. It is for such teachers to teach, and for others to explain and analyze their technique. The majority of teachers must study these people's ways of doing things just as the student of painting or of music must study the

[1] PHELPS, W. L., "Teaching in School and College," The Macmillan Co., New York, 1921, p. 2.

work of the great masters. For until Utopia draws far nearer than it is today the majority of our teachers must be made because they are not "born."

Yet in shunning technique the artistic teacher is not altogether without some excuse. To the new teacher the word "technique" indicates points of view and methods of procedure which seem to her undesirable discussions of what she scornfully refers to as "pedagogy." To her the word "technique" means orthodox technique, as it is expounded in current books on teaching. Of the technique of teaching which she herself uses, very little has, up to the present, gotten into books. In fact, so recent are the new developments in teaching, it is only now that the newer procedures have emerged with sufficient distinctness to make any analysis of technique possible. So, to the new teacher, the word "technique" is practically synonymous with formalized and routinized method of teaching. She may even speak slightingly of the technique of teaching and scornfully of the study of education. She has been compelled to avoid them. She is an individualist. She has learned not from books but by experiment, by trial and error, by fellowship with the comparatively few teachers of her type she has met. These experiences have been supplemented by descriptive books and articles written by others with her views, and by the study of the purely scientific aspects of psychology and education. She has the artist's scorn of technique, but if she is a good teacher, she is a master of technique, in spite of what she says to the contrary. If asked for an exposition of her technique, she may say, "I don't use any particular technique; I just teach." The aphorism is not so profound as it may seem. This teacher fears lest her procedure lose its flexibility and its originality, so that she hesitates to label it. But it *is* technique just the same.

The very conception of teaching as an art and the teacher as an artist implies the technique of teaching. How then shall we define this *sine qua non?* Generally technique is a mode of skilled procedure in which the mind and imagination are active in the pursuit of any art, making practical application of scientific knowledge and principles. Specifically the technique of teaching is a mode of skilled procedure in which the mind and imagination of the teacher are active in the practical application of the science of education. A technique is any such procedure. Thus the sound direction of children's interests, a satisfactory way of looking after the temperature of the room, a tactful method of asking questions which will awaken interest in some historic adventure such as the voyages of Magellan, a skillful type of

THE TECHNIQUE OF TEACHING 63

guidance of some learning experience such as mapping out the neighborhood with blocks, all are techniques of teaching.

That teachers should carry on such things well seems more than obvious. Yet many of the teachers in the new schools have fallen down badly in this respect. It is to be feared that some, influenced by mistaken notions of the undesirability of careful development of technique, have deliberately neglected the matter, and so failed to reach standards which a study even of the older technique might have enabled them to maintain. The complaints made by teachers who visit the new classrooms are frequently only too well justified. They find conditions which they would not tolerate in their own schools. "Why are the children so untidy, and why is their hair, their appearance, their clothing so unkempt?" "Why are they so rude? They talk roughly to one another and to the teacher." "The cups they drink out of are so dirty that they must be unsanitary." "The teacher was teaching arithmetic just as I've seen it taught in many other schools, but she was doing it very poorly."

We are not always so modern or so new as we may think. The comment of a former teacher after observing a lesson in English literature in a fifth grade in one of the best known experimental schools in America was, "I used to teach literature in exactly that way myself, but I think the teacher's lesson was a very poor example of the method." And indeed it had been. Unfortunately, these strictures, oft repeated, are in many cases only too well deserved. I recall a winter morning visit to the class of a well-known exponent of modern methods whose classroom was stuffy and very much overheated. Disorder may be frequently seen, disorder which is still disorder after every allowance is made for "freedom" and "activity." In another classroom of a famous school, where the teacher was using advanced methods with a full activity program, the children's use of language was slovenly, their manners and voices ill-controlled. Frequently in the newer schools wretched enunciation is heard, even among children with very superior home backgrounds. On one occasion, noticing the careless mumbling of the children rehearsing an elaborately developed dramatic presentation, I mentioned this deficiency to the teacher. The children did not speak clearly enough to be heard or understood. I inquired what methods were used to improve the children's enunciation. What was the answer of this teacher, a woman whose understanding of the modern school is far better than that of most teachers engaged in it? She carefully explained that since the life situation involved in presenting the play required good enunciation, it was not necessary for her to bother with it any further!

Such neglect as these examples indicate of elemental and simple technique of teaching is unpardonable. What excuse is there for poor ventilation, irresponsible language, crude behavior or lazy enunciation? Such faults have been avoided or remedied by thousands of good teachers for years, teachers of such skill that no matter what one might think of their method, one could not but admire their technique of teaching.

Lapses in the teaching of the newer teachers are not easily excused. They indicate a lowering of standards which is most undesirable if the new schools are to bear comparison with those which preceded them. Furthermore, the problems of technique are far more cogent and difficult for the new teacher than they were for her predecessor. The organization of school life in terms of conduct is a far more complex arrangement than the older subject-matter type of organization. In fact the complexity of the new teaching has actually been used by certain educators as an argument against it. It is the simplicity of older types of school work which make them appealing, while it is the intricacy of the new modes which puzzle many who fail to understand them. This intricacy is to be noted in several directions. In the first place the beginning points of teaching in children's needs are indefinite and variable. The teacher who decides to discuss the Declaration of Independence in a certain period may begin simply and directly with the subject of her choice. The new teacher, who watches and waits for the moment when the understanding of historical material or the solution of some situation in which the children find themselves depends on knowledge of the Declaration of Independence, finds the beginning of teaching a continually variable problem.

Again the development of bridging activities is very flexible. The teacher who introduces a new arithmetical process by a problem arbitrarily chosen, which she demonstrates at the blackboard, finds her teaching simple compared with that of a teacher whose approach to such a problem may be made in any number of ways, via the school bank, the school shop, the children's questions, the scenery being made for a play, some building that is going on in the yard, the cost of a class excursion—via whatever activity arises which leads in the direction of the values desired. But most hazy of all is the meeting point, the beginning of fusion between the child's responses and the values of the curriculum. The teacher who pursues a direct path, teaching spelling in one period, grammar in another, and punctuation in another, attacks her problem with hammer and tongs. Her subject matter is fixed, her procedure is simple and the learnings per unit of time are easily observed, classified and labeled. The teacher who teaches children not merely to spell words, to describe punctuation and to parrot forth grammar, but to write letters and stories which are properly spelled, well punctuated and in correct English, cannot always tell just when and how class situations will produce these values. Letters are not written at certain prescribed moments, but when a message is to be sent in writing. But the learnings in terms of spelling, punctuation and grammar may go on, not in a logically organized fashion, such as would delight many a formalist, but in a scattered fashion most difficult to describe. They might be accompanied with many other learnings in terms of social intercourse, the content of the letter written and the activities concerned, learnings which cannot be clearly ticketed or described. This haziness which may characterize the meeting point of the child's responses and the values of the curriculum is very confusing to some. In fact the whole matter is so difficult to define or describe that some lack faith to believe that the child actually reaches the goals of the curriculum at all. When such complexities as these exist, analysis becomes not less but even more necessary. It becomes the more imperative to understand and master the technique of the new teaching in which the difficulties and problems are so much more numerous.

The General Problems of Teaching Technique

It is of fundamental importance to make some study and present some analysis of the technique of teaching as it has been worked out by teachers who organize their teaching in terms of conduct. The problems of teaching technique are the problems of bridging the gap which exists between the child and the curriculum. Technique is concerned with the economical conduct of method. By what procedures shall the responses of the child be linked with the goals of the curriculum? There was a time when the gap was bridged by beginning with the subject matter and building across toward the child, by using building materials of subject matter and attempting to fit them to the child's personality. Thus a list of the continents was prepared and children were shown the various continents on the map and expected to learn the list. The technique of teaching was therefore concerned with such matters as the following:

The subject matter had first to be prepared in organized form, say a discussion of continents in the textbook. This subject matter was to be gotten up by the teacher and planned or organized for teaching before she went to class. In class the teacher was faced with the task of awakening the children's interests in continents, and of linking the subject matter to the children by stimulating an effort to learn which would involve its mastery. Finally, it was necessary to keep the children in order and control while this process was going on. Consequently discussions of technique directed toward a maintenance of this régime were concerned with such things as subject matter, units of geography or history and their mastery, the development of prearranged lesson plans, the organization of subject matter into satisfactory lesson types in accordance with its essential structure, the suggestion of devices and artificial forms of awakening the interest of children in the subject matter. Again the problems of order were considered. How might children be kept from misbehaving? If they failed to behave, what forms of punishment were suitable? Punishment frequently became necessary because the child found himself involved in a system which clashed with his nature.

The teacher committed to a more modern form of procedure tends to reverse the process of teaching just described. Instead of beginning with the curriculum, she begins with the responses of the children. Picking these up as she finds them, she guides them into new channels and directs the learning process in such a way that the responses of the children link naturally, and with as little friction as possible, to the values of the curriculum. The children's longing for vicarious romance and adventure may easily find its expression in a desire to follow the heroic and colorful deeds of the great explorers, and to travel with them in imagination as they discovered unknown continents; or the word "continent" might turn up as a perplexing unknown in some of the other work of the class, or some class visitor who had visited several continents might tell the story of his travels, using the map to describe his route from continent to continent. The skillful teacher would follow up such leads and see to it that the children had not merely a mastery of a list of names, but an organized knowledge of continents and a vital concept to associate with each of the names. Thus the process of teaching is not one of crude fitting and building of blocks of subject matter, such as the names of continents. Rather it is the complex webbing and weaving of children's interests and responses into a rich learning pattern involving a significant knowledge and understanding of the continents of the world, and also of many other things.

Teaching of such intricate fabric and pattern is not simple to describe. Consequently, it will not be surprising if the discussions of newer techniques of teaching are less clean-cut and definite than those to which many are accustomed. Generalization is much more difficult. The beginnings of teaching in terms of children's responses, being hypothetical, are less simply discussed. Lesson patterns being more intricate, they will be less adaptable to formal analysis and description in terms of types. The more delicate fitting together of children's responses with curriculum gains should result in an entirely new treatment of class order and behavior, one in which greater knowledge and more delicate handling should result in finer balance and superior conduct. The elimination of a great deal of the friction of the educative process should bring about a happier and pleasanter régime in the schoolroom, one in which the grosser forms of punishment are practically unnecessary.

If the reader is to avoid confusion, it is very necessary that what follows be approached with these limitations and characteristics in mind. Readers should not expect to find in these pages the formal discussions of teaching which occur in other treatises on technique. Such formal analyses based on a generation of experience in public schools are made with comparative ease. Not only would such formal and didactic discussion be impossible, but it is entirely foreign to the spirit of the new teaching which proceeds, not by formula, but by an understanding interpretation and direction of the specific case; not by rules, but by principles.

CHAPTER VII

THE FUNDAMENTAL BASES OF TECHNIQUE

IN ORDER to have a complete understanding of the teaching process as a basis for the technique of teaching, it is necessary to have some clear idea of the actual factors of the educative process, and an understanding of their relationships. Briefly, these factors are the child, the environment, and the teacher.

THE CHILD

Education exists in behalf of the child. Whatever goes on in school should therefore bear a direct relationship to children. Teaching should begin with the child, who is to be regarded as the initiator and the maintainer of his own processes of learning.

THE ENVIRONMENT

The environment will be discussed at length in a succeeding section. It is the world in which the child lives. The curriculum is a very specialized part of the environment. It is a series of goals toward which the child's active process of learning is directed.

THE TEACHER

The teacher is responsible for stimulating children's responses, for accepting from among the responses which they initiate, those which are suitable for school life, and guiding them toward the goals of the curriculum.

The teacher's fulfillment of these responsibilities depends upon her technique of teaching, her way of relating the child and the curriculum. This technique, in turn, depends upon two very important concepts or principles. The first of these is the concept of activities, or units of conduct, as variable bridges between the child and the curriculum. The second is the idea of the maintaining of the flow of the learning process from the child to the curriculum, rather than in the opposite direction. These two fundamental bases of the technique of teaching will be considered in the following paragraphs.

THE FUNDAMENTAL BASES OF TECHNIQUE

1. Arranging Units of Conduct as Variable Bridges Between the Child and the Curriculum

Granted that life is composed of a series of interlocking or interweaving units of conduct, and that school life may be composed of a similar complex of living, it must yet be made clear how the experiencing of such a series of self-initiated units of conduct may secure that desired relating of the child and the curriculum which is called learning. The problem may be clarified by a consideration of the way in which a child acquires skill in handwriting or in manuscript writing. Such a skill may be developed by the carrying on by the child of a series of units of living or units of conduct which involve writing. Such activities are those in which the child writes stories, letters, poems or book reviews. They arise from the child's own needs, and during their progress the child gradually attains the skill of penmanship.

It is obvious that in such cases the units of conduct involved serve as bridges between the child and the curriculum. These bridges are variable bridges. In other words, these units of conduct need not necessarily be the same for each child. For example, certain units of life will involve writing in a book, while others will involve the writing of letters. Furthermore, there need be no fixed sequence of units. It is not necessary to arrange a regular series of units such as one letter a day, one essay a week, and one book report a month. Such an organization is artificial and formal. The units, under such circumstances, would not be the children's own self-initiated activities. Such a mechanical arrangement is not necessary, for genuine units of conduct are variable bridges which span the "gap" between the child and the curriculum.

2. Maintaining the Flow of the Learning Process From the Child to the Curriculum Rather Than in the Opposite Direction

The second fundamental problem of the technique of teaching is the governing of units of conduct in such a way that they arise from children's own self-initiated drives, and are carried on by the children themselves. In other words, it is the problem of maintaining the directional flow of the learning process from the child to the curriculum rather than vice versa.

The teacher must realize that in a very fundamental sense her problems of teaching technique are those of arranging for the initiation and carrying on of units of conduct. By arranging and governing such situations the teacher is fulfilling her responsibility in ideal fashion. Attention has already been called to the fact that normal children are eager and anxious to learn. It is important to note that this fact is attested on every hand. "Children," says Washburne,[1] "are naturally curious about the world in which they live, its nature and its processes. This curiosity is basic for all independent learning, and, if allowed to develop, its driving force continues through school, needing only the guidance of the teacher. Only when it is thwarted and repressed does learning become drudgery. This native interest is fostered in all possible ways. It is stimulated and led into channels related to school work. In this way learning comes from within the child, rather than being imposed as teaching from without."

This statement finds its psychological counterpart in Woodworth's conception of drive as set forth in his "Dynamic Psychology."[2] He points out that an individual, whom we may imagine as standing before us for examination, "contains within himself a large assortment of possible activities. We know that if we show him familiar objects, he will recognize and name them; that if we ask him suitable questions, he will understand and answer; that if we set him suitable tasks, he will perform them; that anger or embarrassment or amusement can be awakened in him by appropriate means; that he can walk, jump, move his eyes, breathe, eat, digest, and, in short, display a large repertory of accomplishments. He is equipped with a whole machine-shop of mechanisms for accomplishing this variety of results. We know, however, that he will not behave in a purely machine-like manner. He may refuse to answer some of our questions; he may object to being detained for further examination, on the plea that he has business of his own to attend to; and if we follow him through the day, we shall observe him at one time start out in quest of food, at another to seek rest. We shall observe him devoting hours of attention and effort to such apparently unstimulating objects as columns of figures or rows of potato plants. He evidently contains within himself a variety of driving forces, as well as a variety of mechanisms to be driven."

This concept of the learning process having its origin in the life force of the child-learner, and being carried forward by him in vital fashion, gives rise to a fundamental theory of teaching, namely, that

[1] WASHBURNE and DUMMER, in *The New Era*, London, July, 1929, p. 167.
[2] WOODWORTH, R. S., "Dynamic Psychology," Columbia University Press, New York, 1918, p. 38.

THE FUNDAMENTAL BASES OF TECHNIQUE 71

teaching is best carried on by maintaining the directional flow of the learning process from the child to the curriculum. To give an initial concrete illustration, such a directional flow might be regarded as maintained when an eight-year-old girl, on her own initiative, chooses a book from the shelf of supplementary readers selected by the teacher, gets permission to take it home over the week-end, reads it through from beginning to end, enjoys its contents, makes, almost unconsciously, new gains in mastery of reading skills, and reports to the other children on Monday what she liked about the book, recommending to them that they read it too.

On the contrary, teaching which attempts to proceed in the opposite direction from the curriculum to the child might be illustrated by a case in which a class engaged in painting pictures which the children are loath to leave unfinished, is informed that since it is ten o'clock they must stop and open their readers at the lesson on page seventy-three, which, according to the teacher's term plan, is the lesson for the day. The teacher then reads through the lesson for the children, pronouncing the new words for them and explaining the meaning as she proceeds. This finished, the children are called on in turn to re-read the material of the text, while they are prompted and corrected whenever they hesitate at a word or make a mistake. No trained teacher anywhere would dream of proceeding as in this last illustration; furthermore, the trained teacher's abhorrence of it is based on her allegiance to the principle that the learning process proceeds from the child toward the curriculum as here maintained.

It is because trained teachers recognize the living, driving quality in the personality of the child that, "the new school organizes itself around the child's intention to learn," [3] rather than around the teacher's intention to teach him. Learning must be regarded as an active process moving forward to establish relationships between the child and the curriculum. A diagrammatic representation may make the exposition clearer. If, for purposes of discussion, we observe the convention of regarding the relationships between the child and the curriculum as represented by a horizontal line,[4] thus—

CHILD ——————————————— CURRICULUM

[3] RUGG and SHUMAKER, "The Child-Centered School," World Book Co., Yonkers-on-the-Hudson, 1928, p. 102.
[4] The horizontal line is used as a diagram here to attain simplicity of exposition. The directional flow of learning is perhaps better indicated as in chapter VIII by the use of a circle. This will not confuse those who realize that diagrams are used to indicate relationships and are not to be regarded as analogies.

having adopted this convention, it is here maintained that the directional movement of the learning process from the child forward toward what he is learning should be indicated by arrow heads, thus—

CHILD >————>————>————> CURRICULUM

rather than *vice versa*, or, thus—

CHILD <————<————<————< CURRICULUM

This fundamental concept will hereafter be used as a principle of reference in developing a consistent theory of teaching.

Some emphasis should be laid upon this idea of the directional flow of the learning process. It is to be hoped that this concept makes it possible to avoid certain phrases which have sometimes been used to indicate important characteristics of modern theories and methods. Some of these have been particularly unfortunate. For instance, the terms "free schools" and "schools of freedom" are most misleading to those who are unfamiliar with their special meaning. The word "freedom" is apt to connote to the popular mind the idea of license and lack of restraint or control. Again, the term "child-centered," or as some learned soul has devised it, "paedo-centric," is undesirable because of its static nature. It seems to connote a child-idol stationary on a pedestal, whom the teacher worships and to whom she bows down. Nothing is further from the good teacher's mind than such an attitude. To her the child is weak and ignorant and unwise, but full of unbounded potentiality for living and growing through experiences. His life is moving on in an integrated stream like a brook over brown stones and among green trees. This child's whole personality is not a stream to be dammed up and thwarted, to be forced through myriad pipes under pressure, nor to be allowed to stray heedlessly and to dissipate itself in a thousand aimless wandering brooklets. Rather is it to flow on in its completeness, enriched by a hundred tributary streams of experience until it flows as a river, broad and deep.

CHAPTER VIII

THE NATURE AND FUNCTION OF INTEREST

THERE are several major problems involved in the initiating and maintaining of units of school life in such a fashion that the directional flow of the learning process may be from the child toward the curriculum. The first of these which will be taken up in this chapter, is the dual problem of interest and effort. If the organization of school life is to be in the terms which have already been discussed, there is urgent necessity that the teacher should be thoroughly acquainted with the nature of interest, a matter which is widely misunderstood. The initiation and continuance of units of conduct depend to a large extent upon interest and upon the exertion of pupil effort.

THE NATURE OF INTEREST AS A MEANS TO EFFORT

1. The Relationships of Interest and Effort

In spite of Dewey's illuminating analysis of the relationship of interest to effort,[1] there continues to be a widespread misunderstanding of the matter. There seems to be considerable apprehension in some quarters lest the reliance of the teacher upon interest is, after all, nothing but an attempt at sugar-coating, and really an indication of soft pedagogy. Consequently, it becomes important to understand, if possible, just why this distrust of interest continues.

In the first place, many of the critics of interest are teachers who habitually think of teaching in terms of subject matter to be taught, rather than in terms of child life.[2] They are confirmed in ways of thinking which interpret the teaching process in terms of subject matter, such as spelling, geography, or French, rather than in terms of conduct, such as writing a mannerly letter to a tourist company for information concerning a trip to France, where one might talk with

---

[1] DEWEY, JOHN, "Interest and Effort," Houghton Mifflin Co., Boston, 1913.
[2] For a more complete presentation of this distinction see "Progressive Teaching," D. Appleton & Co., New York, 1929, Ch. 5.

the French people. They conceive of the materials of teaching as being the inert, quiescent subject matter of the curriculum.

It is important to realize that the synthesis of the problems of interest and effort takes place only when interest is regarded subjectively, as an attribute of a living, dynamic unit of conduct, such as modeling the head of Lincoln or caring for a flock of chickens. Interest has no actual abstract existence separate from the active process of living. Any attempt to isolate interest as a concept and to discuss it aside from the life process of which it is part leads to misunderstanding of teaching. Consequently, any attempt to consider interest in relation to the lifeless, objective, subject matter of the curriculum becomes fallacious and misleading. In a dead curriculum there is no driving force. So the thinker whose modes of thought are in terms of mere subject matter attempts to infuse life into his concepts by the use of the term "effort." Interest to him seems like an attempt to perform a surgical operation on the subject matter to give it a little life. Effort to him means a tapping of the life force of the child in an attempt to set up directional flow of his life force toward the subject matter. He offers a prize to the lad who struggles hardest and makes the highest term record in spelling. Interest becomes a product of teacher effort, a trick of pedagogy, a thing anemic and reprehensible, while effort becomes a manly appeal to the character and personality of the child.

As soon as one drops the subject-matter point of view and considers interest in relation to the conduct of children all the vitality of living returns to the concept. Interest is no longer the pandering attempt of a teacher to furbish up a dull bit of subject matter, but the forceful, vital reaching out of the child's personality toward things which he covets. When a child has an appreciative audience among his school fellows he will hunt widely for good passages to read to them. The active child who wants to learn has a store of effort which follows on where interest leads.

2. *Wasted Effort*

Another source of the general misunderstanding of interest seems to lie in confusion concerning the nature of effort. It is mistakenly supposed that the more disagreeable or unpleasant the task upon which a child determinedly engages, the greater the effort he puts into learning. Consider, for example, the case of a student in high school who is required to study the binomial theorem. He discusses the matter with the teacher of algebra, asking just why a high school boy should study the binomial theorem. The teacher answers, telling him that in all probability the binomial theorem will never be of any use to him in the actual problems of life, but that there are other reasons for studying it. First it trains the mind, secondly, in all probability, there will be several difficult problems concerned with the binomial theorem on the coming examination. Furthermore, if the boy is anxious to get a scholarship in college, he ought to make a high grade in the examination. Under such a stimulus the boy, anxious to do his duty to the best of his ability, refuses an invitation to an evening party and remains at home working abstruse and difficult problems on the binomial theorem. One of the problems proves extremely difficult. In an effort to solve it he sits up working until eleven o'clock, when he becomes so sleepy that he cannot carry on. He might at this point follow what may be regarded as the laudable example of Thomas Platter, a medieval student, who kept himself awake at his midnight studies by placing sand in his mouth! But let us not make of our high school boy so "exemplary" an example. Let us suppose he is just a bright American lad who goes to bed leaving his problem unsolved.

This account is not intended to represent current practice, but to illustrate the point under discussion. For there are some who would maintain that by studying in this determined fashion, the student was putting the maximum of effort into the learning process. It is doubtless true that he was expending a great deal of effort, but that effort was not being expended altogether in learning. Rather a great deal of it was used to overcome various physical and psychological obstacles to learning. It was, from the point of view of learning, wasted effort, effort put forth with the minimum of return in terms of valuable and vital educational gains. So it is not enough for the teacher to secure effort. She must secure fruitful effort, effort which yields the maximum of return in learnings which are significant and useful.

When the pupil is carried on through the arduous process of learning by a real interest, then there is a minimum of wasted effort. It is conceivable that a boy might refuse an invitation to a party because he is called to a committee meeting to work on a real immediate and pressing mathematical problem in assisting the principal of the elementary school to regroup the pupils in accordance with certain findings in a testing program, or that he might remain at home to complete a story which must be handed to the editor of the school paper in the morning. If he is thoroughly interested in these proceedings he puts into them a full degree of effort. The fact that they are agreeable and interesting means that this effort is not partially diverted into the overcoming of obstacles to learning. Rather it goes in its fulness into the activity with its resulting learnings. When interest is at its highest, the fullest degree of the life energy of the learner is most economically conserved and directed into the actual process of learning.

3. The Real and the Superficial Meaning of Interest

Another cause for the distrust of interest in teaching is the confounding of the more superficial, colloquial use of the word with its deeper and technical sense, the only sound sense in which it may be used in a discussion of teaching. The world is full of grown-ups, many, one might say the majority, of whom are badly trained and ill-adjusted to life. Such persons are apt to recognize as interesting only those things which are easy, pleasant, or gratifying to the senses. They are likely to call more intellectual or difficult pursuits "uninteresting." If we should use such adult standards in judging children, it would be no wonder if we were to distrust the use of the word "interest." So people fear that children who are allowed to follow their own interests may become selfish and pleasure-loving, anxious for the easier and more agreeable ways, and repelled by anything stern, which demands moral courage. But fortunately children's interests are not flaccid. They are not the interests of an adult dilettante, or of a self-indulgent esthete. They are wholesome, and embrace life and all its manifestations. Children may become as interested in helping others as in helping themselves. A boy may be as well trained to give the larger "half" to his smaller brother as to grab it for himself. Children are not afraid of work. They are not afraid of what is hard; they are not afraid of self-sacrifice; they are not afraid of effort.

It is for the teacher to protect children's interests from becoming warped. Small children are interested in almost anything when they first come to school. By developing their interests in every valuable direction, the teacher should save them from accepting low and selfish standards of interest. Bad training results in the development of poor habits of interest. If children who are interested in birds, trees, talking, building, singing, paddling, and running are confined to physical inaction, not allowed to talk, forbidden to run, and urged to become engaged in some few interesting tasks such as writing and reading to the exclusion of a hundred others, it is little wonder if these limited interests soon begin to pall, not because they are uninteresting, but because they are overdone. Being overdone, they become obnoxious, and so the formal program of the school may become disliked and uninteresting.

So children's normal interests may be killed, and the school may train them to lose interest in what it regards as of fundamental importance. Bad training may thus prevent the expansion of children's interests, force them to inaction, and consequently put them in a mood to hunt for an easy way out, to escape school tasks for pranks which are interesting. If children's interests are conserved, if they are trained to select from among their interests those which are imperative for the needs of their best living, then they will be trained to live in ways which are sound.

Consequently, teachers who sponsor interest as fundamental to learning must unhesitatingly shoulder the burden of giving an all-round development to children's interests. They must unfailingly and painstakingly train children in the rigid selection of their best interests in accordance with their best needs. Frankness demands the statement that such teachers have not always been facing this responsibility fully. Sometimes children's interests have been confused with their needs. Since children's interests are so wide, it would be impossible to follow them all. It is necessary to select best interests. So teachers must guide children to choose profitable interests such as art and music rather than unprofitable ones such as movies and pugilism. They must guide children to follow their interests in work as well as play. It is essential for the development of sound character in the new schools that teachers who have been neglecting an all-round development of interests should spare no effort in tightening up their method. We need a vigorous, not an idyllic conception of interest.

4. *The Recognition of Interest in the Class Group*

Granted that one clearly understands the nature of interest, there still remains the problem of recognizing interest in the class group. How may teachers know when the group as a whole, or any individual child in the group, is actually interested? Just here teachers seem to have failed. There has been a tendency to assume the presence of interest in the new schools even when it is not actually present. Having given assent to the doctrine of interest and worked out a method which is theoretically in accordance with it, some teachers have tended to argue in a circle and assume that since their method was in accordance with the theory of interest, then the children *must* be interested in their school activities.

But we cannot afford to be so debonair in assuming the presence of interest in the new schools. We must be prepared to answer the charge made by one critic who writes of the loose practice in the classrooms of certain famous experimental schools: "Compare the attitude of the children toward the study of boats, for instance, with the attitude of a traditional class toward the traditional subjects presented by a skillful teacher. You will be surprised to find a lack of interest on the part of the children that is truly alarming." Certainly teachers must be prepared to identify and interpret interest in terms of effort.

Effort is more easily observed and estimated than the interest of which it is a manifestation. It is, therefore, a more suitable barometer of activity than interest alone. Since interest and effort go hand in hand, the one may be taken as the evidence of the other. Thus when activities proceed not under compulsion but freely, having their rise from a satisfactory need, then effort is the best visible criterion of interest. So the teacher and the observer in the new classroom will be continually watching to see what degree of effort children put forth in the pursuit of the goals which they have determined to reach. Are the children who are building playhouses, writing poetry, drilling in arithmetic, or visiting a colonial mansion actually putting their whole energies into the task to which they are devoting themselves? Are they calling on the whole resources of their personalities to carry out the units of conduct upon which they are engaged? Are they expending the maximum of effort in what is, from the point of view of learning, the most economical fashion? Only by rigidly judging her class work by such criteria, and, as nearly as possible, living up to such standards, can the new teacher justify her work to critics accustomed to high standards of performance in traditional schools. Effort is, and ever must be, the most obvious criterion of interest in school work.

5. *Resident and Active Interest*

The distinction may be made at this point between resident and active interests. The use of the word "interest" is very different in each of these two phrases. In the case of resident interest, the word denotes a state of affairs in the organism irrespective of any relationship to specific acts which are going on at the time of speaking. We say that a person is interested in dogs, in sea-weeds, in interior decoration, or in the Einstein theory. By such a statement we do not

THE NATURE AND FUNCTION OF INTEREST 79

mean that the person referred to is actually engaged at the moment upon any one of these concerns, but that due to his inherited responses and his acquired behavior, which have involved him in these matters, he has developed a set of psychological connections which are liable to be made when situations involving these resident readinesses occur. Consequently, we may say that two men playing chess of an evening have different interests, but those resident interests are not manifest until they read the morning paper. At such a time the first individual reads the news of the dog show to the neglect of an article on Einstein's most recent statement which is read by his friend. These interests which were resident when the two played chess were not active or operative until they read the morning paper.

Similarly we may refer to children's resident interests in food, or animals, or fairies, or ships. By this we mean that children's inherited and acquired drives, their curiosities and their tendencies to do or make, have already developed neural patterns which may be called into action when certain situations occur. It is to such resident interests that we refer when we say that an individual has made a study of children's interests in primary reading. We refer to neural patterns or resident readinesses upon which we can rely. Again, it is in a similar sense that Herbart used the phrase, "many-sided interests." He advocated the provision of school experiences in many directions so that after years of schooling children should have acquired resident interests in swimming, art, music, and numerous other things. Thus, in a sense, resident interests are to be relied on as beginning points and looked forward to as ends of the teaching process. When we visit a school studio in which clay modeling is going on, we may find a child who is dabbling with his materials, leaving them frequently and gossiping with his friends, and, on the whole, accomplishing nothing in the way of a concrete result. We ask the question, "Is this child interested in his work—he is not doing anything about it?" The teacher may reply, "That is true just at the moment, but you would be surprised to find how very interested he is in modeling in clay; he is very artistic and always ready to talk about such things; he has a real interest in this kind of work." But the point which the teacher is missing is this: what the child should be expressing during school hours is active interest in the process upon which he is engaged. This interest only, not passive and resident, but active and manifest, is the kind of interest which is the justification of method. Teachers must not salve their consciences for lack of children's interest in, and effort upon the task in hand, by falling back upon resident interest as a defense of their method. Resident interest may be the beginning point and the goal of teaching, but only active interest is an adequate accompaniment of the learning process as it actually goes on in school.

6. *The Teacher's Use and Control of Interest*

It is important for the teacher to distinguish between the function of interest in the initiation of activities, and the function of interest in maintaining them, once they have been initiated. Interests have a very special significance in the initiating of activities. If the directional flow of the learning process is to be initiated by the child, then it must arise via his interests. The teacher should find in them a great wealth of materials which is of very special significance in making beginnings, in getting started on any new line of action. So the robins first seen in the springtime may lead to a study of bird migrations, or the children's interest in a traveler from Alaska may be led on into a study of Alaskan geography. Children's interests are not valuable in and for themselves, but largely because of their leading-on quality.

Once, however, an activity has been initiated by the children need the teacher's attitude toward the children's interests be so tolerant? Should she allow new interests to arise freely and interfere with the progress of others? Should she allow children to pick up and abandon their interests at will, to wander here and there selecting and neglecting them at random? To be more specific, suppose that a group of children has decided to make a garden, and has begun to put the idea into practice. Suppose further that as the work progresses their interest lags, but a new interest in butterflies arises from their experiences in making their garden. Should the children be permitted to give up the garden and pursue their study of insects by making a collection of specimens and by studying the life of the butterfly? Again, should a child who is reading a book give it up in the middle because he has become more interested in cricket and finds no time for reading? Few would advocate any such incoherent form of procedure. Obviously this shifting of interests is not a sound mode of procedure in life and consequently is not a sound mode of procedure in teaching school. A unit of conduct which children have initiated should be carried through to the end.

What then shall we say of flagging interests? It is important to realize that while activities may be initiated by children, the teacher is still faced with the very definite problem of the span of an interest. In the first place, the teacher must help the children select carefully from among numerous interests. In beginning any such unit of conduct as the building of a play city or the study of the way in which man has kept records throughout past generations, she must carefully consider whether or not the interest of the children is sufficiently great to extend, with a reasonable degree of likelihood, to the completion of the unit of conduct initiated. Again, she must be prepared to buttress weakening interest and encourage children to carry out what they have begun. Some teachers seem to have the naïve faith that any interest which is real and vivid to children in the beginning of an activity will have sufficient propulsive quality to carry them through to the end. Children's interests sometimes flare forth at the beginning of an enterprise, such as planning to earn money to send to poor children at Christmas, an enterprise which at first seems rosy with possibilities, only to die down in a few days until they are ready to abandon their plans without encouragement and assistance.

It is important that children learn to realize the *expulsive quality of an interest*. An interest, once adopted, must drive other things away. When an interest such as that of earning money for poor children has been felt, and the individual or group has begun to carry it out, there is a moral responsibility to see it through to its conclusion. When one commits oneself to an interest and to its service, that interest should drive other things from its path. Children who begin to sing in the school chorus should be expected to keep it up, even when the outdoor skating is particularly good and is luring them from rehearsals. But such competition between profitable activities does occur. Children cannot remain at the highest level of interest all through the progress of a unit of conduct on which they have collectively or individually embarked. Consequently, teachers must recognize that their technique must provide for the continual reënforcing of original interests. Teachers must help children to live up to their better interests.

A further problem which complicates the matter of interest in school is that of *group interests* in group enterprises. Clear distinction must be made between the interest of an individual in a unit of conduct which he has himself initiated and the interest of an individual in some coöperative unit of conduct which he helps the whole group to carry on. It is impossible that every member of the group should be equally interested in such a joint activity. It would be reasonable to suppose that the individuals who proposed the activity would be more interested in it than others who have proposed an alternative activity, which failed to carry the majority. Thus children who wanted to study the city's water supply would be less interested in a study of the city's system of waste disposal if the latter carried the class instead of the former. Again, children of greater general ability are likely to be more interested in any activity than duller children. On the other hand, a person of no particular general ability may take a special interest in such a piece of work as the production of a play if she has the leading rôle, while a bright child may be irked by a subsidiary part. To take all such matters into account in the technique of teaching is no simple matter. There is considerable need for the scientific study of group interests and their direction, in order that fresh light may be thrown upon the problem of coöperative group activities.

The Teacher's Attitude Toward Interest

It should be clear, after this lengthy consideration of interest, that teachers should be most careful in their discussions of teaching in terms of interest. We must particularly beware of enthusiasms which find expression in careless use of the term "interest." We should willingly recognize that no teacher, old or new, can maintain interest at white heat throughout all the lessons of the school day. Nor should we pretend to believe that there is anything sacred about children's interests which should allow them to have full sway, or to swing school life this way and that as a wind that bloweth whither it listeth. Interest is no fairy godmother, to wave a magic wand in behalf of the teacher who evokes her aid. Interest is not a gift but an attainment. It is a good teacher indeed under whose guidance children's interests lead on through effort to desirable learning.

CHAPTER IX

THE TECHNIQUE OF ENVIRONMENT AND EQUIPMENT

TEACHERS too often have erred by failing to understand the significance and the function of environment in the development of the child. The environment is what children live by, what they grow by, what they appropriate to themselves and by the strange alchemy of the psychological processes transmute and transform into personality. We have never failed to provide food for hungry bodies because the objective, the gross, the material is so easily understood. We have stacked our environment to provide for physical hunger. But what provision have we made for those other hungers of mind and spirit that cry out for nourishment from a well-provided environment? Too often we have taken children away from the provision that nature makes, unaided, and shut them off in rooms where there was literally no environment but indoor air. True we have provided quantities of ideas and of subject matter for children, but it has been parched, dry, and unpalatable to little organisms thirsty for activity. Environment is the quarry of personality. There children labor and build themselves of the materials they find about them.

Teachers need the conception of a dynamic environment. The environment is a power which molds and builds. Thought, ideals, materials, lie about on every hand, and as the child responds to them he is nourished by them. He lives and grows. Furthermore, there is a very special significance in the way in which the child grows. It is according to the patterns which he develops in childhood that he will live for many years. There is no room for new plants to be set out in the full garden of middle life, for the man is what he was as a child. It is in early childhood that the environment makes its mark.

It is particularly important to understand that the patterns that begin to develop in childhood, that take their form and nourishment from the environment, do not disappear. They are not replaced by other patterns. They grow and expand through the years and become the great fibers of the individual's life. A child whose mother sings and plays to him as an infant, who early learns to sing and play some instrument, is well on toward being a life-long music lover at eighteen. So children find in their environment what is to become part of themselves.

A Child's Size World

The charming phrase, "a child's size world," has been used to describe a good school. It brings before us a picture of the school as a group of children living their own lives happily with one another, in an environment which fits not merely their stature but their children's nature and their growing selves. A good environment for children must be one which is favorable to sound and vigorous growth. Comenius found a key for the understanding of children in the plant and the seed. Since his day the conception of growing childhood has taken a permanent place in our notion of the meaning of education. We find it recurring in Froebel's "Children's Garden" (kindergarten), and it is inherent in Dewey's concept of education as living.

But growth takes place best in a carefully prepared, rich environment. There are some who believe that children should be allowed to develop freely and become whatever they will. Such a theory is as useful to a teacher as to a gardener, no more. Shall we let our garden grow freely and become what it will? Is it of no consequence whether the soil be rich or poor, is it of no consequence whether it be planted with weeds or flowers? There is considerable talk about the danger of interference with the expression of the child's personality, of the error of "imposing" things on the child and of the sins of "indoctrination." We should be clear that we never impose on the child when he adopts, on his own volition, a wise course revealed to him. Nor do we indoctrinate in presenting to him honestly the teachings which are the fruits of ages of race experience. One does not remember the child best by forgetting his environment.

But if we are to make over our schools until the children find themselves in a child's size world, we must build our environment in terms of the lives of growing children. If we are to do so, there must be a world of change in customary ways of school living. How shall we remake the school environment in terms of the child? How shall we arrange school buildings to be the dwellings of the child's world? How shall we provide and equip a school so that it will be a good place for children to grow in? And how shall we guide the life patterns which

THE TECHNIQUE OF ENVIRONMENT AND EQUIPMENT

begin to develop into those of a beautiful and useful life? Such are the problems of environment. We must provide and equip a child's world, for in the environment the child finds himself, and what he finds, he becomes.

THE BUILDINGS OF THE CHILD'S WORLD

We live in houses. So in the child's world we will expect to find houses. Not office buildings, not skyscrapers, not manufacturing plants. There is no room for them. We should keep clearly in mind that the child's school world is a community. It is the big world in little. The school is not a specialized function of a community, but a whole community. If there are to be offices, or industrial plants, they will be there in little. The child's world is a world, a community, a complete organism, not a formalized institution. So we will hope to find our children housed, not in an elaborate stone or concrete structure, but in houses and among workshops which must take the place of many acres of specialized grown-up community living.

In order to get away from that common conception of a school which regards it as a building rather than as a living community, it may be best to describe concretely the way in which some schools have met the problem of housing the child's world. It is characteristic of life that we do not all solve our housing problems in the same way. In great cities people live in skyscrapers, even though it is a poor way to live. Perhaps their children may have to live poorly in great buildings, as their parents do, until some better way is found. In rural communities one small building may be adequate to house all the children who form the school world. The accompanying descriptions are not intended to indicate the only way in which the housing of the child world may be accomplished, but to furnish examples of excellent provisions made under circumstances which made them suitable. Their adequacy lies in the way in which they prove valuable for the living of the school group.

Faced with the opportunity of arranging a child's world practically without restriction, according to her ideals, Mary H. Lewis conceived and worked out the idea of a Primary Village.[1] Hers was the rare privilege of setting the children's village on a great farm and in the apple orchard. Instead of putting up one building, as so many others would have done, this enlightened teacher decided on "a lot of little houses" which were built for children. The little houses were set around

[1] LEWIS, M. H., "An Adventure with Children," Macmillan Co., New York, 1928.

a village green and each was arranged to house two "families" of children. Nor were the little houses all alike when they were built, but variation was secured by consulting the particular needs and requirements of different teachers. In this primary village the children lived and learned, engaged among other things in such real activities as keeping chickens and raising tomatoes, corn and potatoes. Here was a little world where children lived their own lives well.

Perhaps a more concrete idea of the possibilities which lie in a group of small buildings may be gained from the consideration of the way in which the Shady Hill School in Cambridge, Massachusetts, solved its problems. The accompanying plate is very helpful in visualizing the scheme. Beginning with general ideals, which included open-air type of ventilation combined with suitable central heating, sunshine, fresh air, quiet for every classroom and adequate floor space, a plan was worked out by the teachers in coöperation with the architect. From the beginning the teachers were set against artificial ready-made equipment that would interfere with freedom in teaching or limit floor space. Communal arrangement of locker-rooms, lavatories and study-rooms, which might tend to mechanize schedules, and everything savoring of institutionalism was avoided. In considering how these plans might best be worked out, a community of separate buildings was decided upon.[2]

"There are five home-room buildings, besides separate buildings for studio, laboratory, shop, and the main building which will house the offices, library, assembly hall and lunch kitchen. Each home-room building houses two classes, each with its large classroom, its study, lockers, and lavatories. We entirely eliminated the usual large locker-rooms and lavatories for the use of numbers of children.

"There was another reason for our choice of the village plan. It seemed somehow to provide a more natural, simple scheme of life for a school of young children than one large building could have afforded. We planned to place children of approximately the same age in the same house under a scheme of living adapted to their needs, thus avoiding the necessity of framing elaborate rules in order to control with equal fairness children of widely differing maturity."

The teachers testify that this school plant has proved to be both economical and excellent as a scheme to provide for the housing of a children's community.

[2] "The Coöperative Planning of a School," *Progressive Education*, Vol. IV, No. 2, April, 1927, p. 93.

The Shady Hill School.

The Children's Outdoor World

Teachers must restore to children the outdoor world which has been taken away from them. In the past, due to a distorted view of the function of the school, we have failed to remember that a great part of school life may be lived outdoors. It is a great wonder that with their practical minds our school administrators have never thought of this means of reducing school costs!

Our civilization is far too much an indoor one. Doctors are beginning to tell us of the diseases of civilization and of the relation between indoor living and tuberculosis. Gradually we have been realizing this. Windows which some centuries ago were closed at night, have crept open crack by crack. Today we actually indulge in screen doors and outdoor verandahs, and grown up people are beginning to make increasing use of outdoor life. It behooves the school to abandon its within-four-walls policy and show that it is in advance of current practice by getting the children out into the air, not merely to play but to work. We have great problems of school ventilation. Outdoors, there are none. In recent years school men have been realizing that sick children need outdoor air and we have our open-air schools and our open-window classes. "If such fresh air arrangements are indispensable for sick children," asks one astute soul, "why are they not valuable for well ones?"

There are many who will agree with this point of view in theory but insist that it is impossible to put into practice. It is, therefore, important to refute this belief completely and finally by pointing out that so far from being impossible or impracticable, it is actually being lived up to in many schools in many parts of the world, by teachers with the opportunity and the courage to put their principles into practice. A brief mention may be made of some schools, and there are many others, which make a large use of the outdoors during school hours. Such schools are the Ojai Valley School in California; Spring Hill School in Litchfield, Connecticut; and the Unquowa School in Bridgeport, Connecticut. The Carson College for Girls, Flourtown, Pennsylvania, makes continuous use of the outdoors for varied activities. In Downers Grove, Illinois, the children carry on constructive activities in the open. The students of Tower Hill School, Wilmington, Delaware, built a club house for themselves in the open. At Manumit School, Pawling, New York, the pupils are regularly engaged in the care of live stock. Teachers of the Los Angeles public schools take children abroad on nature excursions.

88   THE TECHNIQUE OF PROGRESSIVE TEACHING

In spite of such activities in numerous schools, not only in the United States but in all the countries of Europe, there are still the skeptics of the big cities who insist that there is no outdoor life for children dwelling there. Such individuals are steadfastly refusing to face the possibility of change. They stick determinedly to their conception of school buildings as they are. They will not face the fact that in the most crowded cities there is some outdoors. They are determined to conceive of school life in terms of first costs instead of in terms of final costs and child life. Fortunately, there are some teachers with the courage and initiative to put their ideals into practice. Public school teachers in New York are beginning to make increasing use of the parks and the open. Supervisors are becoming more and more liberal in their attitude toward open-air teaching. Many of the New York Public Schools have found out the value of that undiscovered country on the roofs. The City and Country School, the experimental section of Public School 41 (New York), under the direction of Miss Elisabeth Irwin, make copious use of the outdoor environment. Children from their first coming to school are taken out for trips to the parks, to the fire stations, and to the steamers in dock, until they are able to disentangle the vast web of the great city, confusing in its complexity to many an adult. In the matter of school life out of doors, as in everything else, where there's a will there's a way.

The use of the outdoor environment in teaching does not mean that school life is to be turned into the aimless outdoor play of boys and girls. Far from it. Outdoor life is replete with stimuli which actually generate activity of a kind which the skillful teacher may capitalize and direct into valuable channels of construction and work. The following accounts of boys' responses to a rich outdoor environment are given by Ralph C. Hill.[3] They indicate the way in which, in a suitable environment, valuable educative activities are spontaneously generated.

"Here are Bob and Jim tugging away at an old stump in the midst of a small woody hollow. Bob is eleven and Jim nine. After vigorous pushing and pulling and some talk about what holds the stump fast, they hammer and chop a bit with a light ax. Then they bring a spade into commission, and eventually the old stump yields to their persistent and varied efforts and is rolled away. What is happening?"

The author explains how this activity had its origin due to a stimulus received by the boys in attending a woodcraft council ceremony held by a neighboring group of boys at their camp. Conse-

[3] "Creative Activity in the Summer Camp," *Progressive Education*, Vol. IV, No. 2, pp. 113-115.

quently, their own outdoors environment took on for them a new significance as a possible site for a council ring. So they are engaged in the making of a council ring. It is their own idea and they work on it alone, but in sight of their comrades.

"Day after day they are absorbed in their enterprise. Finally, in a little clearing, reached by a winding path, there is a council ring with neat log seats. In the middle is a stone fireplace whose rocks are covered with thick moss—the finishing touch. Happy in their achievement, these two invite the twenty campers to attend a council fire and marshmallow roast. Bob, the engineer, rises and tells how the trackless jungle was transformed into this fine gathering place. Then Jim, the poet, rises and recounts the transplanting of a little hemlock, the idea of having the moss, the garter snake that they disturbed, and so on.

"Bob and Jim found themselves in a good world, where difficulties are encountered but can be broken down, where one dreams, not to escape an unpleasant routine, but to provide one with work fit for his hands, where one can enjoy a feeling of success without comparing himself to the less successful, where one with ideas need not constantly submit to the will of mightier people. Is there any doubt that they will soon be hatching plans for new and grander enterprises?"

Is it any wonder that some schools, where the environment is restricted, plan school camps when opportunity affords, in order that such rich experience may be capitalized for the group life of the school? The same writer gives two further examples, the first indicating the power of the outdoor environment not merely to stimulate activity but to triumph in its power over the quenching personality of an unwise grown-up.

The second account gives a fine example of a pure combination effected between a boy and environment which fitted his needs.

"A boy of eleven wanted to build a boat. He decided what kind of boat he wanted and how to make it. Then he searched along the lake shore for a piece of driftwood. Having found the right timber, he borrowed a saw and brought home a piece of the right length. He worked with the tools he could get together and sought help now and then when things became pretty difficult. Like the New England boat builders in colonial days, he cut his masts from the woods, and finally his boat was finished. This, too, was quite a handsome model, but it merely happened to be fine looking. The value of the achievement might have been as great had the model been comparatively crude."

Such an activity is a perfect example of a physical, constructive conduct unit. It is the power of a good environment to stimulate valuable units of conduct which makes it imperative for teachers to use the outdoor environment in school work. The educative value of the outdoor environment lays this responsibility upon them and makes its use valuable in a way which leaves the teacher no alternative.

So we may conceive of the school as in large part an outdoor workshop. Space should be provided about and near the school, not merely for play, but for work. If the school can be surrounded with wide acreage, so much the better. What a travesty it is to see children cooped indoors in a rural school, set among hills and woodlands. When such surroundings are not possible, a location near the woods or available free spaces should be influential in determining the site of the school. Somewhere in the locality, on the school grounds, if possible, we might hope to find many things. A brook is a luxury that comparatively few can hope to control. But for those who do, here is a model river to hand. Think of the children in a rural school studying about rivers from a textbook! The brook holds infinite possibilities in the way of building dams, studying water power and transportation, erosion, the source of rivers, floods in relation to human life, natural water life, rainfall and a thousand matters of human interest and concern. One group of children after reading accounts of the remains of villages found in the Swiss lakes set up a miniature village along a brook which flowed through the school grounds. What endless opportunities to begin the study of native life in the Philippines where the women wash clothing in the rivers, the paddy fields and the life of the junk dwellers in China.

Somewhere in the vicinity of the school a pond is a crying necessity. The ideal play pond is that about the fountain in the Luxembourg Gardens in Paris, which is raised up so that children sit on its edge and sail their boats. Next best perhaps is the round pond in Kensington Gardens in London which has a gently sloping edge of asphalt. But any pond has infinite possibilities in the way of physical and imaginative play with boats.

Of great importance is the provision of some rather large space for the construction of a play town such as that in which Mr. Caldwell Cook's boys of the Perse School in England found such delight.[4] Here is a wide field for the study of transportation, building, construction and industry.

A yard for pets is very much needed, and for the younger children a bird bath set well in the open away from danger, and a feeding

[4] See COOK, H. C., *opus cit.*, Ch. VI.

station for birds. Little need be said of the necessity of a school garden carefully planned and provided for from the preparing of the ground to the gathering of the crops, all the year round. Its values are so essential as to be obvious. Provision should also be made for the use of tools outdoors and space provided, perhaps in the environs, for the building by the older children of any such necessity as a clubhouse or a kiln for pottery.

The playground is the most usual aspect of outdoor school life. It should be as spacious as possible and not a mere bit of ground from which the grass has been worn entirely away. It should have trees and grass and places clearly set apart for ball and strenuous games. The equipment for the younger children should not be a mere provision of a few bars and swings, but should be provided for balls and games, with wagons, carts and the sturdy form of playthings which provoke plentiful activity, to the avoidance of merry-go-rounds and such bits of equipment as produce excitement rather than purposeful activity. The matter of playground equipment has been so well and thoroughly treated elsewhere that no further discussion is necessary here. It may well be studied by consulting the references given.[5]

Arrangement and Equipment of the Classroom

It has been well said that the classroom should be half a home and half a workshop. That distinction is indicative of a mechanical arrangement which teachers have found extremely convenient, the provision of a workroom as a supplementary room for each classroom. In this arrangement we see the classroom taking on the semblance of a community. The quiet activities and the group activities which need plenty of floor space may be arranged in the larger room while noisier and more individual activities go on in the workroom. Here again is a world in little; the classroom becomes a place of community living. It takes on the appearance of home and workshop. It has a comfortable, homey, furnished look, there is adequate space for play and work of individuals and groups, there are sufficient materials about the room to provide for the building of ideals, appreciations and values—pictures, books, a phonograph with records

[5] GARRISON, S. C., "Permanent Play Materials for Young Children," Scribners, New York.
HUNT, "A Catalog of Play Equipment" (Pamphlet), Bureau of Educational Experiments, 144 W. 13th St., New York.
Pamphlets of the Recreation and Playground Association of America, 315 Fourth Ave., New York.

to play, a radio and a wealth of books. Such things have been called "materials for impression." In addition there are materials for expression—tools and various things used in arts and crafts.

In the general equipment of the room there are several necessities. The children's chairs and tables are movable and can be variously arranged according to the requirements for work and the necessity for floor space. Blackboards, bulletin boards and windows compete for their share of wall space. There must be bookshelves and a reading table, preferably a round one, which may be set near the classroom library for the use of children consulting or reading books from the shelves. A bit of wall space must be sacrificed to the demands of a bulletin board and considerable space will be taken up with closets for strong materials. Provision may sometimes be needed, especially in the lower classes, for individual lockers for the children's own materials and belongings. Screens—plain, upright and folding ones—are very necessary for setting off sections of the classroom which are not to be seen or disturbed and for use in classroom dramatization. Such an environment by the very amount of careful housekeeping it requires indicates the home aspect of such a classroom.

A still more complex problem is that of the provision of materials which are needed in the manifold activities upon which the children engage. Teachers who are being trained to maintain the flow of the learning process from the child to the curriculum are under the imperative necessity of studying not merely curriculum and subject matter, as were teachers who began to teach with the curriculum, but also activities and materials. The child begins to learn by means of activities and materials. Without such a study the teacher remains almost entirely unconscious of the relationships which exist between a hundred and one simple and useful materials in the environment and the ways in which they fit into school life. To the ordinary individual a used milk bottle cap has no significance. To the teacher it is the stuff of which cart wheels and toy money are manufactured. Shoe buttons are doll's eyes and used kodak films furnish a supply of red or black paper for cutouts.

But these are mere examples. How is the teacher to learn of window-card colors and cardboards and papier-mâché, their sources, appropriate sizes, their prices and where they are to be bought? These questions are the daily problems of teachers in activity schools. This is a mystery with which it is impossible to deal here. But fortunately it is possible to direct the reader to the work of Miss Rose B. Knox who, by providing an account of these very matters in the fullest and most complete fashion has produced a book which no modern teacher can afford to be without as a personal possession. It is the most practical, useful and indispensable book on the materials of new teaching which is available. This book, "School Activities and Equipment," [6] gives a thorough account of the materials for use in construction, literature, art, library, museum, and miscellaneous school work in a form related to the activities in which they are likely to be used. Not only this, but it gives complete directions for their storing, their use, and makes note of their cost, where they may be secured and how they may be used in teaching. It gives concretely, and in detail, the description of the environment of the modern school.

[6] Houghton Mifflin Co., Boston, 1927.

CHAPTER X

INTEREST CENTERS IN THE SCHOOL ENVIRONMENT

IT REMAINS to consider the general technique of the way in which the teacher relates the situations present in the environment to units of conduct valuable for learning. This problem may be better understood by a consideration of what may be called "interest centers" [1] in the environment. Interest centers may be regarded as dynamic points in the environment. They are situations in the environment which are particularly potent in awakening children's interest and activity, although they do not really become potent until children find in them the stimulus. Teachers learn to recognize these situations and are able to judge from experience just what elements in the environment are especially valuable as interest centers. Comenius recognized the importance of object teaching. He advocated the introduction of objects into the classroom and their use while teaching the lesson. His textbook, "Orbis Pictus," was revolutionary in that it contained pictures related to the Latin lessons on the accompanying pages. Here was a step in the direction of re-introducing into the environment stimuli of which it had been deprived by the segregation of children in barren classrooms. Teachers were long in learning the lesson. One of the reasons was that it was not fully clear just wherein the potency of objects as aids to teaching really lay. Unconsciously Comenius was providing interest centers. He discovered empirically points of contact between the child and the curriculum.

Pestalozzi took a further step in this direction. Often, for lack of texts, he discovered the environment as a source of experience, and experience as a source of learning. He discovered new media for learning and established the validity of learning via such activities as working in the soil, spinning and various forms of handicraft.

Yet through all this development there seems to have been a strange lack of realization of the actual potency of environment. The

---

[1] Attention is called to the fact that the term "interest centers" is entirely different in its significance from the term "centers of interest" which has come into use in descriptions of work similar to that done by Dr. DeCroly in Belgium. Centers of interest refer to large units of conduct about which other subsidiary units gather.

INTEREST CENTERS IN THE SCHOOL ENVIRONMENT 95

discovery of new methods seems to have been accidental and their justification pragmatic. The general notion of teaching seems to have been that the teacher was to trick pupils into learning by a series of devices, the use of which was not clearly understood. Real deep-seated faith in the environment as a source of stimuli and a medium for learning seems to have developed but feebly. The attack in studying the problems of learning was deeply colored with notions of curriculum and method. There seems to have been some lack in the understanding of the psychological starting point of learning. Methods were valued as methods. Objects and situations were valued in and for themselves. There was failure to recognize the fact that the environment does not become potent until it enlists the child's attention or interest. There was no clear understanding of the function of interest centers as situations in the environment which may be provided by the teacher but which do not become valid as motivators of learning, and which do not function until the personality of the child draws near to them and so finds in them the beginning points of learning. Interest centers, therefore, are situations in the environment which the teacher may provide because she knows by experience that they are likely to be of interest. They do not become the origin of learning, however; they do not become really potent until the child enlists them in his own behalf.

By providing children with an environment which is rich in interest centers, the teacher will discover that learning will motivate itself. Conduct arises by the child's recognition of a need and the means of its fulfillment. An interest center in the environment may at any moment reveal to a child the possibility of fulfilling some recognized need. Thus activity is initiated. Suppose, for example, that a child finds himself in the schoolroom with nothing to do. He may move to the reading table. On the shelves of the classroom library are forty or fifty books. He looks them over aimlessly. These are forty or fifty interest centers in the environment, but they have absolutely no significance for the learning process of this particular child at this particular time. Suddenly his eye catches a book he has not noticed before, "The Indoor Book for Boys." He takes it from the shelf and examines it. He finds a chapter on book binding. He reads it and decides to bind some copies of *Popular Mechanics* for the school library. He has initiated an activity which may lead on in many valuable ways into various parts of the curriculum such as those concerned in construction and language.

There are many things which may function as interest centers in the school environment. It would be impossible to list them all, but several may be mentioned by way of illustration. Animals as well as plants, or an aquarium or terrarium, are a constant source of interest. Tools and construction materials are always valuable in suggesting activity. Motivation may come from various mechanical devices, from books, from bulletin boards. Blocks, especially the larger forms, are appealing to small children. The school savings bank may become significant. Simple rubber stamp printing sets lend themselves remarkably well to meeting the needs of children in printing records of their trips or excursions, in giving themselves opportunities for self-expression in a form which will be more or less permanent. The printing press fulfills the same purpose for older children. The outdoor environment—with trees, grass, brooks and open spaces, and the thousand and one intriguing mysteries of the ant, the puff ball, the gall, the butterfly, the chips of mica from the rock, the worms, the birds, the sunshine, the shadows—is replete with interest centers which seem to radiate with power to awaken the interest and activity of children.

The Use of Interest Centers in Initiating Activity

One of the first technical problems with which teachers have to deal in directing the learning process is that of guiding the initiating of activity. It is extremely important that the child shall, as far as possible, initiate his own units of conduct. It is at this point that the function of interest centers is significant. The teacher, by providing an environment in which interest centers abound, sets the stage for the progress of learning. Having set the stage, she watches and waits for the drama to begin. If the environment is rich in centers of interest, she will not have long to wait, but will merely wait long enough to choose what is most worth while. When one of the children has discovered an interest center in the environment, the teacher has discovered a beginning point for teaching.

In the Good School Environment Children Want to Learn

It must be obvious from the previous discussion that the school environment should be a social one, that in it there should be other children. Still more obvious is the fact that the teacher is the most important single factor in the good school environment. She is at once part of the environment and the maker of it. The good teacher who understands children constructs an environment in which children

INTEREST CENTERS IN THE SCHOOL ENVIRONMENT

want to learn. Such a teacher builds her environment. In the first place she relies on the potency of interest centers. Furthermore, she relies on children. In the third place she knows that children want to learn. She has solved the problem of the initiation of activity by the children themselves. Her problem is not to find something that children want to do, but to choose from the many activities they are eager to engage in, those which in her judgment will most satisfactorily lead to the goals of the curriculum. So Miss Ellen W. Steele, Head of the Rosemary Junior School, in Greenwich, Connecticut, writes of children whom she was taking over from skilled teachers to teach during the following term: [2]

"Last year the sixth grade group met with me at the end of the year, as I was to direct their next year's work. They came to me as a committee to make a plan for this work and to express their interests and new curiosities, which had more or less arisen from their past experience.

"They wanted to know all the important changes that had taken place after the medieval period that brought the modern world about. They wanted to know how the world gets bigger geographically, what inventions changed the ways of doing things and who the inventors were. They wanted to know how the ways of doing things changed and how the workers changed with the new work. They wanted to know how the nations grew to be so powerful, and how they learned to get on with each other, or, if they didn't get on together, why they didn't. They were interested to find out about the art after the medieval period, and they wished to know who some of the great artists were and to learn some things that were true about them as people. They asked to read some literature that expressed the different great periods of change, as well as some modern literature that expressed today. They wanted to study New York as a great center of modern life, and to compare it with Paris as a great city of today in the Old World. These are a few of the curiosities and interests that they eagerly expressed.

"For my part, I thought it was a better curriculum than a group of teachers could have gotten up in hours of time. The only trouble with it was that it was easily two years' work. As for my part in the story, I was thrilled with the adventure of it, but I felt my unpreparedness to such an extent that I realized that it meant for me a summer of study in order to come back and face the venturing forth into these interests and curiosities in the fall."

[2] *Progressive Education*, Vol. IV, No. 2, April-May-June, 1927, pp. 110-111.

CHAPTER XI

THE SELECTION OF UNITS OF CONDUCT SUITABLE FOR SCHOOL LIFE

TEACHERS have discovered by experiment that not all units of conduct are equally serviceable for use in school. In order to be most valuable as a suitable unit of school experience a unit of conduct must be carefully chosen. Hence, it is desirable to have certain criteria for the selection of units of conduct which will be adapted to economical use in teaching children. Such criteria are presented in this chapter, and are followed by a discussion of the balanced use of conduct units in relation to one another.

ORIGIN

The circumstances from which the unit of conduct arises must be a real life situation. The term "real life situation" seems to puzzle some as to its meaning. It is not so very puzzling if it be taken to mean what it says. Briefly, when children are living a life that is real and natural for them in school or out of school they are involved in life situations. The concept of the real life situation is in harmony with the concept of the school as a miniature community. If one is understood, there should be no difficulty in understanding the other. Real living is going on when children make things they want to make, get their hands dirty doing so, and wash them afterward to get them clean.

But such community living does not begin of itself without a teacher. One writer points out that it is the duty of the school not merely to *select* life situations but to *create* them. This is a varying problem as children pass from the lower to the higher grades of school. When children first come to school they are without any rich background of experience. So in the lower grades it becomes important for the teacher to give them experiences which are suitable and natural for them. This is living for small children. A baby explores the world by sucking his fingers, and gazing at this object and that. A

UNITS OF CONDUCT SUITABLE FOR SCHOOL LIFE

five-year-old, having learned to talk and walk about, is ready to explore the world and the people in it. So teachers in the primary grades take children on trips to places in the neighborhood, the shops, the fields, the homes of people, the gardens or the country. The kindergarten children of the experimental section of Public School 41 in New York are taken to camp in the early summer.

The teacher lives with the children, and they live with the teacher. Consequently, real life situations may become the beginning points for units of conduct involving learning. But once the children have grown older and have continued farther in the journey of living, having once started to live they become more involved and more deeply plunged in living. Experience becomes richer, not poorer, and year by year as they progress through a normal program of living the problem of providing basic experience through widening the direct contact with concrete environment becomes less pressing. The child, in the meanwhile, has been learning to substitute words for experiences, symbols for ideas. He now lives part of his life in terms of symbols and in terms of thoughts representing experience. The teacher's problem becomes less that of providing concrete experiences and more of providing experience in terms of ideas and symbols. So, as we rise higher in the elementary school, we may hunt for the beginning points of real life situations, less and less in terms of concrete objective materials, and more and more in terms of complex experiences, thought, ideas and ideals. Thus, while a kindergarten teacher might take children to visit one of the large ocean liners to create real life experiences which serve as beginning points for the child's units of conduct, a teacher of older children would not need to take them to visit an insurance company when beginning the study of insurance, nor to visit the public library before helping them to appreciate the short story.

So real life situations, which become the beginning points for units of conduct, are plentiful when the life of children in school is like in its aspects and organization to worthy living in the outside world. In the world people work in offices, build buildings, take photographs, give concerts, attend conferences and lectures. In school children may do things which are similar on a suitable level. To units of conduct which arise in such real life situations, teachers may apply a simple test. Do good and right-living adults do things like this? If the answer is yes, then, other things being equal, the unit of conduct may be allowed to develop because of the fruitful promise which it shows.

PROVISION OF USEFUL TRAINING

The unit of conduct must obviously be one which contributes to the growth and development of habits, skills, knowledges, procedures and ideals which will with a high degree of probability be used by the children in the important activities of life.[1] It is to be observed that the fulfillment of criterion one goes far toward the fulfillment of criterion two. In fact, the fulfillment of criterion one is probably the best, the most natural, and indeed the only way in which the second criterion may be fulfilled at all. In other words, it is only real life situations which provide adequate training for real life situations to follow. But all real life situations are not equally valuable. Some teachers seem, at times, to have forgotten this, and to have trusted that all that was necessary for an ideal school life was to allow units of school conduct to develop in real life situations.

Unbelievably grotesque are the extremes to which certain teachers have gone in working out such unbalanced theories in school. A certain teacher relates that she entered a classroom where children were playing and found one on a high cabinet and another on a chair near-by. When asked what they were doing, one child replied, "I'm God and she's the Virgin Mary, but I'm getting tired of being God now and we're going to change." This play was permitted to go on uninterfered with by the teacher, who felt that it was justified as a "real life situation" in which the children were engaged. This teacher failed to realize that some life situations are more valuable for their leading on value than others. Some units of conduct involve a degree and type of growth and advancement which others do not. There is a multiplicity to choose from. So why not choose the best? The teacher should never lose sight of her curriculum goals. It is not enough for the child to live now. He must live well now and in such a way that he may continue to live well later on. In their anxiety that children shall live in a full and rich way, teachers have sometimes forgotten that every moment of the child's life is projected forward and reproduces itself in a myriad other minutes of later life. Just as the tiny tracery of a lantern slide is projected forward on rays of light intercepted by a screen, so each moment of the child's life casts its lights and shadows forward on a thousand life situations. The child's frown or smile, the careless word or the thoughtful one, the task half-finished or carried to conclusion, will reproduce itself in kind through-

---

[1] For this criterion the writer is indebted to CHAPMAN and COUNTS, "Principles of Education," Houghton Mifflin Co., Boston, 1924, p. 371.

out the individual's succeeding days. So, under ordinary circumstances, the children would choose, under the teacher's direction, a unit of conduct involving the understanding and appreciation and study of musical instruments rather than a unit involving the investigation of devices used in playing ball, provided that both were offered or suggested by the children at the same time.

LENGTH

Units of conduct should be carefully selected with regard to their length. Some units of conduct are brief and stand alone. Such units are the making of a printing press, a pictorial map, or giving a party. Some teachers consider this type of unit the more valuable form for school life. There is, however, another and longer type of unit, such as investigating the forms of transportation used in the city, studying Greek civilization, or learning about animals. Such long units are valued by teachers because they are believed to form a general life situation which divides and subdivides into numerous subsidiary units of conduct which lead in the direction of curriculum goals. Thus, in a study of animals, stories of animals provide reading material and material for dramatization. Painting scenery develops artistic tendencies, and designing and erecting the scenery may lead to arithmetic.

Several objections which may be levelled at these longer units make one suspect that they are really little more than a fad of organization, a device or scheme which provides a logical basis for the organization of ideas. In studying the reports of such work, one may often suspect that the units do not arise from a real life situation. One teacher, in discussing the matter, frankly admits that the unit which she carried on in a recent term was predetermined and picked out by her. It did not come from the children in any direct sense, but was part of the teacher's plan. It seems hard to believe that small children can have the judgment, the knowledge, or the fixity of purpose to enable them to choose such a unit as Indian life and carry it through in its various implications through a month or two. One suspects, in such cases, that the work carried on is the teacher's opinion of what the children want, rather than the children's choice. Any skillful teacher may persuade a group of children, in a ten-minute talk, to embark on any of half a dozen so-called units, from the study of the Eskimos to the building of a tunnel in the schoolyard. Is the unifying principle here the children's need and purpose, or is it the teacher's concept of some extensive unit of work? Can children who know little of Indians see two days ahead in such work, let alone two months? Can we pretend that children seriously commit themselves to an undertaking which is largely a blank future to them? A child who plans to make a picture frame to use at home can begin with some unified concept of what he hopes to do. Such is also true of a group of children who plan to make a map of the locality, or to take a trip to visit the grocer and find out how much the food for their intended party may cost. These are unified acts to children, which may be carried on by them with some notion of what they are doing. Can this be said, however, of such a study as that of the Byrd expedition, or the source of the food the children eat, or any other loose and flexible generalized activity? These latter seem rather to be matrices of possible activity which enable the teacher to amuse herself by working out a logically organized plan of procedure. Are these longer inclusive units like the life activities of the world outside the school? Where in the community do we find individuals organizing two or three months of life in terms of the study of textiles, or pursuing the ramifications of Inca life? Does not such a foreordained set of activities in school approach a formal organization of school life? If units of conduct are to be real in origin and vital throughout their progress, it seems that they must arise not from such generalized life needs of children, but rather out of their particular present needs.

In selecting units of conduct careful consideration should be given to the amount of time which will probably be consumed in their accomplishment, and to the possible subsidiary activities into which they may genuinely and profitably lead. Otherwise a long and unwieldly unit which rambles here and there in numerous by-paths may develop into a Frankenstein, which, if it does not destroy its creator, may waste a great deal of his time. Lengthy and unpredictable units of conduct do not lend themselves to economical and even development. If the teacher is to reach her curriculum goals, the class may not indulge in too much aimless wandering. It has happened, on occasion, that a class has spent half a year on some such study as Mexico, via interest in the Panama Canal. Then proceeded to a study of mosquitoes, steam shovels and landslides, in the meantime making models of such things as canals and steamships. Finally it has become clear that there was but half a term left to consider the remainder of North America. Such careless selection and development of units is inexcusable. Units of conduct should have their origin in the children's own needs and interests, should be of a length which makes possible the children's unified comprehension of them, and should be of a duration which is carefully planned in relation to the other work of the class.

BASED NOT ON WHIMS BUT ON FUNDAMENTAL INTERESTS

Units of conduct of any importance or length should not be based on occasional child interest, but on more deeply rooted and firm interest. Teachers need to distinguish between children's whims and fancies, and their real interests. Interest may be a sound indication of suitable activities, but caprice is not. It is absurd to attempt to organize school life in terms of children's interests as they flit here and there, from notice of a passing butterfly to pride in a new dress. Such responses may be useful in teaching small children, and may lead on to other interests, but on the whole they are transitory and not of permanent value. Units of conduct which are valuable usually find their origin in some more fundamental interests. Such interests are a love of living, moving things like animals, joy in constructing things, such as playhouses and various buildings, or that fascination with matters of air transportation which constitutes a larger part of the environment of small boys today than most automobile-minded adults realize.

SUITABLE LEVEL OF DIFFICULTY

Units of conduct must provide activities which are appropriate to the children's level of growth, and which are of suitable difficulty. The use of a thoroughgoing conduct organization of school life is so recent that teachers still know very little about the grading of activities according to difficulty. This is a fruitful field for study and experiment, and the coming years will no doubt do much to clarify the confused procedure of the present time in this respect. Studies of Greek life are regarded by some as suitable material for the third grade, while others believe that they may be more suitably developed with twelve-year-olds. In the meanwhile, it is important for the teacher to use her judgment. She should select from among the activities which the children are ready to engage in, those activities which are of a suitable degree of difficulty, which present an adequate challenge, which are suitable to the children's level of growth, and which provide development on a higher level than that on which the children have lived before. Thus a ten-year-old boy who visits the motor boat show and decides to make a model of a motor boat should not make another of the simple inert models which he built when he was seven, but should work out a real model in which he installs a real engine, and in the execution of which he is faced with really difficult problems of thinking and construction. Furthermore, the result should be one that is worthy of a boy who has had so much training in working with constructive materials. Similarly the child's stories and essays should show an increasing grasp and periodic improvement on his previous writings.

The selection of activities suitable to the children's level of growth should be made, not according to tradition, but according to psychological and educational principles. The haunting echoes of the culture epoch theory seem to be with us still, so that some teachers continue to trust in the magic potency for the lives of small children of the study of primitive social groups. Surely there is nothing actually more remote in terms of time, space or reality. Small children are only in touch with the daily lives of people round about them, with what Mrs. Mitchell calls the "Here and Now." City children are less directly related to the makers of Eskimo huts than to the manufacturers of Eskimo Pies. If there be a time for children to study the far-away primitive origins of things such as fire-making and weaving, surely it is better to wait until they have some knowledge of modern industrial processes that produce the things they use themselves. May we not wait for the age of romance, imagination and adventure in the upper elementary school to teach of

> . . . old, unhappy, far off things,
> And battles long ago.

Directed Toward Curriculum Values

Suitable units of conduct should lead in the direction of curriculum goals. In a well-organized school, in which children are trained in living, far more activities will be suggested than can be carried on. The teacher should guide the children to select those which lead in the direction of curriculum goals rather than allow the aimless choice of whatever suggests itself. Thus the teacher who wishes to lead the children's responses in the direction of the geography of North America would find the children's interests in current discussion of the development of the St. Lawrence waterways a more valuable lead in the development of units of conduct than similar interests in Balkan royalty or in the cost of gasoline. Again, the making and keeping of a

UNITS OF CONDUCT SUITABLE FOR SCHOOL LIFE 105

garden will be of more value in the study of nature and science than the furnishing of a school reception-room or the building of a tennis court. So some units of conduct furnish an abundance of leads into subsidiary units, which in their progress involve the attaining of the values indicated in the curriculum. On the other hand, the making of a tennis court might be more useful than planting a garden to a teacher whose curriculum involved geometry. Thus suitable units of conduct lead on into other units which result in the attainment of the goals of the curriculum.

Related to the Other Work of the Class and School

Units of conduct should be related to the other work of the class and to that of the school in general, and should not follow children's interests aimlessly in rambling fashion. Mr. Micawber's scheme of waiting for something to turn up is a far from adequate one for the teacher. If the teacher accepts any unit of conduct which happens to turn up, allowing it to lead this way and that, in unconcern as to what the children pick up, this lack of organization clashes with the work of other teachers. If the child had but one teacher all his life such rambling might conceivably, for some visionaries, be a method of teaching. As a matter of fact, occasionally teachers do attempt to carry on in this fashion, or there would be no point in this discussion. It may, of course, be amusing for all concerned to start with mudpies, travel to the banks of the Nile, thence to Niagara Falls, water power, electricity, illumination, and the stars. It is not, however, either orderly or temperate. James Joyce may find a satisfactory basis for his novel technique in the stream of consciousness, but it is a poor basis for the organization of school life. Teachers must avoid the haphazard in the selection and guidance of various units of conduct if they are to coöperate with other teachers or develop balanced living in their own pupils.

Sound Relation to Established Knowledge and Standards

In their progress and development, units of conduct should proceed within the limits of available and established knowledge, and in accordance with sound standards of scholarship. It may prove interesting to children to discuss the causes of the Russian Revolution, and to mete out theoretical justice in the case of the Czars versus the followers of Lenin. Is it exactly common sense to expect them to do so? May we not allow children to become overbearing in our enthusiasm for developing critical judgment? Is the whole world to sit at the tribunal of the child?

A youngster of twelve, chatting with me in friendly fashion, said, "I don't believe in God. I don't think there's any God at all." In discussions carried on in the modern school which he attended, this boy had been accustomed to hearing the most profound questions discussed freely by the children, and easily disposed of in a somewhat flippant and superficial manner. Teachers who direct such discussions in history, social science, and literature must not allow light and opinionated talk, in which children mimic their elders, to pass current in the class for "discussion," or pretend to the status of judgments. The man in the street is too ready to pass judgment in matters concerning which he knows little. This should not be the custom in the class. If students are discussing such problems as extraterritoriality in China, or the American policy in the Philippines, there is much actual information to be obtained and studied, and there is a great deal to be said on either side of the question under consideration. Children should not be allowed to base their judgments on ignorance. We do not solve problems by denial or neglect of facts. Loose and unscholarly discussion, followed by immature and ill-founded judgments, is a poor sort of "freedom" to give to young people. Great care should be taken that whatever conduct units are in progress should not develop in shallow or superficial fashion.

THE BALANCED USE OF CONDUCT UNITS

All Types of Units Needed

Up to the present time there has been an almost total neglect of any attempt to gain a balance in the use of units of conduct in the developing of the personality of the individual as a suitable member of the social organism. Hence, the new teaching has been accused of resulting in episodic and unorganized learning, and of failing to teach many things that children ought to know; of dissipating the powers and wasting the time of academically minded students; of permitting a few children to do all the work while others get along with little; of building up the idea that school is only play; and failing to awaken interest in work, in cultivating initiative and responsibility, and neglecting ability to obey, follow directions and persevere. None of these faults are inherent in the organization of school life in terms of conduct. They are merely results of the improper balance in the selection of units of conduct which contribute to the development of well-rounded social personalities.

It seems clear that since all types of activities, units of construction or creation, units of play or recreation, and units of work or duty on each of the three levels, physical, mental and spiritual, take place in the world and are genuine aspects of living, all of these types of units should have their place in children's living. The development of a school program which involves a proper balance of all these types of activities would be a sound one and would no longer be open to the numerous criticisms which are directed against activity schools.

Expression and Restraint Complementary Processes

The greatest confusion may result in the development of programs of activity unless it is clearly realized that an individual develops into a well-balanced social unit by two processes which seem to be opposite in nature, namely, through *free expression* of certain tendencies of the personality and on the other hand by *restraint and control* of other tendencies. Personality patterns develop in two ways. In the first place, by outward expression the individual weaves new ways of appearing. He patterns new thoughts, he tells new stories, he paints new pictures, he reveals new glories. In such activities great freedom is necessary. In the second place, he grows by the development of inward patterns of coördination. He adapts, he controls, he limits himself to modifications which develop skills and techniques.

It is from a failure to understand the relationships of these apparently contradictory principles of education that the controversy between the so-called advocates of *freedom* and the advocates of *discipline* has arisen. This antagonism had better be forgotten. There is room for activities which proceed through freedom to discipline and for others which proceed through discipline to freedom. The only danger lies in the building of a school program based on one of these types to the exclusion of the other. So let us away with our freedom school and our discipline school, and on with our school which believes in a balanced program, including all the forms of activity which go to make up life itself. The problems of organizing such a program are still largely before us. They will provide a fruitful field for experiment and study in the next decade of educational progress. In the meanwhile there are several principles and suggestions which are worthy of attention.

Balance Between In-school and Out-of-school Life

A balanced program of school activities will not duplicate units of conduct which are adequately provided for by out-of-school agencies. To that extent the development of physical activities is cared for by supervised playgrounds, free outdoor after-school play, boy scout organization, junior clubs and societies, and so on. Obviously, the more such provision is made by the community, the less it need be made by the school, and vice versa. The situation will depend much on the nature of the environment. Is it a large or small city? A country town or a village? Such circumstances will have direct bearing on the balanced organization of the school program. Again, the spiritual life of the child is theoretically cared for by the church and the home. When both institutions neglect this factor, what can the school do about it? One sometimes wonders if the back of the school will not be broken by the burdens it carries.

Balanced Use of Play

Another factor which must influence the balance of the school program is the amount of play which is to be provided at various stages of the child's development. Some light may come to the situation by a consideration of the following persuasive argument in behalf of play.[2]

"The main concern in a child's life is that manifold business understood clearly by him and dimly by his elders, as Play. He wakes up in bed even before dawn, and plots out a fairyland of play-doings for the day until he is allowed to get up. Then while the fires are still crackling on the wood you can hear him pattering about the landing or singing on the stairs. Dressing is a nuisance because it requires his presence in one place for some twenty minutes; toys must come to table; food itself must furnish a game. Porridge is an island in a sea of milk, and he would be rather more interested than shocked to find a chicken in every egg. School, above the kindergarten, is a nuisance because there is no play. So he lives on throughout the daylight hours, playing many parts, as pirate, or king-in-a-crown, or beast of prey; in the tree tops, or underground, or sailing merrily on the salt sea, until that little naughty tragedy of bedtime."

Read over this passage, first thinking of a child of five, again thinking of a child of twelve, and once more thinking of a lad of

[2] COOK, CALDWELL, *opus cit.*, p. 1.

sixteen. It is obvious that the older the child grows, the less important is a play approach to the activities of life. So in teaching the parts of speech to nine-year-olds the teacher would find them reveling in the play-stories of the sprite Ram-marg,[3] leading on to the mastery of the parts of speech whereas for secondary school pupils the mastery of grammar would be more directly connected with the language they speak and write. It is obvious that units of play have a fuller place in the early school life of children, while in later school life units involving the mastery of techniques become more important.

Consideration of Individual Needs

It seems obvious that deliberate and careful consideration of individual differences and needs is most important in the arranging of a balanced course for each student. Not only may certain individuals carry through to completion a larger number of units of conduct than others, but certain individuals will attempt what they do on a much larger and more extensive scale. Thus in the mastery of language and writing, one girl may be able to give an account of her summer holidays, while her schoolmate of the same age may write an original short story.

In concluding the discussion of a balanced school program, mention may be made of another field concerning which teachers are at present in almost total ignorance, namely, that of the corrective use of units of conduct. How may units of conduct be so administered and directed as to correct individual variations? What shall be the régime of the student who is academically minded? What shall we do with the boy who reads Shakespeare for pleasure, but who cannot mend a puncture in his bicycle tire? Should he be given a régime which provides him with special opportunities for the development of his academic propensities or should his lack in handling material objects be amended by a special régime of manual work? Probably both. How is such a program to be administered? This is an aspect of the treatment of individual differences which is worthy of careful experimental study.

[3] CARPENTER, J. H., and HOBEN, A. M., "Fairy Grammar," E. P. Dutton & Co., New York, 1929.

CHAPTER XII

THE NATURE OF CURRICULUM

By LIVING through an adequate series of units of conduct a child may reach the goals of the curriculum. The learning process ends when the child attains to curriculum goals. Consequently, any thorough and adequate theory of learning, no matter how enthusiastically it may begin with the child, must, in order to be complete, end with the curriculum. If the learning process begins with the child, from his own self-initiated needs, and is guided forward and onward toward values which supply that need, then the terminal point of the activity involved is curriculum. Furthermore, this is inevitably so in any case when learning goes on. It is so when the values obtained are such as the ability to write a personal letter in correct form, and to recognize Roman numerals to one hundred, values which may be easily predicted and aimed at by the teacher, and which may be clearly described in a printed course of study. It is equally so when the values obtained are unexpected, unpremeditated, and unpredictable at the time when the learning process which achieved them was initiated. Such would be the case when a second-grade child, engaged in making a wooden candlestick, decides to equip it with an electric bulb, and in doing so learns numerous things concerning simple wiring and electricity. It is useless for extremists to shun the idea of curriculum, for, no matter whether the learnings achieved by the child are good or bad, expected or unexpected, clear-cut and logically integrated, or haphazard and nebulously organized, those learnings are actually curriculum.

Misconceptions of "Curriculum"

There seems to be considerable confusion abroad in the use of the word "curriculum." Various extremisms, the denial of the existence of curriculum by some who use language carelessly, the zeal of the methodizers who have confused curriculum and method, and the general tendency away from logically expressed subject-matter curricula, have contributed to the general misunderstanding. But this indefiniteness as to the meaning of words should not go on. Teachers have nothing to gain by confusion of tongues. Already an ill-advised and careless use of terms has brought considerable disfavor on the new teaching. The word "curriculum" is an old one of good standing in the English language and in the field of education. Its meaning is basically that of a race-course, and so figuratively of the course which the child runs in school. The use which is made of it should surely be in harmony with its etymology and its history.

There are three misconceptions which seem to have contributed to the misunderstanding of curriculum and hence to the careless use of the word. The first is that which regards the curriculum as nothing more than a printed account, a foreordained list of subject matter to be mastered by all pupils. But the teacher who regards the curriculum as a printed, preconceived account of values which must be reached by the child in a certain order and at a certain time, is attempting to regard learning in the abstract. She is attempting to regard learning aside from the particular case, to generalize concerning the nature, the time and the sequence of learning. But such procedure is fallacious. If we are to call a part of the printed course of study "curriculum," we do so by an extension of the term. In reality, the learnings which the child actually attains in the course of the learning process are curriculum. When, for the guidance of teaching, any printed record of these is made, it may also, for the sake of convenience, be called curriculum. It is not, however, in the truest sense curriculum. If the teacher is to regard it intelligently, she must regard it as merely a forecast of what may happen. It is merely a compilation descriptive of what has gone on in the past, and consequently, a forecast of what may happen. It is characterized by probability rather than certainty. It is suggestive rather than dictatorial.

It is true, of course, that in certain very objective fields of accomplishment, such as arithmetic, there is a very clear-cut set of minimum essentials which may be simply set forth in writing. In such fields as music, literature, or history, however, the matter is much more complex. For the most part, the moment the teacher forgets the incompleteness of printed curricula, their tentative character, their lack of logical or chronological validity, that moment she becomes confused in her thinking. As soon as one thinks of learning aside from the concrete particular case, one is limited to probabilities. Learning does not go on in the abstract. It is an active, variable process, conditioned in its progress and results by the actual circumstances under which it takes place.

The second misconception which teachers seem, at times, to be guilty of, is of the opposite nature. Such teachers go to the opposite extreme and deny the validity or usefulness of any definitely recorded suggestive printed curricula. These teachers, thoroughly aware of the specific nature of learning, refuse to think in any terms but those of the particular case. This gives the thinking of such a teacher considerable validity while she is actually engaged in the process of teaching. She realizes, in the case of any unit of conduct in progress, just how impossible it is to know fully and completely the end from the beginning. She realizes that during the progress of any activity, such as the keeping of a scrap book, the child not merely learns a number of things which she may forecast, such as the comparative worthlessness of the news in some papers, but many which come as a surprise to her. One fifteen-year-old boy, in the middle of reading a "Tale of Two Cities," announced it as a discovery. "At last I've found a real book," he said, the light of appreciation in his eye. Pointing to several others on the shelf, he continued, "The teacher got me interested in this kind of book, and I sure am glad of it!" Compare the joy of this lad in this remarkable story with the malaise of students whose teachers regard it as a fixed and inevitable bit of curriculum content to be read in a certain year.

So children may not merely learn many things which the teacher did not bargain for, but may actually fail to learn the very things which she would naturally, from experience, have expected. Keeping such things in mind, some teachers maintain that generalizations in the form of printed, suggestive curricula are superfluous. Teachers have even denied the necessity for the recognition of any such conception as curriculum during teaching. They maintain that it is only necessary for the learning process to start well and keep going vigorously, the assumption being that all things will come out well somewhere, sometime. This attitude, by failing to look forward toward desirable curriculum goals, robs the teaching process of rudder and compass. Yet the same teacher who holds it, before setting out for school on a cloudy day, will read the weather forecast in the newspaper, study the sky carefully, consult members of the family, and use her own judgment concerning the possibility of rain before deciding what to wear. If she were to govern her daily actions as she pretends to govern her teaching, she would wear whatever her mood might dictate, and suffer the consequence of her capriciousness, just as her pupils must do.

The truth of the matter is, that while in terms of actual learning the curriculum is that unpredictable series of values which the child

These third graders were so interested in an exhibition of Japanese prints that they built a tea house, made a rickshaw and constructed Japanese books which they used for their arithmetic. The class is that of Mrs. Rayner in the Public Schools of Englewood Cliffs, New Jersey.

THE NATURE OF CURRICULUM

attains in learning, yet that same curriculum, because it is based on previous experience is, to a certain extent, predictable and capable of being set forth in suggestive printed form with considerable degree of probable validity. Error may arise from regarding the printed curriculum as more than suggestive, or actual curriculum as entirely beyond the possibility of forecast.

The third misconception of the nature of the curriculum seems to arise from a confusion of the teacher's notions of curriculum and her notions of method. Changes in method of teaching which have brought about a recasting of the subject matter of the curriculum into various units of conduct, into various activities, have brought about the development of so-called "activity curricula." Thus an account of a large unit of work such as "Studying New York's Food Supply" which tells of all the activities engaged in in the course of reaching certain curriculum goals in English, number, science and so on, may be called curriculum, whereas it is in reality an account of the method which the teacher used, the conduct units which she employed in reaching those goals. The term "activity curricula," sometimes applied to such *in extenso* accounts, and to others which give a list of the activities in which children engage, is inaccurate. It is a misnomer. It is obviously the result of a confusion between the fields of curriculum and method. The moment any involvement of the goals of the curriculum in certain units of conduct in the progress of which they will be obtained occurs, that moment method steps in. If there be any re-statement of curricula, that re-statement should be made in terms of life goals, such as ability to tell the time, ability to write, ability to paint a water color, integrated ideas, knowledges and skills which are the end of the learning process, which are the terminus of its directional flow. If such goals are set up clearly in reorganized curricula, they may, of course, be supplemented. Suggestions may also be given concerning activities in the pursuit of which these goals may possibly be reached. Such tentative lists of possible activities should not, however, be regarded as part of the curriculum proper, nor called "activity curricula." Rather may they be regarded as supplementary aids to method, and termed the school's activity program. This program would then be regarded merely as suggestive and descriptive of work previously carried on in the attainment of the curriculum goals set forth. Otherwise it would be in violation of the very principle of the progress of learning from the child to the curriculum, in accordance with which it was developed.

THE CONSTRUCTION OF CURRICULA

The School's "Eternal Triangle"

A great many of the difficulties which complicate the problems of teaching find their origin in the involved relationships which exist between the three factors of the educative process, the child, the curriculum and the teacher. If these relationships were simple rather than complex, teaching might become a comparatively easy matter. In such a case the whole of teaching might be represented as in the following diagram, the active flow of learning being maintained in the circle in an anti-clockwise direction.

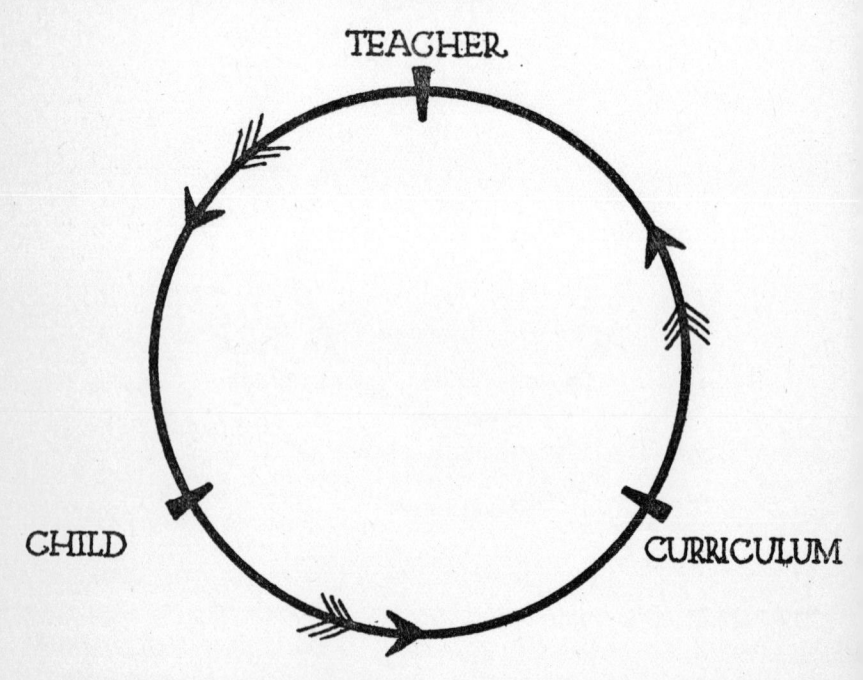

TEACHER

CHILD   CURRICULUM

Thus beginning our description of the teaching process, we might say that the curriculum suggests to the teacher what she must teach, the teacher proceeds to stimulate in the child needs, the fulfillment of which will involve his mastery of curriculum values. But unfortunately the matter is not so easy or so clear. The relationships which exist between any two of these three factors of the teaching process are limited and modified by the third. Thus the relationships between the curriculum and the teacher are conditioned by the child; the relationships between the child and the teacher are conditioned by the curriculum; and the relationships between the child and the curriculum are conditioned by the teacher. As a result of these conditions, the relationships between any two of these factors are not simple or direct, as might be gathered from the first diagram, but are of a more complicated nature. The complexities of the teaching process itself are of necessity reflected in the succeeding paragraphs intended to explore them. Therefore, it is requested that the reader trace them by the aid of the following diagram in terms of which they are expressed.

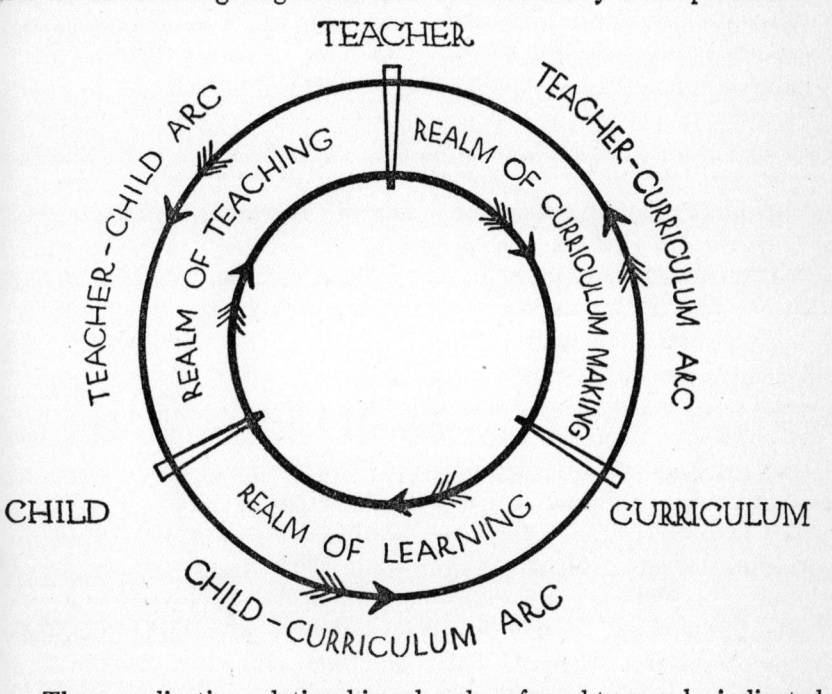

[Diagram: A circular figure labeled with TEACHER at top, CHILD at left, CURRICULUM at right. The outer arcs are labeled TEACHER-CHILD ARC, TEACHER-CURRICULUM ARC, and CHILD-CURRICULUM ARC. The inner regions are labeled REALM OF TEACHING, REALM OF CURRICULUM MAKING, and REALM OF LEARNING, with arrows indicating currents flowing in both directions around the circle.]

The complicating relationships already referred to may be indicated in this fashion. To counter the anti-clockwise motion or current already mentioned there is another motion or current which is contrary to it. Thus in any given arc of the circle one stream must be limited and modified by the other. In the teacher-child arc, which may be regarded as the special realm of *teaching,* not merely does the teacher find it necessary to begin the teaching process with the child, but in doing so she must refer back to the curriculum for guidance. Similarly in the child-curriculum arc, the realm of *learning,* the child may not continue moving forward to attain curriculum goals in his own way, but the process is conditioned by the necessity of referring back to the teacher.

In the teacher-curriculum arc, the realm of *curriculum making*, not merely is the curriculum determined by the teacher, but even in its tentative written form it refers back to the past experiences with children, and to their recognized needs and interests. To express the same thing in different fashion, the teacher's relationships to the child are not merely forward and direct, in an anti-clockwise direction, but also indirect and backward, in a clockwise movement, referring to the child again this time via the curriculum. In the same way the child refers forward directly to the curriculum and again backward to the curriculum via the teacher. The curriculum refers forward toward the teacher, guiding her as to what she should do, but is in turn limited by referring backward to the teacher's approach via the child.

A COMPLETE CONCEPT OF CURRICULUM

It follows that any complete notion of curriculum must involve its relationships with both teacher and child. The curriculum must involve direct relationships with the teacher and indirect relationships with the teacher via the child. It must furthermore involve direct relationships with the child and in addition, indirect relationships with the child via the teacher. Curriculum couched in mere terms of logically arranged subject matter would obviously fail to fulfill all these criteria. While its relationships with the child via the teacher might be established, its relationships with the child directly are not clear. Neither will curricula expressed merely in terms of activities fulfill the criteria listed, for mere listed activities are without clearly established relationships in any direction. They are matters of method rather than elements of curriculum. Curricula should really be expressed in terms of conduct, in terms of abilities which are actually attained or attainable goals. Then, and then only, may curricula be clearly expressed, and with the maximum degree of usefulness, in written suggestive form. Such goals in terms of abilities provide a series of definite objectives for the teacher, which, nevertheless, leave her wide freedom as to her method of teaching, and at the same time are easily and clearly recognizable by the child as meeting definite personal needs.

THE NATURE OF SUITABLE CURRICULUM GOALS

The nature of such desirable and well-expressed curriculum goals may first be presented in the concrete. Unfortunately, however, actual

THE NATURE OF CURRICULUM

material of this description is not plentiful. Consequently, instead of quoting from curriculum material of the school proper, it seems convenient to choose examples of curriculum goals expressed in terms of conduct from the program of the Boy Scout Movement. It will be found that the directors of this movement have worked out an admirable scheme on principles which are extraordinarily sound and useful for the construction of curricula for school life. In fact, the major strength of the Boy Scout Movement lies in its excellent program of activities, which, in reality, is a sort of extra-mural curriculum.

The following quotations from the "Handbook for Boys"[1] are worthy of careful consideration as models for the construction of curricula in terms of conduct. Unfortunately, the fact that they have not been constructed for use in schools, but to fit in with the organization of the Boy Scout system, affects the form in which they are stated so that they are not a perfect model for the making of curricula for schools. Further analysis of their specialized character will be made at the end of the quotations given. For the present it is desirable to notice how almost every goal is stated in the form of a definitely unified and recognizable unit of conduct.

READING

1. Read at least one book a month for a year after becoming a Second Class Scout, including among the twelve books read three standard works and three on some phase of Scouting. Present a list of books read.
2. Present a book review or tell which books he likes best and why.
3. Describe the character he liked best in his fictional reading.
4. If a library is available, have a membership card, which must be presented.
5. List several books he plans to read in the next twelve months.

GARDENING

1. Do two of the following things:

(a) Operate a garden plot of not less than 20 feet square and show a net profit of not less than $5.00 on the season's work. Keep an accurate crop report and show exhibit of garden products produced.

(b) Grow 1/20 acre of potatoes or other garden crops such as tomatoes, sweet corn and popcorn. Select the hills from which seed potatoes are to be taken. Grade potatoes in three divisions—market, medium and culls. Keep an accurate crop report of the season's work.

(c) Keep both back and front yards in good condition for the summer vacation of three months, which will include care of garden, flowers and

[1] Published by Boy Scouts of America, 2 Park Ave., New York.

shrubs, mowing of lawn, keeping the yard neat and clean. Keep an accurate record of the vacation's work.

INTERPRETING

1. Carry on a simple but sustained conversation in a modern foreign language for a period of not less than five minutes.
2. Listen to and translate a statement or address delivered in a modern foreign language, and lasting not less than two minutes, by a person to whom the language is a native tongue.
3. Write a simple letter in a modern foreign language on a subject given by the Counselors.

JOURNALISM

1. "Cover" satisfactorily the following assignments:
(a) Write an article covering a news incident.
(b) Write an article covering a routine club or society meeting.
(c) Write a publicity article.
(d) Write a human interest story, either actual or imaginary.
(e) Write an editorial.
(f) Secure the publication of at least one of these articles.

. . . .

5. Read and correct proof, using the conventional proofreader's signs. (Manuscript of two typewritten pages to be furnished by the Counselor.)
6. Submit four styles of advertising copy for a local newspaper or magazine.

HANDICRAFT

1. Paint a door or a piece of furniture.
2. Whitewash or calsomine a ceiling.
3. Repair gas fittings.
4. Repair sash lines.
5. Repair window and door fastenings.
6. Replace gas mantles, or fuse plugs and electric light bulbs.
7. Replace washers.
8. Solder.
9. Hang pictures and curtains.

Such material may well be studied by teachers and curriculum makers to assist them in re-stating curricula for school use. As has been already pointed out, however, in considering these elements of curriculum it should be realized that they were not prepared for school, but for out-of-school activities. The form in which they are stated is thus sometimes governed by conditions and circumstances which are

THE NATURE OF CURRICULUM

somewhat different from those which govern curricula for use in schools. They cover activities which are intended to be merely supplementary to the formal school program. They consequently leave unprovided for many of the values upon which the formal school program lays great emphasis. Again, the special activities referred to in the above quotations are supplementary to the basic Scout program, and are designed to stimulate individuals to accomplishments which receive recognition by the award of a "merit badge." They are, therefore, couched entirely in individualistic terms. Furthermore, the form in which they are stated is, in some cases, colored by the directions given to pupils for presenting an account of their gains to a Scout examiner (*e. g.* Number 2 under Gardening). When this is so, the element is somewhat distorted in its form as a curriculum goal suitable for school use, since a pure curriculum goal represents not so much an activity or act performed to demonstrate to an examiner, but a clearly denominated and definite ability or accomplishment. All these characteristic deviations should be ignored by teachers who are interested in using this material as a model in re-stating the curriculum in terms of conduct goals.

Further light may be thrown on the problem of curriculum construction by a consideration of the larger categories under which the activities leading to Scout badges are listed. It is important to realize that these badges are entirely optional objectives. A boy chooses as many or as few and in any order he likes. When he fulfills the requirements by attaining the goals set forth all his reward is that of a definite recognition in the form of a cloth badge, which he may wear upon his sleeve that he who runs may read. The list follows:

Agriculture	Carpentry	Plumbing
Angling	Cooking	Pottery
Archery	First Aid	Poultry Keeping
Architecture	Hiking	Printing
Art	Horsemanship	Reptile Study
Astronomy	Insect Life	Scholarship
Aviation	Leathercraft	Sculpture
Bee Keeping	Life Saving	Seamanship
Blacksmithing	Marksmanship	Taxidermy
Camping	Photography	Woodcarving
Canoeing		

It is to be observed that this list practically defies any further classification. Each element stands alone in virtue of its own validity as a type of conduct which goes on in the world. It requires no justification but itself. The intelligent reader will realize that there is not a single thing in the list that, under suitable circumstances, he would not himself be glad to understand and master. In reading it over, the average reader is likely to feel how defective is his own education, and to realize that there are many goals in this list that he himself would be very glad to reach. So it must be with a boy. Given the opportunity to learn he chooses, and having chosen, he commits himself to a course of activities leading to the attainment of the goals listed under that heading.

We are not without schools which have attempted to work out their curricula on similar principles. Having looked into the examples just given from outside the school, we may turn our attention to certain school curricula which may be understood in the light of them. One excellent example of a school system which has curricula something of the nature of those under discussion, is the Bronxville Public Schools, Bronxville, New York. The examples to be quoted, however, are not of the exact type which the writer would like to quote. They are given because of lack of material which is of the type desired in actual use. One of their chief disadvantages for the present purpose is that they are not quoted from the curriculum proper, but from report cards or goal cards used by the children and teachers, and sent home to the parents. The goals stated on them are therefore expressed in the past tense, and are formulated in terms of an accomplishment already performed. The following quotations are from the goal cards used in the Bronxville schools:

WRITTEN ENGLISH (*Upper Elementary*)

Writes stories and experiences
    Having brief clear plan
    Showing mastery of sentence idea
    With interesting fact for beginning
    With significant or surprising observation for ending
    With one high point of interest
Writes friendly letters
    With one or two items elaborated
    Showing personal point of view and consideration for reader
Capitalization
    Names of organizations and all proper nouns
    First word of direct quotation

THE NATURE OF CURRICULUM

ORAL ENGLISH (*Upper Elementary*)

Can express in pantomime a strong emotion
Has conducted informal meetings easily and successfully
Makes brief, accurate reports on reference material
    States facts
    Gives own opinion last

READING (*Upper Elementary*)

Cares for books properly
Reads aloud so that voice inflections contribute to intelligent understanding
    of passage

LIFE SCIENCE (*Upper Elementary*)

Recognition of
    Common roadside plants
    Common garden plants
    Common parts of plants

LITERATURE (*First Junior High Grades*)

Knows and appreciates the writings of early American authors such as:
    Longfellow, Lowell, Irving, Holmes, Franklin, Hawthorne, Whittier, Poe, Bryant, Whitman

MATHEMATICS (*First Junior High Grades*)

Ratio
    Understands meaning of ratio
    Can reduce
    Can find ratio of denominate numbers
    Can divide a number into parts by ratio
    Can change recipes and measurements by scale
    Can apply ratio in problems
Graphs
    Can make and read:
        Bar graphs
        Circle graphs

FORMAL GRAMMAR (*First Junior High Grades*)

Recognizes a sentence as a complete thought
Shows mastery of rules for end punctuation
Recognizes the simple and complete subject
Knows difference between phrase and clause
Knows the difference between an independent and a dependent clause

Attention should be called to the difference in the nature of the general categories used in these goal cards, and the nature of those used in the Boy Scout program quoted above. Whereas in the latter case the categories were forms of conduct such as Bee Keeping, Cooking and Aviation, in the former case they are Written English, Formal Grammar and Mathematics. In other words, the categories are no longer in terms of conduct but in terms of subject matter. The fact that these goal cards are arranged to be sent to parents whose thinking about learning and schools goes on in terms of subjects would explain this. As a fundamental principle of curriculum construction, however, it may be maintained that any basic organization of curricula in terms of subject matter alone is to be treated with great caution in curricula designed for use in modern schools. Such organization may result in a considerable distortion of the nature of curriculum goals.

CURRICULA SHOULD NOT BE STATED IN LOGICAL CATEGORIES

We now approach a principle of curriculum construction which, while it may not be convenient, nevertheless seems inevitable. Curriculum cannot be expressed in logical categories. It is, in a sense, irreducible. It must be presented *in extenso*. At this point we return to a principle which has previously been noted in these pages, namely, that conduct is so complex that it cannot be simply analyzed. Sound curriculum goals expressed in terms of conduct, therefore, may not be determined by a simple process of deduction, but only by a complex and comprehensive search, which makes use of every available method of determining sound and suitable graded life goals.

HOW CURRICULUM MAY BE DETERMINED

Since this book is written primarily for teachers rather than for curriculum makers, the present brief chapter is not the place to develop at length a complete and detailed theory of curriculum construction. Nevertheless, it would not be complete without at least some reference to the problem which may place it in line with the practice of teaching as outlined in these pages. In dealing with the matter it should first of all be pointed out that the curriculum as it is given by the school authorities to the teacher should be the result of long and careful research. Furthermore, such research should make use of every mode of curriculum construction which is in good standing. In fact, each and every mode will be required if the complex process of checking which is necessary for the building of a balanced curriculum is to be adequately carried out. These various methods of curriculum construction are discussed at length in standard texts on the curriculum.[1] Mere mention may here be made of the social survey, job analysis, examination of prevailing practice, analysis of life needs, the study of children's conduct, the picturing of an ideal adult, the canvass of life experiences, the investigation of objective products; all of these methods should be used by curriculum makers, for all are useful. What is more important than the use of any one method, however, is that it shall not be used alone; and what is more important still is that whatever means of investigation be used the final expression of the results should be in terms of conduct goals, expressed as abilities or attainments which are in themselves obviously desirable to the learner in terms of the learner's own needs.

The unfortunate truth seems to be that the process of curriculum construction must be largely a hit-or-miss procedure. The curriculum itself must be largely colored by the sagacious judgment of whatever well-informed, well-trained individual or group of individuals formulates it. For, in the end, the written curriculum must be to a great extent determined by a comparatively few individuals using every means of investigation and research available. Once having carried on such research these individuals are obviously largely dependent upon their own standards and ways of judging in the final determination of desirable goals. If the suggestive, printed curriculum, as turned over by such specialists to the teacher, is stated in terms of such conduct goals as those used by way of illustration in the present chapter, her problem may be immensely simplified. If they are not provided for her in this form, however, it will be necessary for her to re-state her curriculum by the use of the technique described in the following chapter.

These brief suggestions concerning curriculum construction cannot be regarded in any sense as adequate or complete. Curriculum making in the newer schools must for the present be regarded as an unsolved problem. Trends such as those which have been described are only now beginning to be operative in the determination of curricula. Once more it is necessary to point out that the theory advanced in these pages has not yet been worked out in any complete or logical sense in the schools. It is hoped, however, that the analysis here presented may contribute toward the accomplishment of the reality.

[1] KLAPPER, P., "Contemporary Education," D. Appleton & Co., New York, p. 184.

CHAPTER XIII

THE TEACHER'S USE OF THE CURRICULUM

THE TEACHER cannot be responsible for the determination of curriculum goals. The construction of curricula is an undertaking far too complex for the teacher to engage in unassisted. Thus it is that curricula are usually provided for her use by the school or the school system in which she teaches. It is generally true, however, that these curricula are not stated in terms which the progressive teacher will find most useful. Therefore, she is faced with the problem of re-stating the curriculum furnished her in terms which will make it simpler to work with.

RE-STATING THE CURRICULUM IN CONDUCT GOALS

Taking the curriculum in whatever form it is provided for her, the teacher will find it useful to ignore all subject-matter divisions, such as history, geography, or English, and to re-state her curriculum in terms of four types of curriculum goals. These may be referred to as (1) Ability to Do or Make (or achievement in doing or making),[1] (2) Knowledge, (3) Understanding and (4) Personal Appreciation of Worth or Value.

1. *Ability to Do or Make or Achieve*

One of the forms of conduct in which individuals engage is doing things involving the use of complex habits. Thus in the ordinary activities of daily life, such as making beds, repairing an electric bell, handling one's private accounts, or playing the piano, the individual concerned is doing things which call into play dozens of developed habits or skills. These forms of conduct may involve the use of skills customarily referred to in curricula in such terms as addition of whole

---

[1] This classification is based on Palmer's suggestion that learning products are of three types, Ability to Do, Understanding, or Personal Acceptance of Worth and Value. PALMER, A. R., "Progressive Practices in Directing Learning," The Macmillan Co., New York, 1929.

THE TEACHER'S USE OF THE CURRICULUM

numbers, correct use of commas, or electric wiring. These separately denominated skills, however, need to be regrouped and integrated in terms of ability to do or make things if they are to be stated in conduct goals which will be significant for the class teacher.

2. Knowledge

A form of conduct which is most important in every day life is the securing of knowledge or information. In order to secure knowledge, children read books, magazine articles, and newspapers; make excursions and investigations of various sorts. Thus they learn about skyscrapers, the names of common butterflies and moths, the history of the town in which they live.

3. Understanding

Understanding is a little more than knowledge. It frequently precedes the attaining of certain knowledge. Thus it does not require much understanding to know the names of various butterflies, but if one is to distinguish a moth from a butterfly, one will need to understand that the antennae of a butterfly are knobbed, while those of a moth are feathered. Thus one may know the propositions of Euclid without understanding them. There are endless problems such as—What makes ice cream freeze? How does sleep affect health? What causes trade winds?—which require a form of knowledge based on understanding.

4. Personal Appreciation of Worth or Value

The personal appreciation of certain standards of worth, value or beauty is still another form of conduct which involves learning. To hear the story of Pinnochio, not in indifference but with enjoyment and appreciation, involves the acceptance of certain standards of worth. To hear good music and feel that it is good, to recognize cheap writing and intelligently recognize it as poor, is to accept certain standards of judgment as valid. Thus in acknowledging the good others do, and in appreciating the beauties of nature and of art, we are enlarging our own personalities.

The problem of re-stating curricula in terms of these four types of conduct goals or learning products will vary much as the numerous forms of curriculum statement vary. Sometimes curricula, as provided for the teacher, are discursive and worked out in numerous unrelated details. In such case the teacher will find the problem of re-statement a tedious one. In other cases the division of the curriculum into complex subject-matter prescriptions will also be confusing. In whatever form the printed curriculum is stated, however, some attempt may be made to re-group its prescriptions in the terms suggested above. The following example indicates the way in which her third-grade curriculum was re-stated by Mrs. Minnie Rayner:

1. Ability to:
    (a) Write a friendly letter in legible writing.
    (b) Make and address envelopes correctly.
    (c) Compute sums and change.
    (d) Spell certain words.
    (e) Use simple tools and materials.
    (f) Use the abbreviations Mr., Mrs., St., N. J., Mar.
2. Knowledge of:
    (a) Cloud forms.
    (b) Wind and its uses.
    (c) Foreign countries.
    (d) Development of mail carriers.
    (e) Handling of mail.
    (f) Comparative sizes of feet, yards, miles, etc.
    (g) Community geography.
3. Understanding of:
    (a) Progress of time.
    (b) Elections. (Board election was held in February, which caused intense interest in homes.)
4. Personal Appreciation of Worth or Value of:
    (a) "Who Has Seen the Wind," "The Driver," "Old Man March Wind," "The Changing Skies."
    (b) Stories as "The Everywhere Fairy," "The Train and Big Station."
    (c) Songs as "Choo-Choo," and "A Postilion."
    (d) Opinions and Judgments of fellow pupils.
    (e) Good and poor pictures placed on our bulletin board.

SELECTION IN CLASS OF BRIDGING ACTIVITIES

Having re-stated her curriculum in terms of conduct goals the teacher may now select from the various activities developing in class those which will involve the attainment of certain of her curriculum goals. The following account of the way in which Mrs. Rayner en-

THE TEACHER'S USE OF THE CURRICULUM

couraged and guided activities in class leading to the attainment of the goals of her curriculum stated above is an excellent example of what may be done in the introduction of an activity program in a public school where work of this type is new.

Three weeks before Valentine's Day a wooden box, a hammer, some nails and boards were taken to school by the teacher. This, so far as I know, was the first time such implements and materials had entered our school except when brought in by repair men. They were placed in a corner at the front of the room, but were immediately spotted by each arrival, examined and compared with those they had at home. Sly glances were cast toward the teacher, and she heard boasts of how hard and straight each could hammer. After assembly our "Round Table" emphasized the holidays in February, and then that of St. Valentine's Day. Immediately the request for a mail box came forth from a second-grader—but was quickly set aside by a third-grade boy's saying the boys could easily make a "whole Post Office."

That noon we were deluged with wooden boxes, crates, hammers, nails and saws. How the boys worked the next two weeks, building the Post Office, while during that time the girls made Valentines. Our constructive work was something brand new, and from every hand came questions and suggestions. The Post Office was painted, a real ballot election was held, tellers and a chairman appointed, and postmaster, his assistant, mail carriers and such were elected. The responsibility the children felt and enjoyed has thoroughly convinced me that the average child, if properly encouraged and guided, is capable of self-direction and of responsibility.

One icy cold morning, while the activity on the Post Office was still in progress, the teacher placed on the bulletin board a picture of a mail-carrying sled drawn by five Eskimo dogs. "May I paint a sled on the easel before the last bell?" soon came as a request from a little fellow who until recently had shunned the easel. He was told that he might do so, and as each became so interested, I asked how many would like to make a sled another way. We each made a sled, cut free-hand, three or five dogs, which we attached to the sleds, and when finished, had a scene depicting sleds drawn up on shore—while a boat lay out in the distance, on which our Eskimos were trading! Here was something crying out to be sent through the mail. Consequently we made envelopes and learned how to address them to our friends.

Both writing and arithmetic were involved in the children's use of the Post Office. Our arithmetic in the second grade was much aided by the purchase of stamps, which was in reality drill on the two time tables. Writing was necessary in many instances, especially in the sending of a class letter to the other classes in the school, inviting them to the use of our Post Office. Several rules were decided upon by the children, and a copy of them hung on the Post Office, for instance—"Address all mail carefully," "Do not use the Post Office for silly notes."

The next step was to obtain knowledge of different ways in which mail has been carried. An envelope, which had come from the West by airplane, found its way to the bulletin board one morning. That found us burdened at noon with airplanes of every size and appearance, and much interest was aroused in air mail carriers. In our talking we decided that one must know about winds, clouds and stars in order to be a competent flier of mail planes. In the course of this study the children learned the names of several different types of cloud to their great satisfaction. To see a group of children suddenly stop their play and look skyward to say, "Oh, see that lively cirrus cloud," displays a concern deeper than any other I feel that I have ever obtained.

Numerous activities were continually cropping up. In the course of them the children learned to spell many new words, the names of the various clouds, the different mail carriers, and many words which they needed in their own writing. Such occasions would arise when, for instance, letters were written to the primary grades inviting them to come in and enjoy the pictures we had made. A large class picture depicting a Wind Scene had been painted, as well as individual pictures of planes, trains, boats, stage coaches, and clouds. The accumulation of airplanes, boats, trains, and pictures of stage coaches and cloud studies brought in by the children from magazines and for the bulletin board became so great that space had to be provided for them. A scrapbook was suggested and accepted as being "great." Now with tools brought from home, (for as yet none had been provided by the school,) other facilities were added. One second-grader, who had previously not been greatly interested, brought seven crates, and boxes. The materials on hand were painted, and our array of "lockers" is quite attractive.

One morning, during our "Round Table," one of the children asked where the people lived that sent the mail which came to our Post Office by means of the different mail carriers. What an opportunity!—a floor map of our town, marking out the streets—each child making a miniature replica of his home and placing it in a proper setting. We got a large 3' x 9' map of our lovely little Borough, and began our work by having each child draw a sketch of his or her home as a week-end task. A lively discussion of the map revealed that our Borough has but two public buildings—our school and fire house, with no churches and not one store. A great number had not realized that when buying but a loaf of bread, or attending Sunday School, they must go without the bounds of their little town. They have been instilled, during the year, with a deep love for our Palisades, from which we see the majestic sweep of the Hudson. From the very windows of the classroom, we see the towers of the new bridge, across to New York. It stands as a symbol to be translated to the children that we are all dependent on one another for everything we have and are.

One further example of a re-stated curriculum, and the way in which activities were selected by the teacher leading on to the de-

THE TEACHER'S USE OF THE CURRICULUM

sired curriculum goals is to be seen in the following work of Mrs. Grace Cowan, with first-grade children:

RE-STATED CURRICULUM

1. Ability to do or make:
    (a) A bird house.
    (b) A flower book.
    (c) An animal book.
    (d) A rabbit book.
    (e) What is necessary for proper care of goldfish.
    (f) Gather pollywog specimens and other pond forms.
    (g) Label things in our books.
    (h) Read labels written by the teacher.

2. Knowledge of:
    (a) Wild life.
    (b) Pussy willows and where to find them.
    (c) Such tree flowers as those of maple, birch, hazelnut, elm, etc.
    (d) Spring flowers and birds.
    (e) What birds' nests are made of.
    (f) How to pick wild flowers.

3. Understanding of:
    (a) Blooming of pussy willows, maple, alder, hazel, birch, etc.
    (b) How to recognize robins, sparrows, blue jays, flickers, bluebirds, chickadees, starlings.
    (d) Blooming places and naming of forsythia, violets, spring beauties, hepaticae, crocuses, tulips, anemones, bloodroot, etc.

4. Personal Appreciation of Worth or Value of:
    (a) Stories.
    (b) Making books.
    (c) Pictures.
    (d) Poems read and recited.

The activities which developed as a basis of school work in this case were formed about the local environment and generally concerned with "Signs of Spring." The class adopted the slogan "Stop, Look, and Listen."

One day one of the children brought in a little cardboard house she had made at home. I put it on the floor in front of the room. The next morning, in the circle, I asked the children if they liked Jane's house. We talked about houses and our village, and finally it was decided that other children would like to make houses too. So at noon nearly every child brought in some kind of a box and set to work making houses, post office, church, a school and so forth. We painted them and then arranged them in rows and streets like a village. The next morning when I arrived each child, even the most backward and slowest, rushed to me to show me some object he or she had brought for the village. There were cars, trolleys, airplanes, animals, fences, a cannon, and several other things. Each day something new was added to the village. After its completion the second and third grades were invited to see it. For writing and spelling we labelled things, and made up sentences about our town to write. We counted houses, cars, etc. We found pictures of villages and read stories about towns and activities in towns.

While this was going on we went out into the fields and woods in our village. The first thing which interested us was trap rock. Each child carried a piece with him. Then we found sandstone, milky white quartz, and some slate. Next we heard a robin and saw him. Soon we saw a blue jay and some juncos. Returning to class we found pictures of the birds we had seen, and placed them on our "Signs of Spring" chart. We then started a bird calendar. The rocks were labelled and placed in our curiosity corner.

We found a last year's nest, one day, and brought it back with us. This led to talk about birds, and how we might attract them to our houses. Putting out food was suggested, and some one said to make bird houses. I asked the children if they would like to do this, and they were very anxious to do so. Tools and wood were brought from home, and houses were made. In the course of these activities we wrote sentences about birds. I read poems and stories about robins, bluebirds, and wrote about them on the blackboard.

One Monday morning, Nathaniel brought in five or six fine animal pictures cut from the Sunday *Times* picture section. In the circle I showed them to the children. I said, "What shall we do with these fine pictures?" Some one suggested hanging them in the room. The child that brought them in did so. The next day others were brought in, and still more. Finally, I said, "These are fine pictures. It seems as if we should do something else with them." One child said that we could make a book. Out of these suggestions grew a fine animal book, growing bigger and bigger every day. Each child pasted his own pictures in it. It was labelled "First Grade Animal Book." The children decided to leave it in the library for the others next year.

A flower book was started in about the same way. We have a fine flower book now. One boy was particularly interested in it and brought many beautiful pictures every day for several weeks. These two books are looked at very often. The children are proud of them. Every child has contributed something to each book. I gave magazines to some of the slower children to find things in. After a start of this kind, I found that nearly every one would find one or two at home, and bring them the next day.

On one of our walks we picked twigs of maple, alder, beech and willow. We put them in jars of water. Each morning a group of children looked at them and reported to the children in the morning circle of any change in them and showed them to the group. We watched the tight, hard little buds come out into leaf. The children seemed interested and surprised to learn

THE TEACHER'S USE OF THE CURRICULUM

that leaves were all folded up in such tiny, brown buds. On another walk we found skunk cabbage just pushing its purple-streaked hood up through the earth. We saw some of the first bumblebees visiting it to obtain their first load of yellow pollen. From this we knew it was a flower. We plan another trip to see any change which comes over it.

One day we discovered something new about stones. We learned to write on stones with other stones. We learned that some stones are harder than others. This helped us to distinguish various stones in particular by their color, weight, and luster. This was quite a valuable experience as a foundation for later understanding of various rocks.

The first flowers of spring are beginning to be brought in. We write their names on the "Signs of Spring" chart, and we have started a flower calendar. We are having interesting conversations about flowers. I am trying to arouse the children's interest in wild flower conservation, and careful picking of wild flowers. When we go to the woods to pick flowers, I have taught them to pick only several flowers from each clump, and to be sure to leave several blooms in each clump so that they can go to seed, and make more plants next year. The children have caught the spirit, and are very cunning about it. We read stories and poems about flowers. We sing songs and write sentences having the names of flowers in them. We look at good pictures of flowers. What a satisfaction it is when they go to the woods and identify a flower! It is like meeting an old friend.

This is as far as we have gotten with our "Signs of Spring" up to the time this account was written. Such joy the children are having in this new way of working. What opportunities we have had for interesting reading material, writing, dramatization, drawing, and conversation! The children are very happy and full of enthusiasm. It does not seem to be any effort to teach them, or for them to learn things. They have certainly learned the fundamental things necessary for the first grade and more. They have developed an appreciation of things both in and out of doors. It is to be hoped that there has been awakened in them a real desire to "Pause, to Stop, Look and Listen" whenever they are in the woods and fields.

CHECKING ATTAINED CURRICULUM GOALS

Finally, the curriculum may be used by the teacher as a check list of what has been accomplished. This checking process may be carried on with the original *in extenso* written curriculum, such as that usually furnished to public school teachers or, as will be simpler and more convenient, with the curriculum as re-stated by the teacher herself. As any unit of conduct is completed by an individual or by the group, the teacher may check off on her curriculum the goals which have been satisfactorily attained. In order to do this more conveniently, she should keep a careful record of the learnings of the children as each unit develops. This is best done daily. It will be obvious from the examples quoted above that in the progress of the activities described the children attained their curriculum goals. In the case of the first example, for instance, it is obvious that when the work on the post office was completed, the teacher could check off numerous goals from her re-stated curriculum, namely, ability to write a friendly letter, ability to make and address an envelope correctly, use of abbreviations Mr., Mrs., certain spelling and arithmetic, and so on. Matters like spelling and arithmetic need, in addition, special checking which should be arranged for by means of a testing program. In the case in point, for example, Mrs. Rayner's class made the following gains in reading as indicated by the Gates Primary Reading Test-Type I:

	November	*May*
Halvar	43	45
Jack	29	43
Dorothy	28	39
George	18	30
Tammie	34	48
Betsy	12	28
Henry	20	35
Norman	35	48
Marguerite	11	28
Marlen	8	24
Amelia	31	32
Arthur	11	48
Christina	37	46
Dick	17	31

This indicates a satisfactory gain in the reading skills, and, with the remainder of the testing program, completes the teacher's check on the children's attainment of curriculum goals.

The Conclusion of the Teaching Act

So the basic general description of the teaching process here set forth reaches its conclusion. Having begun with the child, it has proceeded forward, discussing the development of bridging activities, and concluding with the curriculum. When the child reaches his curriculum goals the teaching act may be regarded as finished. The teaching process ends with the curriculum; yet in another and secondary sense it may be said to begin there. For learning is, to a certain extent, forecast in the printed curriculum. The teacher's whole previous life, her training, her study of school life and of teaching, her specific preparation for the work of the school year or of the school day are all concerned with her interpretation of curriculum in tentative form. It is in such a general and theoretical sense that teaching may begin with the curriculum. But the child's own learning must begin with him, be guided and directed until the work of the teacher is completed in the fusion of values which occurs when the child is living the curriculum.

Part III
THE TECHNIQUE OF CLASS MANAGEMENT

CHAPTER XIV

PROBLEMS AND TECHNIQUES OF CLASS ADMINISTRATION

IN ADDITION to those generalized techniques which have been discussed in the previous section there are certain techniques of class management which are somewhat more specific. These techniques are concerned with such matters as the organization of class groups, the provision of suitable seating arrangements, the use of the blackboard, the use of textbooks, and the testing of pupils. These matters will be taken up in the present and succeeding chapters.

THE CLASS GROUP

Teachers need a sound conception of the nature of the class group. The idea of a number of children forming a class group is essentially different from that of a classroom full of children, each of whom is to be submitted to the same fixed regimen. A class is much more than an aggregation of children. It is not a mere series of unit children, sitting in rows like puppets, whose relationships are matters of mechanical administrative convenience. Nor is it a group merely in terms of geographical proximity, or the accidents of class grouping. The members of it are bound together by the interweaving of their own personalities. They are vitally related as members of a social community. They have their common interests in the trips they take together, the life they live in common, and the problems they discover and solve by mutual coöperation. There should be an organic unity to the whole class, a unity which is felt by the children and understood by the teacher.

The size of the class is a vital matter in schools which are organized in terms of conduct. The nature of the group as a social organism completely obviates the possibility of large classes. There seem to be very definite limits to the size of a group which can be correctly guided by a single teacher. Teachers of experience agree in placing these limits at from twenty-five to thirty pupils. Many teachers regard twenty-five children as an ideal class. Other skillful teachers state a preference for a class slightly larger than twenty-five, in which, they claim, there is a richer total of experiences and increased social validity. There is a wider diversity of situations, of points of view, and of dispositional traits. All seem convinced, however, that the maximum number of children with which a full activity program can be carried on is thirty. Such are the psychological limits of a correctly functioning class.

It is a notorious fact that the usual public school class in our city schools today is considerably larger than thirty. It is, therefore, indisputable that class work of a kind may be carried on with groups much in excess of thirty children. Nor is it to be disputed that in the early days of public education, a century ago, Lancastrian schools presented the Gargantuan spectacle of one thousand children directed by a single teacher. Thus it would be absurd to pretend that huge classes cannot be maintained in orderly fashion. In fact, the larger the classes the more orderly and stagnant they may become. Nothing can be more correct than a lifeless machine. Accurate functioning of large classes may be secured by routinization, which can only go on at the expense of the functioning organic life of the group. Teachers with excessively large classes should realize that they will be unable to carry on a full unrestricted activity program. The more modern methods of teaching must, for such classes, be modified. The life of the class must be partially routinized to fit the special situation which arises when a group is unavoidably too large.

But teachers whose classes exceed a maximum of thirty need not give up the attempt to organize school life in terms of conduct. In such cases they may carry on by a plan which is a combination of older and newer ways of doing things. A semi-routinization of activities may be worked out in such a unit of conduct as the making of a scrapbook. Each child in the room may keep a scrapbook. In it he may paste whatever he considers most important from the day's newspapers. Again, if a large class wishes to make a mural decoration in a room in which there is not sufficient space to allow the various individuals to coöperate on a single large piece, a compromise may be made. The mural may be first designed on a small scale, and each child at his desk may prepare a cut-out assigned to him to be pasted on the large finished product. Such modifications are restricting and difficult to work out, but in many public schools teachers of initiative and ability are carrying on original modified programs.

It seems important, however, to stress the fact that the small class is absolutely fundamental in a thorough organization of school life in terms of conduct. The class of twenty-five is well able to work together on group problems of research and construction; it is large enough to provide adequate background for live discussion, and is not too large for group instruction and whatever work demands the intellectualizing leadership of the teacher. On the other hand, it is suitable for the carrying on of individualized activities, and to permit children to carry on work which is distinctly their own and different from that of others in the group. School administrators who are concerned with the introduction of an activity program into the classrooms over which they have direction should be perfectly clear that it is their primary problem to see to it that the classes do not exceed a normal size of twenty-five. Until they secure this for their teachers, they cannot expect them to carry on a complete and successful modern program.

System of Class Grouping

To be thoroughly consistent in the matter of functional rather than mechanical organization schools should base their system of grouping children into classes on a principle of the general homogeneity of the children placed together. Traditionally, elementary school pupils have been placed in groups almost entirely on a basis of achievement in the mastery of the subject matter of the course of study, particularly in the tool subjects. Any such organization is obviously based on convenience of instruction and administration rather than upon conditions which facilitate learning. Even if it be granted that the old method of grading was based on intellectual attainment, it can hardly be claimed that it took into adequate consideration the physical, social, or emotional homogeneity of the group.

Yet the physical, social, or emotional maladjustment of the individual to the group in which he is placed may be quite as injurious to his learning, and may produce just as definite and serious distortion of his development as intellectual maladjustment. Social maladjustment, if disregarded in the lower grades, may become cumulative and bring results just as serious for the individual as intellectual failure. Consider, for instance, the case of a fifteen-year-old college freshman of brilliant intellectual attainments. This boy came to college with a history of a very unruly career in high school. In the residential college in which he lived he was a thorn in the flesh of the authorities, and after repeated misdemeanors lost his college scholarship. He was finally expelled at the end of his first year and refused a clear admission to any other college. The plight of such a lad is far worse than that of a college freshman who fails in his examinations. It was caused primarily by a schism between the intellectual and social aspects of the boy's personality, a maladjustment which was produced by a system of promotion based entirely on attainment in examinations.

Emotional maladjustment may also cause unfortunate situations. In spite of all that can be done to prevent it, personal antagonisms sometimes spring up between certain individual children and the teachers in whose classes they are placed. These antagonisms may be caused by a clash of personalities which is too difficult to trace. There are cases on record where children, for reasons that could not be discovered, have been emotional misfits in a certain class, and sometimes in a certain school. Children may, due to some chance remark or experience, conceive a dislike for a teacher before entering her class. One little girl found herself so unhappy in her first year at school that she made repeated refusals to go to class. In this case the trouble was caused by the teacher's antagonism to one of the child's parents, an antagonism which she unconsciously expressed in her attitude toward and treatment of the child. Cases of physical maladjustment are not infrequent, due to the fact that certain children are mentally more or less mature than children of similar bodily development. When such discrepancy occurs the children concerned are restricted in their social intercourse with other children and in participation in competitive games. The restriction of physical activity which results is injurious to the health of the child, and sometimes causes a sense of inferiority with respect to participation in physical activities and games.

It is for such reasons that certain schools have given up the practice of grading into six elementary school grades. The Ojai Valley School, for instance, plans to group boys and girls from five to fourteen on the principle of similarity of interests and abilities into six approximate age groups as follows:

Group 1. Ages 5 and 6
Group 2. Age 7
Group 3. Ages 8 and 9
Group 4. Ages 10 and 11
Group 5. Age 12
Group 6. Age 13

The City and Country School uses a plan, which has been adopted in other schools, of dividing the children into seven groups according to

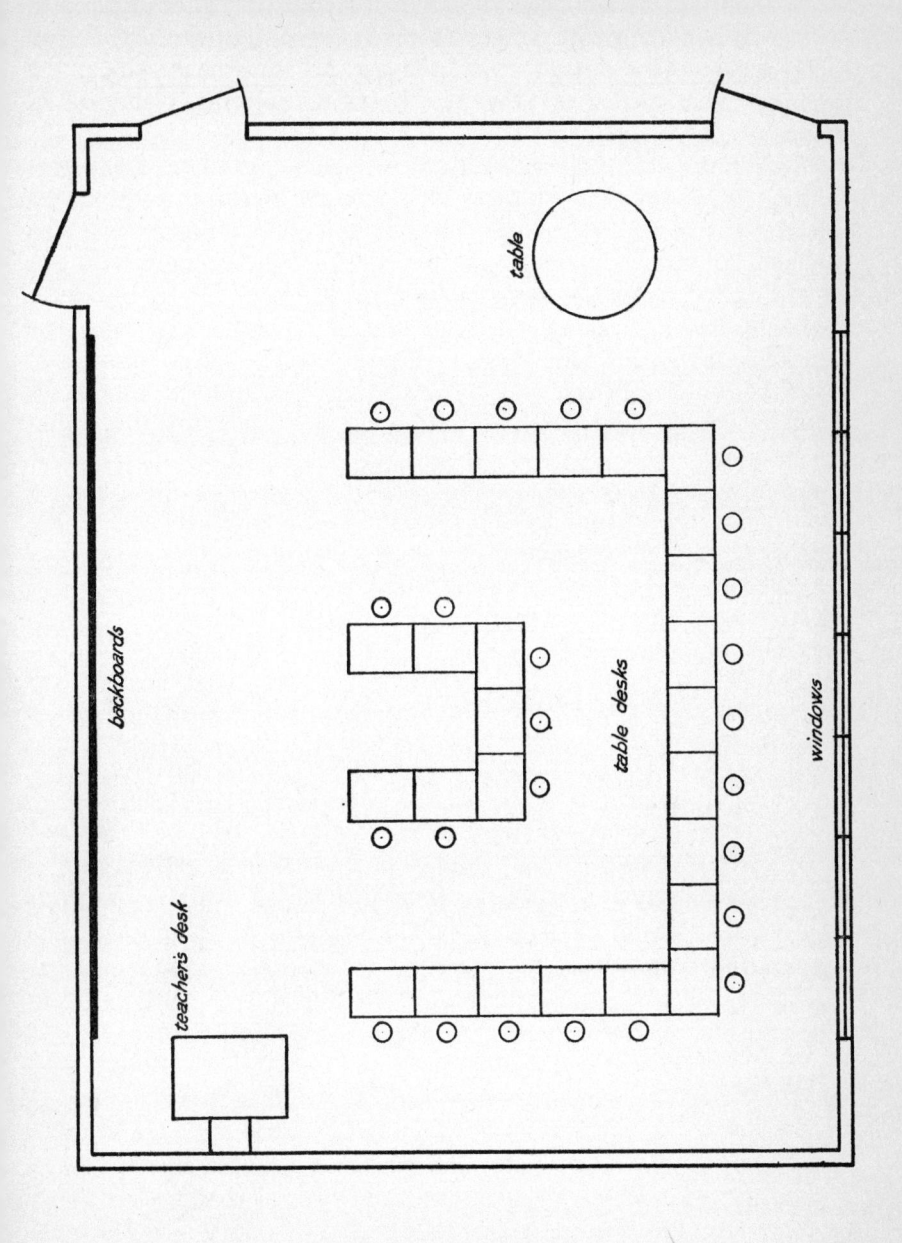

PROBLEMS AND TECHNIQUES OF CLASS ADMINISTRATION 141

approximate ages from three to thirteen. In this school, and in others which use a similar form of organization, the groups are colloquially referred to as the "Sixes" or the "Twelves." In still another school the children are organized into "life classes" according to the activities in which they engage.

The purpose of all such schemes for grouping is to arrange a plan which will allow the maximum of flexibility and permit the shifting of pupils from one group to another for any reason whatever that seems likely to improve the mutual adjustment of the individual and the group, and promote better learning for those concerned.

Not all of the newer schools, however, follow unusual plans of grouping. Many schools, such as the Lincoln School, the Ethical Culture School, and the Francis W. Parker School, follow the customary plan of six elementary school grades. They tend, however, to regard the grade lines as a barrier much less rigid than those of certain other schools. The grade grouping is not made entirely upon a basis of achievement in subject matter, but the whole personality of the child is considered in relation to the group into which he is to fit. Change from group to group may be made for the sake of intellectual, emotional or physical gains. Furthermore, children who are backward or advanced in one or two aspects of school life may carry them on by special arrangement in groups other than their home group. The individual instruction plan used at Winnetka allows for promotion by subjects. A child may be promoted in spelling at one time and in arithmetic at another. Promotion does not necessarily entail change of group. Pupils in the same group may be doing two or even three grades of work. But whatever form of organization is used, the tendency is to work out some plan which will allow as great an amount of flexibility as possible and make the maximum provision for individual variations.

SPACE AND FURNISHINGS

Good teaching which provides children with satisfactory opportunities to live and move about demands adequate space. The classroom itself should be spacious, and whenever possible should have a supplementary activity room. In addition, special rooms are needed, such as a pottery-room, a shop, a laboratory, a library, a music-room and a playroom. To these may be added all out-of-doors.

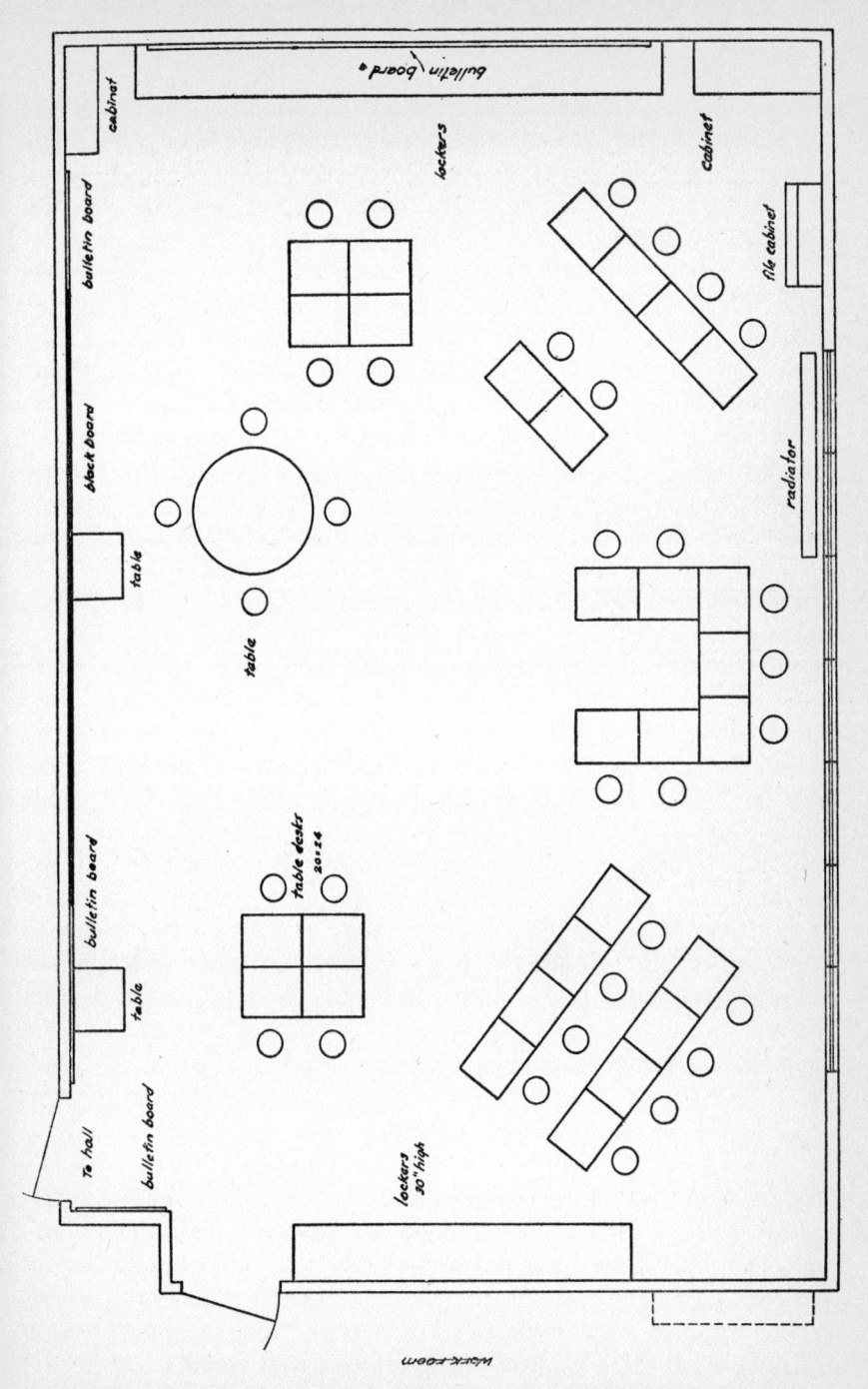

Showing the seating plan of a fifth grade classroom taught by Miss Margaret Batten in the Bronxville Public Schools. The excellence of the arrangement with reference to window lights, blackboards and bulletin boards, as well as to free space for the development of activities, is obvious.

The furnishing of these rooms should be appropriate to the activities carried on in them. Special reference must be made to the type of seats and desks which is desirable. While it is becoming monotonous to hear derogatory references made to screwed-down seats and desks, yet such stationary furniture is still in use in thousands of classrooms. If the expense of the change to movable furniture is pleaded as the cause for not making it, it should be pointed out that it is not absolutely necessary to buy new equipment. The desks and chairs already in use may be screwed to wooden runners instead of being screwed to the floor. While such furniture may be somewhat clumsy, yet it is movable, and anything is preferable to stationary seating.

There are those who seem to be under the impression that movable furniture is desirable for the lower grades but not necessary for the upper grades. Surely such an opinion is not based on the needs of children in the upper elementary school. It seems almost imperative, if teaching of a modern type is to be carried on in the upper grades, that they, too, should have movable chairs and desks. Certainly any teacher carrying on in new ways would be happier with chairs and tables which can be arranged at will.

Teachers who argue in favor of fixed furniture sometimes give as a reason for their preference that the alteration and adjustment of movable furniture may cause a great deal of confusion. Such an argument reveals lack of understanding and poor technique on the part of the teachers who make it. Because chairs and tables are movable it does not necessarily follow that they must be continually moved. The arrangement of seats and desks may remain almost the same for months at a time. Furthermore, there must be something wrong with the order in a class which is unable to look after its seats and desks in quiet and efficient fashion. If children in the upper grades have not developed enough responsibility to look after their own chairs, how may they be regarded as responsible, self-determining children in the other activities of the school?

Desks and seats lose a great deal of their significance in schools in which children spend comparatively little time sitting in them. With less sedentary and more active schoolroom practice, chairs and tables must be relegated to a place in the classroom where they will not interfere with school activities. They are frequently placed around the edges of the room, with just sufficient space between the chairs and the wall to allow free passage. This leaves the center free for various activities. Other interesting arrangements of furniture sometimes used are illustrated in the accompanying diagrams.

As has already been pointed out, whatever the arrangement, it is usually only relatively permanent, and is altered as occasion arises. Thus, at Christmas time, the children may take great pleasure in arranging their chairs for the Christmas week in a circle about the Christmas tree placed in the center. So the arrangement of the seating may assume whatever form suits the needs and desires of the group. Basically this arrangement of furniture should be governed by circumstances and the use to which it is being put at the time. The placing of the furniture may have any degree of formality or informality that the situation demands.

One special circumstance should be mentioned, on account of its significance in the arrangement of seating. One of the important gains which should be secured by a good seating plan is a certain amount of clear space in the classroom. This may be used for materials which are likely to be called for at any moment by some individual or group. Thus a work bench or an easel may find its place in both lower and upper grades of the elementary school. Teachers who find it impossible to rid their classrooms of stationary seats sometimes make use of a bit of open space in whatever part of the classroom they can find it, and occasionally enlarge it by the removal of one or two desks from the classroom, or to another part of the room. In fact, so indispensable is such a portion of free floor space that teachers in public schools who have been unable to find it in their classrooms have gained permission to use the hallways. It is often inconvenient, for one reason or another, for children engaged in some unit of conduct involving the use of special materials to be compelled to go off to the art room, or some supplementary room which is probably in use by others. It is thus obvious that a certain amount of space in the classroom for such supplementary materials for use by individuals is very desirable.

The Daily Program

Certain extremists have maintained that it is undesirable and unnecessary to work out any plan for the daily activities of a class. Experience in the development of activity programs has shown, however, that it is neither wise nor convenient to dispense with them altogether. Rather it seems well to work out schedules which differ

146 THE TECHNIQUE OF PROGRESSIVE TEACHING

from the older type in certain other respects. One hesitates to call these arrangements "time tables" for fear that the term may suggest a rigid organization in terms of clock hours which must be strictly adhered to. Nothing is further from the modern school program than a set, formal organization which is to be determinedly held to. On the contrary, the flexibility which is fundamental to a good time schedule makes its written organization very difficult and its printed form misleading. Several examples of attempts to write out class schedules are here given. They will reward careful examination and consideration.

The following daily program for Grade One is used by Miss Turnbull in Public School 41 in New York City:

    9:00 Work period
    9:50 Recess (Toilet—Milk)
   10:00 Rhythm—Music
   10:40 Outdoors—Yard
   11:10 Discussion
   11:30 Music
   11:45 Lunch
    1:00 Rest
    1:30 Park—Work—Games
    2:30 Stories

Concerning this program several things may be observed. In the first place it is approximately the same for every day of the week, variability being obtained by provision for optional use of given periods. This uniform daily program is suitable for children in the lowest grades because of the desirability for some routinization of the habits of young children, for whom life should not be made too complex. The opening of school with a long free period is to be observed. This allows children to begin work as soon as they reach school on whatever activity they choose. This may be carpentry, block-building, painting, clay-modeling, or any of a number of such things, which they carry on individually, in coöperating pairs, or in small groups. This period is comparatively long, fifty minutes, since it is found that such free individual work cannot be well developed in short periods. Similar long periods are used for outdoor and yard play at 10:40, and for park trips at 1:30. The more intellectualized activities demanding concentration are given shorter tentative allotments of time.

PROBLEMS AND TECHNIQUES OF CLASS ADMINISTRATION

It should be observed that considerable flexibility is allowed by giving merely general denominations to the time periods. The period designated "work period," that referred to as "outdoors—yard," "discussion," and "park—work—games," allow considerable freedom of interpretation as to what actually does go on in the time allowed.

The following program worked out for Grade Three by Miss Baldwin in the Horace Mann School of Columbia University, shows evidence of a number of schemes developed to secure an orderly program with a considerable amount of flexibility:

THIRD GRADE

Time	Monday	Tuesday	Wednesday	Thursday	Friday
8:45	Skills	Skills	Skills	Skills	Skills
9:45	Sciences	Appreciations 10:15 Gymnasium	Sciences	Appreciations 10:15 Gymnasium	
10:45	Recess	Recess	Recess	Recess	Recess
11:00	Fine Arts	10:50 Assembly	Appreciations	10:50 Assembly	10:50 Class Meeting
11:30	Appreciations	11:10 Unassigned	11:30 Fine Arts 12:10 Chorus	11:5 Sciences 11:50 Unassigned	11:10 Unassigned
12:30	Gymnasium	Sciences Shop-work	Unassigned	Gymnasium	12:15 Sciences

The general assignment of the first school hour to the development of skills allows considerable freedom to choose whatever of the work in arithmetic, reading or spelling is most in need of attention at the time. Similar provision is made for experiences in art, literature and music. Other periods, such as those for gymnasium, shop and chorus are fitted in as assigned by the general school program, while provision is made for a weekly class meeting if the children wish to hold it. The inclusion of certain blocks of time marked "unassigned" is another useful feature of this schedule.

The following complete set of programs which were used at one time in the Lincoln School of Columbia University, indicate the way in which programs may coördinate the work of the whole school:

KINDERGARTEN—MISS STEVENS

Time	Monday	Tuesday	Wednesday	Thursday	Friday
9:00 10:00	9:00–10:10	9:00–9:45		9:00–10:10	9:00–9:45
	DISCUSSION OF PLANS AND WORK PERIOD				
10:00		9:50–10:10 MUSIC			9:50–10:10 Music
11:00	10:10–11:10				
	PREPARATION—LUNCHEON—REST				
11:00	11:10–11:30				
	LANGUAGE OR NATURE EXPERIENCES				
12:00	11:30–12:00				
	* ROOF ACTIVITIES OR EXCURSIONS OR STORIES AND DRAMATIZATION				

* Determined by the weather and the need and interest of the group.

GRADE I—MRS. BLISS

Time	Monday	Tuesday	Wednesday	Thursday	Friday
9:00	9:00–9:30 Activities leading to Reading	Household Arts	Assembly or Activities leading to Reading	ACTIVITIES LEADING TO READING	
10:00	9:30–9:50 Gymnasium	Music	Gymnasium	Music	Gymnasium
10:00	9:50–10:10 Music	9:50–10:30 INDUSTRIAL ARTS			9:50–10:30 Language or Science or Number Experiences
	10:10–10:30 Language				
11:00	10:30–11:15				
	LUNCHEON AND REST				
11:00	11:15–11:30				
	ROOF				
12:00	11:30–12:05 Free Creative Activities	11:30–12:30 Free Creative Activities	11:30–12:05 Free Creative Activities	11:30–12:30 FREE CREATIVE ACTIVITIES	
12:00	12:05–12:30 Fine Arts		12:05–12:30 Fine Arts		
1:00	12:30–1:00				
	STORIES AND DRAMATIZATION				

Grade II—Miss Matthews

Time	Monday	Tuesday	Wednesday	Thursday	Friday
9:00	9:00–9:20 *DISCUSSION		9:00–9:30 Assembly		9:00–9:20 DISCUSSION
10:00	9:20–10:00 READING				
10:00	10:00–10:30 Roof	Gymnasium	Roof		GYMNASIUM
11:00	10:30–11:00 LUNCHEON—REST—POEMS—STORIES				
11:00	11:00–11:30 Numbers	Industrial Arts	Numbers	Industrial Arts	Numbers
12:00	11:30–12:00 Fine Arts	Oral Expression of Class Trips and Experiences	Fine Arts	Oral Expression of Class Trips and Experiences	
12:00	12:00–1:00 Creative Period Dramatics Individual Work Period	12:00–12:30 Spelling Writing	12:00–1:00 Creative Period Dramatics Individual Work Period	12:00–12:30 Spelling Writing	Dramatics
1:00		12:30–1:00 Music			12:30–1:00 MUSIC

* Cooking every other Monday.

Grade III—Miss Keelor

Time	Monday	Tuesday	Wednesday	Thursday	Friday
9:00 10:00	9:00–10:00 Industrial Arts	*Room Activities	9:00–9:30 Assembly 9:30–10:45 *Room Activities	9:00–10:00 Household Arts	*Room Activities
10:00	10:00–10:45 *Room Activities	Fine Arts		10:00–10:45 Fine Arts	Industrial Arts
11:00	10:45–11:00	MORNING LUNCH			
11:00	11:00–11:30 Stories or Poems	Creative Music	Singing	Creative Music	Singing
12:00	11:30–12:00	SPELLING AND ARITHMETIC DRILL			
12:00	12:00–12:30	GYMNASIUM			
1:00	12:30–1:00	LIBRARY PERIOD			

* The periods marked Room Activities include various kinds of work needed by the class in written composition, oral discussions, or other subject matter connected with our unit of work.

GRADE IV—Mrs. Eakright

Time	Monday	Tuesday	Wednesday	Thursday	Friday
9:00	9:00–10:00 Fine Arts	9:00–9:30 Arithmetic	9:00–9:45 Assembly	9:00–10:30 ARITHMETIC—SPELLING— READING	
10:00		9:30–10:30 Household Arts	9:45–10:30 Spelling		
10:00	10:00–10:30 Spelling				
11:00	10:30 11:00 Boys' Gym	10:25 11:15 Girls' Swim	10:30–11:00 GYMNASIUM	10:30 11:00 Girls' Gym	10:25 11:15 Boys' Swim	10:30–11:00 GYMNASIUM
11:00	11:00–11:10	MORNING LUNCH			
	11:10–11:30	FRENCH			
12:00	11:30–12:00 Singing	Creative Music	Singing	Creative Music	Remedial Groups
12:00	12:00–12:40 Work Period	Report Period	Industrial Arts	Work Period	Work Period
1:00 1:00 2:00	12:45–2:00	LUNCHEON AND RECREATION			
2:00 3:00	2:00–3:00 Report Period	Library	Creative Work Period	Library	Story Hour

Grade V—Miss Baxter

Time	Monday	Tuesday	Wednesday	Thursday	Friday
9:00–10:00	9:00–9:40 ARITHMETIC		Assembly	9:00–10:00 Industrial Arts	9:00–9:40 Arithmetic
10:00	9:40–10:30 UNIT OF WORK			10:00–10:30 Unit of Work	9:40–10:30 Unit of Work
11:00	10:30–11:00 ENGLISH				
11:00	11:00 11:30 Boys' Gym	10:50 11:40 Girls' Swim	11:00–11:30 Gymnasium	11:00 11:30 Girls' Gym	10:50 11:40 Boys' Swim	11:00–11:30 GYMNASIUM
12:00	11:35–12:00 FRENCH				
12:00	12:00–12:30 Creative Music	Singing	Creative Music	Singing	Library
1:00	12:30–12:45 SPELLING				
1:00–2:00	12:45–2:00 LUNCHEON AND RECREATION				
2:00–3:00	2:00–3:00 Household Arts	Unit of Work	Creative Work Period	Fine Arts	Individual Interests

Grade VI—Miss Barnes

Time	Monday	Tuesday	Wednesday	Thursday	Friday
9:00–10:00	9:00–9:50 *		Assembly		*
10:00	9:50–10:15 FRENCH				
10:00	10:15–10:30 MORNING LUNCH				
11:00	10:30–11:00 *	10:30–11:00 Singing	10:30–11:00 Creative Music	10:30–11:00 Singing	10:30–11:00 Creative Music
11:00	11:00–11:30 Spelling	Report on Council Activities	Spelling		SPELLING
12:00	11:30–12:00 Boys' Gym / 11:15–12:05 Girls' Swim	11:30–12:00 GYMNASIUM	11:30–12:00 Girls' Gym / 11:15–12:05 Boys' Swim		11:30–12:00 GYMNASIUM
12:00–1:00	12:00–12:45 Household Arts	12:00–12:45 ARITHMETIC			
1:00–2:00	12:45–2:00 LUNCHEON AND RECREATION				
2:00–3:00	2:00–3:00 *	*	Creative Work Period	Industrial Arts	Fine Arts
3:00	DISMISSAL				

* Unit of Work—History of Records—or Books Through the Ages.

154 THE TECHNIQUE OF PROGRESSIVE TEACHING

A number of things may be observed in a study of these programs. It is clear that the same simplicity and daily routine to which attention was called in the Grade One program previously discussed is present in these lower grades. Again, the tendency to long periods is to be observed in all the programs. There is, for the most part, the same avoidance of such rigid captions as arithmetic, spelling, geography, history or grammar, and the substitution of more generalized terms such as number interests, discussion, class trips and oral expression. The flexibility of the time schedules is indicated by such terms as "free creative activities," "room activities," "language or nature experiences," "open for class activities and drill," "unit of work," "roof activities or stories or dramatization, determined by the needs and interests of the group."

Attention should again be called to the fact that the very recording of these time tables may be misleading, because in printed form they give an impression of rigidity which is not intended. When teachers find that special circumstances warrant an alteration in the general program, which does not interfere wtih the program of other groups, they have no hesitation in making an alteration. Students who have become specially interested or involved in an activity which could not be dropped and resumed again without considerable loss may be allowed to continue past the allotted time. The whole class may make special arrangements for trips which are not provided for in the schedule. In fact any salutary change may be made at any time, since the time schedule is made for the children, not the children for the time schedule.

USE OF THE BLACKBOARD

Time was when one of the chief uses of a square bit of blackboard was to exhibit the time table. If the supervisor dropped in at any moment, by comparing the class work going on with the class work scheduled and finding them in accord, he was impressed by the accurate and punctual functioning of the school program. The blackboard also fell upon other strange uses. Since it often happened that the upper regions of the board were not merely out of the reach of the children, but of the teacher, something had to be done about it. So the upper borders, by the help of a chair, were sometimes decorated by skillful teachers with drawings in colored chalk, or by the less artistic with stenciled pictures of Dutch boys and girls, hands linked,

PROBLEMS AND TECHNIQUES OF CLASS ADMINISTRATION 155

on the run, or of pussy cats or bunnies. This was all teacher work, intended to brighten a somewhat dingy schoolroom.

But the schoolroom is no longer dingy, and the blackboard belongs not only to the teacher but is shared generously with the children. It has countless uses which make it most valuable in the classroom, especially in the upper grades. In some schools the kindergarten and the first grade have no blackboard space, or very little of it. In these lower grades the uses to which the board can be put are comparatively few, since the children neither read nor write. Many teachers find that the space, if covered with burlap, is more useful as a bulletin board to which paintings and signs may be attached.

In the teaching of arithmetic the board is frequently called into use. Drill is sometimes given by placing numbers on the board for subtraction as follows:

$$\begin{array}{r} 476 \\ 208 \\ \hline \end{array}$$

and calling on individual children to fill in the answers while the class checks their work. Again, arithmetic problems such as the following may be placed on the board for use in oral drill.

÷ 6

1.	20	38	50	29	7	49	42	11	36	55	24
2.	17	48	6	59	34	16	23	58	56	15	60
3.	40	9	41	10	46	37	52	33	18	59	19
4.	28	39	30	31	22	26	13	53	45	12	44
5.	47	21	8	27	35	14	43	31	25	54	56

Questions may be placed on the board during a discussion of short methods of finding simple percentages.

$$\underline{}\% \text{ of } 90 = 30$$

$$30\overline{)3}$$

$$1/3 = 33\ 1/3\%$$

There are several other uses of the blackboard. Either the children or the teacher may use it for demonstrating something which is under discussion. For example, during a report on excavations which are going on in Greece, a student may draw a simple diagram showing how one civilization was buried under another. Sometimes complicated assignments may be conveniently made on the board to avoid confusion, as in the following case where there are certain long numbers involved.

Make a graph showing the output of steel in the United States and other countries in 1927.

          United Kingdom .... 9,086,300 tons
          United States .... 44,935,185 tons
          Germany .... 11,305,330 tons
          France .... 8,275,000 tons

These figures may be left on the board for reference when the assignment is completed and is being discussed.

A frequent use of the blackboard is for the listing of special responsibilities which the children have delegated, or for the making of other lists which may be seen on the boards in some such form as follows:

          Attendance —Herbert
          Lunch   —George
          Fish   —Marian
          Paints   —Ruth
          Tools   —Joan

In the upper grades the blackboard may be called into use whenever it is of assistance in communicating ideas. In practice it is usually the teacher who uses it, as she is more frequently engaged in making visible communications which are intended for the whole group. It is, however, a matter of no importance who writes on or uses the board, as it is used by teachers or students whenever either finds it convenient. The teacher may herself list a committee on the board, or it may be listed by one of the pupils.

In the early teaching of reading, for instance, the blackboard may be very useful as a means of placing significant words in the environment. Daily communications from the teacher to the class may be made if children are trained to watch for them. The children may find an announcement such as the following on the board:

If you wish to read out loud to the rest of the class today, sign your name here.

1. Sandy
2. Ruth
3. Paul
4. Lenora
5. Anne

The board is also helpful when the teacher is dictating. New words may be encountered which are difficult to spell, such as Europe, Renaissance, Civilization, and these may be written on the board as reference is made to them, to aid the pupils in learning their spelling.

Records of class discussions are sometimes conveniently made. On one occasion, for instance, a Grade Two was coöperatively making an Indian play and casting the characters. As they were decided upon by the group, a scribe recorded them with chalk.

The Sons of Kai

Act 1.

Scene 1. Kai Hears a Warning
Scene 2. The Mischief—The God Takes the Boys

Act 2.

Scene 1. To the Home of the Gods
Scene 2. To the West of the Mountain

Act 3.

Scene 1. Working for the Hopis
Scene 2. Home Again

Cast of Characters:

Owl—Joan
Silversmith—Richard
Kai—Rosamond
Twins—George
       Edward

A God—Keith
Hopi—Charles
A God—Marian
A Chief of West Mountain—Anne
Talking God—Herbert

Thus may the blackboard be put to a hundred and one uses by skillful teachers who find it an almost indispensable convenience for the furtherance of teaching.

CHAPTER XV

FURTHER PROBLEMS AND TECHNIQUES OF CLASS ADMINISTRATION

The Use of Demonstration Apparatus

There is a genuine use in the classroom for the various forms of demonstration apparatus, such as maps, globes, diagrams, moving and talking pictures, and radio. Their function should be clearly understood if they are to be wisely used in teaching. Essentially they should be regarded as reference materials, not as beginning points for teaching. In the study of birds, for example, the teacher should not arrange a series of lessons for succeeding days, and introduce each by showing the picture of the bird which she has chosen for that particular lesson. Such a use of pictures or other demonstration materials as beginning points for teaching has been common. Thus whatever material has been used to start off the lesson has been regarded as a means of motivation, and the lesson has often been called an "object lesson."

The procedure which should be followed is quite different from that just outlined. Rather than beginning deliberately with birds the teacher had better wait for the children themselves to begin with birds. Provided the environment were properly set, she would not have to wait long. Sooner or later interest in birds or in some particular bird would arise: some mention of a goldfinch, in other lesson material; some week-end adventure reported to the class by a pupil who has caught a brief vision of a cardinal. In fact, any situation involving reference to a certain bird might lead the children to consult bird charts to give them a clearer picture of the bird in question. A number of such experiences might awaken in children sufficient interest to carry them into a systematic study of pictures and to enable them to identify birds which they had never seen. If such systematic study did develop, however, it is obvious that it would not have been directly initiated by the pictures, but the pictures would have been brought in to assist the progress of activities already under way.

To give a further example, the teacher would not begin a study of Africa by hanging a map of that country in front of the room saying, "This is a picture of Africa, and now we are going to study that country." She would know very well that this "picture" is not a picture at all, and that it is about as unlike Africa as any form of representation could be. It is merely a compilation of relationships for those who are sufficiently interested in Africa to consult it. Consequently, when, in the course of a study of the sources of rubber, it is discovered that a great deal of it comes from Africa, the map or the globe may be referred to, and in this way the pupils may be introduced to a certain amount of map study.

When pupils have been given some familiarity with maps and globes, drill in map location is required to develop a clearer and more abiding knowledge of geographic relationships. This may be carried on by the group together, an individual pointing and the others checking, or by the use of various devices.[1] Maps, globes, and pictures are valuable when their use will amplify and enrich a unit of conduct upon which the children are engaged.

Machines in the Class

The use of such various mechanical aids to teaching as lantern slides, moving and talking pictures, and the radio, is obviously governed by principles similar to those which govern the use of other forms of demonstration apparatus. As the use of these newer devices is obviously on the increase, and as their value if properly related to school programs may become very great, some attention will be given to them here.

Moving and Talking Pictures

First of all it is important to recognize the function of these visual and auditory aids. Their general nature is that of demonstration materials. They should be so regarded by the teacher, and should never be thought of as substitutes for teaching or for teachers. Their purpose is to aid the teaching process, and they may only be used to advantage when they are made subject to the needs of the class and the broader purposes of the teacher.

[1] Rugg, Harold, and Hockett, John A., "Objective Studies in Map Location," Social Science Monograph, No. 1, The Lincoln School, Teachers College, Columbia University, 1925.

The greatest care must be taken in the use of moving pictures, for the teacher must avoid becoming merely a showman. It must not be forgotten that moving pictures may be almost totally uneducative. The listless watching of shadows is probably the lowest ebb of self-activity. Consequently, when moving pictures are used by the teacher their use should be in direct relationship to the needs of the class. The gratuitous introduction of moving pictures into school life in unrelated fashion in order to please or amuse the children is little more than pedagogical pyrotechnics.

There are some teachers in activity schools who feel that moving and talking pictures will be little missed from elementary school classrooms in which they are never shown. The reason for this feeling probably lies in the fact that in schools in which the children are actively engaged in real living and first-hand experiencing, there is comparatively little call for the vicarious experiencing provided by such means. In fact, the more formal and repressive the school program, the more important the moving and talking picture becomes. In schools which are routinized, and in which inactive methods are used, the use of pictures becomes much more important. Moving and talking pictures, when wisely used by teachers, may serve an excellent purpose, for example, in stimulating both the reading and writing activities of children. So it may be that in schools where teachers are not permitted to take the children on walks or on trips which would provide them with first-hand interests and experiences, they may do the second best thing and allow the children to use second-hand experiences as a basis for the more formal learnings. Thus it is that by using moving and talking pictures in repressive schools, teachers acknowledge the principles which they deny.

But even in the best schools there is a place for the moving and talking picture which is really educational in nature, and not a mere advertisement or "show." There is no doubt that moving and talking pictures can overcome time and space, and whenever this is desirable they can be used to great effect in enhancing teaching. A picture which offers a study of a mountain glacier provides something which a class cannot so well secure in any other way. Moving picture enlargements of microscopic life can be most useful. A picture with diagrams worked out to illustrate the Einstein theory may well be of value in presenting that topic. A talking picture which shows a skilled surgeon at work may make it possible to record for thousands of students what could otherwise be witnessed by but a few; and by recording in picture and sound the progress of a demonstration lesson by a skilled teacher, it is possible to set before teachers in training a concrete example of a lesson for evaluation and discussion. It is in cases of this sort that visual aids can be of maximum value in teaching. The fact that pictures can be shown again and again, and that slow motion pictures make it possible to see things which could not be observed by the naked eye, increases the usefulness of good pictures.

If moving and talking pictures are to be used not as substitutes but as aids to teaching, it is important that the teacher's technique be adapted to the requirements of such demonstration work. Teachers should realize that while moving and talking pictures may be of use in teaching, they do not entail less but more effort and energy on the teacher's part. They may increase the teacher's efficiency, but they do not lighten her load. The securing of apparatus and films, and the making of arrangements for their use, are matters which consume much time and strength. If such difficulties have been overcome, the teacher must still keep the following procedure in mind:

1. The teacher should see any film which is to be shown to the class before the class sees it. If this is not possible, she should study the account of it and the sequence of scenes which is usually furnished with good films.
2. She should consider what values in the film are related to the present life of her class, and should hold a discussion with the class before the children see the film, touching on these points, and helping the children decide what special matters they should watch for.
3. The film should, when possible, be shown at least twice, with some discussion between showings.
4. The showing of the film should be followed by class discussion and further study. Impression should be followed by expression.
5. When possible a showing of the film, or at least a review discussion of it, is most desirable.

RADIO

The possibilities for the use of the radio in school are far-reaching, provided that the radio is introduced into school life in the correct fashion. As in the case of moving and talking pictures, it is most important to avoid any tendency to regard the radio as a substitute for the teacher. It can never be such a substitute. Rather it must serve the purposes of the teacher and make itself subject to the needs of the class before it can be of real value.

In all probability little use can be made in school hours of the general broadcast which is made for entertainment and advertising purposes. Specific broadcasts which are made for definite educational purposes may, however, be of considerable value. For some reason or other, which seems difficult to fathom, there is a magnetism in the radio voice which often seems lacking when a living speaker is present. Furthermore, this magnetic voice in specific broadcasts may reach not merely the ears of city children, but of children in far-away rural districts.

If the teacher is to set aside time for radio listening, it is important that some time be spent in class in previous discussion of the subject to be attended to. This can only be so when the teacher has previous announcement of the broadcast. Specific educational broadcasts will be of little value until the broadcasting stations follow a plan which they sometimes use of sending out printed materials to teachers, making it possible for them to prepare their classes for the radio topics announced. Only so may children listen with a purpose which will enable them to make subsequent use of what they hear in discussion or in other school activities. Listening-in is so completely a process of impression, that if it is to be of real educational value definite provision for expression must be provided when the listening-in is over.

Mr. James Egert Allen has made interesting use even of general broadcasting for the improvement of the work of his classes in the New York public schools. In this case the class relied not on class listening but individual listening on the part of those children of the class who had radio equipment in their homes. The radio announcements in the daily papers were scanned by the children in the class, and a listening program was worked out. The listening became a form of homework. Such activities as congressional, presidential and local campaigns formed excellent leads for class discussions. Broadcasts concerning the automobile industry and the rubber industry, for example, assisted the class work in geography. It was discovered by using the radio in this fashion that much was accomplished in the way of furnishing a background for the general work of the class and for oral and written expression. In such fashion a skillful teacher was able to make use of the American system of broadcasting which has not adapted itself to the needs of the schools, but seems on the whole to have sold its soul to advertisers.

Specific educational broadcasts, when adapted to school needs, may be very useful. The descriptive musical broadcasts arranged by the Damrosch School of Music in New York have been found by many schools to be of great interest to the children. Teachers can, by judicious preparation, enlist the children's musical interest in the material they are about to listen to. The class may then meet in the assembly at the proper time to hear the music, and after it is over, they may be given opportunity to tell what they liked about the music. Teachers report that children in the New York elementary schools who have listened to the broadcasting have in many cases developed new interests in musical matters. It may also be possible to benefit from special broadcasts in foreign language teaching where the hearing of the language and the pronunciation of the words is important for the learner. In other words, where the importance of sound predominates as a condition of the learning process, the radio may find a limited use, if it is properly adapted to the needs of school life.

Whatever one's attitude may be toward the use of the radio in schools, there is no denying that many schools are already making use of it, and the number seems to be increasing rapidly. Newer school buildings are frequently equipped with loud speakers for every classroom, and the loud speakers themselves are finding unexpected use as a means for whole school announcements made by the principal, and for fire drill. In some cities school authorities have ordered that every classroom be equipped with receiving facilities. In a recent study 32.6 per cent of school superintendents report radio equipment in the school buildings under their care.

Unfortunately, however, educational broadcasting has not yet been developed as it should be. Although eight State Departments of Public Instruction report repeated use of broadcasting for educational purposes, and 15.2 per cent of all broadcasting in the country purports to have educational purpose, nevertheless the real, efficient use of the radio as an aid to public school life is still in the future. In the meanwhile schools can afford to be cautious lest they waste time by use of the radio as a fad rather than a vital aid to teaching.

Textbooks

In life we read books; in school we read textbooks. At times the distinction has become too marked. The textbooks of years ago were often rigidly organized and badly written. They were prepared to aid ignorant and unresourceful teachers in their task of instruction. They served the function of guides for the inexperienced teacher. The writer of the textbook organized its content in such a way that a teacher might conveniently begin at the beginning of the book and proceed to the end, simply assigning section by section to the pupils. The dependence on the printed page produced a form of teaching which centered itself about the textbook. The teacher assigned a lesson, say in history or geography, for the children to study out of school. During the class period the teacher stood in front of the room, textbook in hand, and persecuted the children with questions, tyrannizing over their closed books with her open one. Thus were developed the techniques of the "recitation." Favorite among them was the art of "questioning," but it was always the teacher and not the pupils who asked the questions.

Such misuse of texts resulted in a revolt against the old haphazardly organized type of school book. Today it has been supplanted by texts which are very much superior and are adapted to use as aids rather than guides to the teacher. These new textbooks may be described as scientifically constructed texts, supplementary texts, and real books.

Doing Without Texts

In the beginning grades of some of the modern schools, the teachers believe that there is no place for textbooks.[2] It is felt that these earliest years are the time when children should have experiences with real things rather than with symbols. Even when the earliest experiences with number and with written language appear, no use is made of printed books. Various learning situations are allowed to develop which do not demand the use of the printed page. Children's sentences may be printed on large cards in script, and the children sometimes print and make their own books. Use may be made of the blackboard, but until the children have developed a certain amount of experimental background and some familiarity with symbols, books are not used.

Scientifically Constructed Texts

To meet the requirements of the modern teacher, textbooks for use in teaching of such skills as those of arithmetic, spelling and reading are constructed with scientific care by educational experts. They exhibit a number of characteristics of which teachers should be thoroughly aware. In the first place, the material in them is *scientifically graded*. In arithmetic texts each of the fundamental processes

[2] Pratt, C., and Stanton, J., "Before Books," Adelphi Co., New York, 1927.

is analyzed into its simplest component steps and adequate exercises and drill material on each of them is provided. In modern spellers the choice of words and the sequence in which they are placed result from careful studies of the words needed by children and of words commonly used by children and adults.

A second characteristic of a scientific textbook is the inclusion of *self-instruction materials.* A textbook need not be constructed in such a way that a teacher becomes a seeming superfluity. On the other hand, the presence of a certain amount of self-instruction material makes it possible for children to use their texts in school as tools which are of actual assistance to them in their learning process. Thus children, after consultation with the teacher, may proceed to work using a certain section of the text as an aid, and may carry on independently while the teacher and the other children are engaged upon different tasks. If anything comes up in the course of the work which needs explanation, the pupil may always refer to the teacher. Thus by consultation and coöperation the teacher and the child may use the textbook as a convenient tool in furthering the learning process.

Drill material is important in a scientifically built textbook in the skill subjects. Drill may stand on its own merits as a work activity arising out of a need to perfect an essential process. By providing a certain amount of drill the textbook may prove of use to the pupil for individual study, may provide material for group drill, and yet leave the teacher free to supplement the work by group drill materials of her own devising, if the need arises.

Textbooks which provide adequate, well-prepared drills are admirably suited to either individual or group study under whatever circumstances happen to be governing the learning of the children at the particular time. They may be used with the most flexible program. The children may work together on a single unit of drill as the teacher directs, either silently or orally. On the other hand, by consultation and arrangement with the teacher, any pupil may progress at his own individual speed.

Provision for the application of newly mastered material is also most desirable in a textbook. At times, when the group is plotting a garden, for example, the text may be called upon to give assistance in linear measurements, and when that assistance has been given the new learning may be used in completing the activities of the life situation from which it has arisen. In other cases, however, the material taken up in the text may be a direct outcome of a desire for arithmetical knowledge which will assist in the problems of measurement in general. Such studies may well be followed by textbook material applying the new learnings.

Such testing material for spelling is provided, for example, in the Mastery Spellers in the form of "100 per cent" tests. These lists are given at regular intervals in the text and the pupils are required to master the words in each test perfectly before proceeding to a new unit of spelling drill. Reviews also are very necessary in a properly constructed scientific text.

THE USE OF SCIENTIFICALLY CONSTRUCTED TEXTS

Scientifically constructed texts should be characterized by a great deal of flexibility, which will permit of their use in various ways according to the varying circumstances and needs of the class. First, they may be used as *reference books*. Such might be the case during the progress of general activities whenever the needs for measurement arise. For instance, in carrying out the measurements involved in the shifting of classroom furniture and equipment, the building of one thing or another, or the marking out of a playground for various sports, the textbook should be a convenient source of information. Second, the book should be adapted to *use with a group*. It frequently happens that a homogeneous group may progress, for a time, together. At other times the teacher may find it convenient to keep members of a small group within the larger group close to one another in their work. Sometimes a number of children happen to pool themselves about a certain type of problem. In such cases group discussion, group testing, or group drill may be carried on by the use of the text. Further, the text frequently must be used by the pupil for individual work. When pupils are progressing individually, or when they are ahead of or behind their group, or when for any other reason they are working independently, they may make use of a good book as the teacher gives them personal direction.

The Use of Texts as Reference Books

At times textbooks should function largely as reference books. A good textbook in geography, for instance, would contain a great deal of material which need not be studied directly under given categories, but which may be called upon as reference material whenever needed. Such a text might contain a diagram of ocean currents, which could be referred to by the children if a question should arise concerning the alleged shifting of the course of the Gulf Stream. Discussion of high altitude flying might demand attention to what the text had to say about winds. Questions concerning methods of weather forecasting might demand reference to material on isotherms. Questions of English usage or of sentence construction might lead the pupils to consult a text on grammar or composition. In such cases the basal texts serve a purpose similar to that served by demonstration apparatus, namely, that of aids rather than beginning points for learning and teaching.

Supplementary Reading Texts

There is coming into increasing use a type of textbook which seems to be about halfway in its characteristics between the textbook and the real book. Such books in appearance and makeup are much like ordinary out-of-school children's books, but they are really arranged for special use in school and generally contain suggestions for the use of the book in the classroom. Such supplementary books are of interest to pupils whose work leads in the direction of special readings. Interest in them is an outcome of class study. They may be regarded as texts which are particularly useful to improve the class environment.

The Use of Real Books

Whenever teachers find it possible, there is a tendency to use real books instead of, or as a supplement to, textbooks. It sometimes happens that the class becomes interested in some special topic, which might be anything from Greek architecture or Elizabethan lyrics to bee keeping. The teacher may even find that she herself knows very little about the matter which has come up. She may not even know anything of the literature of the subject. It may thus become necessary for her to look up the subject in the library and make up a bibliography. From this list several particularly useful books may be chosen as texts, so that each member of the class may secure one. The class as a whole may buy single copies of other books, while still others may be placed on a special shelf in the library. Thus these books may be used for reference, special reports, or class discussion. A considerable amount of the school work, especially in the upper grades, may be done with books which were not written as textbooks, but to fulfill some such need as that which they are called upon to supply in school life.

Tests and Examinations

The status of old-time "examinations" in the new school is indicated by the following conversation held with a ten-year-old pupil of one of the new schools:

"Tell me, Bill, how do you like tests? Do you have tests in your school?"
"I don't like them. They make you work too hard. One day this year Miss ———— gave us a whole lot of them. The Perry tests and the—I can't remember them all."
"That was only once this year, wasn't it?
"Yes, near the beginning."
"Well, have you had a lot of examinations since, do you have examinations every little while?"
At this point the youngster looked somewhat puzzled, so he was asked: "Do you know what examinations are? Do you know what the word means?"
"No," was the slightly bewildered reply, "I don't think I know what you mean."

The practice of incessant detailed quizzes and examinations was one of the results of the old slavery to the textbook which is rapidly passing. It was associated with a régime in which mastery of the material in the textbook was regarded as an aim in itself. According to the study-and-be-examined system, examinations and marks became the goal, and mastery of subject matter without relation to use the result. The desire of pupil and teacher for good grades in examination has probably done more to injure the learning process than any other single factor in the psychological makeup of traditional schools. Furthermore, students seldom regard grades received in examination as measures of themselves. Rather they are measures of their success or luck in "getting grades." Nor do successful responses in examinations necessarily indicate significant mastery of the materials on which the student is examined. Burton tells of a young man who, when criticized for frequent misuse of language and for poor self-expression, defended himself by insisting that he had always received good marks in his English examinations! The traditional school examination was only too often a device to sort out the sheep from the goats in some form with the appearance of justice. This is not the problem of the teacher of today. She is interested in revealing the child to himself as he shows gradual improvement in daily tasks. Furthermore, she wishes to secure his well-rounded development as a social personality and his growth in ways of living. Consequently, the child is encouraged to place constant check on himself. The child who examines himself need not be examined.

The Immeasurables

The learning products which are the distinguishing characteristics of the best schools, and which constitute their chief claim to superiority, are the immeasurables. This is particularly unfortunate because it makes the superiority of the good school less demonstrable. It furthermore makes its advocates particularly liable to the satiric criticisms of gross souls to whom only seeing is believing. Yet a brief consideration of the nature of the values to be obtained in a good school which is organized in terms of conduct will make it obvious that at present there are no instruments designed to measure them. Such values are those of independence, initiative, practical judgment in a complex life situation, ability to carry a task through to a satisfactory conclusion, toleration, a happy outlook on life, good temper, good manners, unselfishness, ability to call all one's resources to the solution of a problem, willingness to coöperate, willingness to accept responsibility, richness of esthetic experience, excellence of esthetic judgment in art, literature and music, originality of thinking, acting and in artistic performance, thoroughgoing integration of the personality, and satisfactory adjustment to life. It must be obvious that there is no battery of educational tests in existence which would enable teachers to estimate the progress their pupils have made in such eminently desirable traits, the acquirement of which is a hundredfold more important for the life of the individual than ability to add and subtract. It is toward the acquirement of just such values that the work of the new schools is directed, and in them the subject matter of the curriculum functions not primarily in and for itself but as a means toward the development of these fundamentally important characteristics.

The Nature and Function of Educational Tests

Yet there is an important place for current educational tests in the school. A correct understanding of that usage depends upon a philosophy of testing which is in accordance with the life of the school, and upon an understanding of the true function of educational tests. This may first be presented negatively, by pointing out certain wrong notions of testing which have gained some currency. It should be clear that a testing program should not be carried on as a scheme of supervision. Certain school administrators with the whiplash theory of supervision have been only too quick to discover in a testing program what they have believed to be a new, and more refined way of discovering whether or not the work of the teacher is up to their notions of performance standards. Tests have been administered to the pupils, and on the basis of the results attempts have been made to evaluate the work of the teacher. Pressure has been exerted upon her to bring her class up to "grade standards" in subject-matter performance, utterly disregarding the far more important factors which may govern the learning process. In order to avoid such a use of tests for purposes of checking efficiency, it is necessary to be clear on the fact that educational tests are not suitable means for evaluating the work of the teacher, the work of the pupil or the method of teaching which is being employed. Their purpose is not to discover any deficiency which may happen to exist among the pupils or teachers and thus to encourage more drill.

When tests are so regarded they assume the nature of the old examination with its false emphasis upon marks. In fact, since they are more refined, they may become even the more pernicious when misused by unwise supervisors. This is likely to happen when those in charge of the direction of school life make the mistake of regarding efficiency in the customary subject-matter skills as the most important product of school life, and when they regard these skills as ends in themselves. Regarding them as ends in themselves, they will be satisfied when test scores are up to regular norms. Thus this more accurate form of school mark may dominate the teaching situation to its detriment. The failure to realize that the desirable school skills in reading and writing and arithmetic are only of value when they are means to a further end, namely, to a good and useful life, may be most unfortunate. It may allow fear to continue its infamous career in the school: fear in the mind of the teacher, in the hearts of the children, fear of the ancient bogey of school marks. So the unhealthful strain and panic of examinations may reappear in the stress of an ill-directed testing program.

On the other hand, when properly used, educational tests may be extremely helpful and salutary in school life. Their application is not to the total life of the school, which is dominated by what have already been referred to as the immeasurables. The realm in which they function is a comparatively small corner or eddy of school life, one concerned with those customary skills, the mastery of which furthers the full living of the group, both in school and in life in the world. The modern teacher usually regards this comparatively small part of school life as of distinctly secondary importance, while she is concerned chiefly with the larger and richer life experiences to which they contribute. She has so many important things to be done, that it is not surprising if she is anxious to have these secondary matters disposed of in as brief a time as possible. It is to be feared that some teachers have, at times, allowed themselves to go too far in their enthusiasm for the fuller life of the school, and have been tempted to neglect the basic social skills. It is to avoid the making of such mistakes that teachers carry on testing programs. Testing thus becomes a safety device, a convenient form of stocktaking in the narrow field of school life concerned with drill in the fundamental operations. By using a battery of tests, and thus taking an inventory of this important but minor part of school activities, teachers may see where they are, see where the class is, see where individual pupils are, and enable the children themselves to get a definite notion of their attainments in this direction. Thus having taken their bearings, teachers and pupils may govern themselves and their activities accordingly.

The Testing Program

The administering of tests should not be regarded as the work of the class teacher. Supervisors cannot expect class teachers to add to their already enormous burdens the mechanical labor of administering, scoring and interpreting tests. Such work should be carried on under the direction of the school psychologist and her staff, and the results furnished by them to the teacher and used coöperatively by all concerned. The collection of endless data by schools which never use them, and the filing away in office record cabinets of accounts which are seldom used, is a serious waste of time and money. It is only by the *use* which is made of the data secured that the expense of a testing program is justified.

The testing is usually centered in one office for the whole school. This office carries a full stock of such tests as are likely to be called into use, either in the regular testing program or whenever special tests for individual pupils are requested by a class teacher. Shortly after he enters school, it is customary to give to every child, in addition to the regular physical examination, a Binet-Simon intelligence test. Two or three times a year a special time is set apart for testing and a group of achievement tests is administered. In some schools the tests are given twice a year, in January and May, or in October and May. In others they are given three times a year, in September, January and May, May being the closing month in many of the schools where this work is carried on. The general plan is to give the tests at the beginning, middle and end of the school year.

The Use of Results

The results of the testing program may be put to numerous valuable uses. The data concerning each individual may be recorded on his personal history card, which is a convenient account that may be consulted whenever the child and his problems are being considered. Furthermore, in schools in which grouping or advancement is connected with subject-matter attainment, the scores obtained on the tests will serve a purpose. Interviews with parents may be held at which the child's individual standing in the tests, when properly related to his intelligence, his habits of work, and his social traits, may form the basis of discussion and further an understanding of his individual development. Again, whenever it seems desirable for the best results, an interview between the psychologist and the child may be arranged for discussion and possibly for further diagnostic investigation.

One of the chief values of test results is their use by the pupils themselves. They provide the children with an objective means of realizing their own development in the factors measured. A most ingenious scheme for this purpose is the "tree of growth" (see figure on page 173) which is used by the pupils of the Beaver Country Day School (Mass.). At the beginning of the year each pupil starts with a copy of the tree mimeographed on paper eight and a half by eleven inches. When tests are given at the beginning of the year the examiner enters a pupil's advancement on his chart in black ink, each skill being entered separately, according to its height of development, somewhere between the ground under the tree and its topmost branches. One of the branches of the tree is the norm for a class for any given testing period. Each pupil is informed of the norm for his class by being told which branch represents that norm for any particular testing period. He is thus able to see his relationship in each skill to the general expectation of his class. At mid-year the results of the second testing are entered in red ink. At the end of the year green ink is used to indicate year-end accomplishment. A new tree is given to the

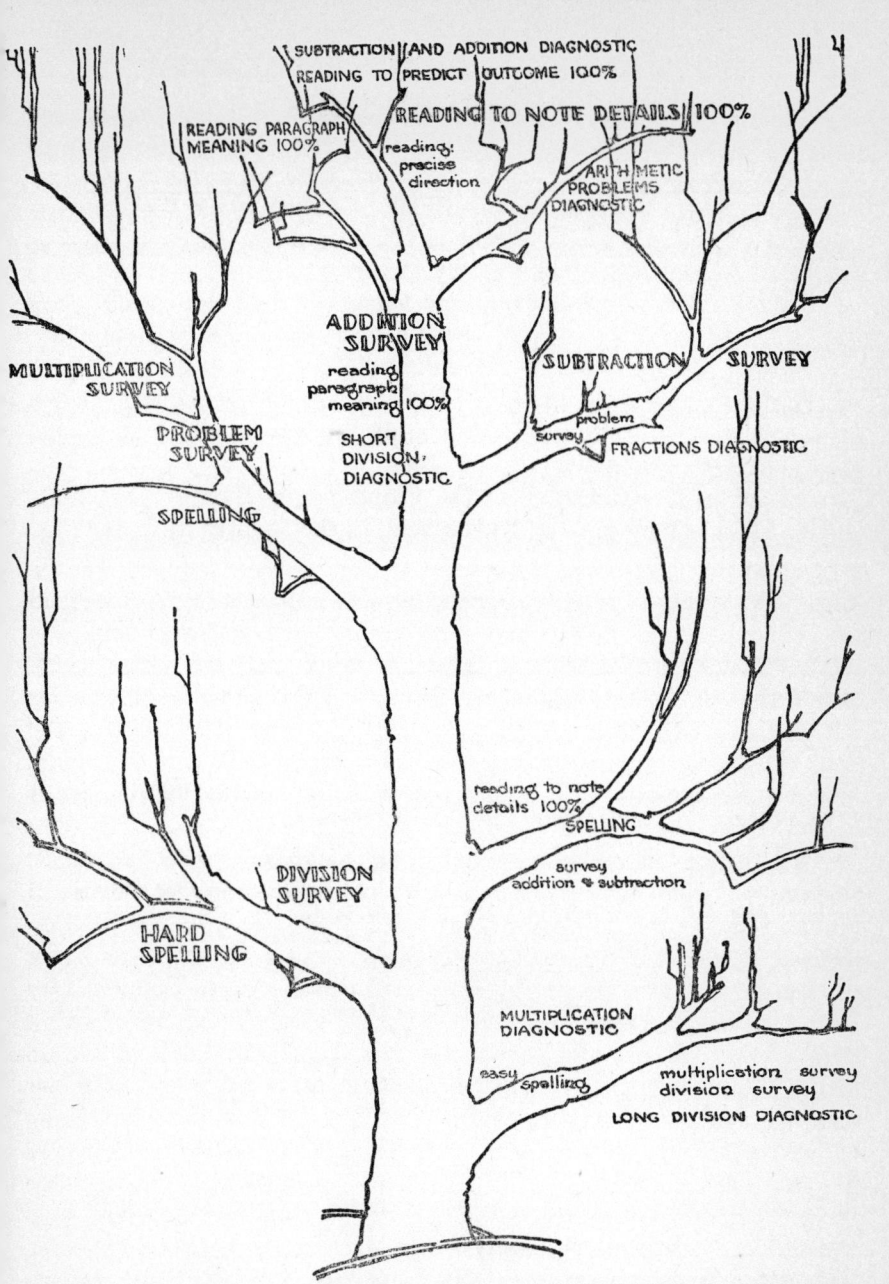

This tree represents one year of growth of one pupil in the fundamental skills. At the beginning of the year the pupil's height of growth is indicated by notations in small letters. At the mid-year testing period his gain is indicated by notations in larger lettering, while the final accomplishment for the year is entered in the largest letters of all. This figure is used through the courtesy of Eugene Randolph Smith, Headmaster of the Beaver Country Day School, Massachusetts. Different size letters are here used instead of the different colored inks mentioned in the text.

pupil for each year of the elementary school. By the end of the year he should normally have climbed the whole tree. Throughout the year the child is able to note in pictorial form his own personal achievement and to act in accordance with the situation which he discovers. As a result unusual improvement is often obtained in correcting any weakness in growth as indicated by the tree.

Probably the most important and valuable use of test results is for diagnosis of individual difficulties as a basis for remedial treatment.[1] A study of the work of the individual child on the tests is of great assistance in revealing the nature of his specific problems. An example may be of assistance in indicating the way in which diagnostic testing may reveal particular difficulties.

Suppose that the section of the Clapp-Young English Test Form A [2] be filled in by the pupil by marking in the squares as follows:

PART II

DIRECTIONS—Mark in the square before the word or group of words that should be used in the blank. DO NOT FILL IN THE BLANK.

16. .....and your mother may come.
  ☒ You
  ☐ Yourself
17. I.....what happened.
  ☐ knowed
  ☒ knew
18. John.....hurt.
  ☐ isn't
  ☒ ain't ←
19. I have.....my lesson.
  ☒ taken
  ☐ took
20. The man.....me a knife.
  ☐ give
  ☒ gave
21. Frank and.....can do it.
  ☐ me
  ☒ I
22. John can eat.....apples.
  ☒ two
  ☐ too
23. Miss Brown,.....I speak to Nellie?
  ☒ can ←
  ☐ may

24. Isabelle.....her lunch.
  ☒ ate
  ☐ eat
25. I like roses better than.....kind of flowers.
  ☐ any
  ☒ any other
26. John could.....keep his eyes open.
  ☒ hardly
  ☐ not hardly
27. He.....away.
  ☐ run
  ☒ ran
28. Where is she.....?
  ☐ going to
  ☒ going
29. Pupils enter the room.....
  ☒ quietly
  ☐ quiet
30. I.....my work.
  ☒ did
  ☐ done
31. We.....but a few left.
  ☒ have
  ☐ haven't

[1] For a treatment of this subject see PALMER, A. R., "Progressive Practices in Directing Learning," The Macmillan Co., New York, 1929, Chs. 10 to 12.
[2] Houghton Mifflin Co., Boston.

FURTHER PROBLEMS AND TECHNIQUES

PART II—*Continued*

32. I.....be late for dinner unless I go now.
    - ☒ shall
    - ☐ will
33. Potatoes are.....here.
    - ☐ plenty
    - ☒ plentiful
34. Fred.....the cider hastily.
    - ☐ drunk
    - ☒ drank
35. Children should not tear.....clothes.
    - ☐ there
    - ☒ their
36. Ted said he.....at once.
    - ☐ came
    - ☒ come   ←
37. May didn't spell.....words correctly.
    - ☒ any
    - ☐ no
38. The pencil was.....
    - ☐ broke
    - ☒ broken
39. I had.....home.
    - ☒ gone
    - ☐ went
40. A brave child.....fear darkness.
    - ☒ doesn't
    - ☐ don't
41. Both Nellie and Susie.....well.
    - ☐ sings
    - ☒ sing
42. You can go as well as.....
    - ☐ me
    - ☒ I
43. When he appeared I.....to run.
    - ☒ began
    - ☐ begun
44. Let us.....and talk.
    - ☐ set
    - ☒ sit
45. I would not go if I.....you.
    - ☒ were
    - ☐ was
46. She should.....down after meals.
    - ☐ lay
    - ☒ lie
47. He is.....to hardship.
    - ☒ used
    - ☐ ust
48. We.....to go to bed early.
    - ☒ have
    - ☐ haft

The teacher may immediately diagnose the child's particular errors by turning over the sheet, when it will be found that the markings caused on the back, by an arrangement of carbon paper, fall in the squares allotted on the back of the paper in all cases except those of 18, 23, and 36. She can thus immediately note that while in most of the specific usages tested the child has no trouble, in these three he is defective. Reading off the words under 18, 23, and 36, she finds that the child who filled in the blank may use *ain't* for *isn't*, *can* in asking permission instead of *may*, and *come* as a past tense instead of *came*. Individual consultation with the child may lead to most economical remedial treatment.

Remedial treatment as a result of special defects discovered by the general testing program or defects discovered in special investigation of difficult cases, is usually to be given by the class teacher. In special cases, however, unusual attention may be given where it is needed. Special defects in the subject-matter skills are often connected with other maladjustments—mental, physical, or social. Consequently, in some schools, weekly conferences are held, attended by the principal, the teacher, the school doctor, the teacher of physical education and the psychologist. Records of the meetings are kept and the results considered in dealing with the case. When the difficulty is a special one, which would demand more attention than could be given it by the class teacher, it receives the special attention of the corrective department of the school.

Adaptation and Development of the Testing Movement

Such are the values and uses of educational tests in the life of the school. It is not necessary to suppose, however, that, as the testing movement develops, its achievement may not be of great assistance in estimating what, for the present, have been termed the immeasurables. Opinion as to the superiority of the products of the modern school, which are held today by its protagonists, are based largely on subjective judgments. By means of subjective comparisons of the children in their schools with children in other schools, they are led to believe that the values obtained by their schools in such matters as initiative, originality, and satisfactory expression in literature and the various forms of art, are in advance of those obtained in the schools with which they compare them.

It may be pointed out that the development of the testing movement up to the present has been in the nature of the development of less subjective and more objective methods of measuring and evaluating learning products. It is not unreasonable to hope that a similar process may lead to the development of less subjective standards which may serve as a basis for the comparison of the less tangible aspects of school life. Such standards of conduct performance would be of real value in the development of the work of the newer schools.

CHAPTER XVI

CLASS DISCIPLINE AND ORDER

The bugbear of many a classroom teacher has been the preservation of order—of what has unfortunately been called "discipline." How might one teacher control and master forty or more mischievous children, bent on getting ahead of her? The attempts to solve this problem have made enmity between teachers and children, and thus pitted friends against friends. They have produced millions of thrashings and resulted in many a pitched battle between pupil and teacher. Teachers have learned to hate teaching and have been compelled to give it up, nervous wrecks. Children have learned to hate school, and have left it prematurely for a world they dreamed of as less harsh. The school of years ago was often made an unhappy place. Unwittingly disorder and unhappiness were promoted in the name of happiness and discipline. When such things go on there is something wrong in the state of the classroom.

What, then, is it that has been wrong? Teachers in such schools have failed completely to understand the real nature of discipline, or the foundations of orderliness in human conduct. Possibly the multifold meaning of the word "discipline" has added to the confusion. The word has several distinct meanings which, while they are certainly related to one another, are sufficiently distinct to cause confusion if the word be used indiscriminately in relation to school life. (1) Discipline is frequently used to mean training. "To discipline" is to put through a series of experiences which will, by the training they give, prepare the individual for situations he is to meet later on. Thus we read of discussions of formal discipline, the doctrine that the study of certain subjects gives results in the development of the individual's personality which are out of proportion to the energy expended upon them. We read that what children learn in school provides discipline which will prepare them later on to cope with the problems which confront them. (2) It sometimes happens that in the progress of school tasks children have failed to meet the standards set by the teachers or to obey the laws which the teachers have ordained. Such breaches have necessitated corrective measures. The training of the individual has demanded that he should make amends. Thus arose the second meaning of the word. "To discipline" came to mean "to punish." Thus, to give a pupil a disagreeable, monotonous, or difficult task, or to give a boy a caning was "to discipline him." Mr. Squeers and his admirers understand this meaning of the word only too well. (3) Out of it and out of a system of school-keeping which depended on enforcing book-learning by compulsion springs the third meaning of the word, "discipline," the maintaining of order. The terms "discipline" and "order" are in such cases regarded as practically synonymous. The good disciplinarian being sharp to detect and quick to punish was thus admirably able to maintain schoolroom order. With a good disciplinarian children would be afraid to do wrong.

Something might be gained if the use of the word "discipline" as it relates to school practice might be restricted to its fundamental root meaning, the first meaning referred to above. Arising from the Latin word *discipulus,* a learner or pupil, it takes its derivation from *disciplina,* meaning learning or receiving teaching. Consequently, it might well be reserved to indicate the meanings suggested by the first definition. Discipline might be regarded as referring to the training values which an individual receives in school. The most desirable form of discipline will, therefore, be that which is received in the pursuit of an activity which is at once useful and significant to the learner performing it and at the same time the best training for the meeting of further life situations.

Such a restricted use of the word "discipline," which will be observed in the following discussion, would provide the added advantage of permitting the clearer use of the word "order." Order in the classroom is that desirable state of affairs according to which classroom activities progress without friction between individuals to a satisfactory conclusion. The separate and distinct use of the word "discipline" to mean a form of curriculum values, and "order" to mean the smooth working of individual and group activities, would obviate the undesirable confusion of either the word "discipline" or the word "order" with the second meaning of the word "discipline" as given above, namely, to punish. This might help teachers to dissociate the word "discipline" from any disagreeable feeling tone. Teachers would be less inclined to the absurd idea that only that which is disagreeable, only the ample provision of punishment produces discipline or learning. In the second place it might help to dissociate the idea of punishment from the maintenance of order, an association which is fundamentally unsound. We might then be free to begin with a real

CLASS DISCIPLINE AND ORDER

understanding of the two diverse matters of discipline and order as a foundation for the sensible building of both.

DISCIPLINARY VALUE OF SCHOOL EXPERIENCES

To consider discipline unrelated to conduct is to misunderstand it. Discipline is the outcome of the satisfactory initiation and conclusion of a desirable unit of conduct. The more wholeheartedly an individual enters into the carrying through of an act such as the planting and raising of the crop of a school garden, or the mastery of the process of division of whole numbers, the more thorough will be the disciplinary value he gains from the activity. It is more desirable for a child studying English to discuss a particular word in terms of its functional relation to the sentence in which it is found and its contribution to verbal expression, than to parse it along with other isolated words in an artificial diagram or arrangement of columns. Similarly there is richer disciplinary value to be gathered from the reading of several of Mrs. Browning's poems, and their discussion in the presence of a good teacher, than from spending half an hour laboriously mastering a description of Mrs. Browning's writings and style in an organized history of English literature. In each case the pleasanter, more natural, and what superficially seems to be the easier way, provides the most satisfactory form of discipline. Satisfactory units of conduct which fulfill a pupil's present needs and are similar in structure to units of conduct in which he is likely to engage later on give the maximum disciplinary value. Discipline comes not from disagreeable but from vital experience.

THE PROMOTION OF ORDER

As in the case of discipline the matter of order is best understood in relation to conduct. Children are orderly in doing. They are disorderly when they have nothing else to do. Disorderliness is a refuge from idleness. Children just cannot do nothing. When there are no orderly activities to carry on, they carry on disorderly ones. When there is no alternative, they become busy doing wrong things. Children who are engaged in the execution of units of conduct which meet their own recognized needs carry them out in the way they have learned to carry them out. If they have learned how to carry on without interfering with others, they will do it that way for their own convenience. Such is the general theory of the maintaining of an orderly classroom. If children are busy doing right, they will not do wrong. This is no new maxim. Teachers have always insisted upon it. Many of them, however have found it difficult to live up to. Children cannot remain continuously busy on subject matter which is not significant to them. It is only as they pursue activities which yield recognized values for living that they may continue busy and in order.

The Self-supporting Structure of Class Order

Good class order depends upon the teacher's knowledge and use of the social structure of the class group. The old type of classroom in which the teacher maintained order in the group is analogous to a great tent of a circus. The teacher in the group is like the central poles which bear the whole weight of the tent. It is by the strength of the central poles that the whole structure is maintained. Every subsidiary pole and every supporting rope is braced against the central supports and the whole is maintained in a state of strain. Such is a classroom in which the order is maintained by the teacher. The moment the teacher leaves the room and her support is withdrawn, the whole thing collapses and the schoolroom falls into confusion.

The best type of order, on the other hand, is self-supporting. The classroom group resembles the firm structure of the skyscraper. Each steel pillar stands firm and upright in its own strength. Each bears its own share of the weight and contributes to the solid stability of the base. So in the schoolroom each child stands alone, engaged in his own responsibilities, bearing his share of the weight of the social structure. The teacher moves about here and there, as it were, from floor to floor. Her duty is not to bear the weight, but rather to watch, lest any part of the structure less unvarying than steel is sickly or tired, and for some reason or other is not bearing its share of the burden. It is not the teacher's strength which maintains order, but the children who maintain it by standing alone.

Building Social Order

But social order does not arise spontaneously. It must be built. It is easy enough to lean upon a tent pole once it is in place. In a school of similar construction, the teacher's effort goes to support a structure too heavy for one pair of shoulders to bear. It takes little effort to build, but immense strength to maintain. But in the school group which is self-supporting the teacher's efforts must be expended in a different fashion. A skyscraper does not spring up of itself. It must be laboriously built; and when it is built, it must be constantly inspected in every beam and kept in repair. School order of similar construction must be built with equal labor and pains in the lower school grades, and when it has been built, in the upper grades it must be preserved and maintained.

Neither children nor adults naturally understand the structure of the social organism. Certain teachers in attempting to give such an understanding have devised various more or less formal or prearranged schemes of self-government and conducted them so that they functioned well and were of some use. Such schemes of self-government are not particularly helpful for classroom organization, however. It is better not to attempt to develop order in a schoolroom by these means unless there are special conditioning circumstances. The problem of order is a more complex one. It is that of patient, slow building of the relationships existing between members of the class group, and a gradual revealing to children of the nature of group living.

Gradual Raising of Conduct Levels in the Classroom

It will be of great assistance to the teacher engaged in building social order in the classroom to realize that a unit of conduct may be carried through on various levels. A recognition of the various levels upon which conduct units may proceed will be most helpful in enabling the teacher to understand just what is her immediate and present problem of class conduct and how to deal with it. McDougall has made a most valuable analysis which enables us to recognize four roughly distinguished levels of conduct.[1] These might be denominated as (1) conduct on a physical level, (2) conduct on a level of immediate social value, (3) conduct on a level of anticipated social advantage, (4) conduct on an ethical level.

(1) A unit of conduct carried out on a *physical level* is one which is modified and controlled by physical pleasure and pain. It is probable that the earliest control which the environment exerts over an infant is of this type. It is not possible to appeal to the child's ill-developed intelligence by means of language. One language only it understands, that of physical sensation. Its responses may be controlled only by physical pain or pleasure. The mother who early detects a case of

[1] McDougall, W., "Introduction to Social Psychology," John W. Luce & Co., Boston.

thumb-sucking and is brave enough to punish the little thumb with a rap from a pencil at every offense will find her purpose accomplished. Control of human conduct by physical pain or pleasure is the lowest form of control possible. It proceeds on the level of simple animal behavior. Thus, teachers who seek to control pupils by the use of physical force, by strapping, beating or caning, are appealing to children on the brute level as if they were not rational beings but creatures beyond ken of mental appeal. There may be times when this gross form of appeal through corporal punishment is necessary. The bully who is continually inflicting pain on others may learn to realize what he is doing by suffering physical pain himself. It is scarcely likely, however, that a bully will be developed in a school which is properly conducted from the lower grades upward. Corporal punishment is a more severe indictment of the teacher who administers it than of the pupil who suffers it.

(2) One of the earliest lessons that children have to learn in school is that group life restricts and limits their actions. They must learn to govern their conduct in terms of *immediate social value*. The social organism automatically administers social rewards and punishments. Such rewards and punishments are administered almost automatically and systematically by the social environment. Conduct so controlled is a somewhat less gross form of control by pains and pleasures. Such control is illustrated by the case of a small girl who had joined the kindergarten group but who refused to learn to skip in the way that was necessary for participation in the class games. At lunch time when the children gathered about the table to drink their milk and chat, she was given her lunch by herself and informed that she did not belong with the other children because every one of them could skip. It was not long before the child understood the meaning of immediate social rewards and learned to skip with alacrity. Control of this kind is one of the most valuable resources of the teacher of the kindergarten and lower grades. It is a form of appeal which children understand and which has the added advantage of enabling them to understand the nature of group living. Teachers of younger children need to be adept in directing children's behavior by means of immediate social rewards and punishments.

(3) A higher form of behavior is that which has been referred to as conduct on the level of *anticipated social advantage*. It is simple enough to understand social rewards and punishments in terms of immediate advantage. It demands experience and imagination to enable individuals to control their behavior in terms of deferred ad-

vantages and disadvantages. Thus, individuals who squander their money are more numerous than those who are thrifty enough to provide for improving their standard of living and assuring their social security. It is frequently necessary to defer present enjoyment for the sake of future advantage.

Children will often put forth great effort for a little recognition or praise from their teacher or classmates. So potent are rewards and punishments of this type that they are frequently abused. They may be used to control the most unnatural and formal conduct by the artificial use of emulation as a stimulus. Emulation when used to motivate the learning process is a form of bribery. One half a class is pitted against another, or half a school against the remainder. One half is called by such a name as the Spartans, while the other is known as the Phoenicians. Points are allotted by the teacher for achievement in subject matter and for proper conduct. The points are summed up and the results announced. Anxiety to win becomes the driving force of conduct. A certain line of conduct becomes desirable not in and for itself, but because of the super-added reward. The teaching conscience is thus soothed into lethargy. Pupils are persuaded into unnatural acts by the potency of emulation. Children are taught to sell themselves for a price.

Properly used, however, control by means of the anticipation of social praise or blame is very useful. The anticipation of the social status he is to assume after graduation is sufficient to help the student teacher or the man who hopes to be a lawyer or a doctor through years of arduous study. So an elementary school child whose work on a report is to be submitted to a class, or whose piece of lithographing is to be exhibited when the parents are invited to school, will work with eagerness because of the approval he hopes to receive.

(4) Units of conduct of the highest type are those on an *ethical level,* those which are regulated or governed by an ideal. Such conduct is controlled by ideas of what is good and bad, right and wrong. It is rational in the best sense of the word and raises the individual above the consideration of mere physical pleasure and pain, above mere social expediency or the pressure of public opinion, to a place where judgments are made in the light of the highest considerations of which the individual is capable. It is conduct on these higher levels which is the goal of character training.

The values of individual development in these highest ranges of the personality are those which the so-called "disciplinarians" have hoped and pretended to attain. When teachers of Latin or Mathematics claim great disciplinary value for their subjects, what they mean is that the study of these subjects produces an integrity of personality, a raising of the status of conduct to the levels of rational and ethical choice. Individuals of this turn of mind point with conviction to certain teachers of these subjects as people of remarkable character. They neglect to realize that only persons of strong intellectual interests, considerable mental acumen, and steady personality, ever embark upon a career of this type. There is also a modicum of truth in the notion that training in such subjects develops restrained and rational conduct. Subject matter which is taught in considerable isolation from any value of use, or any possible application to living, demands the most rigid control for its mastery. Students have to suppress every tendency to wander from the path of study. Rigid rejection of many simple social pleasures and great sacrifices in the form of devoted time are needed for the mastery of such remotely significant subject matter. Again, tasks such as those involved in the memorization of Greek declensions and the structure of Greek sentences according to rule and model, and not according to habit, demand great intellectual effort. Such a subject does, by dint of being taught badly, provide tasks of severe difficulty. So an artificial scheme is arranged to provide the learning process with tasks which are so difficult that only the mentally able and the highly controlled can accomplish them. It is the scarcity of such tasks that has made possible the standard plea that certain subjects "discipline" the mind and character better than others.

But in the end the discipline is attained by engaging the student upon units of conduct which give practice in conduct on higher levels of mental and moral choice. Units of conduct providing satisfactory training must do more than this. They must engage the student in tasks which, in addition, have the semblance of life, which, because they are like life, train for participation in life situations which are difficult. Up to the present there has been an almost total failure of liberal education on the higher levels to provide units of conduct which meet this second criterion for the training of students in secondary schools and colleges. The liberal secondary school is sadly in need of a complete reorganization in terms of conduct. It is urgently necessary that teachers on the secondary level concern themselves with discovering tasks which are first difficult, and second, similar in mold to the activities in which the students are likely to engage. For the secondary school students of moderate abilities this should not be difficult. For students of higher calibre the matter is not so simple. Tasks demanding severe mental efforts are required to satisfy the needs of such students. They should not be sought in the isolated paths of artificially complicated subject matter. Rather we should seek in life for intellectual tasks which are difficult and place their predecessors on the high school program.

Where shall we find such tasks? Shall we find them in the conduct of school campaigns for a better social order, carried out in the community according to the strictest laws of community suitability? May we find them in organized research in any and every field on a secondary school level? Is it not necessary to find opportunity for the development of manual dexterity among such budding musicians and surgeons? Cannot the orchestra work out simple symphonic scores for its own use which will be more suitable than the intricate published compositions? Cannot high school students apply statistics to the many problems of their school? May not boys and girls read Greek literature for pleasure and tell their classmates about it in Greek? What is to prevent children from studying the work of the French and German literary masters for themselves and interpreting it for their classmates? Why should they not write Russian poetry? Cannot the school press with its problems of the daily paper and its publication of books provide activity for students not merely of the mechanically minded in terms of presses and printing, but for the best students in having their works published in the high school series? Whatever type of development the new secondary education takes, it is urgently important for teachers to discover new tasks which are socially useful but challengingly difficult.

The elementary school provides infinite opportunities for children to control their own conduct on the higher levels. Whenever children live in school in ways which involve moral or intellectual choice they are being disciplined by conduct. So the child in kindergarten learns to hunt for some new toy instead of forcibly grabbing that of another child. He learns that he may push over his own block structure but not that of another child. In the middle grades the child learns that the class must not be kept waiting to see his puppet show because he has neglected to have the puppets in order when he began the performance. The older children learn that self-denial is necessary if they are to send a fund to China for other children who would die without food. Thus it is that well-chosen activities develop character.

One of the primary problems of teachers in building class order is the matter of gradually raising the level of conduct upon which the children live. As may be gathered from what has been written, children come to school in the earliest grades with very little knowledge of the nature of group living. Their levels of conduct are, for the most part, those governed by physical pain and pleasure. In the earlier grades they have much to learn of the modifications of behavior which are necessary on the second level of direct social rewards and punishments, and sometimes also on the higher levels of moral ways of doing things. As the children pass on and up through the school, they should learn more and more to govern themselves in higher ways and become as they live increasingly responsible individuals. By the time they leave school they should be independent of their teachers.

Encouraging Growth in Responsibility

In addition to having a clear knowledge of the matter of various levels of conduct, the teacher who would build good classroom order should understand the child's increasing power to accept responsibility. The period from infancy to maturity is one in which the individual grows from a state in which his parents accepted responsibility for all he does to one in which he is a self-determining individual responsible for his own actions. The infant must have everything done for him. He is watched and guided almost entirely by grown-ups. They control his actions and take the responsibility for them. As he grows older, adjustment must be made. The parents and the grown-ups must gradually release the controls which have perhaps been dear to them in the interests of the child's own best development, and the child must take over control with its accompanying responsibility. For the parents to fail to surrender control is to hinder the child's development. On the other hand, for the child to take over control without accepting the complementary responsibility is to allow the child to grow up without learning how to live.

Consequently, in order that as the child grows older he may grow stronger, the teacher learns to allow him to do for himself as much as he can. Teachers of children must learn to keep hands off. It is only by a hands-off policy that children may be trained to take responsibility for what they do. The development of such a technique is not an easy matter. Grown-ups are so much inclined to look upon children as weak little creatures who must be helped in all they do by the older and the stronger. Mothers often do many things for their children which the children should do for themselves, thus robbing them of opportunities to learn. Many grown-ups do not trust children. True, they should not be trusted beyond their strength but they should be trusted to the limits of their strength. The good teacher allows the child to do as much for himself as he can and to accept responsibility for what he does. In visiting a schoolroom on one occasion I witnessed an example of technique which revealed one teacher's unconscious obedience to this law of hands off. A small girl was struggling to fasten a pair of overshoes. The fastening of the "zipper" was not working properly. Noticing the struggles of the youngster to get the thing done herself, the teacher paused, and with her stronger fingers moved the catch an inch forward past the point which caught it, allowing the child to complete the operation herself. In accepting more effort and responsibility for children than we ought, we not only become their servants, but we fail as their teachers.

Children thrive under a régime of responsibility. They have a pride in self-control which is part of the joy of conscious growth. A boy of thirteen playing outdoors with a "catapult" by means of which he shot small missiles of lead, discovered a spider web in which a ball of young spiders just hatched were clustered together. Requested by a grown-up companion to stop shooting at the spiders, he reluctantly gave it up, but a few minutes later returned and was about to begin again.

"Arthur," called his companion, "What are you doing?"

"I'm shooting the spiders."

"You know that's just torturing them?"

"Yes, but I like to do it."

Just here is the dilemma. What is the grown-up sponsor of a boy's conduct to do at this point? He may give up in despair. Perhaps the spiders don't matter so much after all. It is a minor matter. To take this point of view is to neglect the main issue. According to what the boy in the case does, so his character grows. It is in such "minor" matters that life patterns are laid down. Such minor acts have the same insignificance and the same latent significance as seeds. There is still another alternative. The boy may be removed by force. This is a very undignified and very inconvenient method. Furthermore, it may not work. Worst of all it does not accomplish its purpose. It saves the spiders, but it does not save the personality of the learner. What shall the teacher do? The conversation continued.

"Well, you must look after yourself when you're with me. If you continue shooting you must do it on your own responsibility."

"Then, if I've got to do it on my own responsibility, I won't do it," came the reply. The boy got up, moved away and soon found a dozen things to interest him elsewhere. It was "hands off" that won, both for the teacher and for the boy.

This policy of giving over responsibility in the interests of the children's growth is closely connected with another very important matter, that of accepting children's initiative. We are so prone to feel that we must take responsibility for what children do that we hesitate to let them bear the brunt of things themselves. Teachers must be ever on the watch lest they blunt personality. The first efforts of children toward initiating activities are so fragile that they are easily damaged. So it is with older children as they attempt tasks which are difficult for their powers, as they venture ideas which for them are daring, as they venture timidly into the fields of esthetics. It is the refusal to accept initiative which kills development. It is the rejection of these timid venturings forth of personality which must be carefully protected. It is failure in this respect which has brought criticism upon schools which are said to have killed children's intuitions and deadened their personalities.

CHAPTER XVII

BUILDING ORDER IN THE SCHOOL

It is from the guiding of a multitude of incidents that school order grows. The interrelationships between conduct and order are close. Conduct which is normally and responsibly carried out is orderly. So the problem of order is that of continually guiding and directing the units of conduct in which children are engaged from their very first coming to school, and doing so in such a way that they will always be orderly. It is in this infinitely complex way that the teacher may build order.

It would be most convenient if there were some simpler way of building order. It would then be possible in this chapter to give some set of rules for the governing and building of school order. The actual fact is, however, that no valid set of rules can be formulated. The problem of order has all the complexity of human conduct. How, then, is the teacher to know what to do at any given time?

From the very beginning, when children come to school, the teacher must regard the school community itself as her guide. She must analyze the specific structure of the group and in accordance with the principles set forth in this chapter govern the situation. The hostess at an entertainment knows by her experience as a hostess what to do for her guests. So must the teacher, out of a knowledge and understanding of the school community, and of the needs of her children, govern the conduct of the pupils as best she may.

It is not possible to prescribe any scheme of self-government which may be guaranteed to work. By accepting responsibility for their conduct from the very beginning children will soon learn to develop some *modus vivendi* in lieu of government. They will discover, under the teacher's guidance, some scheme for controlling their own group affairs. Miss Pollitzer tells the way in which the plans of one group of children in the Walden School grew up and were modified. In the beginning the children set up a rather elaborate regulative scheme, including a set of rules to be obeyed and a lengthy roll of class officers. The following year the children abandoned this plan. They rejected it because they felt that it was unnecessary to have so many regulations and that all that would be required was for each child to look after himself. In this fashion, they believed, they would have real self-government. They discovered later on, however, that problems may arise which are a concern of the whole group and require group discussion. Consequently, since they could not escape all relationships with the group, they set up new machinery to meet their needs. Once more they organized, this time simply by the election of one officer to preside at meetings whom they called, with considerable directness, the "meeting-runner."

It is not necessary for every class to work things out in this fashion. But it will soon be discovered in any group that some form of class meeting is necessary if the children are to direct their affairs themselves and accept a large measure of responsibility for them. Some groups place this class meeting on the school program, setting aside for it a special period once a week. Others find a less rigid arrangement more satisfactory. At any rate, some form of meeting will almost surely be needed to provide for the discussion of individual and class problems.

It is not to be supposed, however, that children who have been trained for years under a repressive system may be governed easily by methods and principles given here. Whenever a child who has been brought up under a different system enters a class in which the order is of the self-sustaining variety he presents a special problem. Similarly it is not to be supposed that a teacher in taking over a class unused to accepting responsibility for conduct will be able to carry on in the best fashion. Sound order is a result of years of growth and cannot be set up in a minute. The teacher who takes over a class which has been kept in order by compulsion is seriously handicapped. It is not merely necessary to build up new habits but to break down old ones. Such changes can only be made slowly and gradually. In such classes a self-governing régime may only be set up by turning over one part of the responsibility at a time. Even by so doing the class will always be handicapped by its early training, and both individuals and the group are subject at any time to a relapse. Such a case presents special problems.

In schools in which the children have from the very earliest years been carefully trained to live well in a social group the problem of order will be solved. It cannot be pretended that it is solved in any easy way. The way may not be easier for the teacher but it is better for the child. It demands constant care, knowledge and tact in the direction of children's daily actions. School order is built slowly in the course of years. It is the result of constantly directed responsible individual group conduct. In the last analysis character and conduct go hand in hand. The good teacher wants her pupils to behave not for her sake but for their own.

Proponents of older points of view in education seem to have greater difficulty in understanding the way in which order is maintained in the new school than in understanding any other aspect of the newer school life. This is probably due in part to the fact that the *result* of organizing schools in the traditional fashion was disorder. The teacher, therefore, had to combat this malady of school life, to fight it armed with a mighty array of tasks, penalties, and punishments. Such a teacher is not prepared to believe what teachers in the new schools testify is the fact, namely, that the *result* of the *organization* and conduct of schools in terms of life itself is naturally *order*. Consequently, she wishes to approach a school in which order rather than disorder is supreme in old-fashioned panoply of authority and violence. She thinks in terms of disorder rather than order, of punishment rather than precaution, of cure rather than prevention.

Writing in *The New Era* concerning the Tower Hill School of Wilmington, Delaware, the Head Master [1] says:

"When a school becomes the center for the self-initiated, self-directed activities of its students, the question of discipline, in the sense of conduct, seemingly disappears. At least, we have found this to be true at Tower Hill School."

The objector who will not accept the testimony of those who have actually directed children in new schools will, therefore, not be in a position to grasp the supplementary explanation of the way in which deviations from the prevailing orderliness are dealt with.

It is to be carefully observed that such a condition of affairs can be expected only with normal children and when all the remaining conditions of a thoroughgoing organization of school life in terms of life and conduct are maintained. Nothing could be more illogical than to select examples of misbehavior from schools which are organized in traditional fashion, and cite from them cases which could not be handled by newer methods. Such cases would never have arisen in the same form under other conditions. It is beside the point to insist that in great city slum districts, in sections where the children's home background and school experience are drastic and unfortunate, severe disorder may arise which could not be dealt with by the remedial schemes used in schools organized in terms of conduct. Such remedial

[1] BURTON W. FOWLER, in *The New Era*, July, 1929, p. 156.

schemes depend upon the existence of a background in the school, a state of affairs upon which the corrective scheme is dependent and with which it is integrated. In such a school children with a bad home background or a pathological experience would not be allowed to reach the upper grades of the elementary school without effort having been made to rectify the causes of their misbehavior. Consequently, there can be little validity in criticism which cites cases of undesirable conduct which have been aggravated by years of neglect. If the school in which such children had been brought up had been thoroughly organized in the lower grades in terms of conduct, and any behavior variations in children had been understood and remedied from the very beginning, the frequency of disorderliness would certainly diminish. On the other hand, it should be recognized that the régime of responsibility here set forth has usually been worked out with bright children from comparatively comfortable homes. To what extent it would need modification and what specific alterations of technique it would demand if worked out with underprivileged children no one can say with definiteness. The one outstanding example which we have record of, namely, the school which Pestalozzi held at Stanz for the miserable urchins left destitute by the onslaught of the French soldiers, is in this respect one of the most reassuring documents extant. In his letter to his friend, Gessner, Pestalozzi tells his own story.[2]

"I was still without everything but money when the children crowded in; neither kitchen, rooms, nor beds were ready to receive them. At first this was a source of inconceivable confusion. For the first few weeks I was shut up in a very small room; the weather was bad, and the alterations, which made a great dust and filled the corridors with rubbish, rendered the air very unhealthy.

"The want of beds compelled me at first to send some of the poor children home at night; these children generally came back the next day covered with vermin. Most of them on their arrival were very degenerated specimens of humanity. Many of them had a sort of chronic skin-disease, which almost prevented their walking, or sores on their heads, or rags full of vermin; many were almost skeletons, with haggard, careworn faces, and shrinking looks; some brazen, accustomed to begging, hypocrisy, and all sorts of deceit; others broken by misfortune, patient, suspicious, timid, and entirely devoid of affection. There were also some spoilt children amongst them who

[2] QUICK, R. H., "Essays on Educational Reformers," D. Appleton & Co., New York, 1924, pp. 319 and 323.

BUILDING ORDER IN THE SCHOOL

had known the sweets of comfort, and were therefore full of pretensions. . . .

"The entire absence of school learning was what troubled me least, for I trusted in the natural powers that God bestows on even the poorest and most neglected children. I had observed for a long time that behind their coarseness, shyness, and apparent incapacity, are hidden the finest faculties, the most precious powers; and now, even amongst these poor creatures by whom I was surrounded at Stanz, marked natural abilities soon began to show themselves. I knew how useful the common needs of life are in teaching men the relations of things, in bringing out their natural intelligence, in forming their judgment, and in arousing faculties which, buried, as it were, beneath the coarser elements of their nature, cannot become active and useful till they are set free. It was my object to set free these faculties and bring them to bear on the pure and simple circumstances of domestic life, for I was convinced this was all that was wanting, and these natural faculties would show themselves capable of raising the hearts and minds of my pupils to all that I could desire. . . .

"On the return of spring it was evident to everybody that the children were all doing well, growing rapidly, and gaining color. Certain magistrates and ecclesiastics, who saw them some time afterwards, stated that they had improved almost beyond recognition."

Order in the Class

Plans for the building and maintaining of social order involve the life of the whole school. There are also certain plans which may be made by each class to provide for the orderly progress of affairs. The necessity for this repeated reference to the question of order indicates the way in which the matter cuts across the warp and woof of the whole school and is intimately connected with every aspect of school life. It is so closely related to the organic life of the school that the separate discussion of the matter is particularly difficult. It is the orderly carrying out from beginning to end of every unit of conduct undertaken in the school, large or small, individual or group, which brings about school order.

Some form of coöperative consideration by the children of the way in which activities may proceed harmoniously must develop as a need of any class group. In the Lincoln School of Columbia University it has been found wise to make the matter of organization for this purpose very informal. Discussions of class affairs are held under the guidance of the teacher who leads the children to take responsibility for their own behavior and for school welfare in every unit of conduct which they carry out. In the older classes a form of grade council is sometimes worked out. On one occasion a second grade, finding themselves inconvenienced by one of their number, a boy who was something of a problem, became concerned in helping him. Influenced by the idea of their "whole school council," they decided to pass rules against conduct of their members which they found undesirable. The rules were posted together with the names of the members of the class, so that a mark could be placed against the name of any violator of the rule by vote of the class. At the end of the week vote was again taken and if the individual had improved the mark was covered with a piece of white paper. The following list of rules was evolved.[3]

SECOND GRADE LAWS

Courtesy

1. Be careful to say "excuse me" when passing in front of some one.
2. Be careful not to disturb some one at work.
3. Do not push ahead of people in line; be orderly in line.
4. Pass another class quietly in the hall.
5. Be careful not to interrupt.
6. Be careful not to boast.
7. If you annoy some one accidentally, say "excuse me."
8. Be polite to visitors.
9. Answer with a quiet voice.
10. Give other people a chance.

Neatness

1. Pick things up off the floor.
2. Throw scraps in the trash basket.
3. Clean up after work period.
4. Keep the top of your desk clean.
5. Have a neat drawer.
6. Put things where they belong.
7. Do not knock over any chairs.
8. Be careful as you pass people's desks not to knock things off.
9. Hang up your wraps carefully.

[3] "The Student Councils," pamphlet of the Lincoln School of Teachers College, New York City, 1922, p. 32.

Interest in a brand new book with illustrations of the Three Bears led to the need to dramatize the story. This resulted in the building of a bear house with a stone wall in front of it. The walls of the classroom show evidence of many other activities of this grade one class taught by Mrs. Cowan in the Englewood Cliffs Public Schools. Note how different this work is from that of the first grade taught by the same teacher in the previous year. See frontispiece.

Coöperation

1. Work together with the class.
2. Pay attention.
3. Don't disturb the class.
4. Do not hold the class back.

Whatever scheme is worked out it should be worked out by the class and the teacher in school hours to meet the situation in which they find themselves. On certain occasions, especially in older grades, a still more formal type of class council with a formal constitution may be desired. In such a case it may be worked out. In each case, however, it is important that the plan is not one which has been copied from some adult form of government, or even from any other class of children, but rather one which is as simple as possible and worked out to fit the particular needs of the group using it.

Variations from Normal Order

If things are going as they should, teachers and children will find themselves in an orderly school. But in any group there must be deviations from the normal. Simple variations such as carelessness with belongings, lateness, loud talking, being unsocial, will be looked after by the attitudes and governmental plans of the group. In cases which do not yield easily, discussion with the pupil and on occasion with the parents may clear up the difficulty. It is necessary for all concerned to realize that such conduct simply does not go on in the school community. A person who does not act as he should would not be regarded as a member of the group and would not be able to share its privileges until he conformed to its nature.

For example, Dick, a bright ten-year-old, impulsive and overeager, made himself somewhat annoying in class by "smart" remarks. As the class was discussing books, he remarked several times that he thought certain books under discussion were "boring." This pose of oversophistication was obviously an attempt to get special attention. The teacher asked the class if they liked the way Dick was acting. The class insisted that they did not like it at all and suggested that Dick had better go home for the morning. The teacher interceded for him, but when the class voted they decided that they wanted Dick to leave, which he did, very much crestfallen indeed.

This method of isolation is one of particular potency in dealing with minor infringements of order. It is especially useful with small children. Children who are deliberately annoying during the story period, or children who misuse tools or construction materials, may be taken from the room or not allowed to sit with the others at lunch, or may be deprived of some privilege until they are ready to fit into group life.

Sublimation of energies or the substitution of a new habit or activity for an old one frequently accomplishes good results. The following account is given of the way in which children's energies were re-directed at Manumit School: [4]

"These recent incidents in our school life will serve as brief illustrations. Nora was a gentle, nicely behaved little girl of ten who had been gradually led by a divided loyalty to a modern mother and an old-fashioned grandmother into habitual deceit and dishonesty. Billy came to Manumit as a very dirty, combative, but lovable, bright, and exceedingly energetic young lad of nine. There were few in the category of youthful vices of which Billy was not guilty. Jerry came to us a bully and a liar of eleven whom an over-indulgent mother had permitted to do everything he desired. In each instance trouble soon started, but the solution was frankly put up to the children. Punishments, as such, were not resorted to; rather the pressure of the social disapproval of their own group. Nora was put on trial. Billy was expelled from the group and put on 'silence.' Jerry was given a special project in carpentry to work on, where he might prove that he was capable of sticking to one thing and doing it well. Nora concluded the year by writing a real autobiography in which she described how she had been 'saved' by coöperation. Billy was expelled three times before he could fit into his group and community as an integral part. But his dirty, untidy habits were amazingly improved when the children voted to make him inspector of cleanliness and order for the whole school. Jerry is just beginning his project in carpentry, but the kind sympathetic attitude of the children has filled him with the determination to make good."

Another example of the re-direction of a child's activities from harmful to useful channels is given by a teacher of the Medbury Street Infants' School in London.[5]

"The vicious child who interferes with others and spoils apparatus is another great problem. It is generally a good plan to give such a child a responsible position. Arthur was found to be the offender when

---

[4] NELLIE M. SEEDS, Director of the Manumit School, Pawling, New York, *The New Era*, July, 1929.
[5] *The New Era, ibid.*, p. 165.

coats and hats were discovered continually on the floor of one of the cloakrooms. He was made responsible for the tidying up of the cloakroom. He liked this job so much that he was discovered throwing the hats and coats on the floor of the cloakrooms in order to make the job last as long as possible. He lost his position, but in trying to win it back again, he developed a great regard for the property of others. The child who destroys materials can often be taught to take an interest in these by being made responsible for the tidiness and good condition of the apparatus."

More serious cases of non-conformity do arise sometimes. Such cases should be regarded as behavior problems. The instant any child is recognized by the teacher as a behavior problem the child should be placed under special observation in order to determine the cause of his undesirable action. It cannot be too clearly pointed out that the new teacher eagerly pursues the cause of misbehavior rather than blindly punishing its manifestation. In so doing she is not denying the child's moral responsibility, but is assuming the social responsibility that the community bears for the sound direction of child life. It is as though the teacher should turn off the tap rather than try to dam the overflow. If the cause of misconduct is discovered, the remedy will become apparent.

It frequently happens that the cause of the trouble is apparent to a sagacious teacher who understands children. With a small child this is frequently merely the desire to secure more than his share of attention. One curly headed lad, used to a luxurious home and indulgent parents, made frequent bids for attention by "showing off" and attempting to attract attention. The group finding themselves annoyed with the child, the matter was discussed with him. "I know just what is the matter with you," said the teacher to him, as the two talked it over. "You are simply trying to get attention. Now I have too many things to do and so have the rest of us, to give you attention. Until you can learn to do without it you will have to stay by yourself." It was but a matter of minutes before the child decided to coöperate and from then on he made no more trouble.

Professor Joseph Cohen relates the way in which, by his keen understanding of the situation, he was able to deal with two young belligerents in an elementary classroom. With a background of gang life these boys felt that prestige among their companions demanded due show of fistic prowess. Noticing their mutual attitudes, the teacher informed them that since they wished to fight he would arrange the matter for them after class. When the time came, taking them aside, he informed them that he would leave them alone in the classroom to fight the matter to a finish. As the affair was a private one, he promised to say nothing further about it, and requested them to promise that they, too, would not say one word to any one as to what went on in the room or who won the fight. As they agreed to this he left them alone. What went on is, of course, unknown to any but the two boys. The teacher testifies that after ten minutes of intense silence the two boys emerged. If they had fought at all they showed no signs of it, nor was there any further trouble in class, for the glory of fighting had departed.

When infringements of order are more serious and persistent, it may be necessary to place the child concerned under the observation of the principal or the psychiatrist. Sometimes the cause of the trouble can be understood by simply watching the child at work in the class, examining his drawings and other work, and getting at home conditions by consulting the parents. At other times the matter is more obscure, and special studies by the psychologist and possibly a psychiatrist may be needed. The following accounts give some indication of the way in which such cases may be studied and given remedial treatment.

Eddy was a small boy in the primary grades who gave considerable trouble. He was not anxious to learn, and would not put his efforts to worthwhile activities. His case was investigated and it was discovered that he was living under unfortunate home conditions. He was given special attention in school. Careful work was done by the psychologist in teaching him to read by the use of phonetics. At eleven years of age he was questioned as to his prowess in reading and reported to the psychologist that he was the best reader in his class. "How do you account for that?" he was asked. The reply was, "Because you took all that time teaching me to read."

Kenneth had a speech defect of the type so often associated with nervous disturbances. When taken to camp with the other primary children he had tantrums and showed fear of the dark. He was taken from the public school classes and sent by the school to an out-of-town settlement. Here he received special attention. He was given a program involving outdoor activities on the farm and freedom from strain. He soon lost his timid cringing manner and his speech defect disappeared.

Jane was a little girl who was always restless, out of her seat, moving about. She would go to the waste basket, then to the bookcase, sharpen pencils, leave the class frequently, making little sallies about

A GUIDE FOR THE TEACHER'S OBSERVATIONS OF DIFFICULT PUPILS [6]

Undesirable Conduct	Possible Causes	Causal Conditions	Possible Remedies	Aggravative Treatment
1. Superfluous noise	Imitation or Suggestion	Noisy situation Nervous voices Nervous "atmosphere"	Quiet Calm voice Poise	"Desk bell" High, irritable voice Blame Bribing Public discussion
	Muscular fatigue	Misfit seats Insufficient exercise	Adjusted seats Exercise	Calling attention to noise or threatening
	Nerve fatigue	Insufficient rest Improper food Tense work	Relaxation Diet Change of program	Similar work
	Bad air	Ventilation	More fresh air	
	Awkwardness	Has been made self-conscious	Helping others	Public reprimand
	Desire for attention	Has been trained to be vain	Considering others	Personal aggrievedness Personal favor
	Hurry and worry	Habit of fear	Poise Encouragement	Calling him "Noisy"
	Irritation	Disorderly desk or room	Neatness	Visual distractions
2. Wasting time or "visiting"	Lacks educational motive	Does not see course	Explaining uses for work	"Making him do"
	Lacks educational ambition	Lack of satisfaction Work too easy	Good work and private praise More interesting work	Criticism "Drilling"
	Lack of responsibility	Others cared for him	Responsibility	Teacher responsibility

[6] From "Better Schools," by Washburne, Carleton, and Stearns, Myron, The John Day Co, New York, 1928.

200 THE TECHNIQUE OF PROGRESSIVE TEACHING

A GUIDE FOR THE TEACHER'S OBSERVATIONS OF DIFFICULT PUPILS—(Continued)

Undesirable Conduct	Possible Causes	Causal Conditions	Possible Remedies	Aggravative Treatment
	Lacks evaluation	Others judged for him	Comparing and judging	Teacher judging
	Lacks self-direction	Others planned for him	Planning and directing	Teacher directing
	Lack of volition	Others decided for him Weak will	Deciding	Teacher deciding
	Conflict of interest	School tasks bore Undesirable associates Undesirable habits	Choosing own work Put mother on job Put nurse on job	"Driving" Contempt
	Desire for attention	Trained to be vain and selfish	Considering others Shift center of stage	Public
	Nerve fatigue	Malnutrition Irregular hours Unstable nerves	Diet Regularity Frequent relaxation	Scolding Complaining
3. Frequent asking for help	Dependence	Others decided for him	Deciding	Teacher deciding
	Irresponsibility	Others cared for him	Responsibility	Teacher responsibility
	Self-distrust	Failure marks	Satisfactory work	More failure marks
	Lack of self-respect	Public criticism	Private praise	More public criticism
	"Laziness" Auto-intoxication Insufficient exercise Insufficient rest Irregular hours of food and sleep	Malnutrition Exercise Relaxation Regularity	Diet	Pickles, pop and pie "Keeping in", Calling him "Lazy"
	Lack of volition	Others decided for him Weak will	Deciding	Teacher deciding

4. Slow progress	Habit of expecting failure	Failure marks	Satisfactory work	More failure marks Calling him "slow"
	Lack of self-confidence	Criticism	Private praise	Comparing him with others Public criticism
	Faulty preparation	Placed too high	Educational placement	"Drill"
	Weak attack	Teacher direction	Self-direction	Teacher direction
	Lack of volition	Others were responsible Weak will	Responsibility Deciding	"Make him do it" Teacher decision
	Lack of ambition	Lack of satisfaction in work or accomplishment	Good work and praise	Discouragement
	Morbidness	Trained to be self-centered	Considering others Humor	Preaching
	Inattention	Uninteresting work	Change in work Physical examination	Calling him inattentive
	Ill health	Improper food Insufficient exercise Insufficient rest Irregularity in hours	Diet Exercise Relaxation Regularity	Pop, pickles, pie "Keeping in" Too many movies
	Forgetting	Uninteresting work Weak association	Varied presentation Concrete experience	Tell him he forgets
	Childishness	Processes Immature mind	Demotion	Promotion
5. Cheating	Fear of consequences	Ridicule of others Criticism of others Unsuitable penalties Failure marks	Satisfactory work Praise Natural penalties Marking progress	Calling him "Cheat" Public censure More failure marks

A GUIDE FOR THE TEACHER'S OBSERVATIONS OF DIFFICULT PUPILS—(Continued)

Undesirable Conduct	Possible Causes	Causal Conditions	Possible Remedies	Aggravative Treatment
	Self-distrust	Work was not made clear Was placed too high	Encourage questions Correct placement	Sarcasm and criticism Promotion
	Habit of "easiest way"	Others accepted dishonest work	Individual work	Credit for dishonest work
	Habit of copying	Taught through imitation and copying	Constructive planning	Learning by copying
	Habit of working for *answers*	Believes education is for fact getting	Aiming at *training*	Credit given for answers chiefly
	Lack of self-respect	Has done poor work	Private praise	Public censure
	Fascination of the difficult	Given tasks were too easy	Harder, more interesting work	Increasing difficulty to cheat
6. Contrariness and sullenness	Jealousy	Unfair discrimination Home folks not interested Favored brother, sister, classmates	Personal interest	Censure Praise of others
	Sensitiveness	Public criticism Fault finding	Sympathy Private praise	Public censure
	Resentment	Interference Bossiness	Non-interference Independence	Advice and directio
	Unhappiness	Inharmonious home Outside trouble Lack of friendship	Interest Kindness	Sarcasm Severity
	Sticking to first idea	Strong will Weak will	Self-direction	Bossing

Selfishness	Taught to be self-centered Taught to expect his own way	Considering others	Bribing him
Concentration	Strong will	Avoidance of sudden interruptions Courtesy	Nagging
Suspicion	Unfair criticism	Impersonal attitude	Snap judgment
7. Touchiness Habit of expecting criticism Habit of imaginary slights Morbidness	Criticism Unjust suspicion Trained to be self-centered Over-conscientiousness	Praise Fairness Considering Frank discussion Learn to see humor	Censure Snap judgment Seriousness
Nervousness	Improper food Irregular hours Insufficient sleep Neurotic inheritance	Diet Regularity Sleep	Punishment
8. Silliness Self-consciousness	Physical change Overwork	Put mother on job Vacation	Tense work
Conflicting interests, etc. Lack of responsibility Lack of ambition Lack of volition Childishness		(See 2) " " "	
Vanity	Immature mind Taught to be center of stage	Demotion Considering others Shift center of stage	Promotion Resentment Anger Aggrievedness
9. Impertinence Smartness			
Ignorance of proper conduct	Trained to be rude	Surprised silence Extreme politeness Courteous ignoring	Impoliteness

A GUIDE FOR THE TEACHER'S OBSERVATIONS OF DIFFICULT PUPILS—(*Continued*)

Undesirable Conduct	*Possible Causes*	*Causal Conditions*	*Possible Remedies*	*Aggravative Treatment*
	Desire to be hero	Impertinence has been admired	Shift center of stage	Public discussion
	Camouflage	Made ashamed of some condition	Courageous statement of condition	
	Desire for attention	Has not had rightful attention at home	Interest Considering others	Annoyance
	Jealousy	Has not had rightful interest at home Selfishness	Friendliness Considering others	Praise of others
	Lack of self-control	Has had bad example	Calm consideration Suspense Self-punishment	Temper
Teasing			Not to be teased	Temper

the room. When the case was investigated, it was discovered that the child was troubled with a hyper-thyroid condition. She was given medical treatment. Whenever signs of restlessness reappeared she was given special activities of a legitimate kind until her behavior become practically normal.

STAFF COÖPERATION IN BEHAVIOR PROBLEMS

In the good school order is normal. Deviations from order must therefore be regarded as abnormal. They are pathological. They are to be compared to indisposition or sickness of the individual. Disorder is an illness of the social organism. When the individual shows symptoms of illness those concerned in his welfare—the parents, other members of the family, the doctor—seek the cause of the trouble. The cause being understood, the remedy is applied.

So it must be in school. Deviations from normal order must be noted, their cause discovered and the remedy applied. In accordance with the seriousness of the deviation, the obscurity of its cause, and the difficulty of its treatment, so must the school attempt to correct it. Simple deviations are easily understood and dealt with by the teacher. More serious deviations demand, according to their nature and the needs of the particular case, the coöperation of the entire school staff. Any one or all of the regular and special members of the staff, the teacher, the principal, the nurse, the doctor, the psychologist and the visiting teacher, may be called upon to help in the understanding of a behavior problem and in its rectification. In many schools regular periodical meetings of these members of the staff are held. In other schools special meetings are called when specific cases demand discussion.

Although this discussion cannot pretend to give guidance in the handling of behavior problems, in order that teachers may be oriented to the work of other members of the school staff, the following account is given.

It may be profitable to consider in the concrete the rise and treatment of a behavior problem—one little boy, Gerald C., a second grade child, seven years old, in a large public school system. In common with all other children who enter the school he had been given a psychological and physical examination, and the regular records were on file in the school office.

The teacher soon recognized Gerald as a troublesome and restless child. He was of uneven temper, was easily irritated, and on account of these unpleasantnesses was not liked by his companions. He scowled frequently and was a constant source of annoyance to the other children, frequently interfering in their work and bothering them. He was sometimes late for school. Finding that the customary minor forms of guidance were not adequate, the teacher called the attention of the principal to the case as one needing further study.

It should be quite clear that the principal is not regarded as the guardian and responsible head in the matter of school order, as has so often been the case. The appeal to the principal was in no sense a reporting of the child for bad conduct, nor a request for the aid of the principal in correcting the child. One must pity the principal who acts as the chief of police. The report was made by the teacher to the coördinating head of the school because her own interest in the child concerned was keen, and she regarded it as her work to give the child the benefit of the larger services of the school. The principal talked the matter over with the teacher, and it was decided to call on the school doctor, the psychologist and the visiting teacher for special help in understanding the situation.

The psychologist then found time to watch Gerald in the class, about the school, and on the playground. Her notes show that the boy was continually anxious for attention. He would interrupt frequently during stories and discussion and during work periods; when he should have been engaged on what he was doing, he would frequently drop it and run to the teacher about irrelevant and unimportant matters. He was resistant to suggestion, and when asked by the teacher or one of the children to assist, or to carry on some small task such as block moving or cleaning up, was inclined not to coöperate. Furthermore, he had a tendency to organize "gangs," a fact which the teacher had already noticed. He was observed in attempts to set Alfred against Kenneth, and in moves to get one group to fight or oppose another.

In dealing with the matter, the teacher took special occasion to talk with the group. She spoke of the pride which they all had in the class since it had learned to take care of itself, and since each of the pupils had learned how to get along with the others. The children then discussed their disappointment when one child "forgot" and created an unfriendly spirit among them. They spoke of "gangs" and the teacher helped them to make the distinction between "friendships" which are admirable and designed to help one another, and "gangs" which are unfriendly and only try to hinder. The discussion was spoken of as a reminder in which they were all reminding themselves that each one should obey his own rules "by himself," because they had made their rules so that they could live comfortably together without making one another unhappy. The children were interested and entered freely into the discussion, citing various instances which had arisen and talking them over.

The visiting teacher, on one excuse or another, made a special visit to the child's home to talk with his parents. She was able to discover that the child was similarly restless and uncoöperative at home, and that certain of the home conditions were not as they should be. She talked them over with the mother and offered suggestions that might be helpful. The child was staying up very late at nights, his sleep was sometimes troubled, and late rising was the cause of the lateness at school. The doctor, from his special examination of the child, had suggested a bromide occasionally. The visiting teached explained and interpreted this recommendation of the doctor and won the parents to coöperation in the home life of the child.

In a school meeting the various individuals studying the case pooled their information for the benefit of the teacher. With the new understanding she received, she continued her classroom training, carefully checking the child's conduct and gradually gaining his coöperation. This was a very skillful teacher, with an excellent understanding of children accompanied by wise firmness. On one occasion Gerald took an apple, which was already bitten into, from another child and threw it on the floor. The teacher insisted that Gerald pick up the apple, wash it and return it to the child from whom it had been taken. She talked with Gerald and the other children, saying that children must grow up, that children do not do such things, and explained to the boy that he should not want attention from others to look after such matters, he should check himself. Other children, who were inclined to laugh at Gerald's pranks, were taken into confidence. "Georgie," said the teacher to one of them, "if you laugh at Gerald, you are keeping him from growing up." So in every way close watch was kept over the boy's conduct, and such painstaking care, accompanied by the improvement of home conditions, gradually brought the child in the course of the succeeding year increasingly into the line of normal, responsible conduct for a child of his age.

The Visiting Teacher

So very important is the visiting teacher as a member of the school staff that some special reference should be made to her work and her invaluable contribution toward the understanding and improvement of individual living conditions of the children both in and out of school.

The visiting teacher might be called a liaison officer between home and school. It is her function to coördinate these two institutions and bring one to the assistance of the other in order that both may be of maximum assistance to the individual child concerned. Too often these institutions have been antagonistic rather than coöperative. The school has said one thing by word and deed and the home another. The child, mystified by the conflict, has found it only too difficult to pilot his puny course between Scylla and Charybdis.

The visiting teacher must be a person of fine tact and wide experience. She should be a trained social worker who has also had teaching experience. She will then not merely understand children and the problems of school teaching, but will also be in touch with the multifarious social agencies of the community and understand how to call them to the aid of the children and their families whenever necessary. She spends the day from nine till three either at school in her office, where she may be consulted by parents on any matter which has bearing on one of the children, or in visiting homes or in arranging the complex affairs in which she is called upon to assist.

As soon as a child is registered in the school, the visiting teacher does what she is able to get the child's family background. Usually the child is brought to school by one of the parents, and so an initial contact is made at the very beginning. Much may be learned by judicious conversation with the parents. If they are reluctant to answer questions, the matter is never pressed, in order to avoid antagonizing them. The matter may be left until a more convenient season, as it is the first aim of the visiting teacher to make friends of the people whose children are in the school.

If the visiting teacher is watching for an opportunity, it is almost sure to arise sooner or later. In one case, for instance, the mother of a child with infected tonsils had received a report from the school doctor that the child's tonsils should be removed. What could she do about it? The family was poor and could not afford the expense. The visiting teacher, knowing the social resources of the community, was able to arrange for the whole matter in a neighboring hospital. The parents were so grateful that the visiting teacher had ready access to the home. It proved to be one in considerable distress. There were several small children. The father was ill and, consequently, not earning. Arrangements were made for his entrance into a convalescent home where he received proper treatment. When he recovered, he was assisted in finding work. All this was done in the interests of the children in school and of the younger ones who were on their way there.

As soon as any case is handed over to the visiting teacher for investigation, whether it is a teacher's problem or a home problem, it is sent to the social service exchange to be "cleared." The various records of the numerous social agencies of a large city are usually coördinated in a central bureau, so that every case treated by any of the various agencies is reported to the central bureau and kept on file there. When the visiting teacher sends a name, within twenty-four hours she receives a report from this central bureau concerning the family with which she is dealing. She thus knows the record of this family and just what previous association it has had with hospitals, reform institutions, or charity organizations, and is able to handle the case so much the better. Thus, the work of the school may be coördinated with the other social work of the community.

As a consulting expert on any of the hundred and one problems which parents may have concerning their children, the visiting teacher finds much to occupy her time. Parents come to her for all sorts of advice and assistance. It may be that a child is convalescing from measles, and the parent wishes to discuss her return to school. Perhaps it is nearly summer time. The school has arranged special places in an expensive summer camp at a nominal rate of a dollar a day, and the parent wishes to talk over a possible place for her child. Or it may be that a mother has been offered scholarships for her two boys in a well-known private school. She is well satisfied with what this progressive branch of a public school is doing and wishes to know if she should make a change or let her children remain where they are happy and doing well. This and a hundred similar problems are continually arising, and the visiting teacher fulfills her beneficent function of casting oil on troubled waters.

It must be obvious how very salutary is the effect of the visiting teacher on the whole life of the public school. In fact, school systems are beginning to realize that the services of the visiting teacher are essential to the organization of a modern public school. We hear talk of the replacing of the odious truant officer, whose duty was to detect and deliver for punishment, by the visiting teacher whose duty is to prevent maladjustment and to minimize the causes of disorder. Surely the new school looks to the visiting teacher as an absolutely indispensable help to teacher and children.

CHAPTER XVIII

SOME SPECIAL PROBLEMS OF THE TEACHER

The Teacher's Personality

"What does God do in the fourth hour?" asks the Talmud, and the answer is given, "He teaches little children." So high is the function of the teacher in a properly organized society. The personality of the teacher is the most important single factor in the organization of school life. This may seem a truism. If so, it is a truism which receives small recognition either by the man in the street or the man in the school administrator's office. Every scheme and mechanical method of improving school life that can be devised is emphasized to the neglect of the proper selection and training of teachers. A teacher whose personality is so well developed, whose cultural background is so rich that for children to be associated with her many hours a day is a remarkable privilege, is frequently overlooked. On the other hand, precedence may be given to those who have the knack of mechanically and neatly adapting themselves to a school system. The new school, however, belongs to the children and the teacher. Here it is virtually the children who select their teacher because only a real children's teacher can succeed in such a school. Those who select the teachers are the children's delegates, and among them are those who put a high value on teachers having sympathy, character, and culture.

The personality of the teacher should be a rich one. Her experiences should be numerous and varied. It is an advantage for teachers to have had good homes in childhood, where the highest standards of manners, language, and conduct held sway. We need teachers from good homes. Good home experiences should be amplified by a thorough school training and a college training which is not narrowed to the mere vocational aspects of teacher training, but has included a wide exploration in the fields of human interest, such as science and philosophy, art and music. It is also essential that the education of teachers should somewhere and somehow be enriched by a knowledge of the common everyday phenomena of nature. A teacher who does not know the names of the flowers of the garden and the wayside, who cannot

SOME SPECIAL PROBLEMS OF THE TEACHER

recognize the common birds of her locality, and who cannot tell a butterfly from a moth, falls far short of being an ideal teacher of children. Travel, the wider the better, is an enlarging experience which adds untold resources to the teacher as a member of the group. To have seen with one's own eyes is a prized experience. It is to enjoy such privileges that the long summer holiday is given to teachers. Unfortunately, there has sprung up in some quarters a system by which teachers are expected to attend summer schools if they are to find advancement. Summer school work in moderation is desirable, but incessant study at summer school is an enemy of the teacher's fullest development. It is a travesty to give teachers advancement and credit for a six-weeks' period of institutional study and to give no recognition for summer travel. It is essential that in the holiday teachers grow, but they should grow restfully and naturally, by a wise use of leisure.

The good teacher must have a sympathetic attitude toward and a wide knowledge of children. A sympathetic attitude is not to be confused with a sentimental one, nor opinions about children with knowledge of them. The proper attitude for the teacher is a result of the scientific study of children's nature, of careful observation and actual experience in living with children. The teacher who keeps close to children learns to understand what has been called "the child's point of view" without surrendering her own. Children trust her because she trusts them.

The teacher needs wide knowledge of the materials of the whole school environment. She should study these things in their social setting, so that she may be skilled in assembling and integrating her resources about the various interests and activities of children. If the children, during a study of Mexico, should become interested in the making of pottery, the teacher will need to be familiar, to some extent, with the materials involved in such a process. She should also be equipped to discover materials with which she is unfamiliar, and trained to integrate her whole knowledge and experience whether it be gained by reading, travel, or by local visits, so that the resources of her total personality will be available to meet the needs of the children. She should be familiar with clay as a material, with the processes of modeling and perhaps of glazing, and be acquainted with sources whence she may obtain information on the making of pottery. She may, in the same connection, need to become familiar with Mexican or Egyptian history and understand how to obtain library materials and pertinent references should the children become interested in records as men have left them in the form of pottery. In other words, she needs practice in the organizing of the resources of her personality and environment in terms of a unit of conduct upon which the children are engaged.[1]

Little need be said of the character of the teacher lest what is written appear trite. Fundamentally, the work of the teacher is to change people for the better. Everything in the life of the teacher which hinders this process must be a disadvantage, while everything which furthers it must be all to the good. Water cannot rise above its own level nor can teachers raise pupils above their own. It is axiomatic that teachers should be persons of character, but if they are people who meet the requirements of a good teacher as presented in the preceding paragraphs, there is little danger that they will be otherwise. As to the religious life of teachers, differing opinions may be held. Agnostic teachers are found in new schools as in older ones. This is a matter for parents. If parents do not care about such things, how may the schools begin to? But whatever particular interpretation individuals place upon what is virtuous and what is desirable in the teacher's personality, one thing is as undisputed in theory as it is unrecognized today in practice. Children are entitled to the very best people of the community as their teachers.

THE TEACHER'S OUT-OF-CLASS PREPARATION

In preparing for her school work the teacher needs to give very careful study to the surrounding neighborhood. What is the nature of the activities in which the community engages? What industrial plants or activities are maintained? Where are the public buildings, the banks, the post office? What is the nature of the waterfront and the harbor? Where are the piers and what is their relation to the railway and other transportation facilities? Where is the grain shipped from? What is the nature of the shipping? Where are the museums? What special services do they offer to schools? What local exhibitions may be relied on as supplementary to school activities? Where are the headquarters of such organizations as the Boy Scouts? What are the local parks and what others are easily reached by some form of transportation? What outdoor resources are opened up by bus line, steamship or railway? Where are the nearest woods and what is their nature? What is a likely

[1] For a discussion of the teacher's need for keeping data and materials available, see MOSSMAN, L. C., "Principles of Teaching and Learning," Houghton Mifflin Co., Boston, 1929, pp. 279 ff.

SOME SPECIAL PROBLEMS OF THE TEACHER

place for the study of birds, for the discovery of pussy willows or maple blossoms? Where will one be likely to discover mayflowers or lady's-slippers? Where will one find caddice fly larvae or the nymphs of the dragon fly? These and numerous other matters of the local environment should receive attention and investigation from the teacher.

Again the teacher should be familiar with the library resources of the community. What are the possibilities of the school library? How are they supplemented by public libraries in the community? Are there state organizations which forward collections of books or send out traveling libraries? To what extent is it possible to draw on private collections?

Are there societies or organizations which will furnish lantern slides? Is it possible to secure moving picture films from the museum of art or the museum of natural history? Are there individuals in the community whom children may consult in special matters or call on to provide special information? Is there some citizen who has worked in Labrador? Is there a local visitor from India or China? Is there an industrial specialist who can tell of the manufacture of artificial silk, or an engineer who has guided some great piece of scientific engineering, a bridge or a tunnel? It would be a good thing not merely for the children but also for such visitors if they might freshen their contact with life by a half hour spent in answering children's questions.

THE SET-UP

The teacher will also need to spend considerable time in preparing the schoolroom environment, and in arranging for the proper selection and progress of units of work. A teacher of experience usually has, by the beginning of the term, some idea of the particular kind of work she would like done. From her previous knowledge of children, and from particular knowledge and inquiry as to the previous experiences of the pupils coming to her, perhaps from term-end conferences with those very children, she is able to make plans for work which seem likely to materialize. Teachers call this process "setting the stage" or preparing a "set-up." Certain books of significance are placed in the environment. Clay, wood, boxes, pictures, animals, anything bearing on activities which the teacher regards as suitable, are set in place in the schoolroom. When the children come they are allowed to investigate and work with the materials which are themselves suggestive and stimulating. Thus, careful planning is required of the teacher, outside of school hours as well as in school, to prepare suitable set-ups and to select from the activities which arise units of conduct which will develop satisfactorily in the direction of desired values.

The Teacher's Position in the Classroom

The teacher's place is any and everywhere in the classroom and sometimes out of it. She may find herself wherever the children are, though sometimes she may leave them entirely to themselves. Discussions have been carried on in the past as to what position the teacher should hold in the classroom. Front or back? Sitting or standing? Was it best to ask questions from the front, and was it not best to do police duty from the back? Such discussions are beside the point. The good teacher may find herself engaged as a helping partner in any activity in which the children are occupied and may assume most of the attitudes that the children assume in carrying on their work. The position of the teacher is governed by what she has to do, and is adapted to doing it as well as she can. If she is busy with the children, she will be doing as they are. If she leaves them to get some materials or secure certain references, she will do just as the pupils do when sent on such an errand; she will secure what she wants, while most of the children are too busy to observe that she has left.

The Beginning of a Term

It is assumed that by the first day of school the schoolroom has been set in order before the arrival of the children. Any desired set-up has been arranged. The classroom is properly equipped. Things are in their places, the clay is in the jar, the paints where they belong, the blocks on their shelves or perhaps set out where the children will see them. There is no confusion.

The children of the older grades will present no particular problem. They are resuming where they have left off in the previous term. They have endless summer experiences to relate and are ready to report and to exhibit collections which they have gathered during the holiday.[2] The schoolroom, in its general aspects, will be familiar to

---

[2] See "Vacation Activities and the School," The Lincoln School of Teachers College, New York, 1925. This booklet provides suggestions to be given to children for activities during the summer vacation.

SOME SPECIAL PROBLEMS OF THE TEACHER 215

them. They will be used to the handling of materials and to assuming initiative in beginning the term's work. Old materials will be recognized friends, while new materials, which should not be too numerous, will invite exploration.

Small children who have not previously attended school[3] and children in the older grades who have been used to a more formal type of schooling, present a special problem. It is necessary to introduce them to a new environment and in the very beginning teachers should attempt little else. Here is a room to be explored. Here are numerous objects which are strange, the possibilities of which need to be investigated. It is necessary to find a place for coats and other clothing. Materials belonging to individuals may be assigned and labeled with the children's names. There is a group of other children, whose very presence is a new experience to most small children. It is necessary for each child to get used to a group. It takes time for the children to become acquainted with one another; to discover the possibilities of companionship; to learn how to participate in simple activities without excitement; to get used to the teacher and her ways. The beginning of the term is a period of orientation in which ample time should be given for the children to learn how to play freely together according to behavior patterns which will be satisfactory to them.

STARTING THE SCHOOL DAY

The beginning of the school day may be the most informal thing in the world. A business man knows when to get to his office. He is usually there before the time and begins his work when he gets there. So children come to school in the morning and begin work when they arrive. There is small danger of their being late because they have their work to do and are anxious to get at it. The sled or the snowball mortar under construction needs to be ready as soon as possible, so that it can be put to the use for which it is intended. But it is not merely for such constructive activities that children come early to school. It is a common thing for pupils to arrive early to snatch some extra time for some form of work or other. I recently questioned a boy who had arrived twenty minutes before the opening hour and

[3] See Horace Mann Studies in Elementary Education, Teachers College, Columbia University, 1922. This contains an excellent concrete account of a first day with a beginning group.
See also MOSSMAN, L. C., "Principles of Teaching and Learning," Houghton Mifflin Co., Boston, 1929, pp. 1 ff.

had begun writing diligently at his table. It turned out that he was working to catch up on his arithmetic drill book because he had lost time by being unavoidably absent the day before. It may be that no signal at all is needed for the opening of school in the morning. More usually it is desirable to give a signal, such as the tapping of a triangle, a special whistle, or the beating of a light tom-tom, as the teacher prefers. Some teachers find it quieting and simple to have one of the children play a record on the gramophone while the morning activities are beginning. Children should learn to be their own time keepers, but with a group signals are necessary. The teacher will find it useful to have some simple signal which is readily recognized by all the children when the attention of the group is required for any purpose such as a change of program.

THE CARE OF MINOR DETAILS

There are two divergent theories of procedure which govern the way in which different teachers care for the numerous minor details of life in the classroom. There are a hundred and one trifling matters which must have attention from some one. The temperature of the room should be kept at about 66 to 68 degrees Fahrenheit; ventilation, even in classrooms with the most modern mechanical devices, frequently demands the opening and closing of windows; waste paper must be disposed of; desks and materials must be kept in order; the water in the aquarium must be changed; plants must be watered; blackboard brushes must be cleaned; tables must be dusted; in short, good conditions of orderly living must be maintained in the classroom.

TEACHER RESPONSIBILITY

The first of the two theories just referred to is that of teacher responsibility. Those who hold this theory assume the burden of either attending to the details or of seeing that they are properly carried out. Teachers who proceed on this theory must keep all pertinent details in mind and assume responsibility themselves by a careful system of checking. They tend to devise various schemes to routinize attention to certain of these details. An excellent example of such work is daily routinized health inspection carried out in some schools, in which children are given a mimeographed list of the ideals to be maintained, clean face, hands and neck, brushed hair, fresh handkerchief and so on. Each morning the teacher passes down the aisles, pad in hand, noting each child's approximation to the standard and giving here and there a word of criticism or encouragement.

There are other matters which teachers sometimes routinize. One of these is the inspection of desks. At certain set periods, usually at the end of each day, the teacher makes a round of examination to see that there has been no defacement of the school furniture, or to see that the materials in and about the desk are neatly arranged and in order. Again, the disposal of waste paper is sometimes arranged for in a similar way. Just before dismissal a monitor passes about the room with the waste basket into which all waste material is thrown by the pupils.

Shared Responsibility

The second theory of management of the details of class living is that of sharing responsibility. Teachers who hold this theory have little faith in schemes for routinizing attention to details. They might be inclined to ask, with reference to the health inspection just described, what would be the appearance and health habits of the children of the inspected class when they have no inspection on Saturday morning. They believe that the habit which they wish to form in regard to the disposal of waste paper is not that of putting waste paper in a basket which is passed, but of disposing of waste paper by taking it to the basket as one would in an office or home. These teachers attempt to build up in the personality of each child in the group an attitude of responsibility for their own simple concerns and those of the group. This process is not so simple nor mechanical as the mere routinizing of class life. It demands a constant alertness on the part of the teacher to the most inconsequential details of conduct. It involves not merely building in children attitudes and habits which make them look after their own affairs and materials, but attitudes and habits of responsibility toward the affairs and materials of others. This is no simple problem for the teacher. As Miss Barnes of the Lincoln School so aptly expressed it, "It is hard enough to train a child to pick up his own hat, but it is a far more difficult matter to train him to pick up a hat that belongs to somebody else." In other words, children need to learn that what is nobody's business is everybody's business. The various details of keeping the room neat and clean, of caring for your own materials and any others which have chanced to be neglected, the general conditions of living which affect the group, are shared responsibilities in which everybody should do his particular and his general part. Thus, children should keep their own desks clean, dispose of their own waste paper, open a window if the room is really too hot. Whatever tasks children carry out, they should learn to clean up and tidy up the surroundings when they are finished, preferably without checking and without being told.

A great many of the details of school life which have often been looked after by teacher-controlled routine may be cared for by the pupils themselves. Children may, as they grow old enough to do so, keep their own attendance records. A mimeographed sheet distributed from the central office of the school may provide lines and columns for the names of the various members of the class and special columns in which the children may enter a mark if they have purchased milk, orange, apple or crackers for lunch. Again, a box or an envelope fastened in a convenient spot bearing the instructions, "Please put your own absence slips and excuses here," will enable children to look after such mechanical affairs without bothering the teacher. Such matters, in which children assume responsibility for their own conduct, thus serve not merely as convenient devices for the operation of the class affairs, but also as training in living.

The following examples may throw some light on the type of procedure followed by teachers in maintaining conditions which help children in the development of habits of responsibility. On one occasion the teacher of a low primary grade observed that one of the little girls was consistently avoiding her responsibility in a certain situation. It was the custom in this class for the children, when finishing their play, to put away whatever materials they had been using. Instead of joining with the others in putting away the blocks, the child regularly, for several mornings, left the room to go to the lavatory just at the crucial moment. As soon as she noticed the formation of this pattern, the teacher mentioned the matter to the youngster just as she was about to leave. The child insisted that it was necessary for her to leave the room. The teacher insisted that she wait to help in putting away the blocks. The child complied. An hour later she had made no effort to leave the classroom. The teacher then took occasion to inquire if she was not going to the lavatory. The child replied that she had no need to go, and from then on every day she coöperated with the other children in the usual fashion.

On another occasion a fifth grade teacher, entering her classroom in the evening prior to going home, saw the exercises of three children, which had been caught in a gust of wind from the window, lying on the floor. Picking them up, she discovered they were sheets of home work which had been prepared by the children before leaving school but had not been carefully put out of harm's way. Tearing the papers in two, the teacher threw them in the waste basket. In the morning the teacher called for the home work, but that of Fred and Francis was missing. Marjorie had come early, and finding her work lost, had done it over again. The children reported that they had done the work and left it "neatly under a book," anticipating by their excuse the criticism which they expected from this careful teacher for their carelessness. "Oh, no, you didn't," replied the teacher, "because I found that it had blown to the floor, so I tore it up and threw it away!" Thus, in a small item of conduct the children were made to feel the natural consequences of neglecting useful papers. Let those who feel that this is a trifling matter consider in their own case whether or not such a habit might have prevented losses they could ill afford to make. In at least one case, a university student who had completed the research for his doctor's degree lost his briefcase containing the records of years of work.

It is by painstaking attention to such details that teachers may build up in their pupils desirable attitudes. In all such matters of school housekeeping, intelligent and rational conduct should be the order of the day. What a relief it is to any teacher when the children in her class look after themselves.

MODIFYING CIRCUMSTANCES

It may be well to point out just here that while teachers naturally prefer to carry on the work of their class in accordance with the second theory just discussed, such a plan of operation may not always seem wise or feasible. This may be so for many reasons. It may be that the children under her charge have not been accustomed, in previous classes, to the type of control of which the teacher approves. Children with a background of several years of routinized school life cannot readily change. Without the foundation in training in responsibility which should be obtained in the earliest grades, it is almost impossible for children of more mature years to carry on a program of responsible group living. Again, with classes larger than thirty, a teacher cannot expect to carry on entirely by natural group methods. With larger classes the problems of group conduct become so complex that routine becomes necessary. Nor should teachers who find themselves in situations where ideal methods may not apply, have any hesitation in calling upon artificial devices in dealing with material conditions beyond their control. On the other hand, teachers in situations which demand the routinizing of class activities should consult standard works on class management, where they will find full and adequate treatment of methods of procedure which suit their own conditions.[4] The understanding of ideal conditions need be no hindrance to teachers in adapting themselves to less ideal circumstances. Teachers should never desert common sense or attempt to substitute a hypothetical for a real situation.

Dismissal

A signal may be given for dismissal, but it is really not necessary if there be a clock in the classroom. For dismissal may be as informal as the opening of school. Sometimes when children are busy at various activities, they will not notice the time for dismissal, and the teacher may need to tell them that it is time to leave when the room has been cleared. In such cases, when a good deal of construction has been going on, it may be well for the teacher to assign certain bits of tidying for certain children to attend to. "Jean and Mary look after the theater; you boys put away your painting and Dorothy clear off the table." But the children are in no hurry to leave. Several of them keep working at their exercises. John continues painting a bit of scenery at which he is working on the floor. There is no rushing about. The children quietly put things in their places, while the teacher helps them to see anything they have overlooked. The tables and chairs are straightened in line. There is considerable free moving about; one boy is softly whistling, perhaps, and some of the children may be talking, but too gently to disturb several others finishing up the poems they are writing. The children leave unobtrusively but usually with a smile or a good-by for the teacher.[5]

[4] BAGLEY, W. C., "Classroom Management," The Macmillan Co., New York, 1922.
HOLLEY, C. E., "The Teacher's Technique," The Century Co., New York, 1922.
KLAPPER, PAUL, "Contemporary Education," D. Appleton & Co., New York, 1929.
STRAYER, G. D., "A Brief Course in the Teaching Process," The Macmillan Co., New York, 1922.

[5] As sections of the writer's manuscript on *Starting the School Day* and *Dismissal* have been criticized as unduly Utopian, he wishes to note that after careful observation and consideration, he is convinced that these accounts are but descriptions of what may be seen any day in numbers of modern schools. The description in the last paragraph is a literal account of a dismissal of a class in the Bronxville Public Schools.

Part IV

TECHNIQUES FOR DIRECTING LEARNING

CHAPTER XIX

TECHNIQUES FOR DIRECTING LEARNING

Lesson Plans and Records

Just as with all other intelligent procedures, the work of the class must be carefully planned. Part of this planning may be done by the children with the help of the teacher, but a great deal of it must be done by the teacher herself, not only in class, as the rise of new situations demands their immediate consideration, but out of class, in moments of calm and careful thinking. It may be true that a teacher will be unable to forecast, in a complex class situation, just exactly what will happen. Nevertheless, by a keen summing up of the situation as it actually exists in the concrete, and by a clear listing of her objectives, the teacher may make a sharp forecast of much that is likely to occur. Knowing just where the individuals in the class have come from, and the goals toward which she hopes to guide them, the teacher may estimate with a fair degree of accuracy what is just ahead in the life of the class.

There can be no specific directions given the teacher as to how this planning must be done. Notes may be kept in a notebook or on filing cards, in whatever form the teacher finds most convenient. Each teacher must find out for herself the form in which she prefers to write out such plans. She may write down notations of materials, references, objectives, individual problems to be attended to, points to be taken up with the class, appointments and engagements which affect the group, lists of gains or of progress hoped for in certain periods. Dozens of easily forgotten details may be recorded, as well as general sketches of activities extending for some time ahead.

An additional advantage of such plans is that they may also, by a system of checking and annotation, be used as records. So complex does the life of the class become that a system of records is necessary if the teacher is to keep track of what each individual has accomplished, and of the work of the whole group. Here again each teacher must find her own individual solution concerning the method and form which is most suitable. These will depend to a large extent upon the purpose for which the records are designed. They will be of frequent service in the discussion of class work with parents, colleagues, and supervisors in teachers' meetings, and in the writing of reports or accounts of what goes on in the class. In fact, it is characteristic of the new teaching that its records are more detailed, more thorough and more complete than its plans.

The Introduction of an Activity in the Class

The problem of introducing an activity in the class is the problem of getting things started. This might, perhaps, be more accurately stated as the problem of keeping things from getting stopped. It is not wise to attempt to reduce children to a standstill, wind them like clockwork toys with "motivation," and then start them up again. The technique of beginning things is largely that of waiting and watching, while children initiate activities themselves in an environment which has been carefully set. Activities find their origin in the children's present and past experience. The teacher's function is to provide suitable materials and watch the growth and development of activities. There is a sense in which what the children do in the beginning is a matter of comparative indifference to the good teacher. She picks them up while they are under momentum and guides their movements until they are doing something useful and worth while.

Teachers are not always in agreement concerning the proper technique to use in the introduction of new materials, such as crayons or clay. There are those who profess to believe in a thoroughgoing, hands-off policy. Such teachers claim that in introducing such things as construction materials and play apparatus, it is best to allow children to freely explore and experiment. Thus they may find out, by trial and error, the nature of the materials and the laws which govern their adaptation and use. It is intended to allow children the maximum of free expression and to permit them to gain the fullest experience from the activities they engage in.

But comparatively few teachers advocate such a full reliance upon a trial and error procedure. It may be possible, when first introducing such material as clay, to give the children complete freedom of manipulation and exploration. Most teachers agree that it is best to give some explanation and instruction before letting children use comparatively costly materials. Surely it is better to teach children, in the very beginning, that their brushes should be washed before dipping them in a fresh water color, rather than to allow them to ruin jars

TECHNIQUES FOR DIRECTING LEARNING

of color by indiscriminate use. In a similar way, careless destruction of paper, wood, materials and tools used in various types of construction may be avoided by the provision of instruction previous to their use.

It is no adherence to the extreme theory that nature is right which causes the teacher to allow children the maximum sensible amount of freedom in the introduction of activities. Rather, she follows such a plan because the procedure is valuable. It is valuable because in the course of their actions children will reveal sound beginning points which may serve for the development of desirable units of conduct, which the teacher has planned for, or possibly those which she has not foreseen but which are obviously acceptable and desirable. Thus, simple, aimless block building may lead into the development of complex and thoughtful organization of materials, into the study of local geography and the general broadening of the child's interests. Accidental chatter may lead to the development of new language abilities and to sensible group coöperation which may be built on in many and various directions. In the beginning the teacher is seeking for what Klapper calls the "point of contact between the child and the curriculum." When this has been discovered the teacher has found the key which will enable her to proceed in the development of satisfactory lessons.

Distinction may be usefully made, perhaps, between activities initiated by individuals, such as the making of a toy garage or of a dress, and those assumed by the group, such as the holding of an exhibit or the presentation of an assembly program. The latter are the more complex and intricate, the more difficult to plan and to develop soundly. Their initiation is usually from the general life of the class or of the school, and must be attended with considerable class discussion. This discussion is necessary to enable the teacher and the pupils to understand the degree to which an activity is really satisfactory, and to ensure the launching of the program in a fashion which will secure its complete and well-rounded development.

Such a class discussion is particularly necessary if the teacher should find that the class, instead of developing along the lines of some unit of conduct which she has tentatively planned and arranged for, unexpectedly rejects that line of conduct in favor of another which promises to be equally satisfactory. On one occasion a teacher,[1] who started the school year with a carefully set stage, expected oral

[1] See "Curriculum Making in an Elementary School," The Lincoln School Staff, Ginn & Co., New York, 1927, p. 47.

expression and activities to develop out of reading charts and pictures which she had provided, and from the children's relation of their summer experiences. But the children did not take to this form of expression. They seemed restless and those who were reading books soon abandoned them for such activities as making boats, trucks and wagons, painting pictures and playing with blocks and farm animals. The teacher soon realized that the children had no immediate interest in their holiday experiences, but were interested in the here and now. Consequently she surrendered her carefully made plans and faced the task of building lessons not on past experiences, but from present ones which were developing before her eyes. The charts and bulletins she had prepared were useless, but out of their current actions the children helped her to make new sentences for the blackboard and for the bulletins which brought their own reward in vital and meaningful lessons. In beginning activities children must draw from their own significant experiences, past or present.

Activities initiated by single individuals usually have their origin from some specific need, such as the need for a book rack or for a pencil tray to give to a friend, a need which the circumstances of the school environment or his out-of-school life has led the pupil to feel. Such needs are often proposed by the pupil or adopted by the pupil at the teacher's suggestion during the morning conference or in private discussion with the teacher. It is for the teacher to help the child estimate their worth and practicability, and to evaluate them in the light of existing circumstances. If they are suitable, they may be agreed upon and may then be undertaken by the pupil concerned.

THE GOVERNING OF ACTIVITIES

It would be impossible to give any general rule or any brief account which would be adequate for the governing of class activities after they have been initiated. They are so numerous and so varied that no single set procedure can be followed in their development. The whole problem of the governing of activities depends upon one fundamental principle, namely, that the growth of any specific unit of conduct is dependent upon its own inherent nature. In life itself a similar type of procedure is followed. Day by day in going about our work and play we pursue a technique which is, as much as possible, in accordance with the nature of the activity we are pursuing. We evolve a method of doing things which is in accordance with the nature of the situation in which we are involved. The arrangements we make are governed by a process of adapting available resources to the attaining of desired ends. So it should be in school. The particular procedure which is used in the development of any certain unit of conduct must be the result of the intelligent use of the class resources to achieve the desired results.

The Provision of Oral Instruction

The provision of oral instruction as a method of teaching is delightfully satirized in Pagnol's drama, "Topaze." The first act portrays a class in moral philosophy (!) in session. While the youngsters at their barren desks indulge in various forms of disorder such as head slapping, pea shooting, and the playing of popular airs on a fine tooth comb, the teacher sits on his stool behind the desk and recounts egregiously pious examples of hypothetical conduct. Schools of past generations have only too significantly laid themselves open to such ridicule by a limited notion of school life which regarded listening as the most important activity of children in the classroom, the complementary activity of the teacher being that of providing oral instruction.

This conception of the school activity of children as being chiefly listening and occasionally participating by answering of questions pertinent to the teacher's organization of the lesson, has had an enormous influence upon discussions of teaching procedures. Listening is an activity which is comparatively passive. The listener exerts no control over the form his conduct takes in listening. He contributes nothing to the organization of the elements of the situation. He only demands that the lesson which is being taught him be presented by the teacher with the maximum of clarity and effectiveness. He exerts no positive control over the activity in which he is engaged, but allows the teacher full freedom of organization and presentation. Thus it is that teachers have considered themselves free in the provision of oral instruction to base the organization of the lesson on the nature or structure of the subject matter which they desired to teach. This notion of teaching as being largely a matter of providing oral instruction to sitting children has produced numerous accounts of typical methods of organizing subject matter according to its structure and of various so-called "types of teaching."

It would be folly to pretend that the work of the newer class should proceed without a certain amount of listening by the pupils and provision of oral instruction by the teacher. However, in the modern classroom this form of activity is only one of many. It seldom proceeds for long periods and is usually provided for small groups who happen to be engaged upon some common concern, such as a typical difficulty in arithmetic.

Since this type of work does go on, however, it will be all to the good if teachers in the newer schools understand with thoroughness the various types of teaching which have been based on the structure of subject matter and its satisfactory organization for oral presentation. The teachers in the newer schools have nothing to fear and much to gain from a careful study of the current discussions of the structure of subject matter and of teaching types which are to be found in standard textbooks on teaching. Once they are clear on the narrow application of such studies to modern class life, and the limited situations in which they find valid use, they need not hesitate to add them to their total teaching resources. As children grow older, and make increasing use of symbols in learning, their needs for oral instruction increase. It consequently behooves teachers, especially those of older children, to be familiar with the standard types of teaching.

It will not be necessary to duplicate the work of very competent writers who have discussed these standard teaching types. Those who wish to familiarize themselves with this material have only to consult these texts for full discussions.[2] In them may be found presentations of the Herbartian Five Steps, the Inductive Lesson, the Deductive Lesson, the Recitation Lesson, the Drill Lesson, the Review Lesson, and the Lesson in Appreciation. Certain recent writers, notably Burton and Klapper, have broadened and modified the narrower interpretation of the older types of teaching and have given a re-interpretation of them which is more in accordance with newer school procedure, adding to them other types such as those which they call the problem and the project. This modification indicates a movement in the direction of the point of view set forth here, but is, nevertheless, an interpretation

[2] BAGLEY, W. C., "The Educative Process," The Macmillan Co., New York, 1905, Chs. XIX and XX.
BARR and BURTON, "Supervision of Instruction," D. Appleton & Co., New York, 1926.
BURTON, W. H., "The Nature and Direction of Learning," D. Appleton & Co., New York, 1929.
EARHART, L. B., "Types of Teaching," Houghton Mifflin Co., Boston, 1915, Chs. V and VI.
KLAPPER, PAUL, "Contemporary Education," D. Appleton & Co., New York, 1929, Chs. 24-26.
STRAYER, G. D., "A Brief Course in the Teaching Process," The Macmillan Co., New York, 1922.

which is still to a certain extent dominated by a point of view which regards teaching as very largely a matter of oral direction and instruction.

THE PROVISION OF PRINTED INSTRUCTION

Another form of teaching which is, in its genesis, closely associated with the theory that teaching should be carried on in accordance with the structure of the subject matter, is the provision of printed instructions. In this case, however, the procedure, as a general method, rests on much firmer psychological grounds than in the case of the provision of oral instruction. In spite of the fact that the printed instruction materials may be organized in terms of the subject matter which is being presented, such organization need not necessarily be out of relation to the organization which is signified by the type of conduct involved in this form of learning activity. The use of these passive printed materials may be fitted into the total life situation of the school in whatever fashion seems convenient. Furthermore, the nature of the process known as *study* is a very active one, which may take over the comparatively passive materials of the printed instructions and deal with them in terms of the learner's needs and energies. Consequently, in the use of such instructions, the learner may carry on his learning under conditions which are, to a large extent, psychologically sound, inasmuch as they provide for a full amount of initiative and self-activity.

It is important, however, that printed instruction materials should be judiciously used if they are to serve a purpose which is in accordance with the nature of the type of activity for which they are adapted, namely, study. Considerable misuse has frequently been made of printed instruction materials as they occur in textbooks. It has happened only too often that teachers have assigned the larger part of the materials presented in the textbooks, whether in history, arithmetic, geography or any other subject for home "study," thus expecting the children to learn the materials out of school rather than in school under conditions which could not but be unfavorable for study. After various fragmentary attempts at learning, into which hapless parents were often called to give mistaken aid, the children were expected to "recite" what they had learned to the teacher on the following day. Thus arose that unfortunate term, "the recitation," a term which has given countenance to such inane procedures as "quizzing" and "hearing the lesson," forms of cross-examination which suggest the chicanery of poor lawyers rather than the skill of good teachers. So low have some teachers descended in the scale of good sportsmanship that they have even been known to preside over a class of children, record book in hand, stooping to the tyranny of zero.

When printed instruction materials are provided they may generally, especially with younger children, be used best in school hours. It is for this reason that good schools assign the minimum of home work, a device which has disappeared almost entirely in the lower school grades of the present day. In school the proper conditions may be provided for study, and learning may go on for its own sake rather than to mollify a persecuting teacher.

Modern schools have worked out various schemes and plans for the use of specific instructions for study and of printed instruction materials. Among these plans may be mentioned the assignment, contracts, supervised study, the laboratory plan, the mastery technique, and the use of individual instruction materials. Each of these will now be taken up in order and related to the present discussion.

The Assignment

The term "assignment" is somewhat colored by the point of view which regards the teacher as the initiator and governor of the child's learning process. Inasmuch as there are undoubtedly occasions even in the most modern schools when this situation exists, in spite of extremist pretense to the contrary, the term "assignment" may be allowed. There are times when the child expects and desires assignments from the teacher. Such situations might arise during the progress of individual work in arithmetic or even history. The acceptance of such an assignment by the pupil as his own task is as important as the giving of it by the teacher. It partakes less of the nature of a rigid requirement which must be fulfilled by a certain time, and more of a task voluntarily assumed for completion as soon as possible. Its validity lies in the child's desire for mastery, not in the teacher's intention to compel it. Such assignments may often be made in private conference with the teacher. Sometimes an assignment may be made to a group. In such cases all the care which standard discussions of the assignment have urged should be used in the process. The assigning of a piece of work should assume its full dignity as a form of class procedure, and should not be pushed into a corner or squeezed into a snatched moment of time. When teachers are called on to make assignments they should realize that in doing so they are acting as guides to a considerable expenditure of pupil energy. Three minutes saved by the giving of a brief assignment may mean hours of misdirected pupil effort, while ten minutes spent on discussing and clarifying the assignment may ultimately save great quantities of pupil energy.

This is equally true in cases where the assignment is not given by the teacher but is handed over by the class to some individual or individuals. In studying the Russian Revolution, or the local water system, the class often divides the responsibility and apportions certain parts of it to individuals in the form of an assignment. These assignments made by the group to individuals need the most careful group discussion and planning. Their fulfillment develops a sense of responsibility to the group for tasks assumed for the general good.

The Contract

The "contract" is a term very similar to the term "assignment," but it is intended to emphasize the obverse side of the situation, namely, the pupil's assumption of the task involved as his own personal task. It emphasizes the pupil's acceptance of responsibility for the completion of the amount of history, or spelling or geography indicated in the contract within a reasonable given time. The term further connotes the possibility that the contract assumed by any individual may be for a special piece of work which is significant to him, or a special piece of work which he has assumed as a responsibility to the group. It is thus apparent that the word "contract" is but a variant of the word "assignment," and the assuming of contracts may go on much as the making of assignments previously described.

Supervised Study

Supervised study is a form of activity in which the pupil follows the directions which he has accepted in his assignment or contract, usually making use of printed instruction materials of one form or another. This form of activity during school hours is admirably suited to the nature of the learning process. Children, especially in the upper grades, may profitably spend a portion of their school time in supervised study of skills in reading and writing and in the mastery of organized subject matter. The reader is referred to the excellent discussion of Klapper and Burton which need not be repeated here.

The Laboratory Plan

Due to a deep realization of the fact that learning goes on best when children assume the full burden of it, Miss Helen Parkhurst, some years ago, devised a plan which she hoped would facilitate such a state of affairs. This plan, which Miss Parkhurst likes to call the laboratory plan, is to a certain extent indicated by its name. Its essential characteristic is that according to the arrangements which it makes, certain rooms of the school are set apart as laboratories for the carrying on of certain types of activities. Thus, there may be found in the magnificent building which houses the Dalton School in New York, various rooms set apart for painting, construction work, science, arithmetic, French, English, geography and so forth, each of which is under the care of a teacher who is a specialist in the particular work of that laboratory.

There has come into being, wherever the laboratory plan has been worked out in numerous schools, a scheme for the direction of the work of the children above the third grade by means of printed or mimeographed instructions which is not essential to the plan but which seems always to be associated with it. These mimeographed instructions, which are changed from term to term as the situation demands, are devised to assist the children in carrying on their activities during a part of the school day, from 9:35 in the morning to 12:15. These instructions or directions are termed contracts and a contract is given to each child in a Manila folder with a blank record card as soon as he has completed his previous contract. Each child is thus able to proceed at his own rate of speed, assuming a new contract as soon as he has completed the old one.

As the child pursues the study of his contracts or assignments he is free to budget his time in his own way, moving about the school from laboratory to laboratory and staying in each as long as he considers it wise. The work of one contract is normally expected to take four weeks of five days each. Each contract is similarly divided into four parts corresponding roughly to weeks and five units corresponding roughly to days. As the individual completes his units of work in each subject, he enters his line of accomplishment on his own record card.

It is characteristic of the plan that the pupil may work out the units in any order he wishes, spending the time in the appropriate laboratory. It is to be observed, however, that when all the units of a contract in a given subject, say mathematics, are completed, the child must pause to complete the other subjects on his contract before he may secure a new contract. It is not possible, as in the individual instruction plan used at Winnetka, to make progress in one subject without making corresponding progress in the others. It is thus that the laboratory plan makes use of printed instructions in directing learning.

The Mastery Technique

Morrison has pointed out that in the acquiring of skills such as those involved in the study of organized subject matter learning is unitary.[3] That is to say, with respect to such a unit, a pupil either has or has not learned that unit. For example, a boy may or may not be able to spell the word "receive." There is no half way measure. He either knows how to spell it or he does not know how to spell it. There are units of learning in the mastery of skills which are not divisible. To Morrison, in such cases, mastery means completeness. A unit either has or has not been learned by a pupil. If he has learned it he has mastered it and can perform the operation involved perfectly. Consequently, it is necessary for a pupil learning such a complex skill as multiplication to proceed step by step, attaining perfect mastery as he goes. Only so may the complex skills be properly learned. This point of view has resulted in a technique of teaching applicable to the mastery of complex integrated skills which is known as the mastery technique. According to this technique a pupil drills himself on a unit of learning and only passes on to the next when his mastery of the units has been tested and found perfect.

The application of this plan of mastery to the development of assignments and to the working out of printed instruction materials has contributed greatly to the improvement of learning in the field of integrated skills. Morrison's plan has much to contribute to the guidance of activities which demand complete mastery of easily distinguishable units of learning.

The Individual Technique as Worked Out at Winnetka

A very skillful plan for the use of printed instruction materials has been worked out as a subsidiary part of the full activity program

[3] MORRISON, H. C., "The Practice of Teaching in the Secondary School," University of Chicago Press, 1926.

of the Winnetka Public Schools under the direction of Washburne. These individual instruction materials [4] combine in the most skillful fashion the values of printed instruction material, individual drill material, step by step mastery of units, diagnostic testing and provision for individual progress. The materials individualized are just those which are most suitable for such treatment, namely, the commonly needed knowledges and skills such as those involved in number, spelling, reading, writing, and punctuation. It is important to realize that the other activities of the Winnetka program are numerous and varied, the whole program being carried out in thoroughgoing fashion in terms of conduct. The work of the school is so arranged that in a typical class program about half of each morning and half of each afternoon are devoted to the individualized activities while the remainder of the day is taken up with a rich program of activities including discussion, group meetings, field trips, construction and play making.

In preparing the work to be mastered by the pupils the makers of the curriculum began with very definite and specific goals, such as ability to express fractions as per cent, and ability to change decimals to per cent. Special instruction material was then written to enable students by regular study to reach the goals set before them. The practice material in each subject is given the pupil by the teacher and worked out in the home or classroom, not in various subject-matter laboratories as in the Dalton plan. Children may work through their materials as fast as they are able and receive promotion by grades, but not by classrooms, as they proceed. It sometimes happens, therefore, that a child while remaining in the same classroom group may, nevertheless, be of higher or lower standard than his group in terms of attainment in certain school subjects. The following quotations will be of interest as examples of the type of printed instructions and practice materials given to the pupils.

To the Pupil [5]

You can teach yourself with this book. You can correct all your own work. You can test yourself. When you make mistakes in your tests, you can tell just what kind of practice you need.

[4] For a full catalog and price list of these materials teachers may write the Winnetka Individual Materials, Inc., Horace Mann School, Winnetka, Ill.

[5] This material was selected and sent the writer by Dr. Washburne. It is quoted from the Washburne Individual Arithmetics, World Book Co., Yonkers-on-the-Hudson, N. Y., 1929.

TECHNIQUES FOR DIRECTING LEARNING

The work is divided into steps. Each step has just one new thing to learn. At the beginning of each step there is an explanation. Always read this carefully. Have your pencil in your hand and work each part of the examples that are worked for you in the explanation. Be sure you understand what you are doing—you can if you read carefully and do the work.

Then do all the examples under the letter **A**. *Work neatly*—untidy work causes mistakes. When you have finished the **A** examples, turn to the answer page. See whether you have made any mistakes. If every one of your answers is right, you may skip the examples marked **B** and **C** and **D** and go right on to the next step. But if you have made even one mistake in **A**, go back and work the wrong example over to see where you made your mistake. Try to correct it yourself. If you have trouble, go back to the explanation and see if you can find out what you have done wrong. Then do all of **B**. Again turn to the answer page and correct your work. If you have made no mistakes this time, skip **C** and **D** and go right on to the next step. Do **C** if you have made any mistakes in **B**. If you still make mistakes in **C**, ask your teacher for help before you try **D**.

Ask your teacher or another child for help only if you cannot possibly master a step without help. But it is much better to get help than to go on to the next step without thoroughly understanding the step you are doing.

If you *master* each step, the next will not be hard. When you come to tests, you will be able to do them with very little trouble. You will be able to use your arithmetic in solving real problems.

Before beginning this book you have learned the meaning of fractions from Book Eight. If you thoroughly understand the meaning of fractions, you will be able to understand this book.

Step 1

For a long time you have known what $\frac{1}{2}$ means. You also know what $\frac{1}{4}, \frac{1}{3}, \frac{5}{8}, \frac{3}{4}$, and other fractions mean. You know that fractions are made of two numbers—one above the line and one below the line. Each of these numbers has a name: the one above the line is called the *numerator* (nu'mer-a-tor); the one below is called the *denominator* (de-nom'i-na-tor).

$$\frac{2}{3} \begin{array}{l} \leftarrow \text{numerator} \\ \leftarrow \text{denominator} \end{array}$$

In the fraction $\frac{5}{8}$ the numerator is 5 and the denominator is 8.

$$\frac{5}{8} \begin{matrix} \leftarrow \text{numerator} \\ \leftarrow \text{denominator} \end{matrix}$$

A

Copy the following fractions on your scratch paper. Write "numerator" after each numerator and "denominator" after each denominator, like this: 1 *numerator*
(Watch your spelling.)   6 *denominator*

If you make no mistakes in the part marked **A**, you need not work the part marked **B**.

(1) $\frac{1}{2}$ (2) $\frac{1}{3}$ (3) $\frac{3}{8}$ (4) $\frac{7}{12}$ (5) $\frac{3}{4}$ (6) $\frac{5}{8}$

Make fractions as follows:

numerator 7; denominator 8 (Answer: $\frac{7}{8}$)
denominator 6; numerator 5 (Answer: $\frac{5}{6}$)

(7) numerator 1; denominator 12
(8) numerator 3; denominator 8
(9) denominator 3; numerator 1
(10) numerator 2; denominator 3
(11) denominator 5; numerator 4
(12) denominator 8; numerator 7
(13) denominator 10; numerator 3
(14) numerator 5; denominator 12

B

Do the same with these fractions as you did under **A**. (You must work **B** only if you made mistakes in **A**.)

(1) $\frac{5}{12}$ (2) $\frac{3}{10}$ (3) $\frac{1}{2}$ (4) $\frac{2}{3}$ (5) $\frac{1}{6}$ (6) $\frac{4}{5}$

Make fractions as follows:

(7) denominator 2; numerator 1
(8) numerator 9; denominator 10
(9) numerator 1; denominator 12
(10) denominator 8; numerator 5
(11) numerator 3; denominator 4

For answers see page 7.

TECHNIQUES FOR DIRECTING LEARNING

C

Work **C** if you made any mistakes in **B**.

(1) $\frac{1}{10}$ (2) $\frac{5}{12}$ (3) $\frac{7}{8}$ (4) $\frac{3}{5}$ (5) $\frac{4}{5}$ (6) $\frac{5}{8}$

Make fractions as follows:

(7) numerator 5; denominator 8
(8) denominator 5; numerator 3
(9) denominator 3; numerator 1
(10) numerator 9; denominator 12
(11) denominator 10; numerator 7

If you made no mistakes in **C**, you need not work **D**.

D

D is only for children who made mistakes in **C**.

(1) $\frac{11}{22}$ (2) $\frac{7}{10}$ (3) $\frac{3}{8}$ (4) $\frac{5}{6}$ (5) $\frac{3}{4}$ (6) $\frac{1}{5}$

Make fractions as follows:

(7) numerator 1; denominator 3
(8) denominator 4; numerator 3
(9) numerator 2; denominator 5
(10) denominator 6; numerator 5
(11) numerator 3; denominator 10

For answers see page 7.

The instruction materials now proceed to present "Step 2" and so on.

As he proceeds at his own rate through the materials of the unit on which he is working the pupil is free to call upon the teacher for assistance whenever it is necessary. When it is completed the pupil's work is tested by special diagnostic tests prepared by the teacher, and a record is kept of his attainment. This account is kept on a special record card, not in mere terms of marks or grades, but in terms of goals which have been reached. Each goal checked on the record card by the teacher is an evidence of some definite thing mastered. These record cards are kept in order by the teacher, and taken home by the pupil as report cards at the end of every six weeks. Thus the pupils are able to show at home a record of definite achievement and to demonstrate to their parents what they can themselves recognize as very definite and unmistakable growth. By a skillful technique of coördination the teachers relate this work with individual instruction materials to the remainder of the school life and maintain, as much as possible, the correlation and interrelation of all the activities of the whole school. Thus by the use of printed instructions a technique is maintained for the mastery of fundamental skills which, while it may not be the only successful scheme, is certainly an excellent one.

ADDITIONAL NOTES ON THE DALTON PLAN AND THE WINNETKA PLAN

For fear that the presentation which has just been made of one narrow aspect of the Dalton Plan and the Winnetka Plan may be misinterpreted, it may be well to make some further reference to them at this point. The discussion which has just been given of the laboratory plan and the individual instruction technique has dealt with what is merely one part of the total life of these schools. It has been given here merely in its relation to the general topic of the provision of printed instruction as an aid to learning. There seems to be a misconception abroad that these narrow aspects of the schools under discussion are the outstanding and distinguishing characteristics of these schools. This is not so. Miss Parkhurst herself in conversation with me laid emphasis upon the fact that the Dalton School is not a scheme for school administration, but rather a school which is committed to the carrying out of a full modern program of education. One has only to visit this school to see the truth of this statement. The nursery school and the lower grades of the elementary school carry on a modern program which is similar to that which may be seen in progressive schools in different parts of the country. It may also be observed from a study of the contracts given the children that completion of them demands not merely book study, but the carrying out of numerous activities. Provision is also made for coöperative activities such as those worked out in the assemblies, but time is also devoted at the conclusion of the laboratory period to class conferences, and opportunity provided for development of activities during the afternoons. It is to be questioned whether or not in its present form the Dalton Plan, with its long laboratory periods and its specialized laboratories, is the most flexible or adaptable mold for the work of the elementary school. It may be that such an organization is more suitable for the work of the junior high and high schools. It should be realized, however, that the general flexibility of the Dalton Plan would not preclude such a modification in the elementary school should any set of prevailing circumstances seem to make it advisable. Those who learn from it should do so judiciously, not merely taking over in imitative fashion its scheme of administration, but adopting its progressive spirit and only as much of its form of administration as seems advisable.

The Winnetka Plan has been similarly misunderstood in terms of certain of its more superficial characteristics.[6] It is not to be confused with its own plan of providing self-instruction materials. These materials are used because it is believed that they provide the most economical method for providing children in a public school group with the mastery of the commonly needed skills. Thus economical teaching of the skills frees the maximum amount of time for the development of those more enriching activities which go to make up a well-rounded life. Those who have the opportunity to visit Winnetka will come away with the feeling that, with its active and varied air of earnest learning, Winnetka is an oasis in our desert of public education. Others who are less fortunate will find it most informing to read some good brief account of the school.[7]

[6] In a letter to the writer, Dr. Washburne says:
"If you are writing on any other phases of the Individual Technique than this one matter of self-instructive material, I hope you will make note of the fact that one of the basic purposes of individualization at Winnetka, at least, is to clear room for group and creative activities. . . . I very much dislike the tendency of many authors of educational textbooks to refer to the Winnetka work as if it were exclusively a matter of a mechanical arrangement of text material to provide for individual progress."

[7] See DR. WASHBURNE's descriptive article in *School and Society*, Vol. XXIX, No. 733, January 12, 1929.

CHAPTER XX

FURTHER TECHNIQUES FOR DIRECTING LEARNING

The Conference

The conference has a most important and basic function in the progress of class activities. It is, however, neither necessary nor desirable to hold any fixed notion of what a conference should be. It is merely what the word itself signifies, a conferring, which is held between two or more individuals. Its purpose is merely that the two or more persons who confer may work in harmony and coöperation.

Often the class finds it convenient to hold a more or less regular conference at the beginning of the school day, or at the beginning of a period of diverse activities. At this conference general plans for the day are discussed. Trips which are to be made, work to be done on the school paper, anything of common interest may be referred to. But the conference may not be of the full group. In fact, one unconcerned member is a definite drag on any conference. Those who have no purpose for being present should not waste time but should spend it on some other activity. While individuals not concerned are busy on their personal tasks, small groups or committees may meet, with or without the teacher, as the circumstances demand. Individual pupils may confer together or with the teacher. Nor need these conferences be held at any set time. At any time during the progress of activities when it seems convenient any of the types of conference referred to may be arranged. The basic principle of the conference is that individuals may plan together and pupils may have moments of special personal discussion and guidance with the teacher.

The Coördination of Diverse Simultaneous Activities

It is sometimes puzzling to visitors of the new schools to find different children engaged at the same time in many varying activities. One child may be hoisting the carriage of an improvised elevator while another is painting or sawing a pine board. But it is not to be supposed that such a series of activities goes on independent of the

FURTHER TECHNIQUES FOR DIRECTING LEARNING 241

teacher. She is the coördinator of them, and such a schoolroom may only be conducted by a teacher skilled in the technique of teaching. The teacher, who appears to be paying no attention to what is going on, is really paying the most careful attention. She knows very clearly what each of the children is doing. Work is neither begun nor carried on independent of her guidance or direction. If the children are carrying on individual activities they have been arranged for with the teacher in some period of conference. In the conference the teacher and the child came to some agreement as to the unit of conduct for which the child wished to assume responsibility. The teacher made mental or written note of this fact, and consequently knows just what to expect of that individual child. Nor will it be necessary, and children will soon learn this, for a child to keep running to the teacher for directions, since in assuming his piece of work the child should plan it as carefully as possible, getting the teacher's advice and assistance so that reference to her during its progress will be as infrequent as possible.

If the work upon which the child is engaged is not an individual thing, but is part of a whole group activity such as the making and painting of a window to be used as part of the scenery of a class play, the case is similar. The child knows from class discussion and planning the whole of the activity of which this is part; he knows also with whom he should coöperate and confer with respect to it. The teacher, on the other hand, sees the activity as a whole, arranges with the children in conference for a wise and equitable division of labor among the children, and is perfectly clear at any given time as to the part of the whole upon which any particular child or group of children is engaged.

Some teachers find it convenient to carry on diverse activities in a double classroom which is connected by a small anteroom. In one room are carried on such noisy activities as hammering and sawing. In the other, at the far end, are study tables. Teachers who arrange things in this fashion feel that children engaged in original and intellectual work should be alone as much as possible, that quiet is conducive to dignified reflection and self-expression. Such an arrangement of rooms is helpful in the administering of activities of varying types proceeding at the same time. The teacher remaining in or near the anteroom for part of the time may keep an eye on both groups and be close by when assistance must be given. At the same time she may carry on more intimate lessons with a small group of five or six. The pupils who are doing individual work learn to do without the teacher's assistance as much as possible when she is so engaged with a group. They defer their questions and do their best not to interrupt unless it is really necessary.

It should be clear that although the teacher, at any given time, is aware of what each child is doing, she does not attempt to control or administer it in detail. When the child assumes any unit of conduct the teacher hands over to the child as much of the full responsibility as he is able to bear. To visitors who do not understand this, the teacher may appear overbusy. She is not, however, bearing the whole burden of all the activity in progress. Each unit of conduct has a self-supporting center in the personality of the child who is carrying it on. Part of the burden of the activity is being carried by the child. The result is that diverse activities go on smoothly and regularly with the minimum of supervision on the part of the teacher. By careful planning and by keeping accurate mental and written records, the teacher may coördinate the most varied activities.

DIRECTIVE CONVERSATION TECHNIQUE

One of the teacher's most important resources is a good conversational technique. In all of her conversation with the group and with individual children throughout the whole school day, what the teacher says is directive in nature. When the children chatter about this or that, what they say is ordinary conversation, just talk about what they have done, are doing or intend to do. The teacher's conversation, however, is all carefully directed, and while whatever she says may appear to the child to be mere chatting such as he uses himself, it is, on the contrary, carefully worked out in such a way that it may assist and guide the learning process.

Teachers of experience and ability become very skillful in this type of guidance. Miss Jessie M. Stanton, of the Rosemary Junior School, has given the writer some excellent examples of her use of directive conversation in making the experience of small children playing with blocks a real means of growth. Children usually begin to build with blocks in their own way as soon as they have access to them. If, however, a child does not do so, the teacher may hand him some blocks, at the same time reminding him of something he has seen, saying, "You can make it." The child will then probably make some simple arrangement of blocks which may have little meaning. The teacher, however, on seeing it may exclaim, "Why, you've made it!" So by a simple remark the child's responses are encouraged.

FURTHER TECHNIQUES FOR DIRECTING LEARNING

Once an activity is started it may be carefully built upon. Suppose, for example, that a small girl building with her blocks and toys prepares a place for her little horse to sleep by putting down a pillow. In her further manipulation she proceeds to feed a bit of chocolate to her hungry charge. This is the teacher's opportunity. A few well-chosen words may accomplish a great deal. "I have a notion, Mary, that horses don't sleep on pillows, and that they don't eat chocolate. I wonder what they do eat? Don't you think we might go to a place where some horses live and see?" This remark and any discussion of it which follows may lay a basis for a new exploration of the real environment. A trip might be made to some neighboring stalls where the horse's ways of living may be observed. After such a trip the children use their new experiences and learnings in correcting their play. Thus block building and play may assume a new and growing character as the children visit various places, talk about what they have seen and make structures which are more and more elaborate and meaningful.

The teacher may, by a few words now and again, assist the children's imagination in such a way that they may extend and improve their building. This she may do by entering into that imaginative play. Observing a favorite doll left in a house forgotten by its little owner, the teacher says, "Why, Helen, you must be careful of Aunt Ethel." Again, if a child falters in his building, the teacher may ask, "Let me see; what rooms have you there? There's a bedroom; what else?" Or possibly a child pushing an automobile he has made across the floor may be devoting himself to dallying. The teacher asks, "What does your auto carry?" "Coal," is the answer. "Where does it get its coal?" and so the activity is built up and connected with the loading and transporting of materials. The teacher may ask further questions if necessary. "Wouldn't you like to make a garage?" or, in the case of a boat, "Wouldn't you like to make a dock?" So the children's experiences are led on so that they may gain a richer and more accurate realization of the environment and its relationships.

Bright children need comparatively little stimulus, but some children at times are inclined to become lazy or forgetful of their work. In such a case the teacher may say, "May I see your house?" or "Will you show me what you are doing?" This is usually enough to bring the child back to his job. Possibly, after a child has succeeded by great labor in making a boat, others who have not been working hard or helping him like to play in it. They may be asked by the teacher, "Why do you get into the boat? You didn't help to build it."

So a sense of responsibility is gradually fostered. Work becomes respected. Children learn to recognize accomplishment and to realize that it is worth while. So they learn that those who are working should not be interrupted, and the remark may sometimes be heard from the teacher or children, "Don't disturb Fred, he's working." Thus the children learn to live the life of the group amicably and helpfully.

But it is not merely in the lower grades that this form of directing activity by means of conversation is important. All through the activities of the whole school in all grades this technique is most important. In a higher grade, for instance, during the rehearsal of a play in the auditorium, as the children carry on their stage performance, the teacher may need to keep up a running comment of suggestions. "The audience is supposed to be seated now, pull the curtain." "Are you going to leave by the same entrance you came by?" "You said 'git' instead of 'get'." "Say your lines again." "You're not speaking loud enough to be heard." Thus it is obvious that the teacher needs to develop a skillful conversation technique, the habit of saying the right thing, educationally speaking, at the right time. No directions can be given the teacher for the development of such a skill. The most that can be done is to point out the need for it and provide some such examples as those which have been given. Skill will come only by careful self-training in the analysis of children's personalities and modes of reaction. It is important to realize that a great deal of excellent teaching may be done in the guise of simple remarks.

The Development of New Activities from Current Ones

There are two different points of view as to the teacher's duty in the development, from the activities upon which the class is engaged, of other activities which will ensure the logical completion during a given year of the full course of study, for example, in history or geography. How long should a group study be allowed to proceed, when should it be stopped, and how should the untouched elements of the course of study for the year be completely covered?

The first point of view can be put into practice only in a school in which the supervising authorities allow the teacher considerable freedom in the interpretation of the curriculum. Those who hold this point of view are convinced that it is not essential to give to children in the elementary school complete courses in such subjects as history or geography. They feel that the children of a given grade in the elementary school do not need a study of history which will be complete

FURTHER TECHNIQUES FOR DIRECTING LEARNING 245

in terms of subject matter, which will be sure to cover every element of a logical course of study. Rather they believe that the children should delve deeply into some period of history, such as the Colonial Period, as thoroughly, as richly and concretely, and in as much detail as the children wish. Such teachers think it better to give the children full and real experiences even if parts of the suggested curriculum are not covered. They are supported in their convictions by certain upper school teachers who maintain that they do not demand of pupils who come to them complete systematic knowledge in such subjects as history. Partial knowledge, they say, provided that it be complete and rich in the brief field covered, is even more satisfactory than hazy and mechanical knowledge of logical organized surveys. These high school teachers claim that logical, completely organized work is better treated in the upper grades. They prefer that children come to them fresh, without previous thin and poorly digested subject-matter surveys. Thus there are many who prefer for elementary school children episodic learning in such a field as history, as long as this learning is rich in terms of real experience. They have little faith in logically complete knowledge which is, nevertheless, poorly related to the children's total experience.

Others hold a very different point of view. They insist that activities should be developed in such a way that the curriculum for the year will be fully covered. In schools where this opinion is current teachers must assume the burden of completely covering the curriculum. What, then, shall such a teacher do when, toward the end of the term, parts of the work are incomplete? When, due to careful selection and planning, the children have covered the major part of the curriculum, but have left other curriculum essentials untouched? The problem may be better discussed in the concrete. Suppose, for example, that the curriculum in fifth grade geography prescribes for the term the study of the geography of North America, and that the year's work has developed so that a great deal of the geographical material has been covered by various unit studies. First a study was made of the Panama Canal, during which a model of the cut was made by the children, and the whole of its construction investigated. The study of this construction work and the source of supplies, of shipping and the routing of ships and products gave an admirable opportunity for a study of the United States via its transportation facilities. Toward the end of the year, however, it has become increasingly clear that the geography of Canada is being neglected. Here is a large section of the curriculum which has been untouched. What shall the teacher do? Shall she wait to see whether or not the children propose a study which will be concerned with Canadian geography? Or shall she let the matter go? Teachers who are in a teaching situation in which it is required of them to complete the curriculum will deliberately guide the activities of the children by suggestion and the use of materials leading to Canadian affairs. This might be done via a study of Arctic exploration, through international commercial relations in the use of the Great Lakes, through a study of the interchange of products, or via whatever plan seems nearest to the children's developing activities. While it seems unnecessary to suppose that children could not be so guided by a skillful teacher from interest in one part of America to interest in another, yet let us, for the sake of argument allow the possibility. In such a case there is no reason why a teacher should not inform the children that there is a considerable part of their work which is still undone, and suggest the study of some aspect of Canadian life. No teacher need be troubled by her educational conscience who solves a concrete difficulty in practical terms which meet the situation, rather than in theoretical ones which fail to meet it.

But no matter whether teachers approve fewer and more freely developed activities or more thorough and deliberately planned ones, the problem of concluding an activity in which the children are engaged may arise. Suppose the class has spent as much time as the teacher considers wise on a study of Viking life or of Byrd's expedition, but are now becoming still more interested than ever. What shall the teacher do? She does not wish to lose the impetus of this interest, yet she feels that it has gone far enough for present purposes. Consider another case. Suppose that some day a boy from an upper class reports to the group that he would like to give them a lecture on astronomy. The lecture is given. Great interest is aroused. For two months at various times the children carry on this interest, which continues to grow. How long shall it be permitted to go on? In all such cases the teacher must use her judgment and relate the activity to the total class situation. She must judge the developing unit of conduct in relation to the other units upon which the children are engaged, or are about to engage. She should not make the mistake of thinking that children's activity in any given direction is killed because it is discontinued in class. If the children have actually reached the stage where it has become a real interest they will transfer it to out-of-school life, and it will recur in a secondary relation to later class work. The interest in astronomy may, for example, be sublimated into another form by the initiating of an astronomy club. So a teacher must not hesitate to discontinue an activity which seems to her to have fulfilled its purpose.

Discussion

Discussion is group conversation. It is a most important part of class life, since it has a place in nearly all group activities. In fact, it is discussion which gives cohesion to group activities. It is by discussion that the work of the group is bound together and the work of one individual related to that of another. Whenever a number of individuals embark upon a common activity, the activity must be agreed upon by discussion, and its progress worked out by the same means.

But discussion under the new régime in teaching is very different from that under the formal teacher-class organization. According to the latter plan discussion tended to center about a background of subject matter which was being reviewed by the class. This might be, for example, several pages which had been assigned the day before in the history text. The teacher stood before the class asking questions for the pupils to answer. The pupil called upon was expected to answer the teacher's questions while the others were expected to listen. Under the guidance of a skillful teacher such a discussion may be kept very lively. At its best it may awaken a lively interest in the topic before the class and be carefully formulated by the teacher into an organized outcome.

In the newer classroom the discussion is somewhat different. Instead of centering itself about some section of subject matter as presented by the textbook, it tends to center about some enterprise upon which the group is about to embark, such as a trip to an observatory, some problem which has been encountered, such as the raising of a fund for poor children at Christmas, or some aspect of group conduct which cannot progress without the coöperation of the individuals concerned, such as the operating of a school store. It may very definitely deal with subject matter, as, for example, when a class, which is studying the disposal of waste in the city, discusses the relation of the house fly to the general problem; or when the group considering the problem of caring for one's clothing talks over the adequacy of a certain pupil's report on the clothes moth. In such cases, however, the subject matter is neither the end nor the origin of the discussion. On the contrary, it is contributory to the development of some unit of conduct which is in progress. Consequently, the discussion tends to become informal rather than formal, less concerned with subject matter which is not related to some present activity of the group and more concerned with the actual conduct of the children; less concerned with the teacher's questions and more concerned with the questions of the children themselves. Briefly, it is more the children's and less the teacher's discussion.

Training Children to Carry on Discussion

If fruitful and well-governed discussion is to go on in class, children must be very carefully trained to carry it on. Frankness demands the statement that I have seen more disreputable and disorderly discussions in the newer classrooms than in the older ones. Obsessed with false notions of freedom, teachers sometimes allow not merely uncontrolled procedure but actual rudeness during discussion, rudeness which would never be permitted in any well-mannered home. This seems to be one of the danger points in the new schools, where interest in current activities is at such a high pitch that the children all have something to say, and all want to speak at once. Consequently, teachers must be more than usually careful to understand the true nature of the problems of discussion, to train the children to understand them, and to abide by their restricting limitations.

Children do not, without explanation, understand how talking in a group differs from talking to an individual. They have so many questions to ask and so much to say that there is not time for all of it to be said. This and the following points should be explained to children from the very beginning, and as instances violating them arise they should be discussed. What is said in the group must be briefer, more direct, more pointed, less rambling than what is said during ordinary conversation. There must be no interruptions, no wanderings from the point, no mumbling. What is said should be spoken distinctly, and children should be definitely trained to understand that when they speak in class what they say should be directed to the whole group, not to the teacher. When this is expected of them, the other children will complain if what is spoken goes unheard, due to low-toned speaking, poor enunciation, or incoherence. In fact, the children should be one another's critics during discussion, and should be trained to observe whether or not the conditions of orderly discussion are being maintained.

The following criteria of a good discussion may be of use. In the first place, the discussion should be organized about a problem arising

FURTHER TECHNIQUES FOR DIRECTING LEARNING 249

in the course of a unit of conduct which is a concern of the group. Such a problem may be a matter of brief concern which might arise during the course of some activity such as the production of a play. During an early rehearsal of a play, the need for some new piece of property or scenery might be revealed, and the group might be called together to discuss what could be done about it and how it might be secured. In such cases the discussion would last for but a few moments. At other times, when the class is planning some elaborate study or investigation such as the making of a floor map, or considering some important topic such as proper precautions against taking cold, half an hour may be consumed in preliminary discussion and during the several succeeding periods as the work proceeds. Whatever the matter under discussion, if the problem be a real one for the group, the interest will be tense.

In the second place, a good discussion is one which is carefully guided by a teacher skilled in the technique of directing discussion and is participated in by all the children. Unless the children are active yet controlled, and the teacher active in directing with real tact, a great deal of time may be wasted. It is scarcely possible to give rigid rules for the direction of discussion. What the teacher says takes on the form of a more complex and difficult directive conversation technique. The teacher wishes to speak as little as necessary, yet there are times when one word of hers will save hundreds on the part of the children. So she must continually use her own judgment and acumen in directing the remarks and questions of the group. An intelligent teacher who lets the major burden of discussion rest on the children, carefully checking both what she herself says and what the children say, cannot go far wrong.

This matter of checking the children's responses during discussion is an important and difficult one. It is essential that the teacher follow the whole discussion very closely. She will need to watch the pupils continually to see that their questioning and comment is thorough and properly developed, and to keep check on the whole procedure when the children fail to do so. It will be continually necessary to ask such questions as: "Do you think that what George said is a good answer to Mary's question?" "Is there anything that Edward has forgotten?" "Don't you think that we ought to do so and so?" Again, the numerous and frequent criticisms that children offer of the work and remarks of their classmates must be strictly checked. Children need careful training to make them realize that constructive as well as destructive criticism should be offered. Furthermore, it is frequently necessary to ask children who have given adverse criticism of another pupil's work to tell *how* that work might be improved. It is usually wise to remind the complainer that he should, "Give James some help as to how he may make the improvement you have suggested." Through the whole of a class discussion it is necessary to maintain an atmosphere of healthy criticism and to train children not to resent the friendly suggestions of the teacher and the classmates. At best the carrying on of a good discussion is a very complex matter. Observation of a discussion directed by a skillful teacher is most helpful. It takes time and careful self-criticism for any teacher to develop a good discussion technique.

QUESTIONING

The nature of a discussion is so intricate and its satisfactory direction demands so much skill and understanding that, for the most part, the teacher must often be the leader. When all is said and done, there is considerable need for sound questioning by the teacher in directing the activities of children. The following points of good technique on the part of the teacher are valid under both the newer and the older methods of carrying on class work.

The Proper Use of Names in Questioning

When the teacher asks a question which is intended to stimulate the thought of the whole group the name of the pupil chosen to answer should be withheld until all the children have had an opportunity to think over the problem involved. The teacher does not call the name of a pupil before asking the question but says, "Is there anything important which John has left out of his report?" Then, after a pause, choosing from among those offering suggestions, "Elizabeth." Thus the teacher finds opportunity to choose from among those ready to answer as she thinks wise at the moment, or to call on students who fail to respond in order to stimulate them. Occasionally, however, the contrary procedure of calling the name first may be used. In a discussion in which the teacher wishes to emphasize some particular bit of information by asking a question which all will be ready to answer instantly, it may be wise to call some student's name before giving the question, in order to avoid tempting the class to answer all together without permission.

Echoing Answers

Inexperienced teachers need to be warned against repeating pupils' answers to questions which have been asked them. Obviously teachers who expect children to speak so that they may be heard will not fall into this careless habit. If a pupil has answered in a voice too low to be heard and the members of the class do not mention it, the teacher may ask some other pupil in a far part of the room if he has heard clearly. If not the first pupil should repeat his answer.

Repeating Questions

Not only should the teacher refuse to repeat the answers of pupils, but she should refuse to repeat her own questions. If there is any tendency whatever in the class not to pay attention to what is being said, it will certainly be increased if the pupils learn that the teacher will repeat her questions when they have not been attended to. If a pupil has not heard the question in the first place, the teacher should pass on to another for the answer.

On the contrary, there are special occasions when a repetition of the question is desirable. If the answering pupil has obviously misunderstood the question, or if, as often happens, he gives an answer which is irrelevant and the thread of the discussion gets lost, it may be well to return to the original question. Class discussion is essentially directed group thinking, and the clear directional movement of group thinking must be constantly maintained.

"Yes" and "No" Questions

As a general thing questions which may be answered by a simple "yes" or "no" are not worth asking. In such cases it is the teacher rather than the pupils who is doing the thinking. This, however, is not so when the answer "yes" or "no" is to be followed with a series of reasons justifying the answer, that is to say, when the question is really a controversial one. For example, if a class were asked whether or not it wished to assume the responsibility of presenting to another grade an account of some work done on local geology, or nature study, a child might reply "no," and then follow his opinion with its justification. The objection to the simple "yes" or "no" answer is based upon the more general objection to leading questions, which, from their very form, indicate the answer which is expected, such as, "Don't you think the action of the United States on this occasion was really for the best?"

Single Word Answers

The lazy habit of giving single word answers to questions should not be allowed to develop. Pupils tend, at times, to give fragmentary replies, brief words which to them are indicative of what they wish to say but which have little meaning to the remainder of the class. So the pupil who shouts the word "fuselage" when asked if he can tell the class the names of all the main parts of an airplane, should not be allowed to pass muster until he has given a more complete and sensible reply.

GOVERNMENT

One further problem which must be faced in every class is the problem of government. When the teacher is no longer the sole source, judge and arbiter of the children's conduct, it is necessary that arrangements be made which will facilitate another form of government. Children must be taught to govern themselves. Consequently, some place must be given in the school program for the training of pupils in self-government. The following suggestions may form a flexible basis for the working out of some form of class government.

Helping the Children to Recognize the Need for Government

Children are but dimly conscious of the nature of group life. As they live and work together, however, circumstances will occur which will reveal to even the youngest children the necessity for some sort of regulative control. This may become clear to the younger children when they feel irked by the unsocial action of one of their number, who may be quarrelsome, pugnacious, or thoughtless of others. The teacher cannot expect children to know the answer to such social problems. She must seize on the first evidences of discomfort and dissatisfaction and hold a discussion with the children, taking up the question of what must be done, and revealing to them in their own simple terms the need for some form of government.

Setting up a System of Group Government

When the need for some general regulative scheme is clear to the children the question of how it is to be worked out should be taken up with them. Special time must be set aside for this matter when it arises. In this time the children, with the teacher's assistance, should work out some plan which seems to be feasible. With young children in the earliest grades the plan should be a very simple one. Teachers need to be careful not to introduce into the discussion adult notions of government based on a state of affairs which does not exist in a group of children. Usually in the first two or three grades there will be no necessity for any class organization. All that will be necessary is the recognition of the fact that class affairs in general, including deviations from good manners, need to be discussed and considered by the group. The children should be taught to realize that people only live happily together when every one takes responsibility for his own behavior and for the group welfare to as great an extent as his age and experience permit. With older children it may be found desirable to work out some scheme of class organization. Whatever form this takes should be regarded as flexible and subject to change. It is not possible to describe a system of government that will fit all groups of children. A plan must be worked out by them in coöperation with the teacher, and by gradual experimentation as to its suitability for the particular group using it. It is only thus that the governmental function may be adequately related to the particular need of the group.

Provision of Opportunities for the Consideration of Problems of Government

Teachers cannot be too clear upon the fact that any such self-regulative form of behavior cannot be worked out or maintained without an adequate provision of time in which to carry it on. In some classes this time is placed regularly on the program, often as a class meeting. Children have been known, however, to reject the class meeting when it has been found needless. It is not always necessary to have a set time for the discussion of such matters. Whenever it is needed, the time should, however, be definitely set apart. On such occasions the children may bring up matters which have been causing trouble. Perhaps one may suggest that there have been "Too many interruptions when we are working at the bench." Or another may object that at certain times there is "Too much talking out loud." Or the teacher may report that there has been a message from the principal concerning conduct in the corridors, or walking on the lawns, or fire drill, or some such matter of school interest. Whatever problem arises, it should be discussed and solved by the children in such a way that they will realize and accept their responsibility for their own conduct and that of others of the group in respect to the matter being dealt with.

PART V

THE TECHNIQUE OF CLASS TEACHING

I. TYPICAL FORMS OF ENTERPRISE AND THEIR GUIDANCE
II. TEACHING PATTERNS
III. WIDER IMPLICATIONS OF TEACHING

I. TYPICAL FORMS OF ENTERPRISE AND THEIR GUIDANCE

CHAPTER XXI

TYPICAL FORMS OF PUPIL ENTERPRISE AND THEIR GUIDANCE

Typical Forms of Enterprise

ALTHOUGH certain classifications of activities have been provided in preceding chapters, there is still need for further basis of practical distinction. Theoretically speaking, in following out the directional flow of the learning process from the child to the curriculum, as the learner approaches his goals in the curriculum the teaching process becomes more complex. It must deal more and more with subject matter, and less and less with self-initiated responses of children. It must concern itself less with the psychological interpretation of children's responses and more with the logical organization of these responses in terms of the subject matter involved in the end points of the curriculum. There is a sense in which teaching begins with the psychological and ends with the logical. Thus, as we proceed in our discussion of teaching further away from the subjective aspects of teaching in terms of activities, and approach more closely to its objective results in the learner's mastery of the curriculum, it becomes urgently necessary to make an intermediate classification of the processes of learning.

The earlier classification in terms of needs which generate activities (see Chapter V) was a philosophic one. Such a philosophic classification is not, however, adequate to furnish a full understanding of the teaching process. The newer teaching has been seriously hampered up to the present by the failure of its exponents to carry their analyses beyond this point of abstract philosophy into the realms of classroom practice. Kilpatrick has limited his classifications to this abstract realm, suggesting expression projects, enjoyment projects, problem projects and learning projects. Collings, seeming to confuse the philosophic with the practical point of view, has distinguished excursion projects, story projects, hand projects, play projects, and skill projects, and has furnished a discussion of each type. Others have attempted more or less cursory classifications. The present book has provided a primary philosophic classification of units of conduct into three types.[1] This primary classification into units of construction or creation, play or recreation, and work or duty, was based on a psychological consideration of the child. It was subjective, psychological, in terms of activities, and based on the personality of the learner. It was largely concerned with a theoretical understanding of the laws which govern teaching, and especially valuable in its practical application to the problems governing the beginnings of learning and the initiation of activities. It was not, however, a complete guide to the practical problems of teaching, nor are the various units of conduct distinguished to be regarded as teaching plans or types of teaching, as teachers so often regard them.

In order to supplement this philosophical classification, a second classification is given, one which is in harmony with the earlier philosophic concepts, but which is made in different terms, in terms of classroom practice. It is presented here in terms of typical forms of enterprise. An enterprise means, of course, a definite and complex activity, or a complex unit of conduct composed of various interweaving and intermingling units of conduct of varying types. The classification is intended primarily to be of assistance to teachers in understanding the more practical and concrete affairs of the class. In our eagerness that all things shall proceed in terms of the child, we may sometimes forget that there is also a teacher's point of view. If the teacher is to administer school life in terms of the learning processes of children, she will need to be quite clear as to how she may recognize actual class situations which are of definite character. She will need to be able to recognize the various types of enterprises upon which children engage. For it is only by so recognizing them that she may be able to guide them in accordance with their own nature. The teacher must, in the practical situation, be able to recognize *typical forms of enterprise* if she is to be able to guide them in terms of *typical teaching procedures* which are in harmony with the nature of those enterprises.

Consequently, it is necessary to indicate what various types of enterprise children engage upon. But how may such a classification be made? Since it is not to be made philosophically, it must be made practically by an examination of classroom practice as it actually goes on in school. We must regard the things which children actually

[1] See page 49.

do in school, and that people actually carry on in life, and attempt to classify them in terms of some criterion. What, then, shall this criterion be? Obviously, from the teacher's point of view, it should be the necessity for some distinctive procedure in the guidance of the enterprise by the teacher. Since this necessity for some distinct form of guidance must have its counterpart in some distinct characteristic of the enterprise, or activity itself, it will be necessary to distinguish enterprises which involve distinct processes of learning and, consequently, require distinct processes of guidance.

INDIVIDUAL AND GROUP ENTERPRISES

Considering the matter from this point of view, a classification of enterprises in which children engage in school may be suggested. First it seems important to distinguish *individual* and *group* enterprises. Individual enterprises are those activities in which children engage which are distinctly their own. For example, a child may make a toothbrush rack to hold his own toothbrush, or a toy airplane to sail in his leisure time. Group enterprises are activities in which the whole class or some group of class members participates. Such are the organizing of a circus, the raising of poultry, or the holding of a radio party, affairs in which a number of children coöperate.

There are teachers who object to this distinction between individual and group activities. Some have claimed that no matter in what activities children engage while in school, they are still members of a group and, consequently, the distinction between individual and group enterprises is not a sound one. But this contention is merely a confusion of issues. The question with which we are here concerned is not one of social organization but of social adjustment. Within the social group there are individual and group needs, and in the attainment of each the individual must make a sound social adjustment. The distinction between individual and group enterprises is merely the recognition of the age-old problem of the individual-social balance. How may the needs of the individual and the needs of the group be ideally interrelated? Surely there is no better way for the school to train for this inter-relationship than by allowing children to engage in units of conduct which meet their own individual needs while they are living in a social group. Thus by solving in the class the problem of the individual-social balance, we lay a basis for solving it in the community.

Typical Teaching Procedures

With each of the typical forms of enterprise which will be discussed in succeeding pages there is associated a general form of guidance which may be called a *typical teaching procedure*. Special caution is necessary, however, if confusion is to be avoided in understanding the meaning of the term typical teaching procedure. It is important here to avoid a habit of mind which, due to one's previous training, might lead one to misunderstand the nature and purpose of the typical teaching procedures set forth in the following chapters. There is danger lest the reader interpret what are later presented as typical teaching procedures in terms of other analyses of teaching with which he is familiar. Such analyses have described the educative process in terms of "types of teaching" which are far from analogous to the procedures presented here.

It is necessary to avoid an attitude which teachers have held toward the well-known types of teaching. They have been regarded by some as structural models in accordance with which it was possible to plan the teaching of the subject matter of a proposed lesson.

The teacher who had planned her teaching in this fashion presupposed that the lesson she was preparing to teach could be forecast with considerable definiteness. For example, a teacher holding this familiar attitude toward teaching, having decided that she intended to teach a lesson in English dealing with metaphors and similes might proceed as follows: Calling to her aid her studies in pedagogy she might consider the "structure of the subject matter" which would be involved in such a lesson on metaphors and similes. Realizing that this material demands the understanding of an abstract concept by means of concrete examples she might decide that the most suitable mode of conveyance for such a lesson would be an "inductive-deductive" lesson. Knowing, from her study of education, the structure of that type of teaching known as the "inductive-deductive lesson," she might then organize her lesson in accordance with this general plan. Collecting from whatever sources were available a number of concrete examples of metaphors and similes, she might plan to present them to the class in some advantageous series, persuading the pupils to perform an induction to the effect that metaphors call one object by the name of another which it resembles, while similes merely state that the one is like the other. She might further plan to have the pupils hunt up and collect other examples of metaphors and similes in their texts, or in the library, and later have them discussed in class in the

FORMS OF PUPIL ENTERPRISE AND THEIR GUIDANCE 261

light of the definition. She would thus have cast her lesson according to a type of teaching [2] known as the "inductive-deductive lesson."

It is desirable that it be most clearly understood that the typical teaching procedures developed in the following chapters are not intended for use in this fashion. If the teaching process be cast according to the ideals set forth in these pages it will be impossible to forecast with definiteness or exactness just what is to go on in class during any given period of time.[3] It will, consequently, under such circumstances, be relatively difficult to foretell with cold-blooded intellectual precaution just what "type lesson" should be followed in any specific case. The teaching situation which is organized in terms of conduct is far too complex to permit of any such simple procedure in planning and execution. While the teacher in the modern school may expect just as definitely as the teacher in an older school that the question of metaphors will come up some time or other, she cannot be so sure just when or how it will be introduced. It may arise during the writing of a class play, or through the reading of one of the children's poems, or in some other way. When it comes to the fore, the teacher is ready to take advantage of its emergence. She must, keeping her curriculum goals in mind, watch for her opportunity. Then, when it arrives, without warning she must be ready to act. Habits of teaching, techniques which have become to her second nature, must come instantly to her aid. By them she may recognize the nature of the situation and respond in accordance with what seems the most desirable technique.

After being thus clear negatively on attitudes to be avoided it is further necessary to have a definite positive notion of the purpose and function of the typical teaching procedures here set forth. In other words, being clear on what typical teaching procedures are not, let us also be clear upon what they are, and what they are for. They may be regarded as having three distinct values or uses, which are set forth in succeeding paragraphs.

First, typical teaching procedures as here described, while they

[2] There is no intention in this section of minimizing the importance of a study of types of teaching as an aid in understanding instructional forms of teaching. Adequate discussions are presented in many standard texts such as the following:

BAGLEY, W. C., "Classroom Management," The Macmillan Co., New York, 1922, Ch. XIII.

STRAYER, G. D., "A Brief Course in the Teaching Process," The Macmillan Co., New York, 1922, Chs. V and VI.

[3] It is not claimed here, however, that such forecasts cannot sometimes be made with a high degree of probable realization, as, for example, when a period of time is regularly set apart in the program for drill in arithmetic.

are not models to be reproduced in class, nevertheless provide a basis for clear thinking and adequate analysis of teaching. A teacher, like the one to whom reference has just been made, who seizes her opportunity as it arises without warning in class, will be greatly aided in the rapid summoning of her resources if she is in control of concepts which facilitate her rapid analysis of the situation with which she has to deal.

Second, a study of these procedures will assist the teacher-in-training and the inexperienced teacher in her observation and understanding of the work of other teachers, and also help her to understand, study and discuss the teaching patterns given in later chapters of this book, as well as those reported in educational journals. She may study these types not in order to actually reproduce them, but rather to analyze and understand them.

Third, they will assist the teacher while she is working with her class in recognizing the nature of the activities in which the children are engaged, and in guiding those activities in accordance with their nature to their actual completion.

Finally, if the teacher is to make use of these typical teaching procedures in the ways which are here suggested, it is essential that she realize that they are not to be confused with those whole teaching units called lessons. A teaching procedure as here described is a most flexible type of activity. It should not be regarded as coincident with anything but itself; not with a unit of conduct, a class period, or with what is known as a lesson. Each procedure is merely intended to indicate certain structural points which are liable to occur during the progress of certain kinds of activities and which demand the guiding attention of the teacher. They have been prepared with the intention of presenting the matter so as to avoid, as much as possible, any degree of rigidity, and to allow the maximum degree of flexibility. The length of time which they occupy may be a brief few minutes, a day or so, or sometimes a month or so. Other activities may intervene freely during their progress. They are in no sense steps which are to be followed in a certain order. They are discussions which indicate turning points which are likely to occur when children engage in certain activities. They are based upon actual class practice, and upon a survey of what actually has been done by teachers and children in carrying various units of conduct to successful and satisfactory completion.

CHAPTER XXII

GUIDING INDIVIDUAL CONSTRUCTION AND EXPRESSION

INDIVIDUAL CONSTRUCTIVE ACTIVITIES

WHEN an individual child sets out to make something which he needs for himself or for somebody else, he is about to engage on an individual constructive activity. This may be the making of a paper valentine which he wishes to send to some one, or it may be the building of a bird fountain of concrete, elaborately molded and piped from the water supply. In any case, as long as he does practically all the work by himself, and is not merely contributing a part to some larger enterprise, he is engaged upon an individual constructive activity.

There is considerable call for activities of this sort, especially in the lower grades. Just wherein their value lies, however, is not always perfectly clear to teachers. There is danger lest the teacher, accustomed as she is to interpret certain other learning activities in terms of products, attempts to evaluate this constructive work in similar fashion. It is not the product—the crooked waste-paper basket, or the staggering sailboat—which counts the most. It is the fact that the child in making this thing has risen above himself. He sees this product of his own imagination and his own labor, and is dignified in his own eyes as a learning and achieving individual. Its glories are his glories and its deficiencies are his deficiencies. There is infinite value in visioning one's own successes and failures in some such concrete, indisputable embodiment. The objective product may be a poor thing, but it is the child's own.

Again, habits of coöperation and of ability to get along with other people, which are formed in the carrying out of individual enterprises, are most valuable. Children in the lower grades are so very slightly socialized that they cannot coöperate in complex group enterprises such as those which they should increasingly engage in as they reach the higher years of school life. They need to carry out individual enterprises, such as the making of a toy garage or the building of some dock or harbor with blocks. In doing these things they learn to get along with other children. They learn that they must wait for the saw or the hammer until another child is finished, rather than snatch what they want when they want it. They learn not to push, pull and tease, and to be helpful rather than hindering to their fellow workers. They learn to put away their tools when they are done with them and to clean up what dirt they have made when they are finished. They learn, during the progress of their individual enterprises, a hundred and one things which make them socially useful and desirable little human beings.

The technical difficulty which may puzzle the unsophisticated teacher when she considers the progress of individual constructive activities is due, not to the nature of these activities themselves, for they are simple enough, but to the fact that not one child but a number of children are under her care at once. Complexity arises from the fact that numerous children are engaged at the same time in making different objects. A technique of coördination such as that discussed in Chapter XX must be used to handle such a situation. For the work of each individual some plan of guidance like the following must be adopted. The actual procedure in class may be considerably less formal than the following outline might lead one to suppose. The following typical teaching procedures are not to be regarded as a series of steps to be followed in order, but rather as a number of points which require attention, not necessarily in the order here used. Such matters cannot be written down without some sequence. However, this need not compel the teacher to follow this order in her class teaching.

TYPICAL TEACHING PROCEDURE FOR THE GUIDANCE
OF INDIVIDUAL CONSTRUCTIVE ACTIVITIES

1. Holding a Conference

In setting out to make any object which he feels the need for, the pupil must generally find time and opportunity to consult the teacher. There are, of course, occasions when, in the course of some such simple play construction as that involved in the use of building blocks, this will not be necessary. A child may build a house, a fort, or an engine of blocks as he pleases, and all the direction required from the teacher will be that given by the use of directive conversation. But in the case of more complex operations, such as the making of a drum or of a steam engine, which involve the use of tools and specialized materials, a consultation should be held between teacher

GUIDING INDIVIDUAL CONSTRUCTION AND EXPRESSION 265

and pupil before the work is commenced. This conference usually takes place in the morning, at the begining of the school day, but may take place at any time when it can be arranged. Thus, if during the winter a boy wants to make a skating sail, it will be advisable for him to talk with the teacher as to the feasibility of doing so. It will be necessary to consider the time which is available to be devoted to it, the boy's ability to use tools and materials, and the possibility of making use of the sail when it is finished. The cost of materials should also be given careful attention, and clear decisions made as to the assumption by the pupil of whatever part of the expense he is required to bear, if any. In some schools I have seen work left unfinished for one reason or another. In one case a small steamship was left half completed because the boy who began it found the cost of materials for the engine more than he wished to pay. If he had faced this problem in the beginning, he might have saved the time wasted on his abortive product. Some teachers find it convenient to use a small printed form, which can be made by the children, on which each pupil makes a record, with dates, of what work he is engaged upon. This work-slip may be filed in a filing box with that of the other children, and may be removed from the box by the pupil the moment he begins working on this piece of construction. If he keeps this slip on his bench while he is at work, the teacher can see from it just what he is doing and how he is progressing. He may also use it for notes, plans and records which will assist him in carrying on his work. As soon as he stops work, he should, without being told, file his work-slip in the proper place. This plan greatly assists both teacher and pupil in keeping track of the work which is proceeding.

2. *Provision of Directions*

Once it has been agreed upon by teacher and pupil that the latter shall accept responsibility for carrying through some piece of constructive work, the question of directions for carrying on may arise. In certain cases no directions further than the imagination of the child may be necessary. This is so in cases where such simple materials as blocks are used. Often seeing what simple woodwork, boats, and buildings have been made by other children will provide younger children with a sufficient guide. As the children grow older and learn, in the upper grades, how to handle tools and materials, they will wish to embark on more complicated projects. After spending many hours of school life, from the earliest grades, upon constructive work, children in the upper grades should develop considerable sophistication in this type of activity, and should show increasing initiative and ability and embark upon more and more ambitious tasks. Unless this growth and progress appear in the work of the higher grades there must be something seriously wrong with the work of the school. Constructive work is no excuse for dilly-dallying. It should not progress on low levels of dilatory activity.

The increasing difficulty and complexity of the work undertaken by the children will often demand the use of directions given by experts. Unless the pupil has a clear knowledge of what he wishes to do, and how to go about it, some directions will be necessary. In the case of some simple construction a discussion with the teacher will provide adequate guidance. In other cases, it will be necessary for the boy to follow plans which he has discovered for himself, in the library, in some boy's magazine or elsewhere, or plans which are available to the teacher or suggested by her. It is not to be expected that the teacher will know how to make all the various objects which boys and girls may think of making. She will need some experience in such activities as carpentry, cooking, sewing, basket weaving, and many frequently used forms of hand work. Such work should be part of her training school experience. She will need, in addition, a considerable amount of printed materials providing directions and plans for work.

3. *Provision of Tools and Materials*

It will be obvious that when printed directions are given they will make clear to the pupil just what he will need in the way of materials and approximately how much. He should determine these things himself by studying the plan and report to the teacher as to what he needs. Accuracy and care should be expected in such work so that there will be no mistakes or waste of materials. There will be needed, in the instance of the skating sail, two white wood sticks, twelve feet long and one inch and a quarter square, two more sticks five feet six inches long and seven-eighths of an inch square, linen twine, some dark coloring, a little varnish and so on. If the list be presented to the teacher, she can arrange for the securing of this material by whatever means are at her disposal. Funds for this material should be provided in the budget. It is always best to let the pupil secure whatever he can for himself, and help him to realize the cost and value of materials. In such a case as this he may be able to secure materials for the sails himself at home. If he wishes to make something more expensive than the class funds allow, he may be willing to supplement the cost from his own pocket money.

The tools ought to be present in the classroom or the workshop where the construction is carried on. Here ordinary carpenter's tools are required. These should be a part of the available equipment of every class.

4. Supervision of Construction

In addition to supervision provided, during the conference with the pupil as to what he is going to make, and that given by the provision of tools and directions, the teacher should have general supervision of the whole constructive work. She should, of course, allow the work to be done as much as possible by the pupil, but, nevertheless, she should oversee the whole in a general way, and observe whether or not the child is living up to his responsibilities. It is to be assumed that he will live up to them fully. If he fails to do so, however, he ought to be checked. A great deal of teaching in some of the newer schools falls down just at this point. It is not uncommon to see children, who in order to live up to their own intentions and responsibilities should be at work on some supposedly favorite sailboat or airplane, actually idling away their time in useless chatter, or moving about the room in aimless fashion. One of the chief values which should be attained by the use of constructive activities in school is the development in children of sound habits of work. Teachers who do not help their children to live up to high standards of performance because they wish to allow them adequate "freedom" are imbued with a notion of freedom which is as injurious to children as it is fallacious. Children need freedom to develop, not freedom to atrophy.

Knox makes several valuable suggestions for the carrying on of various forms of construction. Teachers, it is maintained, should see that as much of the construction work as possible takes place out of doors. There it will be convenient for children to work and to avoid many of the complications and inevitable confusion of indoor work. Cold need not be a deterrent if children are warmly dressed. Another point of importance is that care must be taken to protect children's clothing. Papers and rugs spread on the floor will avoid a great deal of dirt about the room and on the clothing. In some schools the children wear overalls; in others they use aprons. The children should learn to put on aprons whenever it is necessary, without being told to do so, and to spread papers when carrying on some activity which calls for their use, such as painting. The children should also learn to clean their hands without being told. If there is a wash basin in the room, as there should be in the modern schoolroom, so much the better. If not, shift may be made by the use of cheap toilet paper, or a pan of moist wrapping paper (not newspaper), torn into fairly small pieces. The children learn to wipe their hands on this when occasion demands, and to drop the used paper into the waste paper basket. Finally, children must be taught to clean up whatever dirt they have made when their work is over, and to put their unfinished work in lockers or cupboards where they will find and recognize it, and to put tools and materials in their proper places. It is most essential that children learn to look after these matters meticulously. In certain schools they are sometimes very much neglected. Sometimes maids or servants are provided to do much of this cleaning and tidying in schools where the children are from well-to-do homes and are used to servants. Unfortunately, those who sanction this practice fail to take into consideration the fact that the children under their care are very much in need of the very type of training which would develop habits of tidiness and order. In these seemingly minor points which the teacher may find so tedious to check, she must be infinitely painstaking.

5. *Disposal of the Product*

It is characteristic of constructive work that there is, at its conclusion, some objective product. Certain schools have often allowed such products to collect in the school, or have chosen the best of them for exhibition or display. If it is to be remembered that disposal or exhibition of the product should not be made without the consent of the pupil concerned, and if it be exhibited, it should be returned to the person who made it. Whatever object is made in the school by an individual child should, since it found its source in the child's own need, be regarded as belonging to him. In certain cases, when things are made for the school or for some other individual, they may be disposed of, but the right of their disposal should rest with the child.

It is further important for the teacher to see that the object constructed is actually used, when it has been finished, for the purpose for which it was made. Such things as have been made to meet some actual specific need will almost certainly be called into use. Both the teacher and the other children should know, whenever possible, what use is being made of the various objects made by members of

GUIDING INDIVIDUAL CONSTRUCTION AND EXPRESSION

the class. Thus will the individual's achievement be socially complete, and full recognition accorded him.

ESTHETIC SELF-EXPRESSION

It is somewhat difficult to distinguish absolutely and clearly between individual constructive activities and activities which are carried on for the purpose of esthetic self-expression. Possibly it is not of great importance that this distinction should be made with thorough philosophic clarity. The teaching procedures here set forth are given not for the sake of providing classifications, but in order to facilitate teaching. Therefore, there may be overlapping of types.

It may be convenient, however, to have some distinction made between purely constructive activities and activities involving esthetic self-expression. The former are grosser activities such as the making of tables and chairs. Such constructive activities are, on the whole, dominated by utilitarian motives, and are made for the sake of securing and using the product rather than for the sake of the experience involved in their production. One of their distinguishing characteristics is the fact that the source of the plan is a matter of complete indifference. It may come from a book, the teacher, or another individual. The excellence of the plan, not its degree of originality, is the criterion by which it is judged. Activities which are described as esthetic self-expression, on the contrary, are fine, rather than gross, in their general nature. They are of the type commonly referred to as artistic, or esthetic, such as the writing of a poem or the painting of a picture. They are not inspired by motives of utility, but rather by some emotional or spiritual state of affairs which is but little understood in the psychology of school men.

On the whole it is the *process* which is needed by the individual concerned, not the *product*. The work is undertaken in response to some inner drive, some creative urge which demands an outlet, which calls for the outpouring of one's best in some objective form which may be called good. In their production the individual approaches most nearly to the divinity of creation. It is characteristic that the plan of such work should be original, that it should arise from the innermost self. Any contribution from without must be contamination. One teacher relates the way in which a group of third-grade children cut ships and dragon heads competing with the hope that their own designs might be chosen to decorate a curtain. When the children were asked to choose the best designs, each child chose his own. So it must ever be with the creative self. What we produce is our own image, our own physical embodiment. The process of living forth our own being is esthetic self-expression.

This type of activity is well illustrated and analyzed by a writer in one of the publications of the Francis W. Parker School, who describes the making of a Viking ship.[1]

Such work may be regarded as esthetic self-expression. It may take the form of writing poems or stories, composing music, executing busts or original figures in clay, drawing, painting, dancing, or any other form of action which goes on in accordance with the nature of the creative act.

Lessons which involve the esthetic self-expression of the individual are probably less well understood and less well administered by the average teacher than those of any other type. This may be easily understood if the traditional approach to teaching be taken into consideration. It would be only natural that teaching which began with the curriculum and moved forward toward the children's learning, instead of vice versa, should make its most serious blunders in matters concerned with children's artistic self-expression. For it is in this form of activity that the opposite approach is most necessary. It is here that the child's own self-initiated activity is most essential to his development. It is in matters of esthetics, if anywhere, that education should be really child-centered.

It may be well to consider just why the teaching of the expressive arts ought, more than other types of teaching, to be child-centered. The root of the matter is that they deal with those less tangible manifestations of life which we call the things of the spirit. Little as we understand the affairs of the intellect we understand still less those of the spirit and the emotions. The development of the self-expression of children is concerned with the growth of the least understood, the most impalpable qualities of human personality. Our modern psychologies have lost themselves in the materialistic approach to truth. We wait for a new approach in psychology based on the things of the spirit.

In the meanwhile, it seems clear that the earliest venturings forth of the child's personality in the direction of esthetic self-expression in such realms as those of art and music are the most delicate, the most fragile and the most perishable of children's responses. They need to be watched for carefully and cherished as one cares for the

---

[1] "Creative Effort," The Francis W. Parker School, Studies in Education, Vol. VIII, pp. 139 ff.

GUIDING INDIVIDUAL CONSTRUCTION AND EXPRESSION 271

most delicate flowering plants in the garden. Normally children are eager to give expression to these tendencies. They are ready to sing and to rhyme, and to draw freely without restriction. "Recent collections of children's work in art and in music," says one teacher, "are confirming our feeling that there is much ability in children to create in these forms which is not being discovered early enough, if at all." But in their beginnings children need encouragement. They are timid. The slightest cramping, the least unsympathetic criticism, the mildest repression, is sufficient to stunt this earliest growth. What then must be the result of the bludgeoning and bruising they receive at the hands of teachers armed with veritable battering rams of formal "artistic" technique. Small wonder that the child who survives the process to reach any maturity in the use of the materials of the arts is the very rare exception.

The earliest esthetic responses of children are farthest away from the highly controlled and complex techniques of finished art. Yet these original responses and a certain amount of technique are both essential to satisfactory mature expression. But it is just as important that the earliest efforts of beginners shall be conserved as that the end product shall be a technically skillful artist. Dilemma arises when we consider how two such apparently opposing requirements may be met in the training of the individual.

In attempting to solve this problem teachers have vainly tried to harness the earliest artistic responses of children to the elements of a formal technique. Untold hours of misery, amounting in some cases to torture, have resulted. Little wonder that tiny fingers have abhorred the piano, with its great keys and adult octaves, or that children have felt that music in the form of technical scores was no longer their friend. Such a clumsy approach in any art must be ruinous to the pupil. One may not shorten the bridge over a ravine by bending the end back to meet the beginning. It is necessary to begin at one end of the bridge, and reach the other step by step. So, in matters of esthetic development, it is absolutely essential to begin with the responses of the children, and let them go forward uninjured until they are strong enough to bear the limiting requirements of even the simplest technique. In other words, in the earliest part of their esthetic training children must usually discover what little technique they need for themselves. Their beginnings are so simple that they need little technique. As they develop and feel their pressing needs, they will ask for techniques which offer solution of whatever problems arise.

Of the importance of giving to the beginnings of artistic development the fullest freedom from any technical limitation Mrs. Coleman writes:[2] "It is my belief that the ability for original thought and action is best fostered in the earliest stages of any form of expression, for after habits of following conventional lines have been thoroughly established, it is very hard for the average person to break away into new and original ways. But when the entire field is new, and the child is so young that his ideas are free to flow in one way as in another, it is not so difficult to form habits of finding ways of his own to express his ideas." So in the beginning of training it is essential that whenever a child has an original idea, he be given opportunity and encouragement in expressing it. As the need for technique arises it should be met.

The following outline should make this general process clearer. The examples are chosen chiefly from the field of art and literature, but the general technique is applicable to every field of esthetic self-expression.

Typical Teaching Procedure for the Guidance of Esthetic Self-Expression

1. Provision of Time, and Opportunity for and Encouragement of Freedom in Esthetic Self-Expression

The matter of the beginning points of teaching has already been given considerable attention in the earlier pages of this book, so that it will not be necessary to repeat here what has been said concerning the encouragement of the free self-expression of children. Emphasis should be laid, however, upon the fact that it is in matters of esthetic self-expression that this according of freedom is most important, and most in harmony with the nature of the learning process. In fact, some teachers, carried away by the salutary results of such a régime in matters of art and music, have found the key to their whole method of teaching in their administration of these activities, and have attempted to find in them an analogy for the whole teaching process. Any such extension of one aspect of method to cover the whole field of teaching is as injurious as another. We should allow freedom where freedom is due, and that is essentially in the matter of the initiation and early development of esthetic responses. "Spirit," it has been said, "creates its own form."

[2] Coleman, Satis N., "Creative Music for Children." G. P. Putnam's Sons, New York, 1922, p. 122.

Consequently, the teacher must be ever skillful to see that adequate time is given, and frequent opportunity provided in school time for children to carry on expressive activities. She must be ever on the watch for the occasions in school life which will lead on to this type of activity. She will watch for and reveal to children the romance and daring of whatever history—Greek, Egyptian or American—the children are interested in at the time, for often children's poems are so inspired. Again, the call of the school paper will bring forth stories and poems, and sometimes children with a sympathetic teacher will offer poems out of their own interests and experience, or finished melodies which they have worked out at home by themselves. The numerous needs of the school for wall decoration, for ornamentation of the reception-rooms and offices, all help children to realize their need to express their ideas with paints or with clay. Simple musical rhythms played on the piano will make children eager to respond by various forms of stepping, skipping, galloping, running or hopping. It is this provision of time and presentation of opportunity which stimulate children to feel that artistic self-expression is not something to be suppressed, but rather something which is expected of them as part of a normal child's living and learning.

The gentle guidance which must be given to children who are just beginning to express themselves through artistic materials is well illustrated by an account given by Peppino Mangravite,[3] who writes:

"One of the most difficult situations to meet arises when children say, 'I can't do this.' I always answer, 'Why?' Sometimes they can tell and sometimes they cannot. If they can, I answer, I can help them at once. If not, I must find out why they cannot. Sometimes I say to a child, 'Very well, if you can't draw anything, don't try to, but suppose I should ask you now if there is anything you would love to do.' The child answers perhaps, 'Go swimming.'

" 'Do you like to swim and dive?'

" 'Yes.'

" 'Do you like to go alone?'

" 'No.'

" 'How many should you like to have with you, and do you like children or grown-ups?'

"He answers perhaps, 'About three children.'

" 'Well, do you like to go in the ocean, or a lake, or a pool?'

" 'In a lake.'

" 'Are there trees around the lake? Tell me about it.' You see I

[3] *Progressive Education*, April-May-June, 1926, p. 119.

am developing his mental picture. We are working it out together, but the ideas are all coming from him. When I feel that he has the picture sufficiently in mind I say, 'All right, now draw it for me. Draw me a picture of the place you would like to go swimming in. I should like to see the kind of place you like.' " [4]

2. Provision of Suitable Media of Expression

The finer impulses of human nature thrive only in a specially prepared environment. It is thus important for the teacher to maintain the conditions under which the child may maintain expression. Two distinct problems are involved, that of the general environment and that of the instruments or tools of expression. In the case of art and literature the former is the more important while in the case of music the latter presents a special problem. A concrete presentation may be more helpful than mere abstract discussion. Consequently it may be best to quote first from an excellent article by Cane [5] on the maintenance of a general environment favorable to the development of drawing and painting.

The room should be still when the children enter—expectant; materials ready; plenty of space and light, walls white and undecorated, a fertile world for the imagination to play in; no reproductions of masterpieces on the walls to dull the children into a sense of inferiority, rather some of the most living of the children's work is placed where the color and rhythm and honest crudities stimulates the more sluggish to effort. A few pieces of pure colored velvets are seen about. Some fruits or vegetables or perhaps the presence of a live animal key up unconsciously the latent sense of color or form much more than the work of masters. It is the ingredients of art that stimulate, not the art itself.

The materials used should liberate, not confine. Large sheets of paper are, therefore, used. Small ones tend to cramp the work. Crayons and chalk should be rich colored and soft enough to mark easily. Hard crayons block the intention of the artist, the softer ones accelerate it. For the same reason tempera paints and large brushes are better than the small hard pans of color and little brushes. Charcoal often responds better than pencils, and lithographer chalks and oil crayons are all extremely successful in making the work more broad, daring and individual.

The whole process of creation is extremely complex, but first we must

[4] Another account useful in giving a unified picture of the way in which one teacher encourages musical expression in her children may be found in "Creative Effort," Francis W. Parker School, University of Chicago, Studies in Education, Vol. VIII, p. 58.

[5] CANE, FLORENCE, "Art and the Child's Essential Nature," *Creative Art*, February, 1929.

GUIDING INDIVIDUAL CONSTRUCTION AND EXPRESSION

realize that the body is the instrument through which it occurs. The muscular understanding or kinesthetic sense is the link between conceiving and doing. In our civilization most of us use our bodies in a tense cramped manner or in a drooped flaccid one. Both are useless. We are also accustomed to using chiefly our fingers to draw with, because we have done so in writing, whereas the whole body should be the instrument. The finger tips are after all the last delicate part to convey the message of the mind to the paper, but we are inclined to make them carry the whole burden. A child sitting at his desk in his accustomed position may be blocked in his drawing and totally unable to express himself. If he is placed before a large upright board in a well-balanced position, using large gestures from the shoulders, the problem may be easily solved and the expression of his idea flows out freely. I have even placed a child's work high up on a mantel with a ladder to reach the upper parts and to stretch his body and arms to the farthest reach, with remarkable results. The new position, the wide reach, altered muscular habits, changed the blood stream and the pulse. The effect was to uncover primitive levels in his being, to produce work on a different plane, inaccessible to him during habitual movements. Therefore, I have developed a few simple exercises by means of which the child learns a conscious use of his shoulder, elbow and wrist movements. Some of the exercises are for freedom and some for control. I have seen greater changes occur as a result of them than from any verbal instruction I have ever given. There is doubtless a great deal more for us to learn about the organic functioning of the body with mind and emotions than we have any conception of yet.

The second condition concerns the emotional life of the child. There should, of course, be such sympathy between the teacher and pupil that he loves to come to the studio and is at peace there. Giovanni Gentile, the Italian educator, went so far as to say no teaching can take place without love between the teacher and pupil.

One of the ways of liberating the child's feeling is to permit him always to choose his own subject. The individual life with its own emotional content will come forth, acting as a motor power to carry him through difficulties with a vigor totally different than when the direction comes from the teacher. For example, a boy with a great wish for power, painted horses for a whole year, making them larger and stronger each time until finally he painted a pair of very large strong ones and then was satisfied. He had simultaneously acquired a new power in his work and in his life.

Another instance of the connection between feeling and expression was this: A girl was painting the Birth of Christ. She chose a starlit night, snow scene, a few hamlets half hidden by snow and three angels floating in the sky. I found her crying and when I asked her what the trouble was, she looked up and said: "The sky looks as if Christ were being born, but I can't make the snow look as if Christ were being born." From there on I questioned her to find out what quality she wanted in the snow and then to help her find out how to do it. So the problems of technique appear and are struggled with individually as necessity arises.

The third and most important condition I try to maintain within the child is an awakened spirit. This depends largely on his faith in himself. If one can teach that true knowledge comes from within, one has laid the foundation stone. By my faith in him his own faith grows; by my recognition of individual values each one gains strength to stand against the more external social influences in the world. By encouragement in the use of his imagination, he is enabled to find the language of his inmost being, and enters into the sacred passages leading into infinity. There is no measuring the possible development when that door is open. My work is to find ways of keeping it open when technical problems come to the fore.

By exercises in memory and perception I try to develop experience that will help him solve his own problems; but if he finds an unsurmountable one, he must then have an assurance that there is a solution, that by effort on his part and some new light from the teacher, he will come through. For there is a low point of discouragement in most work. This is the psychological moment when I try to help with fresh stimulus of some sort, but never when the pupil is working to his satisfaction. It may be an intrusion on my part to interrupt at such a time; it may even cut off the stream of interest and the child's power entirely.

A certain balance within is also necessary for him to become expressive. If he is overstimulated, he should be calmed by sitting with his eyes closed, recalling visual images; if he is lethargic or barren, some question may stir him, such as "If you were a great artist and could paint anything you wanted to, what would you paint?" or "How would you like to play with colors and shapes and do just what you want with them?" Such questions often throw off inhibitions when nothing else will; they are an open sesame to unformed but living visions.

The second problem of providing suitable tools or instruments for artistic expression is a distinct one. In the case of painting, for instance, certain artistic media and apparatus—easels, paints, paper, brushes—are more suitable for children than others, but it is in music that we find that especial attention must be paid to this matter. Musical expression of children is hampered first by the great complexity of present-day musical instruments and by our complex system of written music. It takes the ordinary individual years of practice to be able to play the piano even passably well; the violin is a life study; and the complexity of the pipe organ is so great that few ever master it. Written composition is so intricate in its technical requirements that not a fraction of those who might compose ever find time to study a subject so ostracized by curriculum makers. Yet we find children of four and five singing original melodies, and musical expression, if unquenched, running far beyond the individual's ability to perform or record it.

The problem has been determinedly studied by Mrs. Coleman who has made a lasting contribution to the problems of teaching music by the devising of simple instruments suitable for use by children and simple schemes by which they may record sound. Beginning with the human voice the children discover their own tunes or sing simple ones which are familiar. Thus they begin by successful musical experience, and attempt to perform on very simple stringed instruments, gongs, or on a scale built up of tumblers tuned to pitch by various quantities of contained water. These glasses, sometimes distinguished by water of different colors, are set on a cloth and struck with wooden wands. A complete account of this work is given in "Creative Music for Children." It can only be mentioned here. The sounds which children wish recorded may first be written down in terms of the original numbers of the gongs or glasses or strings struck. It is only later on that the children approach complex adult instruments with a basis in their own experience for the understanding of them, and with some knowledge of the principles of notation which will enable them to understand the written form. Thus, under certain circumstances the instruments of expression may need to be worked out on the child's level.

3. *Recognition of the Esthetic Merits of the Product*

If the child's gains in esthetic self-expression are to be conserved, they must receive recognition in accordance with their esthetic merits interpreted in relation to the personality of the individual child. Some children do not and cannot do as well as others. If the product be made the standard or the aim of teaching the whole of the teaching process will be thrown out of joint. A child does not draw to make a masterpiece or play the piano to entrance an audience. The objective result is only important when interpreted in terms of the personality of the individual child concerned. Has he grown, has he drawn a picture or written a poem which has, for a person of his degree of artistic attainment, a satisfactory degree of esthetic merit? A "mastery technique" of teaching has no place in teaching the expressive part of any art.

If a child succeeds in any attainment in esthetic expression that attainment should, for the sake of the child's further development, be recognized. It is the attainment which should be praised, however, and not the child. Recognition given for artistic merit should not be directed toward making the child pleased with himself, but toward making him pleased with his work. Appreciation should be given in terms of the esthetic value of the product. It is permissible to tell a child what you like about his painting or his music and why you enjoy it. Appreciation should be given in terms of the merit of the product, not in terms of admiration of the individual. Children should learn to recognize artistic form, and to realize when they have attained it. They will thus be made conscious of their success in artistic composition or rhythm or in the creation of beautiful melody in music. A simple melody may be harmonized by the teacher for the child's fuller realization of it. Perhaps it may be used, sung or played by several children together. Children's paintings or sculptures in clay are often used to decorate their own rooms or the schoolrooms and halls. Thus, use being made of the product, it takes on a fuller worth for the child. In certain schools the children have furnished parts of the building with original works of art, and in others have decorated the walls of the schoolrooms and school building with colorful friezes. Poems and stories are commonly printed in school papers and certain schools publish small volumes of poems written and printed by the pupils. Thus the worthwhileness of artistic self-expression may be recognized, and the pupils wisely encouraged.

4. *Provision of Technical Training as the Pupil Feels the Need*

Immature performance will not satisfy pupils forever. When the original and more perishable part of the process of self-expression has developed to a sufficient extent to have made such action a real part of the life of the individual, he will want to turn that power toward a fuller realization. As pupils feel this growing need they should be trained to recognize their deficiencies and seek from the teacher the secrets of technique which age-long experimentation in artistic modes has developed. As the desire for more perfect form, more exact knowledge, and a fuller appreciation of historic sources of development and of accurate techniques arise, the teacher, out of a richer experience, may supply the need.

The provision of such technical training demands a teacher who is trained in the art in which she is teaching. In the lower grades, however, a great deal of the work in encouraging esthetic self-expression may be done by the class teacher. When children reach the higher grades, especially beyond the elementary school, special teachers

GUIDING INDIVIDUAL CONSTRUCTION AND EXPRESSION

of training and ability are needed to help the children with the technical problems which arise in their work.

INTELLECTUAL SELF-EXPRESSION

There is a sense in which constructive and esthetic activities are also intellectual, but it may be wise to attempt to distinguish separately those activities which are neither primarily constructive nor primarily esthetic. There is the greatest danger lest, in the pursuit of activities which are novel and interesting, teachers may neglect those fundamental matters which have been the age-long concern of schools, namely, intellectual values. A great many of these intellectual values are secured in the course of activities in which several members of the class participate jointly, in such group activities as a study of Holland, studying bees, or making a farm or dairy. But it is also necessary to encourage individual praticipation in activities which, while they may be largely physical and objective, are yet largely intellectual in their implications, such as making a collection of mosses, caring for a flock of chickens, or engaging upon some private business enterprise.

The matters of intellectual self-expression are, of course, closely allied in their nature to matters of esthetic self-expression. If they are to be distinguished, they may be recognized as less emotional or spiritual in their nature, and more purely mental in their characteristics. Fortunately, the intellectual response is a much more virile and hardy plant than the esthetic response. Children's minds are continually active, and will remain active under ordinary circumstances. It is important that this activity should be directed so that mental effort will produce the maximum and the most valuable satisfactions. Great satisfaction accrues to the individual from properly directed intellectual self-expression. Schools should not fail to provide adequate opportunities for such activity and its development.

Intellectual self-expression might be defined as thinking applied to some actual situation, practical or otherwise, largely because of intelligent mental interest. Thinking does not exist *in vacuo*. Thinking which does not crystallize into action either evaporates or degenerates into dreaming. When either of these things occurs, injury is done to the personality of the individual concerned. It is essential to mental health and development that when thinking goes on it should take definite form. Children should be deliberately encouraged to conserve their thinking in the form of records. I have seen practically nothing of this sort of work done in schools, although it doubtless takes place in certain schools in different parts of the country. A card catalog is of infinite value to any individual who uses his mind in definite self-expression. Such a habit of recording and classifying might well be built up in childhood for those who need it. Collections of stories or poems which they have written might be kept by children in special books or portfolios.

There are numerous collections which might be usefully made by children, the making and organizing of which would provide opportunity for satisfactory intellectual self-expression. Collections of favorite poems, quotations, ballads or folk-songs, collections of leaves, sea-weed, butterflies, insects, plants or a hundred and one things found in nature will meet the needs of different children, or of the same child at different times. These are far more practical sublimations of the collecting impulse than the keeping of stamp books, although the latter is not to be despised as an interest that may lead far afield into many countries if wisely directed by the teacher. In making collections, however, all children should not be expected to make the same kind. The form which intellectual self-expression takes will be very different in different children. Some may find themselves interested in astronomy, while others occupy themselves with chemistry. Caldwell Cook, in his book, "The Play Way," tells most interestingly of the way in which some boys under his care delighted to make "Ilonds," a form of imaginative map, and to deliver lectures on this subject or that to an assembled group of schoolfellows. Little girls are fond of keeping diaries, which are prized possessions when they grow up. It is not beyond possibility that some lad of ability and thoughtful disposition might keep a book entitled "My Opinions," in which he could record whatever ideas and impressions might seem of special interest or value to him. Lewis Carroll, when a boy, was sufficiently precocious to publish a family magazine. Such activities might proceed as follows:

TYPICAL TEACHING PROCEDURE FOR THE GUIDANCE
OF INTELLECTUAL SELF-EXPRESSION

1. The Choice and Limitation of the Field of Activity

It is desirable that every individual, especially in the higher grades, should have a form of intellectual self-expression. Some children may have several. Teachers sometimes have sought to make provision for this type of activity in the mass, by attempting to persuade each child in the class to make some collection such as a set of pressed flowers.

No provision is made for the personality of the learner, no opportunity is given for individual choice, and the response is usually half-hearted indeed. Rather, the teacher, knowing the general trends of the child's personality, might assist him in choosing some form of intellectual self-expression particularly suited to his needs.

The following account given by Salisbury [6] indicates the way in which the teacher may lead a child into an expressive activity which meets his own peculiar need.

"At one time we had a little goat. David, who was very much younger than the other children and not much interested in first grade activities, but much preferred being at home with his mother, was given the little goat to care for. David, up to this time, was late almost every morning, although his mother was trying her best to coöperate and always had him leave home on time. With the little goat David had a real responsibility, for he knew if he did not get to school the little goat would not be fed. Soon David learned to measure a pint of milk which the goat was to drink for each meal. He learned to be thoughtful, kind and considerate."

2. *The Making and Organizing of the Records, Ideas or Materials*

Having decided what form his particular effort is to take, time will be necessary for the pupil to carry it out. Part of this time may be taken in school hours, part of it out of school hours, or part of it in such supplementary parts of the program as that carried on by the Boy Scout Troop or the Hobby Club, or other clubs related to the school life. The amount of time which is devoted to this work in school and out of school must be governed by the circumstances of the case. At any rate, whatever guidance or suggestion is needed may be given by the teacher, whether it has to do with carrying on, collecting and preserving or recording. Records of ideas may be kept in loose-leaf note books, or in card catalogs. Special techniques involved in such work as collecting, drying and mounting moths may be shown to the pupil or he may learn them from written directions. Special butterfly books to assist the pupil in such work and in the problems of organizing and labeling his collections, may be found in the library. A teacher of good background and wide nature interests should be of great assistance in an activity of this sort.

[6] SALISBURY, "An Activity Curriculum for the Kindergarten and the Primary Grades," Harr Wagner Pub. Co., San Francisco, Calif., or from the Southern Branch of the University of California, Los Angeles, Calif., pp. 70-1.

3. The Use of the Product

As in cases previously discussed it is desirable that some use should be made of the product of the pupil's intellectual self-expression. For example, a topic which has been investigated at length by one of the pupils, such as the intricate problems of conjuring and magic, should be prepared in lecture or demonstration form and presented to the whole class, or to the whole school during assembly. Collections which have been made should be exhibited in the classroom or in the display cases in the halls. What pupils have written in the way of records or conclusions should, as much as possible, be read and discussed in class. Thus may the significance and value of the use of the mind in a constructive manner be taught to the children.

CHAPTER XXIII

GUIDANCE FOR INDIVIDUAL MASTERY

THE two types of enterprise to be discussed in this chapter are concerned with (1) the mastery of complex integrated skills, and (2) securing knowledge of organized subject matter. Since they both partake of something of that type of learning which involves control or restraint, they are grouped together under the general head of enterprises which demand the individual's mastery of certain learnings. The use of such an expression should not, however, allow teachers to mistake either of the forms of learning here referred to for that mechanical type of memorization of reproduction-without-comprehension which is sometimes mistaken for mastery. Mastery, as here used, is intended to indicate a power over the learnings concerned which makes possible their functional use by the learner in a life situation. Furthermore, the classification of typical teaching procedures under the general heads of *expression* and *mastery* is not intended to give the impression that in a specific case of learning only one of these processes is at work while the children learn. Rather, it is intended to indicate that in a specific case one of these processes preponderates. Thus when a child writes an original poem the process of expression predominates. When the same child memorizes a poem written by Wordsworth, the learning process is strongly colored by the necessity for mastery.

MASTERY OF COMPLEX INTEGRATED SKILLS

In guiding such individualistic matters as those involved in esthetic self-expression the teacher's method should be more than elsewhere "child-centered." On the contrary, in training children in the mastery of a complex skill the method may be more than elsewhere, though far from entirely, curriculum-centered. Here are two problems of teaching which are very different ones. When a child is engaged in esthetic self-expression, the process may be variable and the result original. In his mastery of a complex skill, however, there can be little variation in the process, and no originality in the result. Originality is not required in multiplying seven and five. The product is standard, specific, uniform. In acquiring mastery of such processes, the child must conform or he does not learn. Therefore, in the development of such skills the teacher must use a technique which will cause the abandonment of caprice, individual variation, and freedom, and secure the subordination of the child's self to the symbol and his willing submission to the control of the thing to be learned.

What is it, then, which may be regarded as a skill? From a broad point of view, any act may be regarded as a habit, because it is a step in the direction of a habit. Similarly, from a broad point of view, any learning may be regarded as a skill. It is particularly necessary in this discussion to regard a skill as something much more than any such beginning of a learning pattern. A skill is here regarded as a learned mode of action which is so thoroughly mastered that ability in carrying it out approaches perfection. It is further distinguished from actions which are obviously but the ripening and maturing of inherited powers, such as ability to walk or run. Skill is controlled action which has been thoroughly learned by the organism.

There are numerous skills which all children need to learn because they meet certain standard needs which necessarily must be encountered by every individual living in a society of the type in which they find themselves. Years ago Indian boys needed to learn the use of the bow and arrow; Roman boys needed to master conversational Latin. Today French boys find it a pressing need to spell French words; and modern children in our Western civilization need to know how to divide whole numbers. It is to be noticed, however, that Indian boys of years ago did not need to master any such complex skill as ability to divide whole numbers any more than modern city boys need to know how to use a bow and arrow. Roman boys had no need to speak modern French, nor do small French boys need to puzzle over the incongruities of English spelling. In other words, such complex integrated skills as those which have been mentioned are merely standard conventions of certain social groupings at certain times. Their whole virtue and nature lies in their standard and unvarying quality. They exist only because of the characteristic of uniformity within the group using them. So it is that by social agreement the Japanese and Chinese may use the same written symbols while speaking different languages. The use of complex integrated skills such as reading and writing are social, not individual matters. The very notion of individual variation in their use is a violation of their essential character. Such complex integrated skills belong not to the individual, but to the group of which he is a member, and to which he must, to a certain extent, submit himself if he is to enjoy to the full the privileges of the group which uses them.

If the individual is to learn these complex integrated skills, he must submit himself to the conventions they impose. They are not the individual's contribution to the group, but the group's offering to the individual, which he may accept only by the process of conformity.

What, then, are the school activities which may be soundly regarded, from the point of view of the teaching process, as complex integrated skills? Confusion in the minds of teachers in this matter has only too frequently led to a widening of the field so that it included not merely those activities properly regarded as complex skills which are socially significant, but others which have no standing at all as skills which should be mastered by children. Such materials when treated according to a teaching technique suitable for the development of complex skills lose all semblance of real life activities. Thus children have been drilled in lists of capes and rivers, and geometry problems have been overlearned to the point of parrot-like repetition by pupils who failed to understand them. Due to a mistaken application of technique, the teaching process has been widely caricatured.

But it is not in such realms of artificialized subject matter that we look for examples of complex skills. It is in the realms in which the resulting learning, while socially useful, is definite, unvarying, and the same for all individuals. Desirable uniformity in the product is an indication of skills which may be mastered in accordance with the technique set forth below. It is obvious, therefore, that the realm of organized bodies of skills is that of such activities as number, where certain processes of an exact kind must be mastered with accuracy, the spelling of words in the way which is sanctioned by general usage, the recognition of symbols which others use in recording meanings in such a way that one may read intelligently, the use of written symbols to communicate one's own thoughts or to record one's musical ideas. Thus do the "tool" activities, reading, writing and arithmetic and a few others, take their places in school life. They are the legitimate realms for the development of complex integrated skills. The technique of their administration may be indicated under the following headings:

TYPICAL TEACHING PROCEDURE FOR GUIDING THE
MASTERY OF COMPLEX INTEGRATED SKILLS

1. Insuring the Child's Early Recognition of His Need

Even in the case of the mastery of organized bodies of skills, it is very necessary that the directional flow of the learning process should originate with the child. The learning of such lessons should wait for the child's own need to make use of the learning involved. This principle has often been violated by those who have been in control of schools. Children have been taught to add, subtract and even multiply when their only conceivable number needs must have been for counting. Infants who could hardly speak have been painfully taught to read. Techniques have been invented and methods advocated for the teaching of such lessons to children who did not need them. Teachers have found themselves in a veritable hysteria of "methods" devised for teaching reading to tiny tots who might have learned almost unaided and overnight had they been permitted to wait a year or two longer.

On the other hand, it should not be supposed that the teacher should pursue a *laissez faire* policy, permitting children to read and figure when and if they begin. One normally endowed child in an extremist experimental school did not learn to read until the age of eleven! This is mere neglect. So far from being indifferent, the teacher is ever active in preparing an environment which will reveal to the children the pressing needs of life for such skills as good speaking and written expression, correct spelling and facility in handwriting and in the use of number. It is necessary during the work of the first two grades of school to maintain constantly a state of affairs which will make children increasingly conscious of their needs in these directions. It is some time during these years that children will be likely to develop sufficient realization of their needs for these skills to awaken in them a desire for their attainment. The teacher may accomplish her end by allowing the children to engage in numerous life activities which are so directed and carried on that the various needs for complex skills are brought to the attention of the children. For example, the number needs of first-grade children may arise in the playing of games, in the keeping by the children of their attendance records, in checking materials such as pencils, crayons, scissors, in counting any objects for the fun of counting, and in dozens of similar activities in which the children engage. Again, in the holding of a Christmas party, or in the use of the doll-house, a great deal of counting in the checking of napkins, plates, doll furniture and so on, is necessary. In the second and third grades more complex activities, such as having a sale or holding a market, introduce the need for more complex figuring. In the fourth and fifth grades controlling the school store or bank brings still other number needs to the fore. The buying of muslin and cloth for the making of a quilt may yield such problems as "the muslin for the blocks cost 30 cents a yard. $1\frac{2}{3}$ yards were required. Find the cost of the muslin." or, "The Peter Pan cloth for the lining cost 36 cents per yard. 1⅔ yards were required. Find the cost of the Peter Pan cloth."

Brief blackboard notices, a bulletin board newspaper, various labels, written directions and stories, and records of their own experiences, the words of which are composed by themselves and printed by the teacher in large letters on cardboard, all stimulate interest in reading. Again, children who have already gained some mastery of reading and are allowed the privilege of reading books to themselves, often invite small groups of non-readers or friends to listen to stories which they read aloud. This makes the non-readers anxious to learn and so gain access to the books which prove so interesting. The needs for spelling soon arise in connection with written English. Miss Keelor of the Lincoln School presented her second grade with a cardboard mail box in which was a letter for each child. This produced a shower of letters from members of the class to one another, and some to others out of class. One morning, she reports, there were thirty-two letters in the box, and on certain days energetic children wrote a letter to every member of the class. So it is that the living environment of the children may become a powerful stimulus driving them to learn reading, writing and arithmetic.

The careful preparation of the environment, coupled with a policy of waiting until the situation has borne down sufficiently on each child, recognizes that the mastery of any complex skill is essentially an individual, and not a group activity. Nowhere is this more so than in the beginnings of such learnings. In each individual case teachers should wait until the child actually feels the pressure of the need to learn. If a child seems slow in responding, the teacher should take special pains to put him in some situation where the particular need will bear upon him with especial cogency. Some children become conscious of a need and so of a desire to read very young. Other normal children have not responded until the age of seven, although this is unusually, one might say undesirably, late. The importance of the teacher's constantly maintaining an environment in which the needs for the basic tools of knowledge may be felt and recognized is obvious. She should be ever on the watch for the time when these needs may be naturally awakened, and should observe and conserve what learning responses arise.

So should the teacher be ever alert throughout the whole development of such a complex integrated skill as arithmetical ability. The need for each new process should be felt when the process is taught.

There can be no fixed rule or procedure for awakening any specific arithmetical need. In the actual instance the method must vary from teacher to teacher and pupil to pupil. Some teachers find that the consciousness of a need for a new process, in a pupil who has reached a certain stage of development, may be awakened by a few words of conversation. Others find that its mere provision as a next stage in instruction materials is sufficient. Certain teachers secure motivation via the other activities of the class, such as construction or play, the making of fudge, the playing of games, or the building of a Dutch home in the classroom. One teacher found the need for fractions arising in the designing of a plan for a palm tree which was to be used as part of the scenery in a class play. The plan for this palm tree was plotted on squared paper and this process of plotting was used as introduction to fractions which the class was expected to learn at about that time. As children advance in growth in these complex skills, motivation is not really difficult. Their value is so obvious in meeting the problems of everyday life that any child who is living normally may realize their essential nature. Teachers, therefore, should not strain themselves to motivate what is already motivated.

2. Analysis of the Complex Skill into Its Simplest Whole Elements

It is not to be supposed that the awakening in children through school activities of a dynamic consciousness of a need for any complex skill will ensure its mastery in the incidental progress of their daily life. Enthusiasts have too often claimed that reading, writing and arithmetic might be learned without supplementary drill, simply by the children's participation in real life activities. Thus it has been thought that the multiplication combinations might be learned by a chart in the school store, which the children could consult in making change, and in similar transactions. Experience in the new schools everywhere is making it indisputably clear that while the origin of the stimulus to master the basic skills may come best from real life situations and genuine units of conduct, yet that stimulus must be used to motivate drill rather than to obviate it. When genuine life activities have awakened in children the desire to read, write and figure, the teaching of those skills is just beginning and must be supplemented by much careful teaching.

Expert analysis of any complex activity into its parts, and of any skill into its components, is necessary if the teacher is to administer it wisely. Thus the teacher of swimming, a comparatively simple skill,

GUIDANCE FOR INDIVIDUAL MASTERY

may break up the process into parts. First, the uninitiated is taught to stand in shallow water and duck. He thus learns to put his head under water without fear. The next step is the dog-paddle from deep to shallow water. When this has been mastered, the crawl is next in order, while the breast stroke, the most difficult of all, comes last. So in the teaching of arithmetical skills the smallest steps must be distinguished and taken up one by one. It is true that the making of such analyses is probably the work of the makers of curricula and textbooks. But the teacher should be familiar with such analyses made by professional educators, and make use of them in her teaching. Courtis, for example, as reported by Monroe, De Voss and Kelly,[1] has indicated the following different types of examples in addition.

"Addition: (1) addition combinations; (2) single-column addition of three figures each; (3) 'bridging the tens,' as $38 + 7$; (4) column addition, seven figures; (5) carrying; (6) column addition with increased attention span, thirteen figures to the column; (7) addition of numbers of different lengths."

The addition combinations mentioned under (1) are further analyzed by Overman according to difficulty of one hundred combinations as follows: [2]

```
0 0 4 1 6 0 0 7 0 3 9 5 2 0 8 0 0
0 3 0 0 0 8 1 0 5 0 0 0 0 4 0 6 9
───────────────────────────────
0 0 1 1 1 4 1 7 6 1 2 1 1 1 2 3 1
2 7 1 2 8 1 5 1 1 3 2 9 6 7 1 3 4
───────────────────────────────
8 4 3 5 5 9 2 3 2 4 3 8 2 6 7 4 3
1 4 1 5 1 1 3 4 6 2 5 2 5 3 2 3 2
───────────────────────────────
5 7 2 2 5 6 3 2 3 9 4 6 4 4 8 7 9
2 3 4 7 3 2 6 8 7 2 7 6 6 8 3 7 4
───────────────────────────────
9 5 8 9 5 7 7 8 6 8 9 7 5 6 8
6 6 5 8 9 5 6 7 5 6 5 9 8 9 9
───────────────────────────────
4 3 6 2 8 3 4 9 7 8 5 9 6 9 5 7 6
5 9 4 9 4 8 9 3 4 8 4 9 7 7 7 8 8
───────────────────────────────
```

[1] MONROE, DEVOSS and KELLY, "Educational Tests and Measurements," Houghton Mifflin Co., Boston, 1917, p. 19. *N.B.* An analysis of subtraction, multiplication and division is given in this book also.

[2] KEELOR, K. L., "Curriculum Studies in the Second Grade," Bureau of Publications, Teachers College, Columbia University, 1925.

Such analyses are of great help in assisting teachers to select step by step each new difficulty which the child will encounter in mastering the whole complex skill.

Care must be taken in such analyses, however, that they are made, as nearly as possible, in terms of conduct, and not in any mere arbitrary scheme of division. Even so astute a teacher as Pestalozzi fell into this error in his syllabaries by dividing reading materials into such bits as *ab, eb* and *ib,* divisions which are logical enough, but which are not in terms of whole-activity of children when they speak in sentences. Many teachers have fallen into similar error and have begun reading by teaching the alphabet, since a letter was the smallest possible particle of subject matter. So in arithmetic, or in recording musical composition in written form, the unit of growth is that which enables the child to solve a new kind of problem. Steps should always be natural steps, and whole steps.

3. Provision of Instruction

This narrow field of the provision of instruction for the mastery of complex skills has widely colored the whole field of traditional teaching. The technique here involved has been widely and indiscriminately applied to every type of teaching, with very harmful results. History, geography, art, and even music have languished under the dominion of the subject-matter teacher, whose total notion of curriculum was subject-matter-to-be-mastered, and whose whole idea of teaching was that of providing instruction in this, that or the other thing. Mastered by this blind spirit, writers on education have manufactured reams of directions for teachers to provide rule-of-thumb instruction to children in every "subject" under the sun. Is it any wonder that the teacher who understands children turns wearily away from textbooks in education which sear her educational conscience?

Instruction may be provided orally by the teacher, by other pupils sometimes called monitors, or by the use of printed materials. In order to facilitate the provision of oral instruction by the teacher certain "types of teaching" have been devised, based largely on the supposition that the teacher will give to the class oral instruction in the lessons which they learn. The type of school organization in which the teacher stands before the class and provides exposition or explanation is still very common. The types of teaching devised to meet the needs of such a teacher are several. The inductive lesson is one in which, by the citation of various examples of some process or phenomenon, the

GUIDANCE FOR INDIVIDUAL MASTERY

general rule involved may be brought to the attention of the pupils who are supposed to be listening. The deductive lesson is one in which the application of a general rule or principle is shown in detail in a particular case. Sometimes a combination of these forms an inductive-deductive lesson. The recitation lesson is one in which the materials studied in another period or at home are brought out orally by class questioning and discussion. The study lesson is one in which the pupils work at assigned material while the teacher oversees their work. The assignment is given and discussed preparatory to its private preparation by the pupils. The drill lesson is one in which the teacher puts the class through a series of exercises, the review lesson is a re-presentation of material previously studied in a fresh way involving new learning as well as a review of the old. The lesson in appreciation is one in which music or literature is presented by the teacher in a way calculated to encourage esthetic enjoyment. These lesson types [3] have been devised, for the most part, with a conception of teaching in mind which was largely based upon the notion of the teacher presenting organized subject matter to a group of children. The nature or structure of the subject matter was regarded as the chief criterion in determining which mode of presentation should be used in giving the lesson. The types were worked out largely for use in group instruction, teaching in which the teacher was comparatively active and the children comparatively passive. In recent years theorists have altered their conceptions of these types, have made them more general and less limited in their application and have added other types intended to supplement their somewhat limited outlook, such as the project, the problem, and the socialized recitation. The organization of theory as presented in this book, however, while it does not obviate the validity of these types within the narrow field of pure instruction, does not logically admit as adequate or complete any such analysis of teaching. It will be found that most of the learning situations dealt with in the well-known "types of teaching" are dealt with in some form or other in these pages. They are not, however, treated in terms of subject

---

[3] A study of the various types of teaching is very valuable in making the teacher conscious of various modes of explanation and exposition, arts of which she should be a thorough master. This matter is treated so thoroughly in standard textbooks that it needs no further presentation here. Excellent discussions are to be found in:
CLAPP, CHASE and MERRIMAN, "Introduction to Teaching," Ginn & Co., New York, 1929, Ch. XVI, p. 496.
KLAPPER, PAUL, "Contemporary Education," D. Appleton & Co., New York, 1929.
STRAYER, G. D., "A Brief Course on the Teaching Process," The Macmillan Co., New York, 1922.

matter to be taught, but in terms of aspects of conduct involved in the learning of individuals.

Oral instruction must always have an important place in teaching. A great deal of it, however, must go on individually by what has been referred to as directive conversation technique. In fact, the full recognition of the importance of individual differences in school has resulted in a decreasing use of group instruction and an increasing use of individual instruction. It follows that the teacher's use of any directive conversation technique would probably benefit from a study of the older types of teaching which have been chiefly used to assist teachers in providing group instruction. Individual differences are so wide that individual progress is almost essential in the mastery of such complex skills as reading or arithmetic. There are times, however, when group instruction will be needed. Little groups of individuals sometimes tend to pool themselves about certain problems which are coming up in class at the same time. Again, certain new work which is of interest to the whole class may sometimes be preceded by explanation or demonstration. Teachers thus find sufficient use for skilled oral instruction.

Printed instructions devised to assist pupils in the mastery of organized subject matter tend in their most recent form to be regarded as "individual instruction materials." Reference has previously been made to the organization and use of such materials so that the discussion need not be carried further at this point.

4. *Provision of Drill*

It is the testimony of many teachers that no matter what methods are used in giving the pupils mastery of complex skills they must include copious drill. When the necessity of overlearning such skills is considered this seems practically obvious. Drill may be provided in any of a number of old-fashioned ways. Wide use is made today of individual instruction materials or of modern textbooks which contain quantities of excellent drill material. The following lesson will give some notion of the way in which fresh drill materials may be derived by the children and the teacher from the regular activities of the class. Whether or not drill materials so derived are superior in nature to the purely formal drills taken from textbooks seems, however, extremely questionable. If drill is to be faced squarely and honestly as drill, it may not be necessary to treat it in this roundabout manner.

GUIDANCE FOR INDIVIDUAL MASTERY

Since such treatment is used by many up-to-date teachers, however, the following example [4] will not be out of place.

MODERN CLEVELAND

Origin:
This study grew out of the class study of a modern city. The pupils wished to make a large book, beautiful and helpful to others interested in Cleveland.

Procedure:
The pupils planned the book and bought the materials. The planning involved class discussion during which pupils decided on the size, style, and contents of the book. Details included the color, design and lettering for the cover, the quality of paper for the leaves, and the clippings and stories to be used.

Illustrative Problems:
 1. Moses Cleveland sailed into Cleveland harbor in 1796. How many years ago did he land?
 2. In 1860 Cleveland had 8 street cars in the city. Now Cleveland has 1,600. What is the increase since 1860?
 3. The Cleveland Railway Company has 110 buses. 50 of these are double-deckers. How many are single?
 4. I can buy 8 tickets for 50 cents. Single fares are 7 cents each. How much is saved in 8 rides by buying such tickets?
 5. The Press costs 2 cents. If my dad gave me 25 cents to give to a newsboy, how much change would I get? Make the biggest change you can.
 6. I stayed at Hotel Statler for one night. My room cost me $3.00, and meals $2.10. I tipped the waiter a quarter. How much change did I have left from a ten-dollar bill?
 7. One night I slept at the Cleveland Hotel. I awoke in the morning, dressed myself and got ready for breakfast. My room and breakfast cost $3.65. How much change did I get if I gave the cashier a five-dollar bill?

5. *Testing*

It is necessary for the pupil, as he progresses in the mastery of any set of complex skills, to test himself in order to see his degree of growth, in order to make an estimate of his proficiency. This matter has been discussed elsewhere (p. 172), so that it need receive little further attention here. Most modern texts or sets of individual instruction materials provide adequate testing materials. When they are missing, the teacher may use whatever tests seem convenient or devise tests which meet her own needs.

[4] "Activity Problems in Second- and Third-Grade Arithmetic," ALICE HANTHORN in *American Childhood*, March, 1929, p. 24.

Testing may be made significant to children by frequent reference to standards. If, for example, informal tests for rate and comprehension in reading are made each week children are anxious to improve their record and to see from a chart, if one be kept, how their work compares with that of their friends in the same class, and how close they approach mastery which is average for their grade. A list like the following showing the average rates as indicated from standard tests, or a similar list giving the standards for their own school, may be provided for the children to refer to.

>   Grade   I,   80–100 words per minute
>   "   II,   100–140   "   "   "
>   "   III,   120–160   "   "   "
>   "   IV,   140–180   "   "   "
>   "   V,   160–200   "   "   "
>   "   VI,   180–220   "   "   "
>   "   VII,   190–230   "   "   "
>   "   VIII,   200–240   "   "   "

In some schools the teachers have worked out diagnostic self-testing materials suitable to their own needs, by means of which the pupil may, at the end of a unit of drill such as the study of a new spelling list, test himself to discover whether or not he has complete mastery of the unit of work, and if not, just what particular part of it needs further drill. When he has found himself proficient in a number of units, he may report to the teacher. The teacher may then give a test of her own to the pupil in order to verify his results and keep check on his progress. As he masters a unit of work, and is successful in the testing of it, he may pass on to the next unit.

6. *Use of the Newly Mastered Skill*

Whenever it is at all possible, students should find immediate use for any newly acquired skill. In fact, it would seem that in the case of mastery of skills the final use of the newly acquired power in a unit of conduct in which it is valuable is more important than its origin in some life activity. Thus Boy Scouts who are easily persuaded to spend long periods drilling on the tying of various knots need to use these knots in camping and boating if they are to acquire any ability to use the knots where they are needed. Many a Boy Scout who has passed his tests in knot tying with flying colors uses a "granny" knot to tie up a parcel or moor a boat. So arithmetic and spelling and composition take on real significance as they are used in the practical affairs of the school bank, the school paper and the writing of social and business letters which arise out of school activities. Thus does the pupil become rewarded for the effort he has put forth.

It should not be supposed, however, that every skill, or every small unit of skill which is newly acquired, can be put into immediate use in school. It might be desirable if this were possible, but unfortunately it cannot be so. Although we may have no natural ready application of any skill there is no reason why we should not teach it. Children can have little life need for the addition of four-column numbers, yet their need for drill in number relations is sufficient reason for their doing this work. When it is possible to make use of newly acquired learnings it is desirable, but when it is not, the learning experience must in this respect remain incomplete.

SECURING KNOWLEDGE OF ORGANIZED SUBJECT MATTER

There is still another form of activity which has so dominated much of the life of the traditional school that the new schools have been tempted to neglect it, namely, the mastery of organized subject matter. This is one further realm in which conformity to patterns laid down by others is essential. No matter how eagerly the new schools may embrace an activity program, they should never forget that intellectual activity which conforms to the thought patterns of others as recorded in books is one of the basic activities of present-day mental life.

The careful teacher will encourage children to make themselves conform to accurate knowledge rather than to express half-formed opinion. Such was the case with a fifth-grade teacher in whose class the children had become very much interested in architecture. After some study along these lines they were dealing with the Renaissance style. The teacher asked the children to make a trip to the library whenever they could find time during the day, to consider available sources and bring to class written on a slip of paper "in the words of the author of the book or article" the best sentence each child could find descriptive of the nature of the Renaissance. It is obvious that in carrying out this task the children would have to do considerable reading and thinking. Consequently, the plan seemed a bit irksome to some of the children who had been brought up in earlier grades under a régime of considerable "freedom." Several, therefore, coaxed for permission not to be tied down to the author's words, and sought permission to write what was required in their own way. This would have been easier and would have freed the children from the discipline of careful reading. But this was a wise teacher who knew children's weaknesses and how to correct them. She insisted that the reports be made "in the words of the book." [5]

There has been the widest misunderstanding, not merely as to what subject matter should be mastered, but also as to what mastery of it really is.

In their search for organized subject matter difficult to master, curriculum makers and teachers have wearied children with useless and meaningless lists, valueless facts, and such artificially complicated subject matter as declensions and conjugations. They have agreed with Mr. Gradgrind, if not in theory then certainly in practice, as to "the necessity of infinite grinding at the mill of knowledge, as per system, schedule, blue book, report, and tabular statements A to Z." But further still, having piled up mountains of collated facts, they have sinned against the learning process by mistaking memorizing for mastery. To all such absurdities children will inevitably answer in terms of Tom Gradgrind, "I wish I could collect all the Facts we hear so much about, and all the Figures, and all the people who found them out: and I wish I could put a thousand barrels of gunpowder under them, and blow them all up together!" To which sentiments the good teacher is sorely, though not wisely, tempted to cry "Amen!"

Let us hasten to point out, lest enthusiasm for change carry us too far, that useful facts, information and knowledge which can be obtained from books is of priceless worth to any intelligent child. No teacher can neglect organized subject matter as it is found in books, articles and records except to the detriment of children. As normal children grow older, they develop a wide curiosity concerning facts and information of every kind. So the pupils of a good teacher are not stuffed with facts but are hungry for them. The brighter the children the wider and more omnivorous is this search for written truth. Just as the physical infant devoted himself to exploration of the physical world by manipulation and roaming, so the mental infant now seeks to explore the world of information and ideas. He delights in books and magazines which tell of the mystery of machinery, electricity, nature in sea and on land, and mankind in strange climes and stirring adventures. He glories in a hundred esoteric realms of fact and fancy.

The life of people and their doings is most interesting subject mat-

[5] The teacher in this case was Miss Emily Ann Barnes of the Lincoln School of Columbia University.

ter to all of us. If this is what is called history, or geography, or the social sciences, or science, or nature study, well and good. Then the children will find it as interesting as their teacher does; possibly more so, but certainly no less. Having once determined on such endless vasts of suitable organized subject matter, the next concern may arise from the impossibility of a complete exploration of such forests of knowledge. It is in the solution of this problem that teachers may still make an ancient mistake of curriculum makers. Faced with the impossibility of covering all knowledge, curriculum makers have taken upon themselves the burden of combing vast masses of subject matter for what they regarded as the most important facts and information and of organizing the residuum for rapid consumption by earnest learners. In doing so they have committed two fallacies. In the first place they have made the mistake of thinking that facts and information can always be selected for learning irrespective of the learning situations of specific children. In the second place they have assumed that all children will need and will learn very much the same information. There is, of course, a certain degree of truth in each of these assumptions. In spite of this, however, the assumptions do a good deal of violence to the conditions under which children actually learn. The organized subject matter which a child really learns is, to a large extent, dependent upon what he is interested in at the time, and upon what are his temporary needs for organized subject matter. The child who is collecting sea-weed will read through pages of a book on seaweeds which a child fascinated by tales of the French Revolution might scarcely glance at. The selection of organized subject matter for children in the elementary school should not be made on an encyclopedic basis. Those who have made the mistake of thinking so have missed the very important point that the organization of subject matter to be mastered is not primarily the duty of the curriculum maker or of the teacher, but of the learner.

Granted that it is more important for children in elementary school to know a lot about some things rather than a little about everything, there remains the problem of how children may gain a mastery over the facts and information they do set out to learn. In order to be clear on this we need to realize first of all that memorization of organized subject matter should not be confused with its mastery. A student who has memorized the first book of Euclid may be far from having mastered it. Mastery over facts and over organized subject matter means possession of the ability to use it when it meets life's needs and purposes. Nor is thoroughness to be confused with the ability to repeat by rote or to reproduce, under cross examination, what has been learned. "Thoroughness of the better type," writes Charles McMurry,[6] "is that which rests first upon complete understanding of the thing to be learned. To see a thing clearly in its beginnings, growth, and essential relations, to comprehend it in its bearings on reality, to get an experimental, usable knowledge of a thing is to know it thoroughly. The thoroughness of knowledge that makes it efficient in use is what we want. There is a fictitious, rather pretentious, kind of thoroughness based upon verbal drills and oft repeated reviews, which has a strong resemblance to knowledge. But the best kind of knowledge is that which takes deep root and, like a young plant, soon acquires powers of independent assimilation and growth."

Too much stress cannot be laid on the fact that it is by his own organization of ideas, facts and information that the pupil gains mastery over organized subject matter. It is only by such activity that he can relate what he studies to his own thoughts, knowledge and ideas, to his apperceptive mass. Furthermore, only as the individual relates the new subject matter to his own mental life can he be said to have mastered or learned it. Constructive work, such as the making of a bird pole or a chair, is organizing materials. The mastery of subject matter is similarly the organizing of facts and ideas.

So it is that Mrs. Mitchell talks approvingly of the making of a "creative map," a map in which the children put in what they know: "When our eight-year-olds went to the docks, I realized that the children had no sense of what a channel was at all. I asked them to draw me an island, and did all that I could to get the children below the water. One of the things I did was to give them pilot maps and let them paint all numbers under forty in one shade of blue, and all over forty in another shade, a symbol they could understand. I also remember teaching a group of twelve-year-olds who were going to study modern European history, and wanted to get a geographic background beforehand. I brought them a map, which I had painted, of roughnesses and smoothnesses, and said, 'If you knew nothing about Europe, excepting that there had to be a great many nations settled in this country, where would you put your dividing lines?' They looked up where the forests were, where the lakes and rivers were, and then they began to divide up with that as a basis. We then compared

---

[6] "Type Studies and Lesson Plans," George Peabody College for Teachers, Nashville, Tenn., Vol. III, No. 1, August, 1922, p. 33.

GUIDANCE FOR INDIVIDUAL MASTERY

this with the actual political boundaries."[7] It is surely obvious that in doing such things children are mastering the subject matter of geography. Again, when a child carefully prepares material with graphs for a lecture to his class on the gas engine, or prepares a report in the library to present to his group, he is gaining a mastery over organized subject matter.

As children grow older and pass into the higher grades of school, they need less direct experiencing as a basis for organizing ideas. They may learn vicariously and via the symbol, by reorganizing in their own terms the materials they read on the printed page. The older individuals become the less they are dependent on direct experiencing in learning. Their basic experiences being continually wider, and more and more understood in terms of language symbols, they are more and more equipped to learn indirectly via the short cut of organized subject matter. Thus books become increasingly important in the educative process. The following outline may be useful to the teacher for the direction of such learning activities.

TYPICAL TEACHING PROCEDURE FOR GUIDING
THE SECURING OF ORGANIZED KNOWLEDGE

1. Care that Subject Matter to be Mastered Should be Such as Fulfills an Understood Need

The needs for the study of organized subject matter are many and various in the good school. There are needs for historical information, needs for social information, needs for information about nature, science, and such definite matters as costuming and designing. These needs arise out of the activities of a good school life, out of the various units of conduct on which the children are engaged, such as giving a marionette show, studying the local environment in such a way that it expands into the national and world environment, or collecting frogs' eggs and watching the tadpoles change into frogs.

There are, however, needs for organized subject matter which are not so simply explained in terms of current daily happenings. The love of knowledge for its own sake must ever be one of the most pressing and one of the finest motives for learning. We must never overlook the fact that children will rummage through any available

---

[7] From an address by Mrs. Lucy Sprague Mitchell at the Sixth Annual Conference of the Manumit Associates, Manumit School, Pawling, New York. Published in a pamphlet by the School.

library, for no other apparent reason than that it opens an unknown and unexplored world, and will read books on every subject from hypnotism to post-impressionism. They thirst for information which is not obscured by pedantry and impenetrability of style. This active urge, this ceaseless curiosity creates a real need for knowledge, a need which should not be underestimated because it is not expressed in terms of immediate interests and activities. There is a positive delight in knowing which is entirely apart from utilitarian value.

Though children should be encouraged to indulge such high yearnings, there are more prosaic calls for the mastery of organized subject matter. In the course of the lesson in literature it may become evident that it is extremely inconvenient not to know "by heart" the names of the books in the Bible. Again, a number of pupils wishing to try out for a part in "The Tempest" which is being produced by the class, may find it necessary to learn lines of the play by rote. Or possibly a class engaged in a study of the sanitation of their city may formulate a list of outcomes which are of direct personal significance to each pupil in doing his share in maintaining public and private health. In all such cases it seems clear that the pupil would encounter subject matter which ought to be brought under his control.

2. The Subject Matter to be Mastered Should be Reorganized in Some Way by the Pupil

There are numerous ways in which subject matter may be reorganized to make the learning of it possible. It may be organized in discussion after the class has made a trip to the fire engine house or to the grocery store. As each individual makes his contributions to the discussion or listens to the contribution of others he is organizing ideas and relationships. As Mrs. Mitchell has so well expressed it, the child in imitating a train engine he has been watching makes the synthesis, "The thing that smokes is the same thing that whistles." Subject matter may be reorganized in the very familiar forms of underlining, annotating, outlining, map and diagram making, and essay or report writing. Older children need to be taught with great care how to carry on each of these activities in whatever reading materials are sufficiently important as temporary or permanent acquirements. Most of the directions usually given in books on "How to Study" are intended to assist the student in reorganizing organized subject matter. There is, further, a generalized habit of mentally organizing whatever one reads which is most important. Children should acquire this habit, which might be broadly called that of thoughtful reading. The writing of book reviews of what the children read will greatly facilitate them in the habit of reorganizing as they read.

3. Overlearning, Memorizing or Drill

Understanding what is read is a very real preliminary to the mastery of it. Overlearning is equally necessary if the material is to be retained in the memory. Thus rereading repetition, the formation of fresh associations with the material learned, and review are often necessary. In the case of lines to be spoken in a play actual memorization is, of course, desirable, as it is in cases where one is so taken by some excerpt of poetry that one wishes to have it always in one's possession. Usually, in the mastery of organized subject matter, some time and effort beyond that of passing attention will be required if the material being studied is to be available to the student when required by him in subsequent thought and action.

4. Use of the Subject Matter Learned

The test of the successful mastery of subject matter is evident during its use. The individual who finds himself able to use the subject matter he has studied at a time when he needs it in discussion or sensible conversation, has learned it satisfactorily. What is beyond recall at the time when it is needed is, other things being equal, not adequately learned. Consequently, students should, whenever possible, be given opportunities to test their powers in conduct which will make their degree of attainment obvious in a social situation. It is, without doubt, impossible to provide such opportunities for the immediate use of all subject matter which has been learned. Hence the temptation to provide an artificial possibility by the giving of examinations. If work which involves the mastery of subject matter could be so conducted that the functioning of the learning becomes subject to social approval, the artificialities of an examination system which makes learning abortive could be done away with. It is when the mastery of organized subject matter becomes really incident to the satisfactory progress of some significant unit of conduct, such as giving a hobby show, or issuing a class magazine, that it is both adequately motivated and satisfactorily tested. The way in which class activities may initiate and carry forward to completion the mastery of organized subject matter is indicated by the following report of a fifth grade teacher.[8]

"One day in the fall term our most versatile initiator announced his readiness to give the class a talk on the four-stroke cycle of the gas-engine. While I welcomed the subject, I was still surprised at the clearness with which he developed his points through chalk diagrams: intake, compression, power, and exhaust strokes. The essential differences between the internal combustion engine and the steam-engine came out pretty clearly. Other problems likewise opened up; Why do you have to crank a gas-engine? What are spark plugs? What is the carburetor for? How does it work? What is evaporation? What is the cut-out? What does the muffler do and how does it work? In what ways does the steam-engine differ from the gas-engine? What is the reason the gas-engine has many cylinders while the steam-engine has only one? Why does not the steam-engine need cranking? Why does the steamer have an advantage on starting on a hill? What is the arrangement of valves in the steam-chest? We had a toy steam-engine that we operated in the room and it showed the valve action pretty well. It also demonstrated the need of the flywheel."

It is clear that this individual study and presentation of this material on the gas-engine leading on, as it did later, to a study of transportation and industry, involved a great deal of study of materials and books, and the mastery by the individual concerned and the class to which he belonged of a great deal of organized subject matter.

[8] Francis W. Parker School Yearbook, The Course in Science, Vol. V, July, 1918, p. 84.

CHAPTER XXIV

THE DIRECTION OF PLAY

IN CONSIDERING the play of children we must not become too formal. There can be no advantage gained by giving separate attention to individual and group play. The nature of each is so similar and the technique for the direction of each is so simple, that there is no particular point in distinguishing between them. Consequently the present chapter will not make the distinction between individual and group activities which is made in the immediately preceding and immediately following chapters. It will serve rather as a transition between the pages on individual and those on group activities. We may find it profitable, however, to distinguish here between several different kinds of children's play.

UNDIRECTED PLAY

When children carry on almost aimless free activities their play is undirected. Using whatever materials and opportunities that come to hand, they sometimes wander carelessly and thoughtlessly from one thing to another. Any fine day in summer youngsters may be seen climbing trees, paddling in the water, making mud pies and playing chase. Such activities usually occur in out-of-school play time. Since they are entirely undirected they may progress without any attention from the teacher. They spring up naturally in entire independence of adults. Even city children, deprived of the wider opportunities of country life, may still be seen building with old bricks in city lots, or damming the gutters after the rain.

Yet there is a place for such play in school, especially in the lower grades. It is distinctly valuable to the teacher because it may become the beginning point for learning. Free activities which spring up in time which is allotted for recreation may be carefully watched and made use of. I recently observed children in an old type rural school during recess time. They were intently engaged upon setting up a simple bridge-like structure, with apparently little intent. Such play leads nowhere of itself, and stops as suddenly as it begins.

Its value to the teacher lies in the way in which it can be picked up and led on into directed play. The schoolyard activity just referred to might with due encouragement have led on to constructive and social activities of considerable value.[1] Thus undirected play may by a process of simple transition become a valuable introduction to learning.

Directed Play

Directed play is free, spontaneous activity which goes on, nevertheless, in a deliberately limited environment. It is play in which the child's activity is directed by a carefully prepared environment in which the teacher has seen to it that there are few stimuli to undesirable action and numerous stimuli likely to call forth action which is desirable. The teacher herself may be a very important factor in such an environment.

Knox describes the nature and guidance of directed play in the following words:[2]

"At first this play consists of very simple activities with no organization and with quick changes. Little or nothing is needed to help out. Any box is a train, a wagon, and a car in quick succession; a rolled-up towel is a satisfactory baby. But by the kindergarten period a baby doll is preferred to the towel, a doll's bed to an empty box, and playthings which represent real things are eagerly chosen. Gradually the disconnected play of 'being the ice man,' 'talking over the 'phone,' 'being mamma,' shade into playing house or store and imitating other sustained activities. This later playing is organized and quite realized and quite realistic in the primary grades, and more material is needed to help out the imaginative play. A 'play' store must now have bags, boxes, counters, a cash register, and regulation stock.

"Detail and conformity to fact become definitely marked in the upper grades as the children quickly act out certain points or phases of history, geography, literature or industrial life that have caught their attention—as the story of William Tell, trip to Holland, a guild of the Middle Ages.

---

[1] For an excellent example of the leading on of play activities see the Francis W. Parker School Yearbook, The Social Motive in School Work, Vol. 1, June, 1912, p. 46.

[2] KNOX, ROSE B., "School Activities and Equipment," Houghton Mifflin Co., New York, 1927, p. 175.

"The words *free* and *spontaneous* describe the method of all this type of play. With the younger children the teacher sees that the essential needs are provided; that each has a fair chance; that there is no danger of chaos; that done, she keeps hands off, leaving them free to play in their own way. The older children need some help in selecting the topic, but otherwise they should be left free to develop things as they choose."

TYPES OF DIRECTED PLAY

1. Physical Enjoyment

One type of directed play is that which provides physical enjoyment: walking, swimming, skating, horseback riding, canoeing, boating and others. Such play, if engaged upon in school time, may be regarded as directed, inasmuch as it requires a specialized environment. It fulfills the criteria of health and desirable activity in a way in which smoking, street corner loafing, and disorderly conduct do not. The teacher's directive function is obvious when children choose such desirable activities rather than other comparatively useless ones. Furthermore, in the supervision of these activities teachers have a real responsibility for the safety of the children under their charge. Active, strenuous play of children, such as swimming, skating, and unorganized ball playing, should be carefully supervised. A twelve-year-old boy engaged in excited hockey playing, stumbled over a board on the ice and snapped off a front tooth. This happened on the school pond, when teachers were present, under circumstances which seemed entirely unnecessary if the teachers had been intelligently directing the children's play. In another instance a boy under the care of a teacher conducting a recreational group of children from a well-known experimental school had his finger broken by a hard baseball. Surely in consideration of the hundreds of accidents caused by hard balls teachers should have sufficient common sense to see that preadolescents use only indoor baseballs, sponge balls, or some other form of soft ball. There are teachers who regard this as over-precaution. It is presumable that they have never been called upon on such occasions to pay the doctors' bills. Many physical play activities are cared for at summer camps and during outings. When they are not provided for in any other way the school should do what is possible to arrange for them.

2. Intellectual Enjoyment

A second type of directed play is that which provides intellectual enjoyment. If properly directed, children will find it in reading or listening to the "Three Bears," "Just So Stories," "Hiawatha," Froissart's "Chronicles," "The Faerie Queene" or "Adam Bede." They will prefer them to the vulgarisms of the comic strip, cheaply romantic magazine fiction, or the vacuous type of boys' and girls' books only too cheap and too prevalent. Removing poor material from the environment and stocking the class book shelf wisely, will aid in the direction of this type of play.

3. Esthetic Enjoyment

The third type of directed play is that in which the individual experiences esthetic enjoyment. Looking at pictures of a satisfactory kind is such an activity. These may be found in museums or in magazines containing lithographed copies of masterpieces. Further examples are the enjoyment of statuary, good music or any form of art; appreciation of poetry; and enjoyment of nature. Children need to be given time and opportunity to discover beauty for themselves. Otherwise they may develop the habit of neglecting the beauty of their physical surroundings, of nature and of art. Many an individual whose tastes were unprejudiced in childhood has learned to prefer cheap forms of jazz to good music, and, more pitiful still, to be esthetically blind to the beauty in a flower or a cloud.

If children are to learn to enjoy music, they must be given opportunity to listen to it. In many a kindergarten the phonograph is used to play selections from the works of standard composers. As the youngsters become familiar with the music they enjoy informal recognition tests as a sort of game. This early listening and watching for familiar passages is a sound foundation on which to build a later taste for music of the better sort. As the children grow older they may be introduced to longer compositions. What child would not appreciate Saint-Saëns' "Carnival of the Animals," the quirks and cries of the chickens, the lurching gait of the elephant, or the stately movement of the swan? By hearing such music children learn to enjoy it.

ORGANIZED GAMES

Organized games are simply a form of directed group play. They have their place chiefly in periods devoted to physical recreation. A large part of the time allowed for such recreation should be used in this way rather than in ways in which the time has often been occupied. There has been a tendency to a belief that formal drill and calisthenics provide suitable activity for the physical training of children. Recent investigation, however, has tended to support the view that there is small place for formal gymnastics arranged in a routine program for the physical development of children. Free play and games seem better suited to meet the requirement of keeping bodies already healthy in normal condition. In the case of special defects, exercises, if really corrective and prescribed by a director who actually understands what he is doing, are valuable. For the ordinary healthy child, informally organized play and games are better than gymnastics.

Salisbury mentions among other games, Puss in the Circle, Cat and Rat, Frog in the Middle, Toad's Mistake, and the Ringmaster, as suitable games for small children, giving directions for playing each of them.[3] The familiar, organized games—tennis, basketball, and others—are suitable for older children. Such organized play when carried on under the auspices of the school should, as much as possible, be supervised by a class teacher rather than by a professional athlete or physical director. It is only a teacher thoroughly familiar with children and their ways, and well trained to understand and teach them, who is capable of properly handling such work. When pupils are trained by a special supervisor the tendency is for the work to become formal and not naturally related to the other activities of the class. Thus an undesirable separation and lack of unity is introduced into the school life. In administering such games teachers should take care that no undue rivalry is stirred up between participating groups. The games should be played largely for enjoyment and for the development in grace and skill which may be secured by all who participate in them. Winning or losing is not an end in itself but merely a means to make games interesting. Consequently, interclass and interschool games, if arranged at all, should be rare.

It seems scarcely necessary after this discussion of play to append any lengthy discussion of the teacher's technique in its direction. The two following points may be mentioned, largely by way of repetition and summary.

[3] SALISBURY, "An Activity Curriculum for the Kindergarten and Primary Grades," Harr Wagner, San Francisco, 1924, p. 43.

TYPICAL TEACHING PROCEDURE FOR
THE DIRECTION OF PLAY

1. Keeping Hands Off

Play only develops in a régime of freedom. Consequently, if children are really to enjoy themselves, the teacher must let them alone. She may make suggestions, but it is only when children are arbiters, in the fullest sense, of their own conduct, that they may be said to be really playing. Children taken on a visit to the woods at their own request make most interesting use of the time if left to themselves and permitted to benefit by any suggestions which are offered. This is evident from the following account of such a visit made by first-grade children.

"The problems of construction are made more realistic to the children by a day spent in the woods, where they make a playhouse of brush, twigs, and vines. The children begin to build this house as an eagle builds her nest, by gathering sticks and twigs and throwing them into a pile. But they soon see that a better protection can be made by weaving together small branches and tying them into place with stout weeds and vines. When the little hut is finished, they make a carpet of red and yellow leaves.

"Some children make bows and arrows of twigs and vines, with which to hunt imaginary lions and tigers; others bring in, as their imagination suggests, wild fruits and nuts, or small game, such as rabbits or squirrels caught with their hands. They search the woods to select trees with spreading branches, so formed that a shelter might be made among them. They choose one that could be quickly climbed when the dweller sought refuge from wild animals." [4]

2. The Selection and Leading on of Play Activities

So very important is this technique of selecting and leading on children's play responses into other activities that, at the risk of saying the same thing twice, it is mentioned again at this point. The play experiences of the children during their visit to the woods just referred to are picked up by the teacher later on when the children have returned to the classroom and made part of their continuing experience. Colored leaves which have been collected are used in handwork. A hut is built in the schoolyard from brush left from trimming

[4] Francis W. Parker School, Studies in Education, Social Science Series, The Course in History, Vol. VII, p. 20.

trees; interest has been created in tree dwellers and the children have gained, from their observation of trees, an experimental basis for the understanding of stories about tree dwellers. This is easily led on to stories of cave men and so forth, affecting the work of the children in its various uses of sand, clay, or dramatization.

Similarly numerous play activities may be led on in an ever expanding way into channels which are useful. A visit to the farm may awaken interest in fodder, grain and milk or other foodstuff. Digging may lead on to the planting of wheat or corn, which the children may watch as it grows; stories or simple conversation may lead to little blackboard stories. The following example [5] gives an interesting account of the way in which play responses may be picked up by the teacher and made to serve her purposes in securing learning:

"In our beginners' room we enjoyed the first day of school thoroughly, watching our canary bird take his bath. His pretty yellow and black wings splashed water all about to the intense delight of the children, who readily came together as a social group to watch and help care for their pet. It was necessary to think together to choose his name, decide on the safest place to hang him, and determine the best place to keep his food and sand. Several children undertook interesting duties in connection with giving the bird fresh water, seed and a clean cage. This experience over and the bird safely hung by the window, the children were told that I would write about it on the blackboard so that others coming into the room would know what had happened. It was suggested that we save a part of the blackboard for sentences just about the bird. Our first entry that day was, 'Our bird took a bath.' This was proudly displayed to the few visitors of the day who heard this story read. It was read and reread, as were the succeeding notes added day by day. At the end of the first week of school, we had a fairly complete diary of the bird.

> The bird took a bath.
> The bird has a swing.
> Pete swings and swings.
> The bird is yellow and black.
> The bird sings and sings.
> The bird eats seed."

So what seems to be aimless activity may be a means to natural learning.

[5] ALICE KELIHER in *American Childhood*, Vol. XIV, March, 1929, No. 7, p. 16.

CHAPTER XXV

GUIDING GROUP CONSTRUCTION AND EXPRESSION

THE administration of group enterprises is, in a sense, more complex than the administration of individual activities. This is due to the fact that the responses of the children composing the group must be related and interrelated in such a way that during the progress of the enterprise all the children are active. In the case of individual activities each child is busy about his own personal affairs. In the case of group activities it is difficult to organize them so that all the children will be working all the time. Furthermore, the work of the various children must be so arranged that although each child is not necessarily engaged upon the same sort of work, yet the contribution of each bears an essential relation to the whole activity. In the past teachers have often sought to coördinate the work of different children by providing the same activity for each child during a certain period of time, and allowing them to carry on simultaneously. Such routinized procedure is far different from the approach which demands of the children, not uniformity in pursuing tasks which are identical, but variation. Thus, in the building of a house, each child may carry on a part of the whole task, a part which may be related to but different from that of some of the other children, but at the same time contributory to the whole.

SOCIALIZED CONSTRUCTIVE ACTIVITIES

There are a number of constructive activities which, although they are very diverse in their external aspect, may be discussed together because they may be similarly directed by the teacher. Such activities are the preparing of the daily lunch, the making of a wooden press to print linoleum blocks carved by the children, or the building of a kiln for pottery. They are often concerned with constructive work such as building or furnishing and decorating a school kitchen. These activities are those that are likely to come out of the everyday problems of living. They arise out of common surroundings, common needs, and social circumstances in which coöperation would make life more worth living. They differ from individual, constructive activities chiefly in the fact that they are more extensive, and require for their execution a number of individuals. Since the nature of such activities has been adequately presented in a previous chapter, no lengthy discussion of their nature is needed here.

The following conditions governing their growth and developments may be of assistance in their guidance:

TYPICAL TEACHING PROCEDURE FOR GUIDING
SOCIALIZED CONSTRUCTIVE ACTIVITIES

1. Recognition by Each Member of the Group of the Group Need for the Enterprise to be Engaged in

It is obvious that a group enterprise cannot be one's own in the way in which an individual enterprise may be. Consequently, such an activity must be initiated in response to a need which is common to the group. Furthermore, it is necessary to establish in each child the realization that there is a real group need, and that that need will only be satisfied if he himself makes his contribution. In short, each individual should recognize in connection with the proposed enterprise a personal significance and a social responsibility.

The teacher should make sure in the beginning of any group enterprise that each child realizes his personal need and his personal responsibility. If the children are engaged in preparing the daily lunch, for instance, the personal need and responsibility should be obvious to each child. If it is not, it should be made clear during the preliminary discussion. But the need for an activity is not always so personal or direct. It may on other occasions arise out of the larger conditions and needs of the school community. In some schools the seventh grade is expected to assume the responsibility for the printed materials used by the school. This need may be presented to them by the teacher and the class may discuss its willingness to assume this community responsibility. If, however, the need for printing is a more direct one, it should be similarly understood. The class may wish to print a booklet of their favorite poems, or of their own poems, so that each may have a copy for himself. In such a case the social and personal value of the activity should be so treated that it is clear to every participating individual. When children find themselves thus personally related to what is going on they give themselves to it willingly.

2. The Planning of the Proposed Enterprise

The planning of the work may be carried on in different ways, depending on the enterprise and the particular circumstances of the case. This planning may perhaps be experimental. Children of a second grade who have agreed to care for the school flock of chickens may make a personal examination of the chicken run and chicken house, and pool their information while discussing their plans for carrying on. The planning may be merely general. If there is no flock of chickens in the school, but the children are anxious to have them, the problems of securing the chickens and proper quarters in which to keep them will arise. A certain amount of abstract discussion will be necessary to launch the enterprise. Such would be the case if an older grade decided to set up a colonial house in the school room, or an eighth grade to build a club house. Just how the planning would go on in each case would be dependent upon the circumstances. A third type of planning may involve instruction given by some one else. If printing presses, unfamiliar to the children, were to be used, and unfamiliar type-setting engaged in, instruction as to how to proceed would need to be given by either the teacher or older pupils used to the work.

3. The Assignment of Various Parts of the Enterprise to Groups or to Individuals

The planning of a piece of work is very likely to involve a division of labor. If this be the case, it will be necessary for the group to designate very definitely certain individuals who are willing to assume responsibility for the completion of a certain part of the work. For instance, in the construction of a toy grocery store there are many tasks to be completed. There is the construction of a counter of old cases or boxes, the securing of cans, boxes, bags and sacks for materials, the making of a telephone and a telephone book, the making of several types of merchandise from clay, and the painting and shellacking of the same. It is obvious that all the children cannot be engaged on each of these activities. Consequently, the work needs to be apportioned among various children during some conference period or discussion. No matter what the activity is, whether it be chicken raising, printing, or building a log cabin, this apportioning or assigning of work by the group to individuals will be necessary for orderly progress.

4. The Work of Individuals or Small Coöperating Groups on the Assigned Task

Once an individual has accepted responsibility for any piece of work, it assumes the nature of an individual enterprise. Thus any assigned task, such as the making of the wheels for a train engine, now assumes the nature of an individual constructive enterprise. It may proceed, therefore, as far as the individual and the teacher are concerned, much as in the case of such an activity. This work may be carried on by nearly all the children at the same time during some denominated activity period, or different individuals may carry on their assigned work during some free period, when each individual is engaged upon what is, for him, most pressing. Again, the work may be carried on at any time during the school day or after it, when the individual concerned finds time and opportunity, irrespective of what other pupils are doing at the time.

5. The Coördination of the Various Parts of the Finished Work

From the original planning the pupils should have gained an understanding of the relation of their own individual work to the whole. The assembling of the completed work of all the children into whatever final form they have been working for should be an occasion for great satisfaction. This assembling may take place gradually, as in building a cabin, or the whole may wait for the assembling of various parts, as in the making of a train with engine and cars. The coördination of the whole may need considerable checking and supervision by the teacher, and extra work of alteration and modification may need to be assumed by the children.

6. The Use of the Product

So much work is sure to issue in a concrete result. The chicken raisers will have a fund from the sale of eggs. The builders will have a building to make use of. The printers will have forms to distribute, or books to cherish. Whatever disposal is suitable will be made of the product. There is little danger that what has been so dearly earned will not be put to good use when it is completed.

GROUP EXPRESSION

Another type of social enterprise is that in which the group gives expression coöperatively to some emotional or esthetic urge. Such would be the case when children are genuinely eager to form a toy orchestra, coöperate on some piece of mural decoration, or perform a play. Enterprises of this sort differ from group constructive activities chiefly in that they are concerned with the finer rather than the grosser things of life. They are esthetic in their nature and may be called "creative." A full and detailed account of how such matters may be carried out must be left to books dealing with method. The following points, however, may be characteristic of their development.

TYPICAL TEACHING PROCEDURE FOR
GUIDING GROUP EXPRESSION

1. Insuring Consciousness Within the Group of Emotional and Esthetic Values Which Need Expression

In work which is genuinely group expression, it is essential that the activities involved take their rise from a genuinely emotional or esthetic experience shared by the group. This is quite as important, if not more so, in the case of group expression than it is in the case of individual self-expression. So a group which decides to work out and present a play based on the life of Daniel Boone, should do so in response to a deep emotional appreciation of the character and personality of the hero. Similarly the need for a toy orchestra should grow out of a desire on the part of the children to build up their esthetic experience in the composition and performance of their own melodies. Again, delight in the imaginative qualities of "A Midsummer Night's Dream" might lead children to a desire to perform some part of it. It is only when group expression finds its origin in such genuine experiences that it can have its fullest and highest educational value.

Teachers, even in some of the best schools, have often failed to understand the importance of a genuine emotional or esthetic origin for group expression. They have mistaken the grossest imitation and the most slavish nose-leading of children for this type of esthetic activity. They have regarded dramatic work as fashionable and educative in some mysterious way. Plays have been held for their own sake. They have been written and performed for no reason at all. Teachers have sometimes forgotten that "the play's the thing" is a theatrical, not an educational, maxim.

It is to be carefully noted, however, that a great many educational values are secured in carrying on even the less genuine kinds of dramatic work. It demands graceful and interpretive use of the body, it provides numerous interesting activities, it motivates the correct use of speech and good habits of enunciation. It may provide hand work in costume making and construction of scenery. It may even contribute to the work in spelling and arithmetic. Such incidental gains, however, are not an adequate basis on which to found a sound philosophic justification for dramatic work. They might all be secured via some other equally complex and ingenious scheme of class procedure. No matter how desirable such educational gains may be, they are secondary and incidental. If they are to be of maximum educational value, they should arise during the progress of group expression which is not mere imitation but the real thing. Group expression which is real expression finding its origin in a genuine esthetic or emotional drive is infused with a life and reality which contributes to the progress of every part of the total activity.

It is not necessary, or possible, on the other hand, that this original emotional or esthetic experience should be a complete or comprehensive appreciation of the situation from which it arises. It would be absurd to maintain that a full emotional appreciation of "A Midsummer Night's Dream" is required for a proper initiation of its performance. No such full appreciation is required, but some glimpse of inherent values should inspire pupils toward its presentation. It is the original spark which will strike fire. So their initial esthetic experience will result in the fuller unfolding and appreciation of the beauties of the play.

Consequently, in the origin of such work as the writing of a play, the painting of a large piece of decoration, the giving of a puppet show, the performing of a symphony, the writing by the group of the words of a school song, it is important that the emotional or esthetic spring of the work be felt by every member of the group. Such activities may have their origin in the common experiences of the class. These may be real experiences, for instance a trip to the woods may contribute to a nature play, or literary experiences, when children dramatize nursery rhymes, or group interests as in such cases where the study of Greek or Colonial history or the history of the locality inspires the making of a frieze or the writing of a play derived from these common group interests. Whatever be the source, teachers should take care that each participating child is touched by the esthetic or emotional origin of the activity.[1]

[1] For an excellent discussion of the values of Dramatic Expression see Francis W. Parker School Yearbook, "The Social Motive in School Work," Vol. 1, June, 1912, p. 54.

2. The Development and Coördination of the Activity by the Use of the Special Technique Involved

Each type of group expression, whether it be artistic, musical, literary or of some other type, requires for its development a special technique.[2] The presentation of such complex matters of procedure must be left to writers on method of teaching. It is frequently necessary to develop the technique at the time, in accordance with the requirements of the case.

The following quotation provides examples of the use of special technique in the coördination of group expression:

In the preparation of a Greek play, two fifth grade boys one year evolved a chant for the setting of a long original poem on the deeds of Odysseus. They started by repeating the poem clearly, marking the rise and fall of their voices and the importance of certain words. They went to work at it as they imagined the primitive Greeks to have done. As they recited the poem, they drew on the board a curving line showing by the relative height of the curves the rise and fall of their voices, and the relative importance of certain words. In this manner each line of the verse was analyzed and developed from the inflection of the voice, into a definite melody. The result is not what could, by any possibility, be termed beautiful, but is interesting, has form and a good melodic base, and has been a profitable experience for the boys, as well as the teacher.

A really remarkable little melody was conceived by a fourth grade through great interest in a fairy play which they gave, and the song, which is a pixie spinning song, shows an unusual amount of originality of conception. Three fairies assemble at night, and in secret, in the humble home where dwells the little girl Rosadew, noted for her gentle disposition and unselfish deeds. Here they spin a garment of wondrous hue for the little girl, and sing a song in praise of her true loveliness, as they spin. The play had a great influence on the fourth grade, and every child in the class was eager to have a share in the making of a melody for the words of the fairy song. In all, they spent one and one-half periods on it, every member of the class working at great tension. They said the poem again and again, they thought it, felt it, acted it. A spinning wheel was brought up to the music room and put in motion to help in the feeling and rhythm. They were unanimous in wanting the song to give the impression of a spinning wheel in action. Hence the first two measures,—"Twirl and Turn," and the repetition. After much subdued humming one child thought out this musical idea which was instantly seized upon by the rest of the class with great enthusiasm. It was fairy-like and, so said the children, very characteristic of a spinning wheel.

[2] BROWN, CORINNE, "Creative Drama in the Lower School," D. Appleton & Co., New York, 1929.

Fairies' Spinning Song

CONSTANCE Mac KAYE　　　　　　　　　　Fourth Grade 1910-11

Twirl and turn, twirl and turn, Thistlekin Flittermouse Seed o' fern

Wondrous the gar-ment we pre-pare, Fit for a true prin-cess to wear;

Gold-en the thread on the spin-dle flies, Pearl-y the tears of Ros-a-dew's eyes

Twirl and turn, twirl and turn, Thistlekin Flitt-er-mouse Seed o' fern.

317

318   THE TECHNIQUE OF PROGRESSIVE TEACHING

Now that the start was made, suggestions for the following lines came flooding in. One phrase after another was written on the board, criticized, rejected, till the class found the one which suited the words and the music of the preceding line, each child contributing his musical setting and good-naturedly and impartially rejecting it for the one he considered better than his own in expressing the right idea.

The repetitions used in the song were not done unconsciously, nor for lack of new ideas. They were conscientiously thought out, and used because, according to the children, certain ideas needed repetition. Especially in the last two lines is this true. Many melodies were given and put on the board for criticism, but none of them satisfied the children until finally one child, with radiant face, suggested the spinning motif, and the children immediately adopted the idea and sank back satisfied in the knowledge that the song now sounded complete, as they themselves expressed it. Thus a perfect form was established through their own initiative, and one of the loveliest of their efforts was brought to a close.[3]

HELLAS

Oh! I'm thinking of Hellas
Of far away Hellas,
Where the green fields are lying
Where the sunlight is dying,
O'er the far stretching fields of my Hellas—
My far away Hellas.

Oh! I'm thinking of Hellas
Of far away Hellas,
Where the cattle are lowing
Where the waters are flowing,
On the wide sunlight fields of my Hellas—
My far away Hellas.

FAIRIES' SPINNING SONG

Twirl and turn, twirl and turn,
  Thistlekin Flittermouse Seed o' fern
Wondrous the garment we prepare,
  Fit for a true princess to wear;
Golden the thread on the spindle flies,
  Pearly the tears of Rosadew's eyes
Twirl and turn, twirl and turn,
  Thistlekin Flittermouse Seed o' fern.

[3] Francis W. Parker School Yearbook, The Social Motive in School Work, Vol. 1, June, 1912, p. 88.

Hellas

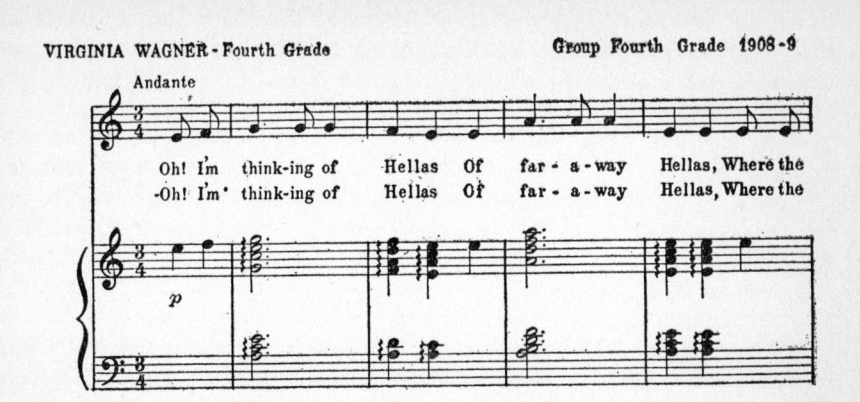

VIRGINIA WAGNER - Fourth Grade   Group Fourth Grade 1908-9

Oh! I'm think-ing of Hellas Of far - a - way Hellas, Where the
-Oh! I'm think-ing of Hellas Of far - a - way Hellas, Where the

green fields are ly-ing Where the sun-light is dy - ing, O'er the far stretch-ing
cat - tle are low-ing Where the wat-ers are flow-ing, On the wide sun-light

Last ending
fields of my Hel-las   My far. a way Hel - las.
fields of my Hel-las

3. The Use of the Coördinated Product

Little need be said of the use of the product of group expression. A play finds performance since that is, in the minds of the children at least, its chief end. Music which is composed will reach performance in the group, and large pieces of mural decoration may take a permanent place in the school.[4]

GROUP EXHIBITS

There is a type of group enterprise which is very much of the nature of intellectual expression such as that which has already been discussed in relation to individuals. This may take the form of a class exhibit. Such exhibits are often the outgrowth of the current activities of the class, and indicate a desire of the group to give some ordered and classified expression to the activities they have been engaged in. "For instance" writes Knox,[5] "a study of feudalism. There are pictures cut from magazines, mounted and labeled, and sketches of their own showing costumes, armor, a court-yard, a moat and other carefully reproduced details and another sketch showing a craftsman shop. There are also perhaps some miniature reproductions: a group of good-sized dolls dressed as noble, peasant, and middle-class people; some furniture; a cardboard shield, large enough to show decoration; a coat-of-arms. There are booklets with interesting descriptions of the period—one of each topic or phase—and on the book table a collection of books about the period—story or history.

"Or perhaps the fourth grade has been studying paper. The children have made, dyed, and used their own product and assembled samples of all kinds of paper; and they have also worked out a chart showing all the processes of making and dying—not only of their own work, but of the commercial products. Details have been carefully and accurately worked out. A period, an industry, or an art stands forth clearly. So others are invited to see the achievement. The fact that it is the work of children has nothing to do with it. The young workers should themselves understand this and judge their own products impersonally."

[4] An interesting example of group expression describing the making of a frieze based on Greek life is described in Curriculum Bulletin No. 5, "Teaching in Grades Four, Five and Six," Mildred English, Editor, Raleigh Public Schools, Raleigh, N. C., p. 111.

[5] KNOX, ROSE B., "School Activities and Equipment," Houghton Mifflin Co., Boston, 1927, p. 256.

When children have so much to show for their work, they are anxious for others to see their accomplishments. Consequently, an exhibit may be looked forward to in anticipation of some occasion on which visitors or parents are to visit the school, possibly toward the close of the term. By an exhibit is here meant any exhibition of the products of the children's activities, or, by extension of the term any exhibition of the children's activities themselves, such as choral singing, dancing, or some other performance or program largely the result of intellectual rather than emotional stimulus. The following elements will usually have bearing on the holding of an exhibit:

TYPICAL TEACHING PROCEDURE FOR
GUIDING A CLASS EXHIBIT

1. Early Recognition of the Intention to Have an Exhibit

At some time fairly early in the term, for such an activity should be a very occasional one, it is wise for the teacher to draw the attention of the children to the opportunity which will probably be presented at the term end or year end for some exhibit of the work they have been doing. The closing exercises of the school, or some similar function would provide the opportunity. Since visitors and parents come to the school to see what has been done during the term, there is a real need for the preparing of some sort of welcome. The children may early reach a decision as to whether or not they wish to hold a term end program or exhibit. If so, any tentative plans which ought to be made may be worked out and recorded.

2. Occasional Term Work Directed Toward the Exhibition

During the term plans for the exhibit should be somewhat refined. Occasional reference to the matter by the teacher when necessary, may help the children to remember their goal. In the case of choral work, in which regular practice periods are held, children may need to be made conscious of their responsibility to attend choral practice with regularity. A hockey game on the roof may prove a sore temptation to the pupil who is due at orchestra or choral practice. It may be necessary for the teacher to keep clearly before the children the fact that they have committed themselves to the more restrictive activity, and remind them of the purpose of their work.

3. Planning of the Program

As the time for the exhibit approaches, special attention should be given in class to the perfecting of the plans and organization. The program of activities, when the exhibition involves any type of performance, should be carefully worked out. If the program is to be printed in the school, arrangements must be made. If it is to be decorated by the children, some design must be selected, whether by choice of the children's previous work, by assignment to one able child, or by competition, as the circumstances of the case seem to warrant.

4. Final Preparations

Whatever final preparations are made should be made by the pupils themselves, not by the teacher. In the case of regular performances in which the school auditorium is used, little preparation further than that of arranging for the hall, and a rehearsal or two need be made. If the exhibit is of the children's hobbies, paintings— or other art work, or of some collection they have made, the whole problem of setting out and labeling must be faced. Sometimes the exhibit is not a temporary one of only a day or two's duration, but is a matter of a week or two. Such exhibits are those which are sometimes set up in hall cases so that they may be viewed by the remainder of the school or by any passing visitors. The cases must be carefully and attractively arranged so as to make a satisfactory visual appeal.

5. The Clearing of the Special Arrangements

Enthusiasm is likely to wane at a startling rate when once the gala occasion is over.

> "The tumult and the shouting dies,
> The captains and the kings depart."

But the children should not be permitted to go with them. The taking down and clearing of exhibits, and the returning of materials to the owners is as much a part of a well-planned exhibit as the setting up. Certain types of activities clear themselves away, such as the performance of an orchestral program. Others need more arduous labor. Such work should be carefully planned for and carried on, not by the teacher, but by the pupils.

CHAPTER XXVI

GUIDING THE GROUP SEARCH FOR KNOWLEDGE

CHILDREN are eager to secure knowledge, and the activities of the group should further their opportunities for doing so. In the first place, knowledge may be secured through direct experiencing, through *visits or excursions*. In the second place, especially as pupils grow older, knowledge may be attained from secondary sources, via the reports of others or via written or printed symbols. This knowledge is most coveted by the learning individual at a time when he is faced with some definite problem, the solution of which requires the knowledge he is seeking. Thus pupils are willing to study what is written when it will serve in the solution of *group problems*.

Knowledge which is thus gained by direct experiencing in the form of trips or excursions, or in the solution of problems, is very different from mere information which in the popular mind passes for education. Since it is functionally related to the needs of the learners, it becomes related to their personalities, and so may be regarded as genuine knowledge rather than as mere information.

GROUP EXCURSIONS OR VISITS

There are numerous activities which may be referred to under the general heading of excursions and visits. One of the chief of these types of activity is outdoor trips or visits made either to some natural spot, where science and nature may be studied directly, or to near-by places in the community which children should see and understand. Thus a class may take a trip to the mountains or hills to follow the nature trails which have been prepared for nature lovers. Or they may make such a trip as that made by Mrs. Mitchell's kindergarten class (Public School 41, in New York City), to a near-by stable, and at another time to the elevated railroad. An older class in the same school visited the steamship *Berengaria* in port. Again, manufacturing plants are sources of valuable knowledge and information. They provide excellent opportunities for the study of science via its applications to industry. Museums, especially in the large cities, are a veritable mine of materials valuable in teaching. Unfortunately, however, teachers often make very poor and inefficient use of them. Museum visits which are mere pleasure excursions may amuse the children, but they have little value. Classes of children troop through the great museums in the city of London. In the Natural History Museum they may be seen almost any day, marching from exhibit to exhibit with unseeing eyes. In the Science Museum, so replete with endless materials on land, water and air transportation, youngsters stand about aimlessly pressing the buttons to watch the wheels of the model engines go round. Thus they receive the least possible educational value for the school time spent in the museum. Such visits should be made only with a definite object in view, and usually confined to the sections or exhibits which are pertinent. Children studying the steamboat might make a trip to the museum to study primitive types of boats, and confine their attention to the Pacific Island out-rigger, the Eskimo kayak, or the Indian canoe.

Attending a moving picture performance may be classed as an excursion or visit. At times children have opportunity to visit talking or moving pictures in the school auditorium or some special showing in some local theater. A great deal of time may be wasted in this way unless the work is carried on carefully and soundly. Some modern elementary schools are finding that they can make comparatively little advantageous use of moving pictures in school work. They seem inclined to allow moving pictures in school time only if an exceptional film becomes available. When such pictures are shown there should, in the first place, be no doubt about the educational value of the picture. It should certainly be definitely related in some way to the general needs of children. Furthermore, it should not be aimlessly viewed. Fortunately the educational effect of a moving picture may be practically negligible, or we might well worry over the millions of our children who visit the "movies" once or twice a week. If children visit moving or talking pictures in school time, the subject should be one of importance and worth, and preparation should be carefully made for the visit.

Other types of trips may be mentioned. Possibly the school might visit a local exhibition or fair, or take a trip to see a play or hear a symphony concert. Even listening to a radio performance may, in a sense, be regarded as a visit. Again, unless such work is carefully prepared for and supplemented, it may become very wasteful. The following general points are more or less applicable to lessons which have the nature of trips or visits.

Typical Teaching Procedure for the Guidance of Excursions or Visits

1. The Occurrence of the Occasion or Need for the Visit or Excursion

If trips and visits are to be of real value, they must be closely related to the work which the children are doing in class. They are most significant when they arise from a need which is definitely felt in connection with other activities carried on by the class. So children who are interested in birds but have little opportunity to see them, might plan an early morning bird trip; or boys who are building a cabin might visit a house under construction and talk with the carpenters. On account of their organized nature, museums are particularly useful. Students studying some branch of life activity which is concerned with science will find museum trips of great value. In certain other cases, however, the need is not so obvious to the children. Some teachers are convinced that young children need to be introduced to their environment by frequent neighborhood trips. In such cases, the general desire to see and hear and feel will motivate a trip which the teacher suggests, or which is chosen by the children in conference with the teacher. Classes sometimes make trips to stores to buy materials used in class or to discover for themselves the answer to some question that has come up. In fact, children are always ready to go on a trip. It is necessary for the teacher to guard against trips which would be comparatively wasteful of time and productive of little educational value. Only the most worthwhile and necessary trips should be carried out.

2. The Planning of the Trip

Before the children go on the trip, class time must be taken to plan both the trip out and the return. Such arrangements need to be carefully made and time clearly set apart in which to make them.

3. Planning of the Visit

It is in the planning of the visit, however, that the greatest care must be taken. Unplanned visits are practically useless. It is necessary, in the first place, for the children to realize why they are going on the trip. Suppose that a New York class has been studying the Panama

Canal, and the significance of the mosquito in the completion of that work comes to the fore. It may occur to the teacher or to the class that in the Museum of Natural History is a model of the mosquito, with considerable organized material concerning its life and habits. The class may decide on a trip to secure what information it can on the subject of the mosquito and its relation to disease. Again, if the class has been studying the housefly or is likely to encounter problems concerned with it, it might be well to make a study of the models and material on that topic at the same time. On the other hand, such may not prove to be advisable. The class should decide what it will do. Possibly it may decide to limit the study to the mosquito and malaria.

When the decision is made the pupils should collect what available materials they have and make some preliminary study of the subject. This work should be treated, according to its dimensions, somewhat as a class problem. It is necessary for the children to be acquainted in a general way with the matter they are to see and what the museum exhibit has to offer. Perhaps a scout may be sent for a preliminary visit to the museum to make a class report which will be helpful in planning. The class should list what it is to look for. Perhaps a set of questions which need answers may be written on the board. If the exhibit is a large one, there may be a division of labor so that groups of two or three may make studies and sketches of special parts of the exhibit in their notebooks. Special class reports may be given on these at a later time. Whatever specific plans are made the children should be clear before leaving the school as to their special purpose, knowing specifically what they want to see. They should have made plans for a thorough study of the whole exhibit in its bearings on the topic they are concerned with.

4. The Visit

During the actual visit itself, the children should carry out the plans they have made. If the visit has been well planned, there will be no idle children. During a museum visit the children should not wander to various parts of the museum unless a large general exhibit is being viewed. They should concentrate about the parts of the museum with which they are concerned and should spend fifteen or twenty minutes actively engaged in investigating and recording the information in their notebooks, and talking over the problems which arise with one another.

In the case of a visit to a manufacturing concern less freedom may be possible for the pupils. The children may have arranged beforehand for certain individuals to ask special questions of the guide at special times.

5. Discussion, Organization of Information, Use and Evaluation of the Results of the Visit

A visit should not be considered finished as soon as the actual trip is made. It is necessary to correlate the information obtained and to reach some sort of organized outcome. Thus, time must be set apart a day or so later, when the unimportant details have faded somewhat, for discussion of the trip and the presentation and organization of the materials gained. The pupils should be careful to evaluate their own activities in the light of their object in making the visit. They should be careful to note whether or not the purpose of the work has been satisfactorily accomplished.

Group Problems

A group problem is a special type of group enterprise which is not chiefly concerned with direct first-hand experiences of an outward and material kind, but rather with ideas, information or special subject matter. It does not deal, like trips or visits, with first-hand sense expressions and experiences, but largely with vicarious experiences as expressed in language or in written symbols. It deals with ideas rather than gross realities. It is usually concerned little with hand work, and more with head work. It involves thinking rather than overt doing or making.

Such problems arise continually during the progress of school life, usually with increasing frequency and in more extensive form in the higher grades. As the mental grasp of the children increases, it is natural that they should deal less with mere things, and increasingly with ideas and information. For example, in the course of their study of community life, the seventh grade may become interested in the problem of how a person of another country may become a citizen of the United States, or of conditions governing immigration, or of the purpose of passports. Or possibly in the course of work in science, interest may be aroused concerning various ways in which people have kept time. This may lead to the study of the sun dial, the water clock and the spring and electric clock.

It is becoming well established that facts and information are not so well learned separately as they are when related to some specific situation in which they function, or on which they have a bearing.[1] Thus it is that teachers tend to organize much of the actual and informational work in geography, history and the social studies in terms of problems. These problems organize the materials to be mastered about situations which involve the use of these materials in thinking. Consequently the learning of the subject matter of the curriculum takes place in a setting in which it has significance. Such problems as—How is the purity of the city water supply secured? Why did the United States purchase Alaska? Why is Kingsford-Smith called the Magellan of the Air? What is the purpose of the Boulder Dam?—all lead far afield and under the direction of a skillful teacher will carry the class into the studies that will be well worthwhile. Teachers should realize that the children's environment may offer many problems in the solution of which they are vitally interested. By picking up pupils on the level of their real interest in problems of living which they themselves realize, or problems which are revealed to them by the teacher, they may be led in profitable directions. Thus they may gain an understanding and mastery of history, geography, science, or nature study, in a context both desirable and useful.

The origin and scope of these problems may vary enormously. A simple problem may arise with the younger children as to how the ice in their drinking water is made, or why "dry ice" doesn't melt. On the other hand, problems of wide reach and significance may arise in the older groups, such as the nature of American policy in Mexico, British policy in India, or the problem of extraterritoriality in China. While the guidance of activities involved in the solution of such problems is similar to that given to socialized enterprises in general, it is thought better, for the sake of clarity, to give separate suggestions for carrying on this type of work.

TYPICAL TEACHING PROCEDURE FOR
THE GUIDANCE OF GROUP PROBLEMS

1. Arranging the Group's Acceptance of the Problem as Their Own

One's intellectual interests are apt to be more diverse from those of others than one's mere physical needs. Consequently, the securing

[1] It should be noted that this does not mean that facts learned incidentally do not need drill if they are to be retained over a long period.

of group unanimity in the study of any particular problem may be more difficult than the securing of interest of small children in such an amusing adventure as constructing a Play Town. In a healthy class many more problems will arise than can receive attention from the whole class. Thus in a class of small children interested in gardens, different children may suggest different problems: What should we do with toads in the garden? Can we change the color of flower petals? What flowers attract humming-birds? From these problems, and many similar, the group must choose one which they recognize as of significance to all concerned. It is important that the teacher aid the children by suggestions and discussion in committing themselves only to problems of general interest and value. The nearer the group approaches to unanimity in recognizing the need for the solution of the problem on which the group is engaged, the better that problem will be as a suitable spring for group activity.

2. Group Planning for the Solution of the Problem

Once any problem has been adopted by the class as its own, it must be discussed and analyzed by the group. Thus, a class interested in cotton cloth and how it is manufactured, might ask such subsidiary questions as: Why is cotton sent from the South to the North to be manufactured and then sent South again? Is cotton raised in our state? What manufactured products do we get from New England and do we send any there?

The following account [2] gives a good example of the way in which a larger problem may be broken up by a class into its various parts for further study:

The children were anxious to know something about the state in which they lived. They wanted to know where the people of North Carolina came from, how they lived, dressed and traveled in the early days, so they decided to study about the Pioneer Days of North Carolina first. They studied many of the scenes of the early days, also many of the activities.

When this was finished they wanted to know what part North Carolina had in the Revolutionary War, and what part North Carolina had in the Civil War. Then they were interested in the Reconstruction Days and the development of North Carolina from the Civil War to the present day. Many problems arose with this large unit of work, "Know Your State." It

[2] SENTER, MRS. HERMAN, Teacher of the Sixth Grade, Boylan Heights School, Raleigh, N. C., in Curriculum Bulletin No. 5, "Teaching in Grades Four, Five and Six," Raleigh Public Schools, Raleigh, N. C., 1929, p. 120.

required a great deal of reading and much collecting of material. In geography they tried to develop North Carolina from the early days, when North Carolina's resources were not well enough known to fix its present standing, "The Fifth State."

Problems Worked Out in the Study of North Carolina:

1. Who's Who in Early North Carolina?
2. The Development of the Water Power of North Carolina.
3. Where North Carolina Leads.
4. Early Governors of North Carolina and the chief event of each term.
5. Where North Carolina Leads in Minerals.
6. Forestry Facts.
7. Governors of North Carolina from 1836-1928; the chief event of each term.
8. Much material was collected on North Carolina Folk Lore, as follows:

    1. What is Folk Lore?
    2. North Carolina Folk Lore Superstitions.
    3. North Carolina Folk Lore Riddles.
    4. North Carolina Folk Lore Games.
    5. North Carolina Folk Lore Songs.
    6. Ballads traced from the beginnings.
    7. North Carolina Ballads.
    9. North Carolina Folk Lore Plays.

3. *The Apportioning and Acceptance of Responsibility*

As in the case of all units of conduct in which a group coöperates there must be some division of responsibility. In a case in which children study problems concerned with their own state, different parts of the work may be carried on in different ways. Possibly certain of the problems may be dealt with by the whole group, each member looking up what he is able to find on the subject. The teacher may find it necessary to use her superior knowledge and ability in securing special books and directing the children by means of specially prepared bibliographies to certain pertinent materials. Further discussion may lead to the assigning of reports to certain individuals for special investigation. In the study of North Carolina just quoted, for example, various children reported at certain times on "Early Cities of North Carolina," "The Albemarle Colony," "A Summary of Fishing in North Carolina," "The Wealthy People of Early North Carolina," and several other subjects. Again, a class that is studying the problem of how ice is made may divide up the work among them in one way or another, according to the time which can be spared for the work and other circumstances. Perhaps, for instance, the division of labor might be in part as follows: One pupil might consult magazines to discover what she can on the subject. Another might consult certain references supplied by the teacher, and prepare a report. A third might visit a factory where ice is made, while a fourth might prepare a diagram, a chart, or a piece of demonstration apparatus, as the need of the case demanded. This apportioning or assigning of responsibility need not, of course, be made all at once. As the problem unfolds and becomes the better understood various pupils may accept responsibility for the investigation of whatever aspects of the situation need study.

4. The Work of Individuals on Assignments

Having accepted the assignment of a problem the individual concerned will then set to work on it independently, making use of whatever aids are afforded by the library or the community. The work becomes virtually an individual enterprise, which is being carried on for the good of the group. Children need to be trained to carry on work of this sort, which is in reality a simple form of research. They will need to be taught how to use the library and reference material. They need to be encouraged in such activities as making visits, carrying on experiments, making investigations, securing information in out-of-the-way places. Their best habits of individual study will be called into play in such work. It is obvious that a youngster preparing a report on "Insect Enemies of Wheat," "Customs of Central Africans," or "The Use of the Cocoanut Shell to Tell the Time," will have to work hard to get the material in good shape to present it to the class. Such work may be carried on in school time if the individual's program permits it, or in out-of-school time, as the case may be.

5. The Coördination of Individual Assignments in the Solution of the Whole Problem

The coördination of various parts of the work must, of course, be carried on when the class is meeting as a group. This will usually be done in the case of class problems by the presentation, criticism, and discussion of whatever material is being set before the class. Suppose, for instance, during a study of the cause of the extraordinary growth of New York a child is making a report on rates of growth in the population of the city. When the child has reported that New York has, by the most recent census, a population of 6,955,363 and is expected to pass the 7,000,000 in the very near future, since the average gain is 357 a day, the report will be open for discussion. Presumably some one may raise the question as to whether or not New York is now larger than London. This may lead to the securing of the supplementary information that the estimated population for London in comparative figures is 7,900,000. Further data indicate that London is spread out over 693 square miles, while New York's seven millions are contained within an area of only 299 square miles. These facts may readily lead to a lively discussion concerning congestion and the importance of the fact that Manhattan Island is completely surrounded by water. The conclusions that the concentration of population in a small area and the large waterfront have been significant factors in the growth of the city should be duly recorded as throwing light on the general topic of the causes of the phenomenal growth of New York. When the various reports and discussions have all been completed, the outcomes of each should be formulated into some form of final summary providing the answer to the original problem. These summaries and the clear recognition of outcomes are most important if work of this kind is not to be rambling and slipshod.

6. *The Evaluation of the Class Work on the Problem*

This evaluation of the work of the class on the whole problem may include an evaluation of the way in which the work was carried on and also of the final solution. Was the problem a worthwhile one? Did the class handle it satisfactorily? Does each member of the class understand how the final conclusions were reached? Is the solution a satisfactory one? In the case of problems such as those of national policy the class should learn not to take its own decisions too seriously. The degree of thoroughness of the investigation should be taken into consideration, and its adequacy discussed. Thus by the estimating of results preparation may be made for a more careful handling of similar units of work later on.

It is particularly important that both the teacher and the class be adequately critical of the reports given by the pupils. A great deal of time may be wasted in poor class reporting. Good class reports are not a gift of the gods. They are the result of careful training on the part of the teacher. Pupils reporting need to be developed by constant attention on the part of the teacher and the class to the quality of the reports offered. This is particularly important in the higher grades, where the subjects dealt with are less concrete and more easily neglected and prepared in careless fashion. It will be found, however, that children who have been trained to habits of responsibility, and who are used to class coöperation throughout their whole school life, will be well prepared to carry on more serious work as they reach the higher grades.

II. TEACHING PATTERNS

CHAPTER XXVII

TEACHING PATTERNS

Lessons as they actually occur in the classroom defy classification. Never is this more true than when teaching is organized in terms of conduct. The complexity and variety of class procedure reflects the complexity and variety of life itself. To be accurately apprehended, teaching must be regarded in its unity. Analysis of teaching can, at best, be partial and artificially descriptive. It may contribute to an understanding of the actual process of teaching, but it cannot be an exact and full representation of class procedure as it really takes place.

Consequently, it is not sufficient to present, as has been done in Chapter V, a general classification of units of conduct into three general types: constructive units, play units, and work units. Nor is it sufficient to present a further classification of activities in terms of typical forms of enterprise and typical teaching procedures, as has been done in the immediately preceding chapters. Something further is necessary. It is desirable to have whole pictures, concrete descriptions of the actual teaching of lessons, if the matter is to be presented in its unity, and the various analyses properly subordinated and related to actual class teaching.

It is obvious that typical teaching procedures do not present an adequate, full view of whole or complete units of teaching. They are phases of whole teaching patterns. A single teaching pattern may be composed of numerous activities which are so diverse that they may be governed by several varying procedures. For example, in the course of a whole teaching pattern, such as the writing and performance of a play based on local history, several teaching procedures will be followed. The writing of the play may be guided in a fashion suitable for group expression, the making of posters by that suitable for esthetic self-expression, the making of costumes and scenery by that suitable for group construction, and individual work on assigned costumes or properties by that suitable for individual construction, or individual self-expression, as the case may be. Consequently, if a whole view of teaching is to be obtained, something more than a study of typical procedures is required, namely, the study of a series of actual teaching patterns.

Such a presentation of unified pictures of lessons and teaching is not a simple matter. Nevertheless, if teaching is to be regarded in its unity, it must be regarded in its complexity. The opportunism of life, its ever-changing conditions, its manifold and varied activities, its uncertainty of pattern and issue, all must have counterpart in school life which is really living.

How may any such activity as collecting rocks, finding out why boats float, or putting electric buzzers into a play village, be smugly classified into any particular mold and referred to as a "type of lesson?" One might as well classify one's thoughts, or one's meals, or one's visits to the country into type thoughts, type meals, or type visits. Human life and conduct, in school or out of it, is so infinitely intricate that it defies simple analysis, and practically invalidates generalization. Genuine whole-activities will not fit accurately into descriptive molds. The best that can be done is to analyze and plot behavior patterns, to study cases in the hope that in such fashion some knowledge may be obtained which will serve in cases which are similar. We should not lose sight of the whole in the analysis of its parts.

Perhaps in the matter of teaching we can do little better than this. The various forms which the life of the school may take are so ephemeral, so varied, that each hour of the school day defies prediction. It is an individual lesson. It can neither be exactly imitated nor copied. It is in the mold of life itself. It can be described, but if it is to be fully described, it must be described as an individual case, not as a "type" to be reproduced or mechanically imitated. Teaching patterns and learning patterns may be well studied *in extenso*. Hence the preparation of case studies is most important for teaching.

Such *in extenso* case reports of teaching are here referred to as teaching patterns. The use of the word "patterns" is intended to be regarded in something of the same sense in which it is used in the term "behavior pattern." The word "patterns" is by no means intended in the sense of a pattern from which a coat or dress is made. Such a pattern is one to be observed closely and accurately followed. In the case of teaching patterns, the contrary is true. In the sense in which it is here used it is intended to refer to a resident design or pattern to be observed in a lesson or series of lessons. It is used in a similar sense to that in which we say that we find patterns in leaves, in clouds and on spiders' backs. This pattern is observed and recorded, not for imitation, but because it gives essential interest and individuality to the matter reported or observed. By neglecting unessentials it yet presents the unit described in its individual character.

The teaching patterns are presented for study analysis and inspiration rather than for imitation. The situation is similar to one in which one examines pictures in a museum. The picture is a unified piece of art. It may not be classified into one of half a dozen or so types of painting. It is as individual as the artist himself and as the moods which inspired it. One views it not to classify or to imitate it, but to appreciate, enjoy, and possibly to evaluate and analyze it. The technique of the brushwork is noted, the juxtaposition of color and nature of the design. So in the study of a single teaching pattern one may admire the skillful organization of the complexities of the situation, one may observe a gleaming facet of discussion, admire a phrase of conversational technique, or the skillful direction of some creative impulse.

Classroom procedure which superficially examined is apparently formless and transitory, may partake of the characteristics of several types of teaching at once. The total organization and pattern, however, is not necessarily that of any given type, but rather that given to it by some concrete situation, some bit of living. *The organization and development of the lesson is guided by the inherent structure of the unit of conduct involved.* The teacher is not guided by any rule of procedure but the organization of learning and teaching is governed by the inner nature of the activity in progress. In its development the teacher has been a creative artist, relying not on established modes, but rather continually developing new patterns to meet current needs.

Consequently, in order to complete the picture presented by the theory of teaching as here outlined, it is necessary to give some concrete accounts of actual teaching patterns in the hope that teachers will be encouraged to keep such records of their work for the benefit of others who would be anxious to study their patterns. In the presentation of the technique of teaching in the present pages, teaching has been described as the maintaining of a directional flow of the learning process from the child to the curriculum. An attempt has been made to analyze, step by step, the directing of the children's self-initiated responses by means of desirable units of conduct toward the realization of the values of the curriculum. As the analysis gradually reaches the fuller and more complete description of teaching, it becomes more and more complex. The weaving process, which is living, becomes more and more clear and definite in practice, yet less and less simple of description. The teaching patterns presented in the following pages should help to make clear in final and definite form how teaching, as here described, may issue in a definite teaching procedure which results in sound and adequate learning. It is hoped that they will give some brief picture of the actual synthesis of the child's responses with the values inherent in the curriculum.

It will not be possible here to include a large or comprehensive group of teaching patterns. In the present state of experimental teaching records are comparatively scarce and the process of reporting is haphazard and ill-organized. What patterns are given are carefully chosen from among many for the purposes for which they are designed. It has not been possible to present patterns which are perfect in every respect of artistic teaching. It is intended rather to present a series of brief, valuable and interesting teaching patterns with an analysis which will assist in their understanding and appreciation in the terms of the technique set forth in this book. After careful study of these lessons, it will be possible to examine into various reports in magazines and current literature of the newer teaching with greater profit. Furthermore, such study will assist teachers themselves to make a clearer and more definite analysis of their own teaching. In accordance with what has been said above, no attempt will be made at classification. Rather the teaching patterns will be given in whatever form seems profitable in each case, with notes and analyses which seem appropriate for discussion.

I

Teaching Pattern Involving Geographical
Orientation, Block Building and Language

*Five-Year-Old Group, Experimental Section,
Public School 41, New York City*

The following is a splendid example of the way in which an exceptional teacher may work out original teaching patterns which are distinctive and different from the work of other teachers while, nevertheless, they are in many respects similar. It is of additional interest in that it illustrates the way in which Mrs. Lucy Sprague Mitchell finds in children's real experiences the basis for her published stories which are so beloved by children all over the country.[1] Mrs. Mitchell believes that with very young children it is of prime importance that they should be given experiences which will enable them to find themselves in a complex environment and to orient themselves geographically and in every sense to the environment in which they live. It was my privilege to spend a morning with Mrs. Mitchell in her classroom and to go with her and her group of New York Public School five-year-olds on the morning trip to the subway which is referred to in the following account:

The children visited the subway, going down into the ground at one entrance, watching the trains for a few moments through the gates, and crossing underground to come out on the other side of the street. Outside the steam shovel, "Biting Marion," was just beginning its work of excavation.

Before leaving the classroom for the morning walk, the children were reminded of their previous trips into the neighborhood, impressions of which they had been working out in their blockbuilding. They were asked to keep careful watch, to see and hear whatever they could so that they might tell about it later. Leaving the classroom, the children walked along Greenwich Avenue to the corner and visited the subway as related above, returning in about a quarter of an hour the way they had come. During the adventure they were frequently reminded, as well as they could be for the roar of the city, to "use their eyes and ears." To see the children walking two by two along the sidewalk it might seem to the unsophisticated observer that they were merely taking an aimless morning walk. How different from this was the actual situation! The results of the trip make quite clear how this apparently ordinary situation was conditioned by the children's own experiences carefully guided by the teacher.

Discussion of the trip did not begin until a day or two later. The way in which it developed and an account of the various class activities which ensued are given below from Mrs. Mitchell's own records.

Origin of the Activities

The trip taken on March 7th was partly for orientation and partly to see the subway and subway construction. Tunnels appear frequently in blockbuilding play in spite of the practical difficulties of constructing anything which seems underground. I have records of tunnels in blockbuilding on eleven out of the possible nineteen days of school.

[1] Mitchell, L. S., "The Here and Now Story Book," Dutton, New York, 1921.

TEACHING PATTERNS

These tunnels were for automobiles and wagons. The only record I have of spontaneous references to subways (aside from the construction going on on Greenwich and Seventh Avenues), appear in an individual story of a child who used to live in the Bronx, and in block-building construction on the day of the trip.

RECORDS OF CLASS ACTIVITIES AND DISCUSSIONS

March 7—

Albert: This is supposed to be a tunnel. That's where the trolley car is and here's where the trains are.

After the trip I have the following records of blockbuilding:

March 12—

Herman, Lawrence and Edgar built together a long structure crossing the entire room consisting of the long blocks stood on edge, wide enough for the train to pass between. At intervals bridges crossed this structure. Very sketchy station at one end.

Herman: This is where the train runs. This is a tunnel. This here is where it makes a turn.

Lawrence: This is where the trains run. These are tunnels. We are going to make a station but we got no time to make it.

Edgar: This is where the train goes all the way through the tunnel and it turns here and another train goes through the other little tunnel.

He had left a space in the long blocks so that a train could pass at right angles.

Since then we have had some kind of train play every day except one, sometimes with and sometimes without a tunnel—March fourteen, fifteen, eighteen, nineteen, twenty, twenty-one, twenty-two, twenty-six, twenty-seven, twenty-eight,—eleven out of twelve days in March. The commonest type of track is a row of the long blocks with the smaller blocks stood on edge on either side like a fence. I think this is the influence of the subway. The details of the building have sometimes included stations and red and green lights, but not always. No reference to steam or electricity on the part of the children except in response to direct questioning.

Subways have not appeared in painting, drawing, or carpentry.

DISCUSSIONS

The day before the subway trip I have the following record concerning subways gathered from observations on a former trip:

Some child: I saw a big hole. It was because they were making a new sidewalk.

Herman: No, they were making a subway. They were making a subway. They have to go down in the hole to make the subway.

I asked them to tell me about subways—

Various children:

> To carry people.
> A train goes in a subway.
> A big, heavy train made out of steel.
> It runs on tracks.
> It runs under the street.

The following discussion is recorded the day after our trip. I asked what had been seen yesterday.

Chorus: The subway.
Herman: We went down under the street. We came up on the other side.

I asked where the street was when we were in the subway station. Herman, Alexander, Edgar and perhaps six others pointed upwards. One child said, "The street was up on our heads." Several children, laughing, "The cars and the people were going up on our heads."

Edgar: I saw a derrick. He took up the sand like this. (Showing with his arms.) He opened up like this.
Three or four children: He opened his mouth and took up the dirt.
Teacher: Where was he getting the dirt?
One child: From way down in the big hole.
Teacher: What kind of a hole?
Herman: Very deep. Deeper than the room.
Teacher: What did you see in the hole, Herman?
Herman: I saw pieces of wood holding up the whole street.
Charles R.: I see the dirt. There were walls of dirt.
Judith: I saw a horse on the sidewalk, and I said "Somebody will have to go to Police Court."

March 12

I told them I had seen something on the way to school. It wasn't an animal but it could move and make a noise and it was very big.

Helen: That's the big thing that goes up and down. It's in the street. It makes the sand go up and down.
Judith: Helen means a derrick. It's a big thing and looks like a shovel.

These kindergartners are adventuring in their own neighborhood. They have seen the sights of the fire-house and the way the firemen live there. Later this experience emerged in block building, drawing and outdoor yard play. The class is that of Mrs. Mitchell in Public School 41, New York City.

Edgar: Why don't you ask me? I could tell you. It picks up the sand like this (with his arms). It is a big thing. It is to make a subway.
Rosalind: It took up the sand with a steam shovel.
Kenneth: (Laughing) He opens his mouth and he shuts his mouth. (All the children took up the chorus.) "He opens his mouth and he shuts his mouth."

Trip on March 19

After a nap at eleven o'clock we went to Gansevoort Market. The children were slow walkers. They could not keep their places and the street crossings were difficult. At the end of Greenwich Avenue and Seventh the little automobile was standing by the hole. Some child asked one of the men what it did. He answered—"It is to haul lumber."

Herman: Didn't I tell you it was a lumber auto?

The policemen helped us across Seventh Avenue. We stood by the street where we had looked down into the deep hole on the trip of March the seventh. It was fully boarded over. There stood a cart of boiling tar. Chunks of hard tar lay on the ground. The children all saw the fire which was heating the tar. We also saw the big steam shovel walking off down the road.

March 25

I took the table with the milk bottles out of the center of the classroom and pushed the chairs back to a larger circle leaving an opening toward the west. I asked two children who were not drinking milk to build us a little school. Kenneth and one other child quickly built a three-story house with two chimneys. I asked what street we were on—Chorus of "Greenwich Avenue." I asked who could lay the long blocks for Greenwich Avenue. Thomas P. cried "Me, me." I gave him two blocks, but he placed them one growing out of the school one way, and one growing out another way. Lloyd placed them correctly to the south of the school saying, "We ought to have sidewalks." I told him we had not time and let him build the street two blocks wide in both directions. I asked what we would come to if we walked in that direction, pointing west. Chorus of "Market." I called one of the tables "the market." Coming back to the school, I asked—

"What do you come to as you walk along Greenwich Avenue?"
Kenneth: The water tank.

He puts it in place.
Some child says "Seventh Avenue." Herman takes two long blocks and lays out Seventh Avenue parallel to Greenwich. I bring him back to the school and make him walk on Greenwich saying "Do you cross Seventh

Avenue?" He immediately changes the blocks to run at right angles. I help him place them diagonally without comment. What else do you come to?

Rosalind: The show.

She with two others quickly built the moving picture theater on the corner of Greenwich and Seventh.

Kenneth: The subway.
Teacher: Yes, but I am afraid we can't build the subway.
Judith: I can build the subway.

She takes a long block, lifts the block which stands for Seventh Avenue, puts hers underneath and replaces Seventh Avenue, perfectly satisfied.

USE OF THE RESULTS. STORIES PREPARED AND READ TO THE CHILDREN

Stories Which Came Out of the Trips

The following stories have come out of the trip. The first one is what I call a group story and is in the children's own words with the other somewhat changed.

The second and third stories are mine. They have been read to the children. The first is too long and too old—that is, too much in terms of function for these five-year-olds. I shall see how the six-year-olds react to it. The second is better but needs shortening. These children seem to need more dramatic material than other five-year-olds I have taught. I am now trying to write a subway story from the point of view of a small dog. Sarah Cone Bryant has written a good street paving story in which the little dog buries his bone in a soft pile and cannot find it after the tar and steam roller have passed over it! This story the children have heard and dramatized.

(Made from children's own words somewhat re-organized. Two discussions.)

We went to see the subway. The subway is down under the street. A train goes in a subway. We saw a train. It was in the subway and it was going. We were at the station. The train was stopped when we came into the station. It is a big heavy train made out of steel. It runs on tracks down under the street. We went down under the street. We came up on the other side. The street was up on our heads. The cars and the people were going up on our heads! (much laughter)

The street was Seventh Avenue. It is the big street with the traffic lights. We saw a funny kind of bus. It was yellow. We saw a funny taxi. It had yellow and orange and green and all different colors. We saw a white bus and a black and white taxi. We saw many busses and taxis on the big street.

We saw a big hole. It was because they were making a new subway. They have to go down in a hole to make a subway. We saw a derrick. He took the sand up like this (showing with his arms.) He opened up like this. He opened up his mouth and took up the dirt. He took the dirt from way down in the big hole. The hole was very deep, deeper than this room. Down in the wall we saw pieces of wood holding up the whole street. We saw dirt. These were walls of dirt.

Another day we saw a funny little engine. We watched it and we had to laugh. It looked so comical. We asked the man what it did. He said it was a lumber auto. It put the lumber down the deep hole.

When we were on the sidewalk we heard a noise coming from down, down, down, from 'way down. We saw iron bars across the hole. We looked down and saw dirt and sand. It was d—e—e—p!

The Workmen Build the Subway

In the big city there is another street. It is not quite so wide or quite so long as the big street with the traffic lights. Somewhere it runs across the big street. For the big city is full of streets, some running one way and some running the other way. So that the city is full of street crossings.

One day a lot of workmen came to this street. For the city wanted to build a subway down under the street. The workmen came with tools—pickaxes with sharp beaks and long-handled spades. And all up and down the street the workmen began making holes. They swung the pickaxes over their shoulders and with a stroke brought down the sharp beaks in the pavement. Swing up, stroke down, swing up, stroke down, until a chunk was loose. Another swing up, stroke down, swing up, stroke down, until another chunk was loose. Then when the top of the pavement was broken into chunks, they shovelled the chunks into trucks that carted them away.

But in some places the workmen kept on digging, making holes. And when the holes were big enough the workmen with the pickaxes and the shovels went away.

But more workmen came. One morning some workmen came down the street riding on a kind of a huge monster that moved without any wheels. The monster jolted and jounced as it slowly made its way down the street, for it was enormous and heavy and clumsy. It was like a big square box full of many belts and wheels. In front it had a huge derrick that reared up into the air two stories high. From this derrick came strong cables that held a huge iron scoop that could split in the middle and open and close. For the monster is a steam shovel.

The wheels and belts in the big square box are really a little engine which the workmen manage. This engine puffs and snorts when it works. The derrick slowly dips, the great iron scoop swings open its huge jaws. Into the loose earth it bites, gathering the dirt into its mouth. The jaws close.

Up comes the derrick slowly, up, up, up. Little pieces of dirt dribble out of the mouth. The derrick swings to the side. The mouth opens. Out pours the dirt into the truck below. Bang comes the dirt down into the truck. Back again, derrick. Down again, derrick. Open your jaws again. Fill your mouth with dirt, again. Close your jaws again. Up, up, up—steady—keep your jaws closed—don't drool and dribble so much dirt. Swing, swing, till your scoops are over the waiting truck. Now, you are just right. Open your mouth, wide, wider. Bang! That was a good hit! The dirt landed just on the middle of the truck.

So the steam shovel and workmen dig the holes deeper and deeper and deeper into the street.

Then more workmen come. These are the truck-drivers. First comes a lumber truck carrying huge heavy wooden beams. Bump! the driver dumps the wooden beams down on the side of the street. Then comes a truck with huger, heavier iron beams. Bang! the driver whangs the iron beams down on the side of the street. Then comes a truck with long planks. Flop! the driver drops the planks down on the side of the street. And when the truck-drivers have gone away with their trucks, the sides of the streets are piled with wooden beams, iron beams and planks. For they need the wooden beams to hold up the dirt walls in the deep holes, and they need the iron beams to make the strong walls for the subway. And they need the planks to lay over the torn-up street while they are building the subway below.

Then comes the very funniest little automobile in the world, I do believe. It is so comical that if you should see it you would laugh and laugh. That's what some little boys and girls did who were watching from the sidewalk. They just laughed and laughed! This comical little automobile has no body like a taxi. It is just an engine with a seat behind for the driver and a long arm that stretches far in front or high into the air. But it is strong, this comical little engine! For after the driver has tied one of the huge wooden beams to the long arm, the little engine raises its arm high into the air with the huge wooden beam dangling from it. Then it starts full speed for the deep hole that the steam shovel has bitten. Do be careful, comical little engine, with your huge dangling beam! You look so little and the beam looks so big. How dare you race so fast? How dare you chase down the rough street? Now the little engine stops close to the deep hole. Slowly it bends its long arm. Down goes the rope with the beam tied to it, down, down, down into the deep, deep hole.

And way down below some other workmen untie the heavy beam and put it into place. Back and forth races the comical little engine bringing the heavy wooden beams and the heavier iron beams to the workmen down in the deep hole to hold up the earth walls and to build the strong walls of the subway.

So the many workmen work that the city may have a new subway down under the street.

With pick and with shovel the workmen come,
   Can you hear the sharp picks
   With a swing and a stroke?

With derrick and scoop the steam shovel bites,
   Can you see the mouth open?
   With a roar the dirt falls!

With beams and with planks the truck-drivers come,
   Thump! they are dumping!
   Can you feel the ground shake?

With speed and with snorting, the small auto comes,
   Can he swing up that iron
   With his comical might?

So the workmen keep working, keep working all day. Till at last they will make us another subway.

One cannot fail to be impressed by the freshness and the spontaneity of this lesson. There is no question as to the naturalness of its origin, and throughout its course there is a complete lack of any forcing or overdirection of the children's responses. On their trip to the subway there is no lecturing, no rasping of the vacillating attention of the children, no orders to watch this that or the other thing. Just an adequate stimulus for the children to be alive, and to live fully in their own environment. Again, in their later discussion, it is the children who speak, the children who bubble over with something to tell. The teacher merely directs and helps the children to express their thoughts and coördinate their imaginations.

It is important to realize that this work is only a partial account of the activities of these children during the days concerning which the reports are made. In certain schools attempts might be made to prolong and attenuate the experience of the children into a continuing unit, from which the rest of their school work would be derived. Thus they might be persuaded to draw steam shovels, (art) compose workmen's songs, (music) and write poetry about subways, (creative English). Such forcing of children's activities is sometimes carried on in progressive schools, while teachers delude themselves in the belief that they are following the children's interests. This organizing of school life in terms of teachers' notions rather than children's needs is as much a violation of the psychological by the logical as the older subject-matter programs ever were. The work done by Mrs. Mitchell's group was obviously not of this sort. In the case of these children their experiences actually led to certain activities on their own momentum. The numerous other activities of the school, such as painting, woodwork, number work, and music were the outcomes of other experiences which actually produced these activities.

The high imaginative plane on which the work was carried on is to be noted. This was partly due to the personality of the teacher, but also, in part, to the technique of teaching which was employed. Impression in the course of one activity preceded expression in the course of others. The children saw, heard, smelled and felt during their outdoor trip. Later on in the group they talked, used their imaginations, and finally rejoiced in reliving these experiences coördinated in story form. They were learning the way in which stories grow even before they could use a pencil themselves. Furthermore, they were gaining not merely power over ideas, over their own imagination, and over language, but they were disentangling their own environment, and coördinating their own experiences. They were learning to live by living together in a child's size world.

II

Teaching Pattern of a Study of Foods

Fourth Grade Children

Miss Goodlander of the Ethical Culture School gives an account of a teaching pattern which developed very freely in a fourth grade.[1]

Origins of the Activity

Before school opened I had not planned to take up the subject of food with the children; but the example of the older pupils, who were all preserving foods, led my class to can a few tomatoes which were brought in by one of our members. The success of the first small group in carrying through the various steps of cold-pack canning, led to further work of the same sort, as various vegetables were given us. The children also dried apples and lima beans which they gathered themselves at the school farm.

[1] Goodlander, Mabel R., "Education Through Experience," Bureau of Educational Experiments, 144 W. 13th St., New York, 1922, pp. 10-13.

Progress of Activities

That the interest in this rather exacting work was sustained for two months was doubtless due to the fact that the children had a genuine purpose in canning a large quantity of vegetables. For early in the work, upon the suggestion of one of the class, it had been decided to have a sale and to use the proceeds to buy milk for a sick baby. Although I had not thought of this plan myself, I was glad to lend it my support.

The final preparation for the sale occupied a large share of the school time for several weeks. The chief consideration from the children's point of view seemed to be who should take charge of the business of selling. They had conducted a play store intermittently during the fall, but, upon testing it, it was found that most of the class were ill-prepared to act as sales people. The children readily recognized this fact and willingly went to work to drill on addition and subtraction. The most successful drill was accomplished by means of a dramatic rehearsal of the forthcoming sale, some children impersonating the visitors and the others the salesmen. Real money, correct prices, and the actual jars of vegetables and fruit were used for this play. The need of invitations, of price lists, and of bookkeepers the day of the sale, was also recognized and led to much needed practice in written English. The prices were determined by a study of the latest Park & Tilford catalog, a small group with a teacher undertaking this work. It necessitated the use of an alphabetical index, and in some cases the calculation of the price of pints, when only quarts were listed, as we had used both pint and quart jars.

Further preparation consisted in making of labels for the jars and of posters for the room. The art teacher, when called in to advise, taught the children how to make accurate square letters, which they used in various sizes for the labels and posters. The making of fifty or more small labels with half-inch letters proved irksome to the little people but they showed much persistence in completing the task because of their interest in the sale. The eight children who made the final large posters did a great deal of intelligent, painstaking work. From the artistic point of view, the posters were noteworthy, but they represented the children's own suggestions.

The sale was conducted by the children, who made their own change, kept records of sales and wrapped up purchases. The various duties were agreed upon by the class, in accordance with each one's proved ability to carry them out, and every one had some share.

ACTIVITIES DEVELOPING OUT OF THE ORIGINAL UNIT

Running parallel with the work of canning there was some study of the sources of food and of methods of distribution. This was accomplished by means of talks, pictures, and excursions. Besides the trip to the school garden, the excursions included a visit to Park & Tilford's store, where we saw the retail department and also the large stock of canned goods, a trip to the fruit dock of the Erie Railroad, a visit to Ward's Bakery, and later a day at a farm.

The dock trip was especially interesting. We were shown every activity connected with the handling of fruit, from the unloading of the cars on the floats which brought them from the New Jersey Railroad terminal, until the fruit was carried away in wagons by the market man.

Following this trip, several groups of children constructed from peglock blocks a dock, a float, and a market wagon. One boy brought toy cars from home, and other children made from clay fruit, vegetables, and a tug. Then, for several weeks, the children conducted a self-organized, dramatic play which at one time or another involved every member of the class. The play included the playhouse and store, the newly made dock, and two other places in the room, respectively called California and New Jersey. The fruit was loaded on the cars at California, brought to New Jersey, and taken across the river on the float to the dock. The storekeeper sent men to the dock to buy fruit, which, in turn, the family in the house bought at the store—toy money being the medium of exchange. This game was of value chiefly because it increased the children's power of initiative and self-direction, and furthered the spirit of social coöperation in the class. But also, the play, in connection with the excursions and talks, helped in some degree to give the children an appreciation of the number of people and of the amount of work involved in providing the food which we obtain so easily.

This study of foods is a good example of a firmly knit series of units, which are related to one another and develop soundly out of one another. It is not so large in its scope as to be beyond the children's actual grasp. It is soundly motivated by an actual need arising out of a life situation, and is not unduly drawn out or prolonged. Neither is it so extensive that it crowds out other activities from school life, and compels the teacher to artificially link the activities of the unit with her curriculum goals. Used in this way it is a sound and valuable unit of work. Dragged out as food study sometimes is and twisted and manipulated so that it would form a single basic unit to fill the activity program of the whole term, it might become an anemic thing indeed.

Attention is called to the various teaching patterns reported in the publications of the Francis Parker School. (See bibliography.) The reporting of these lessons is of a very superior character which makes them well worthy of study.

III

TEACHING PATTERN OF A UNIT OF SOCIAL SERVICE

High School Grades

The following teaching pattern is admirably reported. It is an account of activity in the Francis Parker School of the University of Chicago.[1]

THE SPIRIT OF GIVING AS DEVELOPED AT THANKSGIVING AND CHRISTMAS

STATEMENT OF GOALS

The demands of good citizenship require that the school gradually develop in the child a growing social consciousness. The self-centered individual of the kindergarten and primary grades should become, as the school years pass by, more sympathetic and tolerant towards those of various temperaments and conditions of life.

Opportunity for social endeavor within the school community is provided in abundant measure by the needs and activities of classroom and school. The need for contact with social activities and conditions outside the school is not so well recognized, nor so abundantly supplied. Christmas and Thanksgiving, however, present an unique opportunity for this larger social service, possibly a greater opportunity than at any

[1] Francis Parker School Yearbook, Vol. I, June, 1912. Published by the Faculty of the Francis W. Parker School, Chicago, pp. 15-19.

other time of the school year, and one which schools as a rule have not used to the best advantage. It is believed that by the methods we have used in this school our pupils have been helped to develop character along coöperative and unselfish lines. Our endeavor in handling questions of sharing and giving such as arise at Christmas and Thanksgiving, has been to create a sympathetic and respectful attitude on the part of the pupils toward others in less fortunate circumstances.

ORIGIN OF THE SOURCE OF ACTIVITY IN THE CHILDREN'S EXPERIENCE

The Spirit of Thanksgiving in the School

The spirit of Thanksgiving differs somewhat from that of Christmas. At Thanksgiving thoughts of relief of the more elemental needs, such as food and clothing, are uppermost. At Christmas, however, while these are present to some extent, they are overshadowed by the thought of providing good cheer, mainly through less material means. Naturally Christmas is the time when the joyous spirit of childhood can with the greatest pleasure enter into such work. So it would seem at first glance that the contact with the material needs of the Thanksgiving season would be such as would not come within the experience of childhood. This need not be so. The younger children, of course, should not be overburdened with the problems of the poverty and distress of others, but there is much that can be done without actual contact with these conditions. With the classroom teacher and settlement and charity worker as intermediaries, each class in the school becomes for the time being a relief and aid society for the assistance of a small group of people, usually a family in which there are several children.

To secure the coöperation of the parents, a circular letter is sent to all the members of the Parents' Association to invite their assistance in the work.

PROGRESS OF THE ACTIVITY

The first step consists in securing information of a trustworthy nature concerning the family to be helped. This is usually furnished by reports written or oral, from settlement and charity workers. In some instances, however, the teacher and a few pupils visit the homes in question, generally in company with a friend of the family, the charity worker, who is intimately and sympathetically acquainted with their problems. This closer contact brings in the personal element, which is desirable and has been found to be possible under proper direction in the upper grades of high school. Very often it may be the first opportunity of a pleasure-loving thoughtless girl of high school age, shielded and nurtured in comfortable surroundings, to get a glimpse of "how the other half lives." Let it not be understood that any "case" which comes within the scope of the organized charity worker would be suitable for such a visit. Both the receiver of the gifts and the giver are considered. Thought should be given to avoiding conditions which would present harmful influences and to selecting those where present need is plainly apparent to the young investigator, and which offer opportunities for such endeavors as are within his power. A hint or word of explanation dropped by one who is familiar with the history of the conditions, will fall on fertile ground. It is needless to say that the boy or girl returns from such a visit in a much different frame of mind, less patronizing and more sympathetic and democratic in spirit.

From reports gathered from these sources the class has data for discussing the various needs of the family. With the aid of the classroom teacher, such articles of food and clothing are obtained as will best serve these needs. Frequently, after class discussion, each pupil is delegated to provide for one individual. Thus he pictures to himself "Martha, aged nine" or "Johnnie, aged six," and sets about to select a complete outfit of good serviceable garments for the coming winter. Often this will mean trips to other rooms in the school to see what is available, the school thus becoming a clearing house for these useful gifts. Serious and thoughtful discussions are often overheard regarding size, fitness and condition of garments. Contributions of money are devoted to many important needs, a part being used for the repair of shoes which have been brought in. Often a month's rent or a ton of coal is provided to tide over an emergency. In most cases a Thanksgiving dinner is sent. For the sick, special delicacies are included.

Results

On the day before Thanksgiving all is activity. Hammers are busy nailing up boxes of provisions. Sheets of heavy wrapping paper and stout twine are in great demand, for by two o'clock all packages, duly labeled, are to be ready in the lower hall for distribution. The value of this appeal to the physical activity of the child cannot be emphasized too strongly. The emotions aroused in the classroom discussion would fail to register lasting impressions on the brain were it not for the abundant opportunity to handle and wrap up articles of food and clothing, tie bundles, nail up boxes, and fill barrels and baskets until they tax the strength of the young worker to lift them. Thus he is giving of himself in a most effective way. Compare the vivid impressions thus created with those called forth by the stereotyped appeal for donations to "give to the poor," an appeal which results merely in bringing articles of food and clothing from a plentifully supplied home. The value of this endeavor should be measured by the amount and quality of personal effort on the part of the pupil rather than by mere quantity of material things.

When the bundles are gathered together ready for distribution, there are volunteers to assist in loading wagons and other conveyances. Routes have been mapped out and directions carefully prepared so that no mistake may be made in locating "third floor rears" or basement tenements. Here again is opportunity for lessons in democracy and the proper spirit of giving. The guide or teacher can many times call attention to conditions from which the pupils who are assisting cannot fail to draw their own conclusions. This may be done by chance remarks without the slightest evidence of pointing a moral, but that the lesson "goes home" is shown in many ways; sometimes by the silent, thoughtful attitude of an otherwise thoughtless, talkative boy after a visit to some dark basement lodging, or by the remarks of admiration called forth by evidences of thrift and cleanliness.

This teaching pattern illustrates the sound use of a background unit in the development of subsidiary units which are a real and vital part of the whole activity, and yet vary as widely as do clerical work, discussion, and hammering in the tops of boxes. The whole unit is one which is extensive in time, since it is a matter of weeks, rather than of one or two consecutive periods, yet it is really unified due to the strong validity of such an activity for adolescent boys and girls, and to its simplicity and directness of purpose.

It is commendable in that it recognizes not the mere gross needs of young people, such as those for food and figures, but their very real need for the expression of altruistic ideas and emotions. It translates these higher needs of the personality into a form of concrete expression, which enables the pupils to find joy in their fulfillment and fruition. It transmutes the spiritual values of unselfishness from precept and imagination into the shining reality of slums and sacrifice. The teachers who sponsored it are more than justified and rewarded for their unusual clarity of aims and goals by the sound and indubitable growth of their pupils in spirit and character.

CHAPTER XXVIII

TEACHING PATTERNS (Continued)

IV

Teaching Pattern of a Unit of Dramatization

Sixth Grade

The following is a descriptive account of the way in which a dramatic presentation was originated and carried on. It is an example of a teaching pattern which developed as a unit subsidiary to a larger unit. The large unit from which the smaller unit of dramatization developed was a study of animals.

Origin of the Central Unit from Which the Unit of Dramatization Developed

The teacher approached the work of the term with a general notion of what the class was to do. She knew the work which this group had done in previous years, and she felt that a study of animals would be a suitable follow-up for children of the age and training of the new class. On the other hand, however, the teacher was prepared to discuss with the class the problem of what they were to work on during the term. She was ready, if the children really wished to reject this unit, to consider with them the substitution of another, although considering the suitability of the unit she thought it unlikely that they would do so. If such were the case, however, she had in mind the suggestion of another unit centering about the personality of Edison. This would involve the study of electricity. Another suitable unit to be suggested if necessary was one concerned with aviation. There still remained the possibility that in the initial discussion some unexpected unit might be suggested by the children, and preferred to any of the other units suggested. In such a case, if the unit showed every likelihood of being a profitable one the children would have been assisted in carrying it through. In the meanwhile, before the teacher discussed the matter

354 THE TECHNIQUE OF PROGRESSIVE TEACHING

with the class, actual preparation had been carefully made for an approach to the unit of animal study. In the actual event, as was to be expected, the unit was most acceptable to the children.

Various Subsidiary Units Which Developed from the Central Unit

In the course of the school activities the following, among other subsidiary units, developed:

1. The study of jungle life.
2. Aspects of the life of animals (taught in the class in Life Science, by a coöperating special teacher).
3. People who explored Africa.
4. Poems and stories written about animals.
5. The making of a fantastic decorative frieze in colors, based in animal motifs.
6. A study of great men interested in animals.
7. The reading of Hugh Lofting's "Dr. Dolittle."

The Rise of the Unit of Dramatization from the Children's Self-Initiated Responses Based on a Background of Interest and Experience

During the reading and discussion of the story, "Dr. Dolittle," the children expressed a desire to make it into a play. They were aware of the fact that each year the class to which they belonged usually presented a play near the end of the year. In all probability they had been reminded of this by receiving from the school committee, or school officer concerned, an invitation to prepare the entertainment. When such conditions prevail no class will be likely to reject such an opportunity. Consequently, the children decided that they would write, rehearse and present a play based on the amusing and delightful story of the animal doctor.

The Progress of the Activity

Once this decision had been made two distinct problems had to be faced, the making of costumes and scenery, and second, the writing and acting of the play. The making of the costumes and scenery provided work for individual, constructive activities, and at the same time was used to motivate arithmetic via the needs for measurement. The scenery was designed and painted. Groups of children were assigned by the class to various tasks. Each pupil was made responsible for some part of the construction work, or for the painting of part of the scenery. Thus an opportunity was afforded for coöperative group construction.

When the parts were cast each child became responsible for his own costume. He might, however, call on other members of the class to assist him with it, if necessary. Thus one youngster might have been seen on a busy morning kneeling on the clean hardwood floor of his classroom cutting from brown paper a pattern for a monkey tail. He himself with the coöperation of the art teacher had made the design which he used for this purpose. Once the pattern had been completed it was to be reproduced in cloth, doubled and sewed up into a tail. The sewing process, if it later proved beyond the boy's ability in this direction, might be taken home for completion by his mother or sister. There were other kinds of costumes. As the tail was being manufactured another boy was to be seen working on his costume. He had to fit himself out to play the part of a sick horse, applying to Dr. Dolittle for the treatment of his eye. He was therefore engaged in making a large mask to wear over his head. The lifelike representation he strove to make had nothing less than a genuine mane attached.[1]

The writing of the play went on bit by bit during the discussion and rehearsals. At first, when the story was thoroughly understood by every member of the class, the piece was roughly acted out. In this first attempt the children used their own words. Other members of the class wrote out the parts after they were spoken. Then the whole was assembled, criticized, revised by the class, and finally typed. Try-outs for the main parts followed at rehearsals.

Suppose that we are privileged to visit a rehearsal in the auditorium as the play nears its final performance. The children who are responsible for the various stage properties are busy with them. Those who have nothing to do for the moment sit in the auditorium, watching critically. The teacher gives a signal and the curtain is drawn.

The stage is illuminated with the proper footlights, for one pupil is looking after the lighting. The setting is simple. The plain, dark back curtains are relieved by a bristol board room-angle in the way of scenery. It indicates a plain boarded room. On the wall hangs the

---

[1] Valuable help for the teacher doing such work is to be had in the article, "Masks and Wigs in Schoolroom Dramatics," by FRANK M. RICH, in *American Childhood*, February, 1929, p. 9.

sign, "No Smoking," a rope dangles near the middle of the stage, convenient for human monkeys. On a near-by pedestal sits a potential parrot in the form of a boy without his parrot costume.

The dialogue begins and the play goes on, until, in a moment of haste the boy, acting Dr. Dolittle, speaks too crossly and rudely to a "case" who is dismissed with an unkindliness most unlike what is to be expected from the gentle Dr. Dolittle. The "case" drops suddenly into the guise of a mere pupil and interrupts the rehearsal to complain to the audience that he was almost "shoved" out of the doctor's office. The group quickly decided that this is poor acting on the part of the doctor, that certainly he would not treat his "case" so rudely unless he wished to lose his last patient. The young actor then defends his virtuosity by reacting the scene in a more controlled fashion.

But now a venturesome monkey speaks his lines in violation of all good grammar, "my tail sweeps worser than it did before." The teacher suggests that since some of the pupils object to this poor usage he had better "fix it up." This, however, brings a storm of protests from certain other children, "If he wants to say it that way let him say it," —"Don't be so perfect." So the bad grammar is permitted to remain in the interests of artistic performance.

The Use of the Organized Result

The play is thus satisfactorily brought to the point of production, and is given at commencement where it is received with enthusiasm and approval. It is not necessary here to discuss what curricular values were gained, as such work is now accepted practically everywhere as of sound educational value.[2]

The teaching pattern is particularly interesting because of the light it throws upon the technique used by the teacher in carrying on a unit of dramatization. It is of further interest since it indicates the way in which such a unit may be integrated with and related to other activities of the class. The writer must take exception, however, to one aspect of this relationship. The organization of the term's activity work into such a lengthy and ill-defined unit as the study of animals, or of some other equally diffuse and discursive topic, seems to be in many senses artificial and arbitrary. It must seem obvious that the dramatic work done on "Dr. Dolittle," and all the subsidiary activities developing out of and related to this work, might have arisen

[2] See Francis W. Parker School, *Studies in Education*, Vol. I, June, 1912, p. 54. "The Function of Dramatic Expression in Education."

TEACHING PATTERNS

quite as readily out of a much simpler background. The reading of the book by the children needed no more elaborate motivation than the presence of the book in the environment, with possibly a reference to it in discussion. The teaching pattern is presented here, however, not for the sake of these words of negative criticism, but for the many positive values exhibited in its careful handling by an exceptionally skillful and understanding teacher.

V

TEACHING PATTERN INVOLVING THE
WRITING OF AN ANIMAL POEM

The following account is given because it presents a teaching pattern of a very brief unit, involving a simple piece of esthetic expression by a girl student who was one of the group which carried on the unit of dramatization reported in the previous teaching pattern. It is not given on account of the merit of the poem but as an illustration of a teaching pattern different from the others given.

During the course of the term the principal sent an announcement to the various classes that he would offer a prize for a poem written by the children. The following poem was written as an individual effort and a copy of it made for me at my request.

PUFF AND JOEY

Puffy was a kitten,
Joey was a dog,
Puff's favorite thing was to sit by the fire
But Joey did not like to retire,
Joey liked to catch frogs,
He prowled around all the bogs,
And when he saw a squirming snake,
Oh how his little tail would shake.

One day Puff saw beside a tree,
A drooping Joey did she see,
Poor little Joey was all bloody,
And little Joey was all muddy,
A snarling cat was spitting at him.

> Our little Puff ran out,
> My how she knocked that cat about,
> She'd run up a tree and let it drop,
> When 'round the corner came a cop,
> Goodness what did happen then,
> They were in the house ere you could count ten!

This poem was carefully copied in the best lettering of its author, enclosed in a sealed envelope and sent in to the contest under a pseudonym.

Here is a little bit of teaching in the mold of life itself. In school we find a little girl doing on her level what grown-ups do on theirs, and finding joy in self-expression and in the activity involved. It is to be observed that only those children competed who wished to compete, yet the environment was so arranged as to encourage writing. The prize giving would provide a basis for judging the activity and the publication of suitable poems in the school paper would provide for their use. The fact should not be overlooked that the teacher by a general inspirational attitude and an appreciative presentation of literature provides an atmosphere in which original writing may flourish.

VI

Teaching Pattern Involving the Publication by the Sixth Grade of the School Paper

Another activity carried on by the class just referred to received its initiating stimulus from the general activities of the whole school. The smaller class groups all have a responsibility to the larger school community for their share of work in the publication of the school paper. The school magazine, *School Life*, is a mimeographed paper, several pages of which are here given.

Whole School Coöperative Arrangements for Publication of the Monthly Paper

It is the custom of the school to publish every month of the school year a school paper written and edited by the children. The arrangement is that each month one school class looks after the publication. Early in the term the principal sends to each class asking when that class will find opportunity to take its month of responsibility. Arrangements are made in this fashion so that a given grade knows just in what month it must do the work involved.

ORIGIN OF THE UNIT OF CONDUCT

The need to publish and edit the book is the origin of the activities involved. It is a matter of recognized group responsibility.

PROGRESS OF THE UNIT OF CONDUCT

In carrying on this work the children feel their own responsibility and take the initiative entirely. The first step is the appointment of a staff.

The problems with which the class had to deal are well defined. They were:

1. Collection and editing of contributions from the whole school;
2. Writing of letters concerning various problems which arise;
3. Provision of illustrations, cover designs, and cartoons;
4. Attention to all business arising in course of publication;
5. The selling of the magazine, and keeping accurate account of all expenditures and money received.

In order to deal with the problems the class organized itself into a number of committees. A delegate visited other classrooms and announced that the paper was to be published on a certain set date. He asked for contributions by a certain date. The school responded by sending in materials which were discussed by the class from the point of view of their suitability for publication. The following quotation gives some idea of the nature of the material which the children chose for their paper:

EDITORIALS

319 MILES PER HOUR

On November 4, 1928, Flight Lieutenant D'Arcy Creig of the Royal Air Force at Calshot, England developed the fastest speed ever made by a pilot under official observation. Although he flew at three hundred nineteen and fifty-seven miles per hour, he did not establish the five mile margin necessary to set a new record. The super marine Napier S5 seaplane was powered with a 1000 horse power engine, of the same type as the one that powered the

Golden Arrow, the car in which Major H. O. D. Segrave set a world's record of 231 M. P. H. at Daytona Beach.

NEWS

The 3A class is studying about airplanes. They are finding it very interesting. Three children have brought airplanes to school to give the class an idea of how airplanes are made.

Miss Merritt is helping the 3A class with their vegetable study. The children are making window boxes and will plant vegetable seeds in them.

Jimmy Colquhoun in the 3A class had an experience on Saturday. He and his mother were driving just off the Parkway to New York. They were going down a hill. All of a sudden they struck a deep hole filled with water. There was a great splash! The windshield was so spattered with mud and water that they had to wash the window before they could go any further.

3A Class.

WHO MADE THE FIRST AIRPLANE

Two boys were waiting for their father to come home. Their names were Wilbur and Orville Wright. Soon they caught sight of their father. They ran up to meet him. They noticed that their father held one hand in back of him.

Daddy brought out a queer object that looked like a box kite. They asked him what it was called. Daddy said it was called a helicopter. The boys called it a bat. "All right," said Daddy, "it is called a bat."

"I will throw it on the ground," said Daddy, and he did. The boys tried to catch it.

"If birds fly why can't we?"

"Because we have no wings," Daddy answered.

"But why can't we make wings?" Orville wanted to know.

"Perhaps it wouldn't work," Daddy said.

"But when you grow to be big like me you can make yourself a pair of wings."

One day when the boys were out in the meadows with their father Orville said, "Wilbur is going to make a big kite."

These things happened in 1878. The year 1900 came. Wilbur and Orville were young men and they went into the motorcycle business.

One day Orville said to Wilbur, "You never made your kite and you never made your wings."

"Let's take a vacation," Wilbur said. So they made their kite.

When they were at home one day they looked up some old geography books that they used in school. Wilbur ran his finger up the sea coast until he saw a little city called Kitty Hawk. Wilbur said to Orville, "We can take a vacation on this island to study the birds."

So they packed up their glider and went to Kitty Hawk to get help if they needed it. When they got to Kitty Hawk they went to the sea coast to watch the birds. They watched the birds hours and hours. They noticed that the birds didn't flap their wings long distances and also they noticed that the birds tipped their wings to steer.

"Now that we have watched the birds fly we will try our glider," Wilbur said. So they went to a sand dune and gave their glider a little push. They saw it go off the slope. The air current caught the wings, and the glider swept off the slope.

When the glider came back Wilbur got into the glider and Orville gave a little push. Still the glider rose into the air. Wilbur was riding in the air.

When Wilbur came back he said to Orville. "We must learn to balance and steer."

When they learned to balance and steer, they went to West Hill and everything went well.

One day Orville said to Wilbur, "Let us put a motor in our glider so that we don't have to give our glider a push."

So they made the motor and fastened it to their glider, and although the motor was heavy it rose into the air and carried a passenger in it.

It was known all over that the name glider was changed into airplane.

If Daddy Wright hadn't brought home the little bat, both brothers would not have had an idea of an airplane.

A. D.

The editorials for such a paper are written by the members of the staff and discussed in class. "Dry English" is avoided as much as possible. Thus the work is provided for the class day by day and receives attention for the most part in the period allotted to English. The finished product when mimeographed is sold for ten cents a copy.

This work on the school paper differs from other teaching patterns reported here in that the need for its initiation arises not out of the school life of the class as a group, but out of the life of the larger community, the whole school. Thus the life of the smaller group is related to that of the larger by means of significant responsibilities and activities which lead to the attainment of many valuable curriculum goals.

CHAPTER XXIX

TEACHING PATTERNS (Continued)

VII

A Teaching Pattern Describing a Miniature Pioneer Home Reported With Reference to Outcomes in Arithmetic

Fifth Grade

The accompanying account, which clearly indicates the way in which a unit of conduct involving measurement may become a source of problems in arithmetic is an interesting study. It is reported by R. G. Jones, Superintendent in the Cleveland Public Schools.[1]

Building a Miniature Pioneer Home

Origin: In the study of pioneer life the children became so interested that they wished to build a miniature home and to furnish it.

Objective A.—Measurements. Drawing to scale.

Procedure: Through extensive reading and picture study, information was gathered about the homes and lives of the pioneers, their furniture and clothing. The children built their house 22″ long x 18″ wide x 9″ high modeled after a 22′ x 18′ x 9′ cabin. It was decided that only three sides of the house would be built. The poles which the children brought to use for logs were about 1″ in thickness. The problem arose as to how many logs would be needed for the three walls. This involved division. After much drill in simple division problems the children found that 27 logs were needed to build their homes. Then they sawed 18 logs 18″ long for the sides, and 9 logs 22″ long for the back of the cabin. They planned and located the fireplace.

Objective B.—Fractions. Subtraction of fractions.

The back wall of the house measured 16″ inside measurement. The children decided on a 1½″ fireplace to be placed in the center of back wall.

[1] Jones, R. G., "Activities in Fifth Grade Arithmetic," from *American Childhood*, The Milton Bradley Co., New York, June, 1929, Volume 14, No. 10, pp. 12-14.

16   " .... length of back wall
8½" .... length of fireplace
7½" .... space left

½ of 7½" equals 3¾", or the space on each side of the chimney.

The children found the actual width of the opening. The side walls of our fireplace were 2" thick. 2" × 2 equals 4", width of two side walls of the fireplace. The width of the fireplace was 8½", of the side walls 4", and of the opening 4½".

The pupils designed and placed the crane. The first problem in this connection was to find how much wire would be needed to make the crane. They wanted it to extend into the middle of the opening of the fireplace. They allowed ⅛" for the curve at the end of the crane on which to hang the kettles.

They felt that the wire should be fastened in the side wall of the fireplace and then curve downward about ¾" in order to hold the crane securely.

OBJECTIVE C.—Multiplication of fractions.

Pupils found the length of the extension of the crane into the opening. The opening was 4½" wide. Since they wanted to have the crane extend halfway into the opening the problem was to find ½ of 4½". They found the length of the extension into the side wall. Since the side wall was 2" thick and the crane was to extend halfway in, the problem was to find ½ of 2". They found the amount of wire needed.

2¼" extended into the opening.
1" extended into the side wall.
⅛" was used for the hook at the end.
¾" was used for the downward extension.

The sum, 4⅛", was the amount of wire needed.

The pupils made furnishings. The furnishings for the interior were worked out in much the same way as the cabin itself. Problems for making the curtains, sheets, quilts and pillow-cases were worked out according to dimensions decided upon by the class. The following is a typical example:

How much cloth will be needed for the table cover?

The table was 4⅞" long and 2⅜" wide.
The cloth was to hang over ¾" on each side and end.
The hem was to be ⅜" on all four sides.
¾" × 2 equals 1½", amount of cloth that hangs over.
⅜" × 2 equals ¾", cloth that is needed for hem.
4⅞" .... length of table
1½" .... cloth that hangs over on two ends
¾" .... hem on two ends
7½" .... length of cover

2¾" ....width of table
1½" ....cloth that hangs over
¾" ....hems on two sides
4⅝" ....width of cover

The cover must be 7⅛" long, 4⅝" wide when cut.

Tools and materials used:
Books
Pictures
Stones for the fireplace
Yarns for rugs and quilts
Wire
Hammers
Magazines
Poles for the cabin and furniture
Fur
Cloth
Clay
Cardboard
Nails
Saws.

ILLUSTRATIVE PROBLEMS: Pupils admired the results of their united efforts and decided to work out some furnishings for rooms at home. Problems related to furnishing a dining-room follow:

Curtains, 3 windows, length 1¾"
Table cover, length 2½'
Buffet runner, length 1½'
Floor, rug 9' x 12'
Table, 1
Chairs, 6
Buffet, 1

If curtain material cost $0.98 per yard and 2 lengths were placed at each window, how much did the dining-room curtains cost?

If the table cover cost $1.50 per yard, how much was paid for the tablecloth?

If the buffet runner cost $1.75 per yard, what did it cost?

The rug cost $67.50
The table cost $52.50
The chairs cost $8.75 each
The buffet cost $105.25
Find cost of dining-room furniture.

TEACHING PATTERNS

Find entire cost of equipping the dining-room for use. Formulate and solve enough problems, keeping within the pupil's experience, to develop necessary skills in problem solving.

SUPPLEMENTARY OUTCOMES: Pupils became interested in the dimensions of furniture at home and in the comparative dimensions required for the furniture in the miniature pioneer house at school. Pupils constructed small cabins at home, furnished them, and exhibited them at school. They also expressed an interest in and an appreciation of proper proportion in good design.

Through help extended from group or individuals to those having difficulties, pupils learned coöperation.

This teaching pattern is particularly interesting on account of the point of view from which it is reported. It indicates the way in which certain curriculum goals in arithmetic were reached via what might seem a remote activity, the making of a pioneer home. This activity undertaken by the children entirely independent of any intention connected with arithmetic is so directed by the teacher that the curriculum goals which are set before her for the class, are actually attained via the activity engaged in by the children. Observe that the teacher begins with the following objectives in arithmetic for her fifth grade:

Drawing to scale.
Subtraction of fractions.
Multiplication of fractions.

These objectives in arithmetic she has before her, as well as many other objectives concerned with other school subjects. She expects these objectives to be reached via drill activities strongly and intelligently motivated by the fact they take their rise from situations involving the use of the arithmetical processes involved. Thus she intends to use the living conduct of the children as a vehicle for the reaching of curriculum goals. Whether the unit of conduct initiated by the children is the making of a pioneer home, or some other equally suitable activity, is not a matter of great concern to the teacher. All that she does is to maintain such conditions that suitable activities of some sort will arise. When a suitable activity arises, in this case the building of a pioneer home, it serves her purpose in the reaching of her objectives. Since this activity is here reported with the intention of indicating arithmetical outcomes, its richer contribution to the life of the school is merely mentioned. This should not blind the reader to its fuller and more varied contribution to the whole life of the class.

VIII

The Store at Pooh Corner [1]
Its Arithmetical Implications

The Sixth Grade, Tower Hill School

The following account of an activity involving the attainment of arithmetical values may be of assistance in enabling the reader to better understand the wider meaning and the general orientation of the previous account in the life of the whole school.

Like true business men the children looked about to find some need at school that they might be able to meet. Prompted by the knowledge that many students remain after school hours to engage in sports and games, and by their own convictions that a little "smakeral" of something to eat in mid-afternoon is most desirable, they decided to open a store. There were discussions in which the values of such an enterprise were listed and studied, suggestions were offered, evaluated, accepted, or rejected, advice of real business people was sought, and finally definite plans of procedure formulated. The children had been reading "The House at Pooh Corner," and had so thoroughly loved Pooh Bear for his devotion to his honey pots, and his constant thought of a little "smakeral" of something about eleven o'clock in the morning, that they could think of no name so suitable as "The Store at Pooh Corner." At the outset it was agreed that the greatest possibilities of the venture were serving a real need, developing within themselves a spirit of coöperative responsibility, and, best of all to them, making arithmetic a live thing.

On October 22nd, the business was launched. Prior to this it had been necessary to negotiate a loan of two dollars from the Tower Hill School bank with which to purchase the first supplies. Interest at six per cent plus the principal was guaranteed by three members of the class who signed the note, thus agreeing to make good the amount from their personal accounts in case the business failed. Considerable anxiety was felt by the entire group, and much enthusiasm was given

[1] Announcement of the Tower Hill School, Wilmington, Delaware, Seventeenth Street and Tower Road, 1929-30. P. 69.

to verbal advertising lest there be a failure. Large posters announcing the formal opening were made under the supervision of the art teacher, and displayed through the halls of the school.

Local wholesale dealers were interviewed, and stock selected from salesmen's samples. Fruits, and plain and fancy crackers were chosen as staple goods. Buying in quantity produced the problem of fixing retail prices, all of which involved much addition, subtraction, multiplication and division.

The labor was divided among groups, a plan which has been strictly adhered to. A leader arranged the rotation of duties so that every member serves in each capacity in turn. All committees are appointed on Friday and serve for one week.

At the close of the second week the profits were sufficient to repay the loan, and the cancelled note was deposited in the "strong box" with mingled feelings of relief and joy. Since then there has been no question as to the success of the venture. When it was discovered that one dollar offered five per cent discount for a certain amount of goods bought, and larger discounts in proportion, much effort was made to increase our sales that we might take advantage of the larger discount. Quite recently a second dealer offered goods at higher prices, but with a greater discount. We have had our losses. Unwise buying of fruits resulted unfavorably for the Pooh Store. Obviously the arithmetic at these points was not teacher enforced. Rather it was a situation in which the class felt the need, and demanded instruction. Figuring discount, interest, profit and loss, percentage of profit, making change accurately and quickly have been interesting and real.

Each morning the sales of the previous day are reported, the cash checked, bills submitted, deposits in the school bank made, checks written if necessary, and orders checked. Accounts are kept in a very simple way. Before the weekly call of the salesman, it is necessary to take inventory of stock, refer to the sales book, and make out satisfactory orders for goods. The store has been no small venture, several hundred dollars having been handled by the children, and a handsome profit estimated for the year.

In addition to such practical arithmetic, the children are given daily drill in fundamentals. Work books are used, careful diagnosis of difficulties made with the help of the individual, and a program of remedial work outlined to aid in overcoming them. Common fractions are reviewed, and all practices with decimal fractions taught. Problem-solving enters into discussions concerning various time divisions in history, size of Greek stadia, length of race courses, Roman navy and army, medieval castles, printing presses, and extent of early English trade.

The freshness and vigor of the children's entrance into the activities here described is obvious. It is something of a contrast to the activity of building a pioneer home described in the preceding account. In the latter case the reader is left to guess whether the building of this pioneer home was really a genuine child-developed activity, even to fear that it was a piece of work imposed on the children by a teacher who found pioneer homes convenient as arithmetical vehicles. This account of "The Store at Pooh Corner" is sufficiently breezy to enable one to recognize the swing of a genuine unit of conduct. Furthermore, while one might seriously suspect children's genuine interest in anything so remote as a pioneer home, one cannot doubt their interest in anything so near and dear to youngsters as the various comestibles of the "Store." Neither can one doubt the vital and practical nature of the children's venture into real finance.

IX

TEACHING PATTERN DESIGNED
AROUND PILGRIM LIFE

Third Grade

Time: Columbus Day to Thanksgiving.

The following account of a unit school procedure is an example of a longer teaching pattern which seems to have, on the whole, considerable validity for children of the third grade. It involves a great deal of activity on the play level. If small children are to become interested in such far-away matters as those concerned with pioneer life, and there must be a considerable amount of doubt as to whether they can so be genuinely interested, they might well become so in some such natural way as this. It is reported by Katherine Tierney.[1]

INITIATION OF THE UNIT OF CONDUCT BY THE CHILDREN

The pilgrim project was initiated by the children, although its final form and direction were influenced by the teacher. Shortly after

[1] *Progressive Education*, April-May-June, 1929, Vol. VI, No. 2, pp. 190-193.

Columbus Day, the group was discussing the explorers and the early settlers of this country. The members of the group contributed interesting information about the Pilgrims; in fact, they seemed to be so much interested in the subject that several volunteered to bring books and pictures. One child spoke of a book, "Pilgrim Stories," by Margaret Pumphrey, which her sister had read when in the third grade. When the teacher offered to order this book for the children, if it was not too difficult, the idea was enthusiastically received. The book was brought to school, and it was found that all but four could read it readily. These children promised to read on in their readers in class time if they might have the book to take home or follow when the others were reading.

Progress and Development of Activities

While taking a walk a day or two later, the group discovered a clump of small trees with underbrush. As they begged to play Pilgrims and Indians, various scenes from the story of the Pilgrims were dramatized. They had a glorious time in spite of the multiplicity of Captain Standishes and Massasoits. This free play continued for several days and became better organized as time went on. Some of the children chose names and addressed one another by them. Another group set about making an enclosure of brush and sticks which they called a cabin. Several days of rain and cold weather put a stop to the outdoor trips. One of the children remarked that if the cabin had only been a real one, the weather wouldn't have mattered. This remark and the sight of tall packing cases piled near the school window led to the suggestion that a cabin be built using the cases as logs. These crates were about sixteen inches square and six feet high. They could have been used as logs for a huge and rather unsightly cabin. This group when in the first grade had made an outdoor village from large packing cases so the idea of building appealed to them. Though not convinced of the feasibility of the plan, yet wishing to respect initiative, the teacher promised to investigate.

Since the head janitor is a skillful workman with a real understanding of little children, his advice is often sought. He suggested a smaller cabin in the schoolroom. This plan was discussed in a group meeting. As the weather continued disagreeable, the new idea was unanimously accepted. The third grade room was a busy, noisy and happy place for the next few weeks. The children reveled in the pounding, hammering, sawing, and joyous confusion as only children can.

Since the group was a small one composed entirely of girls, the whole burden of construction was not allowed to rest entirely upon them. Help was given by the room teacher and by the art teacher whenever difficulties seemed so great that there was danger of undeservedly thwarting effort. The janitor also advised and assisted frequently. He was much interested in the venture and besides making the roof, a problem which it was unsafe for the children to attempt, he contributed a charming door with an old fashioned latch and real hinges. This was a problem which the children might have solved but their joy in its perfection perhaps made up for the educational loss.

Four of the locker crates were used as corner posts. A plank was nailed near the bottom of each side to make a framework. The two sides were then squared and the front and back planks nailed in place. Beaver board was nailed to this framework. An opening was left for the door and a window was measured and cut. It was found that because of lack of planning, about six inches of heavy board, as well as the beaver board had to be cut. This taught the workers a valuable lesson, as sawing with a keyhole saw through a heavy plank is a painful operation. They constantly reminded one another to plan carefully. "Remember that window" became a slogan. Paper was greased and put in the window but was removed in a short time as it made the cabin too dark.

The two back crates were used to make a fireplace. The two sides of the front ones were knocked out when the cabin was finished. Two children asked if they might make the fireplace alone. They measured and fitted all the beaver board, with the exception of the door to the Dutch oven. The janitor made a crane and a brass kettle was donated.

The cabin was painted a dark grey inside and out. The art teacher showed the children how to paint logs on the cabin. Each child helped to make a log under her direction. After painting the front in this way, the children tired of the rather arduous work and decided that the rest of the house looked very well as it was. Since they were satisfied, a higher standard was not demanded.

After the cabin was completed the class wished to make furniture. The kinds of furniture used and the materials and tools available at that time were discussed. It was decided to make a stool, a chair, a table, a bed, and a trundle bed. The children divided into groups and each group made one article. The bed was made with only two legs and fastened to the wall. The mattresses were stuffed with cornstalks. A rug was started and a patchwork quilt was planned, but the approaching Thanksgiving entertainment made it necessary to complete these furnishings at a later date.

Curricular Implications

Many other worthwhile activities were outgrowths of the interest which the making and furnishing of the cabin aroused. The history and geography lessons consisted of discussions of the food, clothing and shelter which the Pilgrims had to solve. The children were led to compare these problems with those their own parents had to meet. To make these problems more real, the class was given the experience of drying apples, making tomato butter, washing, combing and attempting to spin wool with a very crude spindle. The children saw a wool spinning-wheel at the museum but a flax wheel was the only one available for use in the room. No actual spinning was done but the principles of mechanics were demonstrated. The children enjoyed trying to count the number of revolutions made by the spindle with each turn of the wheel. The fact that both the spinning-wheel and the loom were simple machines was emphasized.

Organized Conclusion of the Unit

The program for Thanksgiving summed up all the work of the unit. The children invited their parents to come and see the cabin and took pleasure in explaining to their visitors every detail of the processes of building, candle dipping, spinning, and weaving.

The following record was made by the class to explain the cabin to the friends and patrons who attended a reception when the school was not in session:

Our Cabin

Our cabin is five feet wide and six feet long. It is in our schoolroom.

We wanted to have a log cabin because we were studying about the Pilgrims. We played Indians and Pilgrims outdoors in the woods near our school. At first we thought it would be better to build our cabin outdoors. But the class decided to have it in the room, so we could play when the weather was stormy.

Our cabin is made of beaver board and wood. We used the packing cases that the lockers came in because they were so tall. We could not get logs so easily as the Pilgrims. We have better tools than they had. We found it takes a lot of planning and measuring and sawing to make a house. It takes a great deal of arithmetic, too. Charles, our janitor, helped us a great deal.

He made the ridge pole and put on the roof. We could not have made the cabin without his help. We think it will be fun to play in our cabin when it is finished. But we think making it has been fun too.

THE CLASS

Candle Dipping

The third grade made candles. We made them just as the Pilgrims did. We dipped our candles in paraffin. The Pilgrims used tallow, wax, and bayberry.

We are going to tell you just how we did it. First we melted six cakes of paraffin. Miss Tierney put in some dye to make the candles green. Each girl cut a piece of wick about twenty inches long. We doubled the wick and twisted it around a little stick. Then we dipped the wick in the melted paraffin. After they were cool we dipped again. We dipped a long time. Slowly the candles grew larger and larger. At last they were big enough to be real candles. How happy we were to see them!

Drying Apples

We have been talking about getting ready for winter. The Pilgrims dried things. Our mothers can things instead of drying. We dried some apples and made some tomato butter. We took it home for our mothers on Hallowe'en.

LEADING ON VALUES

Contrary to our expectations, Thanksgiving did not end the children's interest in the enterprise. The children begged to have the cabin left in the room because they had worked so hard to make it and were enjoying it so much. Before school and during their free time, there was usually a group playing house. Before Thanksgiving the teacher presented to the group a Pilgrim doll which was named Priscilla. Her many loving mothers begged to give Priscilla a Merry Christmas in the cabin. The teacher explained that the Pilgrims had never celebrated this holiday. Thereupon it was decided to change the Pilgrim house to a pioneer cabin. Stockings were hung and lantern, wreaths and holly were used for decoration. There were several stimulating discussions concerning the differences between pioneer life and Pilgrim life. Some interesting stories and pictures were found. A visit which had been made to the Cleveland Historical Museum helped to make the gradual advance of the frontier clear. It is hoped that this work will link up with a study of early Cleveland which will be made later.

After Christmas the rug and quilt were completed as belated gifts to Priscilla. The rug woven was a rag rug as it was thought one of yarn would work up too slowly. This gave the class an opportunity to cut and sew the strips as well as learn to operate the heddle and wind the shuttle. Two children usually wove at a time, one to push the shuttle through, the other to operate the heddle and catch the shuttle. The class dipped candles which were given as Christmas presents to the mothers. Since dipping candles is a long process, each child made a little apron, cap and kerchief.

The cabin was finally demolished to make way for other activities; it is, however, still lovingly mentioned and its loss is sometimes mourned.

GENERAL CURRICULUM GOALS ATTAINED BY THE GROUP

Activities in Connection with the Unit

Art:
A series of pictures was made to go above the blackboard. Each child chose an episode in the Pilgrim Story and illustrated it.

Music:
Spinning Song.

Science:
The drying of apples led to a discussion of the causes of evaporation. Several simple experiments were performed to make them clear. Sterilization as related to canning was demonstrated. The mechanical principles of the pulley and wheel and axle were discussed.

English:
Opportunity was given for much oral English in class discussions and in the preparation for the Thanksgiving entertainment.
Dramatization of scenes from the Pilgrim Story. Free play in the cabin.
Written accounts of the various activities for use in the exhibit case and for the school paper. Letters arranging for visits to the museum and invitations to the party.

History:
The study of wool and the experience in weaving led to an interesting study of clothing.

Industrial Art:
Building a cabin.
Making furniture.
Drying apples.
Making tomato butter.
Study of wool.

Weaving a rag rug.
Making a patchwork quilt.
Dipping candles.
Making Pilgrim caps and aprons.

The clear indication of curricular implications is one of the valuable features of this account. Unfortunately, however, one cannot follow them with complete agreement. It is hard to believe that children in the third grade would freely, without a certain amount of pedagogical "log-rolling" on the part of the teacher, be inspired by their interests in pioneers to devote their art activities to illustrating the Pilgrim Story. One suspects the "spinning" song, and also some of the more meandering ramifications of the pilgrim activity. In spite of these suspicions, which may not be justified, the unit of work must be allowed a great deal of validity, and awaken admiration for the ability of the teacher who directed it.

THE RELATIONSHIP OF UNITS WITHIN THE TOTAL CLASS PROGRAM

It may be advisable to close this section with a brief discussion of the way in which various units of conduct may be arranged to the best advantage in patterns of teaching which are most economical. There are several schemes or arrangements which are favored by different teachers. In certain classes teachers tend to arrange the class work in a succession of comparatively short units, one following as the other is completed. Thus the work of the class might develop first by the holding of a sale, later by the giving of a birthday party, later by the building of a miniature farm, and so on, each unit being taken up as the preceding one is completed. There may be something to be said for this form of procedure in classes which are so large that teachers cannot carry on in them a full activity program. A teacher might, therefore, use this semi-artificial device of promoting useful activities.

Another type of organization which it seems well to avoid, although it is at present in considerable vogue, is the artificial scheme of adopting, at the beginning of a term, a single basic activity, which is in some cases rather a mere theme than a genuine activity, and deriving the work of the class for the term from the subsidiary units which arise. Thus the basic topic or theme is used as a matrix from which the other activities of the class are supposed to be developed. For example, in the third grade, Indian life might be chosen as the unit. Certain teachers claim that their unit is initiated by the children, while others are willing to admit that it is often simply a piece of manipulation by the teacher. In the course of the term's work, the larger part of the school's activity program is developed out of this unit, which is sometimes called a "Center of Interest." During the course of the term such varying activities as making an Indian play, reading Indian stories, making a pueblo and a tepee, chipping arrowheads and spearheads, stringing a shell necklace, arranging an Indian exhibit and working out Indian rhythms and dramatizations in the gymnasium. These "Centers of Interest" are often vaguely stated as *A Study of Milk, Water Transportation,* or *How Man Has Made Records*. Reports which are current and the study of such work in operation in certain schools tempt us to believe that this plan is just another teacher-manipulated "scheme," for educating children, like the theories of Correlation, Concentration, and the Culture Epochs it will have its day and pass away. The origin of the basic activities seems to lack genuineness, and the contention that children are really psychologically identified with these activities seems scarcely credible. The activities are often vague in their meaning, beyond the initial comprehension of the children, and sometimes based on remote interests. The real reason for their successful career seems to lie in the skill of the teachers in experimental schools who could make any scheme of procedure an ostensible success.

The only sound scheme for the carrying on of a full activity program in thorough accord with the point of view set forth in this book would be considerably different from the two plans just referred to. If we are to find in school the likeness to life in the world, there must be a genuineness to the children's activities which can scarcely be secured by either of the schemes mentioned. In our everyday life it is our general experiences, the situations in which we find ourselves which are the motivators of our conduct. The units of conduct which we carry on are neither entirely consecutive, nor are they all related to one another directly or to any single core activity. In the course of a month's time a man may play golf, buy a piano, carry on his routine business at the office, live according to his daily habits of eating and sleeping, give a lecture, and take a trip to California. It must be obvious that these activities are genuine ones, each having its own separate existence. They are not necessarily related to any central plan, which runs through the whole. They are independent and real. Furthermore, they are neither consecutive nor coterminous. The buying of a house, for instance, may be a matter of weeks, the activity lying in abeyance while a dozen other important matters are attended to. The buying of a piano, on the other hand, may be the work of an hour or two. So it should be in the life of the ideal school. The units of conduct in which the children engage, if they are genuine, if they actually do arise from the children's real living, will be a series of units which grow neither singly and separately nor consecutively. They will be haphazard in their appearance, and frequently unrelated in their organization. Thus the most diverse activities may be carried on simultaneously in school, and teaching patterns may be woven of units of conduct in the genuine mode of real living.

CHAPTER XXX

THE RECORDING AND REPORTING OF TEACHING PATTERNS

THERE is considerable need for eye-witness reports of new and original teaching patterns. The coming years, no doubt, will produce a great deal of literature of this type. As the newer ways of teaching take increasing hold upon the life of the public school, there will be even greater need for the reporting and recording of the teaching which is going on in the best schools. The need for such accounts is even now being felt in institutions for the training of teachers. Much of the abundant material which is available in current texts is no longer suitable to meet new needs. In fact, educational literature must be almost entirely rewritten if it is to meet current needs of teachers in training. It is, therefore, fitting to consider the matter of the form in which teaching patterns should be reported. What is it that those who read these records and reports desire to know? What should be included, and what left out? How may the records be presented in a way which will be most useful to teachers who study them? Some of these matters will be dealt with here.

AVOIDANCE OF FORMALIZED REPORTS

In the reporting of teaching patterns it should never be forgotten that each pattern is an individual pattern, unlike any other. Every effort should be made to avoid the use of a formalized report, with certain fixed steps arranged in readiness to be filled in. Such a form of reporting can only result in a new formalizing of the teaching process. Teachers who read such reports will attempt to work out lesson plans which are based on these reported steps. This can only work havoc with the process of teaching. When teaching is organized in terms of conduct, there can be no certain order of steps to be rigidly followed through a teaching pattern. It is true that there are certain typical teaching procedures which may be helpful in organizing aspects of class work, but that is an entirely different matter. In such cases the teaching procedure is merely one kind of teaching which takes place during the progress of the whole lesson. Reports of class work should, as much as possible, be made individual and distinctive if they are to be most helpful.

This does not mean, however, that system and order may not characterize such reports. There are certain things which teachers studying the reports will want to know. While each report may be individual and may include material which is interesting and suggestive because it is different, nevertheless, there are certain things which must be made clear if readers are actually to understand how the lessons under discussion were really taught. Some of these matters are referred to in what follows. Those who have opportunities to study other teachers at work may also observe actual teaching with more profit if they will consider similar matters with respect to the teaching they are studying.

SUGGESTIONS FOR THE SYSTEMATIC
REPORTING OF TEACHING PATTERNS

1. There Should Be a Clearly Indicated and Definite Statement of the Minimum Curriculum Goals Which the Lessons Were Instituted to Attain

This statement of goals may present many problems which must be solved in the light of the circumstances involved. A number of difficulties will immediately be encountered in making such a report. It is comparatively simple, for instance, to forecast goals in the realm of complex skills, such as those involved in the teaching of punctuation or spelling. The matter is far from simple, however, when goals in history are to be stated, or goals to be attained in a unit of individual play or construction. Thus various units will present particular difficulties to those reporting them. How these difficulties may be overcome must be left to the teacher or eye-witness who is preparing the account.

If the lessons reported are to be really convincing, however, it is most desirable that a statement of the goals aimed at should be made. Unfortunately, it is impossible to forecast concretely and with definiteness all the goals that will be attained in the development of a unit of conduct, especially when the course of that unit may not be fully forecast. On the other hand, satisfaction may accrue from the later opportunity of listing goals which were unplanned for and unexpected.

RECORDING AND REPORTING OF TEACHING PATTERNS

2. *Throughout the Report the Time Element Should Be Given Attention*

It is important for the securing of clarity in the reporting of teaching patterns that the reader be given an account of the time element involved. Therefore, it is necessary to make clear, somewhere near the beginning of the report, just how much time was taken in the development of the unit of conduct under discussion. This helps to give the reader some idea of the size of the unit. In the case of long units it is most helpful to indicate, whenever possible, the amount of time consumed in whatever parts of the procedure may be recognized as separate wholes. It is most important that a unit of conduct used in school work should be justified, not merely in terms of objective accomplishment, but also in terms of time consumed.

3. *The General Plan of Organization of Units Should Be Given*

If the reader is to understand fully the way in which the work of any special unit is related to the class work in general, some account must be given of the way in which the whole term's work is organized. In order that readers may become quickly oriented to the whole class situation an explanation of the relation of the unit of conduct under discussion to other units is necessary. The recorder will receive some assistance in recognizing the type of organization of class work which is being used by consulting the discussion of this matter on page 374 of this book. It may be that the teacher has been using one of the schemes of organization there referred to. If some other form of organization has been worked out, the reader will be most anxious to have it brought to his attention.

4. *The Origin of the Activity Should Be Accurately Accounted For*

The closest attention should be paid to the giving of an accurate account of the way in which the unit of conduct under discussion originated. Teachers who study reports of lessons will scrutinize the text most carefully to see just how the activity involved in the lesson originated. This is a crucial point in the understanding of the nature of any teaching pattern. To just what extent was the activity concerned really initiated by the child or children concerned, and to what extent was it a teacher-stimulated unit? There is a temptation to slur over this matter in giving a report. It is fashionable in "child-centered" schools to maintain the fiction that activities are initiated independent of the teacher. What we really need is frankness in this matter. We want to know to just what extent teachers have actually kept hands off, and to what extent they have guided and planned even the earliest initiated responses of the children. Teachers who are not scientifically faithful and accurate in such reporting can do the cause for which they work infinite harm. We need to be more clear on this matter than we are at present. It is one in which certain individuals hold extreme views. Accurate unwavering reports, which give a lucid account of the part of both teacher and children in initiating activities reported will prove most helpful to students of the subject. After all, it is the teacher who should know best, not the theorist. The theorist depends upon the teacher to criticize his views, and must ever learn from her experience.

5. *The Account of the Progress of the Activity Should Be Concrete, and Interestingly Written*

The largest section of any report will probably be taken up in reporting the progress of the activities. It is here that the reader hopes to discover a vivid picture, full of interesting scraps of detail, containing records of the actual words of teacher and pupils which would add to the description. It will be most useful to find a clear and somewhat detailed account of just how the developing activity was planned by the children. In the description of the actual details of the work a great deal of ingenuity will be needed. The art of the matter is that of leaving out nothing which is essential, pictorial or interestingly descriptive, yet at the same time omitting a great deal of what was actually said and done. Limitations of space will make it necessary to follow some such plan in reporting long units. Brief units may often be reported stenographically to good advantage. It is in this main body of the account that the teacher will find ample opportunity for presentation in terms of the individual case.

6. *The Use Which Is Made of the Result Should Be Clearly Set Forth*

In cases where the activity issues in any objective result or any definite learning the use to which this is put by the pupil should be made clear. There is a tendency in current reports to neglect this aspect of the situation.

7. A Report Should Be Given of the Way in Which Evaluation Was Made

Readers will be anxious to know whether or not the pupils finally made any check on the activity they were engaged in. Did they judge the adequacy of the product, whether that product was a material object, or something less tangible? Did they consider whether the resulting learnings were satisfactory or not? Was the original need met? Were the curriculum goals which were definitely aimed at by the pupils actually reached? Again, did the class conduct the work in a satisfactory manner? If not, in what ways could they improve their procedure on future occasions? The teaching pattern which is thus well rounded out and complete is convincing and satisfactory because it leaves the reader with a feeling of completeness and a confidence that the work has issued in discipline and character development.

8. A Final Statement of Attained Curriculum Goals Should Be Given

Critics of educational procedure will wish to be given a clear account of curricular gains resulting from the unit of conduct reported. It is, therefore, necessary to give in some form such an accounting. This may be a brief statement that the goals aimed at have been reached. On the other hand, it may indicate just where the unit has failed in this respect, and give a helpful account of the probable reasons. Again, it may include an account of many curriculum goals attained which were in addition to those hoped for. It is usually better not to claim such generalized attainments as improved powers of concentration, added ability to think, or fuller understanding of fairness or sportsmanship. Such claims usually weaken rather than strengthen the case, since they may be claimed with equal validity for almost any sort of school work. Statements of attained curriculum goals should be definite, specific and concrete.

III. WIDER IMPLICATIONS OF TEACHING

CHAPTER XXXI

THE LIFE OF THE WHOLE SCHOOL

ALL that has been written in these pages has been set forth from the point of view of the class teacher. Everything has been regarded from the teacher's standpoint, and has, consequently, dealt chiefly with the teacher's attitude and techniques. The teacher is primarily interested in her own class. Nevertheless, she must take a wider view than this. A class is not an isolated group, nor may it be soundly regarded as a separate social entity. It is but a part of the larger school community. Therefore, both the teacher and the members of her class should be conscious of this larger outlook and of the responsibilities and privileges it involves. The present chapter will, therefore, while still keeping to the teacher's point of view, make reference to the wider school life of which the class forms a part, and in which it must coöperate.

Children should have a developing consciousness of their membership not only in the class group, but in that larger community, the whole school. Only when this is so is there any such thing as "school spirit." The school spirit is the life of the school. It is a manifestation of an organic school community. Each pupil should be proud of the school without knowing it, not because it is his school rather than somebody else's, but because this school has life, unity, individuality, and a significant existence in the world in general.

If these things are to be a reality, the school must verily be a community. Organic unity is not secured by writing it on the school curriculum or the school calendar. It exists only when the children in the school find opportunity to coöperate with one another, to embark upon joint enterprises. A school is only a community when the children live in it together. In what follows, an account is given of some of the ways in which the lives of individuals and classes merge and intermingle in the larger school life.

The Assembly

One of the most obvious opportunities for the whole school to coöperate and live together is provided by the assembly. This meeting together of the school is not the old-time opening exercise, to which the pupils came with nothing in mind, and left in the same condition. It is a vitalized assembly, in which matters of importance or interest which develop in the course of community living may be conveniently dealt with. Thus, if the fourth grade has been investigating the making of artificial silk from wood pulp, and has arrived at an interesting organization of the results of its study, it may pass on to the whole school what it has discovered; or to the children of another class, who have worked out a play worth seeing, may present it to the larger group.

This assembly of the whole school has advantages which are both social and individual. The sharing of all the children in certain activities of common interest serves to make them conscious of membership in the larger group. They may realize that, in spite of their separation for the greater part of the time into classes, they are yet all members of a larger family, a group which has that unity which comes of common interests. Advantage to the individual results from the fact that the children themselves, not the teachers, take charge of the assembly. This brings about numerous opportunities for children to appear before a larger group, and to develop the power to meet an audience without the self-consciousness which tortures many an individual brought up without benefit of assembly. Even simple programs should be rehearsed by the group presenting them, so that the children may be sure of themselves and fully confident when appearing before the group.

The activities which may be carried on during assembly are numerous and varied. Music has its place, so that children who have composed, or who perform, may entertain the group. Poetry, stories, singing, or rhythms worked out by the children may be presented. There may be moving pictures, or slides to illustrate some phase of living which is interesting, such as the life of the bee. The assembly period belongs to the children and is an organic growth to which the life of the whole school contributes. It is an outcome of school life, not an appendage to it. Teachers belong there as interested members of the group who have their part on appropriate but comparatively rare occasions, just as the children have their part at appropriate times. Again, the assembly affords an excellent opportunity for the working out of plans for any enterprise upon which the school is to embark as a whole, such as the holding of a school fair or the arranging of the commencement program, or the planning of some benevolent enterprise in which the school is to take part. In fact, every matter which has educational value and interest for the larger group deserves its place on the assembly program.

It seems scarcely necessary to emphasize that the children control and govern their own assemblies; that good assemblies are not teacher-manufactured and teacher-run activities. The school administration may assist in the arranging of the schedule, but the assemblies are usually arranged for by the children and conducted by individuals chosen in one way or another to carry on. Schools which have an elementary school council may have an assembly committee as part of the council to make plans for assemblies and arrange for the giving of notices concerning seating or any matter of group responsibility. The meetings are presided over by one of the children chosen by the committee, by the class holding the assembly, or in some other way.

The time at which the assembly is held is usually the early morning, but it may be at some different time according to the programs of various schools. Whenever it is held it should be short. It may be as frequent as the particular situation demands. In certain schools it may be developed more readily and needed more often than in others. Some schools hold an assembly practically every day, others but once a week. More customarily they are held about four times a week. One school holds fifteen-minute assemblies three times a week, at which such matters as devotional exercises, singing, and reports on current events are given attention, and in addition one forty-five-minute period a week at which the children present longer programs, such as the result of some unit of work, a "moving picture" of Dutch life, a program for Book Week, or an original play. Certain schools find it necessary to modify assembly arrangements so that only certain groups attend at certain times. The children of the lower grades may not be present when matters too mature for their interest or understanding are presented. Sometimes a class may decide in consultation with the teacher whether or not they will attend on certain specific occasions. In matters of assemblies, as elsewhere, common sense contributes greatly to good living.

SUMMER ACTIVITIES

The Tower Hill School, of Wilmington, Delaware, has sometimes held an assembly program built on summer activities and based on questionnaires distributed soon after school opens.[1]

[1] Announcement of the Tower Hill School, Wilmington, Delaware, 1929-30, p. 153.

"To show the aggregate gain and weight of the school two sets of gigantic cardboard men were made, the shorter and thinner representing weight and height in June, the taller and fatter showing September figures. A large book, its pages slowly turned by two animated book-ends, revealed the number of books read by each grade during the summer. A procession of fourth grade children, each carrying a map of one of the United States with a conspicuous numeral on the map, indicated the states visited by pupils during the summer. A long procession of craftsmen, each group distinguished by its own banner such as 'Woodworkers,' 'Silversmiths,' 'Gardeners,' 'Painters,' and each member carrying something made by his own hands, gave some idea of the creative activities of the vacation period. By means of dramatization of the 'Tower Hill School Employment Agency' twenty or thirty types of work done during the summer were shown. In connection with this assembly very interesting exhibits were arranged in cases and on tables in the halls. This long program, representing types of activity was followed by a series of short programs in which individual pupils gave informal talks on interesting places they had visited, people they had met, or things they had done or made."

This is but one example of the way in which the summer experiences of the children contribute to the life of the school. These free experiences of children form an invaluable background for the class work. Many activities may be based on activities arising as a result of what the children have done during the summer. It is for this reason, and because the school is bound to be interested in developing sound habits of recreation in its pupils, that the modern school tries to do something to guide the summer activities of its pupils. The prospective use of the children's summer experiences in school later on will be a real stimulus to them to engage in something worth while during the holidays so that they may have something to show for their time in school later on. It is necessary, however, to provide the children with some printed suggestions before they leave school for the holidays if the school intends to make use of their summer experiences when they return.[1]

Whole School Activities

It has been mentioned that there are certain activities in which the school as a whole takes part, some of which may be introduced

[1] Some such list may be worked out as that which is used by the Francis Parker School of the University of Chicago. See Catalog and Course of Study of the Francis W. Parker School, University of Chicago, pp. 18 ff.

or planned during the morning assembly. The first type is that in which the whole school participates. Such an occasion would be the arranging of a school festival of the type described by Chubb,[1] or the arranging of a school fair, in which the whole school participates from the little girl who may exhibit a "home-made" rag doll to a boy who shows a collection of coins.[2]

The carrying on of the Santa Claus Toy Shop by the children of the Francis W. Parker School [3] is another example of the way in which the whole school may engage on a coöperative enterprise. Each year, for the two weeks following the Thanksgiving recess, all time usually devoted to art, gymnasium and hand work is set free, and the children use these periods and any other time they can spare to work in the toy shop, repairing and renovating toys which have been collected. They have the work divided into different departments, such as dressmaking, metal work, doll repair, book and game repair. All is carefully organized, and when Christmas time comes, the distribution of toys among those who would otherwise be without them helps to make the children realize that the school is itself a part of a still larger community about it.

A second type of whole school activity is that which is carried on by the school for special individual members of the various class groups who are interested in a special activity, such as the school orchestra. In such work the children find opportunity to use the special talents which they have trained in a way that enables them to get used to contributing to the public good. They not only thus prepare themselves for later possible playing with a professional group, but meet other members of the school and contribute to the whole school life by public performance.

The Use of the Whole School Environment as a Stimulus to Activities

The school organization and environment, because of the fact that the school is a living organism, a community itself, provides many occasions and opportunities for pupil activity. The school is not an iron-bound pattern into which the pupils must fit. Rather it is a

---

[1] Chubb, P., "Festivals and Plays," Harper.

[2] For an account of a Fall Fair which is well worked out, see "The Parker School Fall Fair," by Flora J. Cooke, *Progressive Education*, April-May-June, 1929, Vol. VI, No. 2, p. 166. An account of the technique of exhibits is given by Knox in "School Activities and Equipment," Houghton Mifflin Co., Boston, pp. 255-260.

[3] See The Francis W. Parker School Yearbook, Vol. I, June, 1912, p. 21.

THE LIFE OF THE WHOLE SCHOOL

flexible, vital situation which the pupil himself helps to create. The children are part of the motive power of the school. They participate in their own government by some scheme or other. They may work together with the manager of the lunch room or with the librarian for the improvement of these special branches. The school store, the gymnasium, in fact any aspect of daily activity may be an opportunity for developing the life of the school and the children living there. So in cases where the school is faced with some special need, the children learn by coöperating to supply it. Miss Lewis [1] relates the way in which the children in a school under her direction took over a vacant cottage on the school property and made it into a playhouse, with its living-room, bedrooms, and kitchen, and so by their own efforts added a definite asset to the life of the school. A visitor to the Walden School, in New York, will see in the reception-room, a large painting five feet square, the work of one of the pupils, while the room is decorated with the children's own work in plastic arts. In the cafeteria of some schools children who have reached the goal of legibility in script are allowed to write the day's menu on the cafeteria blackboard. So learning becomes a mature rather than a callow product.

Supplementary School Activities

In addition to the regular class work, well-organized schools provide for supplementary activities after class hours, activities which use the school equipment and are supervised by special members of the school staff. The playground and the gymnasium may be so used. If children have opportunity to play on the school grounds, they will not have to hunt about town for ways in which to fill in time. So on the playground the children may play such games as speed ball, kick ball, soccer, and hand ball. Provision may be made for hockey, cricket, baseball and archery. The art rooms and the school shop, if kept open, will provide opportunity for those not athletically inclined. A Boy Scout cabin, the property of a scout troop with a scoutmaster who is a trained teacher, is a center of valuable activity. Again, afternoon clubs and Saturday clubs provide for the satisfactory use of leisure time. The work of such clubs may be supplemented by "hikes" and by trips to the school cabin in the country.

In all such activities care should be taken that the children assume

[1] Lewis, M. H., "An Adventure With Children," The Macmillan Co., New York, 1928, p. 182.

as much of the responsibility for the making and securing of their own play equipment as the circumstances permit. The mere provision of money and the purchase of equipment can never be so satisfactory as an arrangement by which the children make, build and buy from their own earned money the equipment which they use for play. This will not always be possible. It is unwise for any group to attempt to lift a weight too heavy for it. Under certain circumstances it will be necessary for the school to provide. As much as possible, however, the children's own efforts should provide for their recreational equipment and needs. Otherwise children are trained to buy recreation or to demand it free rather than to find joy in creating it.

The Health of the Whole School

While it is true that, in a general sense, the health of the school child is an interest of the teacher, yet the actual care of the health of the child must, to a large extent, be delegated to the school administration. It is an occasion for specialized service. Nevertheless, so important is the health of the child in relation to his learning that some account will be given here of a school health program in order that the teacher may orient herself to the general health plans of a school.

The Health Program

If a community were compelled to choose between looking after the health of its children and teaching them, surely it would be better to bring up healthy children untaught rather than children who are trained but unhealthy. Fortunately, it is not necessary to choose between such unnatural alternatives. The problem of health and the problem of education are so intimately interrelated that the educational program itself should be a health program. This is, however, a very different thing from saying that the schools should be agencies for health propaganda. Filled with mistaken zeal, some school systems have been lured into artificial and ill-conceived health drives. To promote such drives principals and teachers have been suborned by an administration which had failed in its duty of maintaining a health program, to interfere with the regular educational program of the schools by causing a health-mania to throw the remainder of the program out of kilter. Thus children have been expected to make health posters, write health stories, make and present health fairy plays, until the very program of health became if not unhealthy, at least irksome. Such patching-up schemes tend rather to make children overconscious rather than healthy. The whole attitude of the school should be a positive one of maintaining healthy living and, consequently, taking health for granted.

This maintaining of healthy living will be much promoted by schools which carry on the maximum amount of school living out of doors. Previous mention has already been made of the educational advantages of an outdoor environment. Such an environment is equally advantageous from the point of view of the good health of children, not to mention teachers. Many schools which still carry on most of their activities indoors have, nevertheless, worked out programs of physical training and athletics which are carried on almost entirely in the open air. Thus the physical training work, in addition to various forms of ball playing, includes skating, walking on stilts, hoop-rolling, rope-jumping, and archery, as well as trips abroad in the countryside where hill and rock-climbing may become strenuous enough.

The development of health habits which become an integral part of the children's living is a primary duty of the school. Such habits are an important part of the work of the nursery school, so that schools which lack this initial unit in their program are already at a disadvantage in this respect when the children come to kindergarten. The kindergarten and primary grades continue to lay emphasis on this matter by providing an unusually hygienic environment, and a schedule of living which provides the correct amount of physical activity and rest. The children in these grades are trained to live in healthy fashion by actually maintaining such healthy habits as washing their hands in the school. In the upper grades children are taught the bearings of science on healthy living, and are encouraged to maintain correct habits by, for example, the use of proper food in the lunch room. They are also taught to keep check on their own habits by the use of such devices as sleep charts. Some schools find it advantageous to use some additional form of checking. The more formal school sometimes used such drastic methods as a regular morning inspection by the teacher, in which she passed down each row watching for dirty hands and clothing, or for a child without a handkerchief. On the other hand, the writer has visited "progressive" schools in which the children, youngsters from privileged homes, were slovenly, untidy and unwashed. One is puzzled to know whether the overdirection in the one case is more pernicious than the underdirection of the other. Certainly, when health habits learned in the lower grades are not being kept up, the class should consider the problem very seriously, and plan a scheme for improvement. Health habits are best taught by being maintained through the whole of the school program as the foundation of their further maintenance through life.

In many communities and schools the plan of providing mid-morning milk lunches has been adopted as a regular part of the health program. The distribution of the bottles on trays to the various rooms, the keeping of accounts involved, the setting of the table in the primary grades, and the passing of bottles and straws in the older grades are activities which all contribute to the activity program of the school. They should be worked out to suit the specific needs of each school with the general matter of their contribution to school activities in mind.

The Hygienic Program

Adequate medical inspection of children is necessary if hygienic conditions are to be maintained. During a year a complete physical examination of each child should be made either by the family or the school physician. It is usually wise to notify the parents when such physical examinations are to be given, and invite them to be present. An account of the results of the examination should be sent to each parent, with a report of remediable defects which have been noticed, and advice to consult the regular physician of the family or to visit clinics suggested on the report. In addition to the provision of these physical examinations, the physical education department of some schools makes certain further examinations. "Foot-o-graph" prints are made each year of the children's feet, with special attention to those whose arches are poor. Posture silhouettes are made in the nude through a translucent screen. The silhouettes, which are kept in a locked file in the school office, are of great value in revealing defects of the shoulders, spine, or hips, and are most useful in indicating improvement due to corrective work. Certain schools arrange for a periodic weighing and measuring of the children, the results of which are entered on a Classroom Weight Record. This is hung in the classroom at a height which makes it visible to the children. It may become a source of considerable investigation and calculation, and if correctly used, a valuable aid to motivating the maintenance of good health habits.

Every school should have a full-time school nurse, with an office or health clinic in the school. All absences should be reported to the nurse early in the day. The nurse is then able to telephone the family of the absentee during the morning. The nurse assists in the general hygienic program of the school. She keeps check on the readmission of children after sicknesses, such as scarlet fever, mumps, or measles, and sees that children with colds are kept at home. She also assists in the follow-up work of the school, visiting families when necessary to explain the nature of defects revealed in the physical examination. In certain cases she takes the child needing attention to a clinic or hospital, or in matters of home hygiene, calls at the home.

A corrective régime is maintained for children who are underweight, undernourished, or of bad posture. According to the needs of the case, provision is made for mid-morning milk, for monthly weighing and measuring, for special diet, or for attendance in special health classes meeting once a week, or special classes in the open air. In matters of posture, teachers should give attention to the setting up of good standards for all the children, but in cases of deviation, special exercises must be provided. Roaring like a lion, for instance, induces deep breathing and squaring of the shoulders; flat feet are corrected by playing at being a tight-rope walker; and trying to be a giraffe helps the general posture. When defects in posture, spine, or feet are detected, special exercises are prescribed by the department of physical education, and the child is shown how to perform these exercises, if possible, in the presence of the teacher and the parent. Thus both teacher and parent are able to supervise such special exercises at home or in school.

LAW AND ORDER IN THE SCHOOL COMMUNITY

The matter of school order has been previously treated from the point of view of the classroom teacher. It must receive separate and distinct consideration in its relationships to the whole school. For in a disorderly school there is little hope of an orderly class. The essence of successful order in the class group is the membership of that class in a larger school community which is itself orderly. It is important for the teacher to realize this relationship. One teacher with a disorderly group may destroy the order of the whole school. In this matter the school must be one. Each child must feel that because things go well about him on every side, it is not for him to prevent their proper functioning. Such a feeling is school pride. There is a real joy in belonging to a smoothly running community of high standards.

The maintenance of a school community of high standards provides the only satisfactory background for well-behaving individuals. Consciousness on the part of the children of that well-ordered, large-group living is the basis upon which the order of the whole school is maintained. When there is such a state of affairs on every side, children are ashamed to do wrong, if not in the doing, at least when the deed is done. When they regard themselves in the light of their proud community, they find themselves wanting. It is as though a boy with filthy hands sits down to table with a dozen other boys whose hands are washed. He may not notice it at the time, but the moment it is directed to his attention, he feels ashamed. He is ashamed to be dirty when others are clean. So a boy is ashamed of doing wrong when he is among others who do right. It thus becomes clear how very essential it is that the whole school shall be a spotless community. It is only so that children may feel their own delinquencies.

There are three general ways in which the checking of children who vary from standards of order may be made. The first is by the children themselves. In a school in which children have pride in their community life, the children will naturally and simply tell others who are making trouble to stop. This is not the priggishness and self-importance that make some children boss others in schools where repression is the order of the day. It is a simple rebuke given when disorder of one child interferes with another. So in the classroom one pupil may tell another not to talk so loud.

The second and third ways of checking children are by sending them to the principal or before the elementary school council. Circumstances must govern to which a child must go. On the whole teachers who find a pupil determinedly troublesome may well refer his case to the elementary school council. It is best to arrange matters so that any sending of a child to the principal shall in no way be associated with the idea of punishment. Rather such a visit should be regarded as a report.[1] The child assumes the burden of reporting that he has not lived up to his responsibility. So, in the case of such a clear matter of law and order as playing on forbidden lawn, about which there is a definite regulation, a younger child may be asked by an older one to go to see the principal to talk over the matter. The idea is not that the child is to go to the principal for a scolding, much less a punishment, but to get the matter straightened out. It is possible that the child has not understood the regulation, or possibly has not realized its importance. Approaching the principal, not in fear,

[1] In some schools children are never sent to the principal in cases of conduct deviation.

possibly in shame, but certainly as though going to a friend, the child may bring up the reason for his visit.

In talking to children, the manner of the principal should always be positive and sympathetic. It is wise for the teacher to assume an attitude of trust in the child. She assumes that if the child has made a mistake, he will certainly not do it again. Sometimes the teacher may talk with the child until he sees that there has been some wrong done. In such a case he will agree to the necessity of spoiling his office record card with a mark. This mark may be removed after a month if the child does not return in the same type of trouble during that period. It is assumed that the slip was merely a slip and has been rectified. The child may learn to see himself in his record and be anxious to keep clean.

The elementary school council may deal with problems of discipline when necessary, but it is very desirable that these matters shall be the least and most infrequent of their concerns. Such a council may be elected by the children to suit the particular needs of the school. In an ordinary school two members, a boy and a girl from each grade above the second, with optional representation from grades one and two, may compose the council, which meets together with an adult adviser. This council may deal with any joint problems of the school which the administration may be able to hand over to them: the provision of a piece of school equipment not provided for in the budget, the participation of the school in some larger community enterprise, or any such problem as one arising from food complaints or confusion in the lunchroom. The Lincoln School [1] at times finds the origin for group activities in social service from the determinations of this council. Whatever problems of individuals out of order seem advisable to bring before the council, they should be simply dealt with under the guidance of the council's adviser, as the circumstances of the case dictate.[2]

One other point concerning the development of the order of the whole school is significant in schools which are changing from the old ideas of discipline to the newer ideas of self-sustaining order. A special problem is created in such schools by the fact that children accustomed to the older methods of control do not respond easily to the new. It is only in schools in which children have lived under a self-determining régime from the very beginning that such a reliance

---

[1] "Curriculum Making in an Elementary School," pp. 12-19.
[2] Cox, W. L., "Creative School Control," J. B. Lippincott & Co., Philadelphia, 1927, Ch. XI, p. 219.

upon them is warranted. Children and even teachers who have used other modes of behavior for years will continually revert to the older way of looking at things. In schools which are attempting to change from the old order to the new, special problems must be expected which are directly due to the making of the change itself. When such changes are made it may possibly be best to begin from the bottom of the school and change gradually through a period of years.

Special reference may also be made to schools which are situated in parts of a large city in which there are a great number of underprivileged children whose home and social environment may be undesirable, or even vicious. No final dictum can be issued at present as to whether the methods of control set forth in this book will be found adequate to meet such situations. There are those who maintain vigorously, and a little fearsomely, that they will not. On the other hand, there are many teachers who believe that with slight modifications they will. The proof of the controversy will lie in the actual attempt to work out school life in terms of such special environments, an educational experiment which, as far as my knowledge extends, has never yet been made. It may possibly be that a program of social training such as has been outlined in these pages will not prove adequate to meet the specialized problems of unfortunate city environments. In such cases those in charge of the schools will fall back on the older views and schemes of punishments so adequately and unsparingly set forth by many writers on education. Until such time, however, there are many whose larger faith in children's ability to learn, will lead them to insist that in an orderly school normal children will be orderly, to insist that even in matters of order the whole may not be greater than its parts.

Imitation in Whole School Organization

In these matters of order, and in other matters of whole school organization, schools which would organize themselves according to newer methods may at first be imitative. In the struggle for reorganization schools may well do what others have done. Those responsible for the organization of the school may study school practice and follow it imitatively, reproducing, as nearly as may be, what they have seen elsewhere. But such an imitative policy should not be followed blindly or for long. One form or another must be tried out and either adopted or discarded. Each school is an individual school. It has its own special characteristics and its own individual problems. Gradually the school, by exploring its own needs, must solve its own problems. The school must grow and change and find its own form of expression. So continually by experiment and alteration and growth, the individual school may become a unique organism, with a structure determined by its permanent and changing functions. So may the life of the school be the living of the children.

BIBLIOGRAPHY

BOOKS ON PROGRESSIVE TEACHING

Specially Recommended Books are Starred *

Activity Curriculums at Work (Criteria for Units of Work, p. 7), National Education Association, 1929.
BURKE, A., and Others, *A Conduct Curriculum*, Scribners, N. Y., 1923.
CLAUSER, L. W., and MILLIKAN, C. E., *Kindergarten Primary Activities Based on Community Life*, The Macmillan Co., N. Y., 1929.
DYER, S., "Objectives in the First Three Grades," *Childhood Education*, April, 1926, pp. 384-391.
Eight Year Old Merchants, Greenberg, Publisher, Inc., N. Y., 1928.
GREEN, *Making a Movie in the Second Grade*, Wauwatosa, Wis., The Kenyon Press, 1926.
HILL, *A Conduct Curriculum for the Kindergarten and First Grade*, Charles Scribner's Sons, N. Y., 1923.
KEELOR, K. L., *Curriculum Studies in the Second Grade*, Bureau of Publications, Teachers College, Columbia Univ., 1925.
* KNOX, ROSE B., *School Activities and Equipment*, The Houghton Mifflin Co., Boston, 1927.
KRACKOWITZER, *Projects in the Primary Grades*, J. B. Lippincott Co., Philadelphia, 1919.
LACY, NAN, *A Method of Curriculum Reorganization*, The Raleigh Public Schools, 1926.
Lincoln Elementary School Staff, *Curriculum Making in an Elementary School*, Ginn & Co., N. Y., 1927.
MELVIN, A. GORDON, *Progressive Teaching*, D. Appleton & Co., N. Y., 1929.
Milwaukee, Wis., *Creative Activities in Eighth Grade*, A Christmas Play, State Normal, Curriculum Series, 1926.
POLLITZER, MARGARET, "Education for Creative Living," *The World of Tomorrow*, May, 1924.
* PORTER, MARTHA PECK, *The Teacher in the New School*, The World Book Co., Yonkers-on-the-Hudson, 1930.
PRATT, C., *Experimental Practice in the City and Country School*, E. P. Dutton, N. Y.
PRATT, C., and STANTON, J., *Before Books*, Adelphi Co., N. Y., 1927.
* Publications of the Francis W. Parker School, The University of Chicago:
The Social Motive in School Work, Vol. 1, June, 1912.
The Course in Science, Vol. 5, July, 1918.
The Individual and the Curriculum, Vol. 6.
Social Science Series, Vol. 7.
Creative Effort, Vol. 8.
Catalog and Course of Study.

Public Schools of San Francisco, Calif., *Furnishing the Setting for an Activity Program in the Kindergarten and Primary Grades,* April, 1927.
Raleigh Public Schools, *Statement of Aims and Educational Program* (Mimeographed), 1928.
Raleigh Public Schools, Raleigh, N. C. (Mimeographed and Bound). Payment required in advance. Prices here as quoted 1930:
   Bulletin No. 1—*A Suggested List of Activities for Grades 1-6,* 66 pages, 1928, $ .50. (This pamphlet is printed.)
   Bulletin No. 2—*Statement of Aims and Educational Program,* 151 pages, 1928, $1.50.
   Bulletin No. 3—*Teaching in the First Grade,* 199 pages, 1928, $1.25.
   Bulletin No. 4—*Teaching in Grades 2 and 3,* 121 pages, 1928, $1.40.
   Bulletin No. 5—*Teaching in Grades 4, 5, and 6,* 136 pages, 1929, $1.45.
   Bulletin No. 6—*Art Education* (Grades 1-11), 119 pages, 1929, $1.75.
SALISBURY, *An Activity Curriculum for Kindergarten and Primary Grades,* Harr Wagner, San Francisco, 1924.
* SLOMAN, LAURA GILLMORE, *Some Primary Methods,* The Macmillan Co., N. Y., 1927.
* STEVENS, M. P., *The Activities Curriculum in the Primary Grades,* D. C. Heath & Co., N. Y., 1931.
STOTT, L. V., *Adventuring with Twelve Year Olds,* Greenberg, Publisher, Inc., N. Y., 1927.
* *Teachers Guide to Child Development,* Bulletin, 1930, No. 36, United States Department of the Interior, Washington.
The City and Country School, N. Y., *Record of Group Six.*

TEACHING PATTERNS

"Adventure Island," Charles A. Kinney in *Progressive Education,* Vol. VI, Number 2, April-May-June, 1929, p. 173.
"Bringing the Tree-Dwellers into the Schoolroom," article by Dorothea Jackson, Seattle Public Schools, *American Childhood,* Vol. 14, No. 8, April, 1929, p. 8.
"Investigation Lane," *University of Chicago Studies in Education,* Vol. 1.
"Japanese Art," a stenographic report of a class lesson, *Francis W. Parker School Studies in Education,* Vol. VI, 1920, p. 13.
"Research Work in the Museum for Ten Year Olds," Hannah Falk in *Progressive Education,* July-Aug.-Sept., 1928, p. 234.
"Six Year Old Explorers in New York City," article by Jessie M. Stanton in *Progressive Education,* Vol. V, No. 3, July-Aug.-Sept., 1928, p. 224.
"The Sevens Discover How the City Gets Bread," article by Avah Hughes in *Progressive Education,* July-Aug.-Sept., 1928, p. 229.
"Twelve-year-olds Investigate the Textile Industry," same issue of *Progressive Education,* p. 238, article by Ellen W. Steele.
"When the Circus Comes to School," article by Carlotta Alexander, The Out-of-Door School, Sarasota, Florida, *American Childhood,* Vol. 14, No. 9, May, 1929, p. 9.

BIBLIOGRAPHY

Other Valuable Concrete Reports of Teaching Patterns in

STEVENS, M. P., *The Activities Curriculum in the Primary Grades,* D. C. Heath & Co., N. Y., 1931.
Teachers Guide to Child Development, Bulletin, 1930, No. 36, United States Department of the Interior, Washington.
Publications of The Francis W. Parker School, University of Chicago.

ART

CANE, FLORENCE, "Teaching Children to Paint," *The Arts,* August, 1924.
CHENEY, SHELDON, *A Primer of Modern Art,* Boni & Liveright.
CIZEK, FRANZ, *The Child as an Artist,* Cizek Exhibit, Greenwich, Conn.
FURNISS, DOROTHY, *Drawing for Beginners,* Bridgman, Publishers, Pelham, N. Y.
MATHIAS, *The Beginnings of Art in the Public Schools,* Charles Scribner's Sons, N. Y., 1924.
Progressive Education, April, 1926, "Creative Expression Through Art."
Progressive Education, January, 1927, "Creative Expression Through Art."
Raleigh Public Schools, Raleigh, N. C., *Art Education,* Grades 1-11, (Mimeographed), 119 pages, 1929.
SARGENT and MILLER, *How Children Learn to Draw,* Ginn & Co., N. Y., 1927.
The New Era, April, 1926, "A New Approach to Drawing in Vienna Schools."
The New Era, "Creative Effort in Childhood," Franz Cizek, October, 1923.
WILSON, FRANCESCA, *A Lecture of Professor Cizek,* Cizek Exhibit, Greenwich, Conn.
ZACHRY, CAROLINE B., *Illustration of English Work in Junior High,* Lincoln School, Columbia University, N. Y., 1925.

DRAMATICS

BROWN, CORINNE, *Creative Drama in the Lower School,* D. Appleton & Co., N. Y., 1929.
CHUBB, P., *Festivals and Plays,* Harper & Bros., 1912.
Progressive Education, January, 1928, "Adventures with Puppets."
Progressive Education, January, 1931, "Creative Expression Through Dramatics."
Progressive Education, January, 1927, "Place of the Festival in Modern Life."
Progressive Education, January, 1928.
Teachers of the Shady Hill School, *Acting Things Out.*
WARD, *Creative Dramatics,* D. Appleton & Co., N. Y.

LITERATURE

AUSLANDER, JOSEPH and HILL, FRANK E., *The Winged Horse,* Doubleday Doran & Co., A History of Poetry for Young People.
Progressive Education, January, 1928, "Creative Expression Through Literature."

MUSIC

CADY, CALVIN B., *Music Education,* Clayton F. Summy Co.
CANFIELD, JULIA, *Original Composition,* Francis Parker Yearbook, Univ. of Chicago, Vol. 1.

CLEMENTS, KATHERINE, *Music Moods in Pastel and Charcoal*, Francis Parker Yearbook, Univ. of Chicago, Vol. VI.
COLEMAN, SATIS N., *Creative Music for Children*, Putnam.
———, *Creative Music in the Home*, Lewis E. Meyers & Co., Valparaiso, Ind.
———, *First Steps in Playing and Composing*, A Music Book for Children, The Lincoln School, 425 West 123rd Street, New York City, 1926.
COLEMAN, SATIS N., and THORN, A. G., *Singing Time*, A Book of Songs for Little Children, The John Day Co., N. Y.
DALCROZE, EMILE JACQUES, *Rhythm, Music and Education*, G. P. Putnam, N. Y., 1925.
GOODRICH, HELEN, *Creative Effort in Melody*, Francis W. Parker Yearbook, The University of Chicago, Vol. I.
———, *Creative Effort in Melody*, Francis Parker Yearbook, University of Chicago, Vol. VIII.
KERN, M. R., "Elementary Music Teaching in the Laboratory School," *Elementary School Teacher*, September, 1903.
———, "Song Composition," *Elementary School Record*, No. 2.
KINNEY, CHARLES M., *Work with Children Backward in Music*, Francis Parker Yearbook, University of Chicago, Vol. I.
NEWMAN, ELIZABETH, *How to Teach Music to Children*, Fischer.
Progressive Education, January, 1927, "Creative Expression Through Music."
The New Era, April, 1926, "Musical Design," MURIEL MACKENZIE.
TROTTER, T. H. YORKE, *Making of Musicians*, Dutton.
VANDEVER, J. LILIAN, *The Toy Symphony Orchestra*, Birchard.

RHYTHMICS

COLEMAN, SATIS N., *The Beginnings of Music*, The Making and Use of Instruments for Rhythm, The Lincoln School, Columbia Univ., Experimental Edition, 1925.
DALCROZE, EMILE JACQUES, *Rhythm, Music and Education*, G. P. Putnam, N. Y., 1925.
DOING, RUTH, "Rythmics," *Progressive Education*, Jan., 1927.
HARRIGAN, OLIVE K., *Creative Activities in Physical Education*, A. S. Barnes & Co., N. Y., 1929.

SPECIAL ACTIVITIES

ADAMS, J. H., *Harper's Indoor Book for Boys*, Harper & Bros., N. Y., 1908.
BONSER and MOSSMAN, *Industrial Arts in the Elementary Schools*, The Macmillan Co., N. Y., 1927.
BUTLER, EVA L., *Along the Shore*, The John Day Co., N. Y.
BRIGHAM, LOUISE, *Box Furniture*, The Century Co., N. Y., 1919.
COLEMAN, SATIS N., *Bells*, Their History, Legends, Making, and Uses, Rand McNally Co., N. Y., 1928.
FULLER, R. T., *Walk, Look, and Listen*, The John Day Co., N. Y.
FURST, HERBERT, *The Modern Woodcut*, Dodd Mead & Co.
MCKENNY, MARGARET, *Mushrooms of Field and Wood*, The John Day Co., N. Y.
SHOOK, ANNA NOTT, *The Book of Weaving*, The John Day Co., N. Y.

SPRAGUE, CURTISS, *How to Make Linoleum Blocks*, Bridgman Publishers, Pelham, N. Y., 1928.

MISCELLANEOUS

A LIST OF PROGRESSIVE SCHOOLS is published by the Progressive Education Association, Washington.
ANNOUNCEMENT OF THE TOWER HILL SCHOOL, 17th St. and Tower Rd., Wilmington, Delaware.
Functions of the Department of Psychological Measurement, by Gertrude Hildreth (Pamphlet), Bureau of Publications, Teachers College, Columbia University, N. Y., 1927.
Horace Mann Studies in Elementary Education, Teachers College, Columbia University, 1922.
Journal of the National Education Association, November, 1930, p. 245, "The Visiting Teacher at Work," By Josephine Chase.
Lincoln School, Columbia University, N. Y., *Field Work*, Charles Finley and James S. Tippett, 1925.
MELVIN, A. GORDON, *Progressive Education*, June, 1930, "Temperance and Technique."
Materials for the Individual Technique. Pamphlet listing materials for reading, spelling, arithmetic, language, social studies and general science. Winnetka Individual Materials Incorporated, Horace Mann School, Winnetka, Ill. Sent on request.
Parent-Teacher Organizations of the Lincoln School (Pamphlet), The Lincoln School of Teachers College, 425 W. 123rd Street, N. Y., 1926.
PRACTICE TESTS
  McCall and Crabbs—Standard Test Lessons in Reading.
  Courtis Spelling Practice Test.
  Courtis Standard Practice Test in Handwriting.
  Studebaker Economy Practice—Exercises in Arithmetic (Fundamentals).
  Greene—Studebaker—Knight—Ruch—Economy Problem-solving Exercise Cards.
  Courtis Standard Practice Tests in Arithmetic.
Price List of the Industrial Arts Co-operative Service, 519 W. 121st St., New York City. An excellent Bureau for the purchase of materials for equipment of the school environment. Special rates to members.
Progressive Education, April-May-June, 1928, "The Three R's."
Progressive Education, Magazine of the Progressive Education Association, Washington, D. C.
The New Era, Magazine of the New Education Fellowship, 11 Tavistock Square, London, England.
Vacation Activities and the School, The Lincoln School of Teachers College, 425 West 123d St., N. Y., 1925.
WHIPPLE, H. D., *Making Citizens of the Mentally Limited* (A Curriculum for Special Classes). Public School Publishing Co., Bloomington, Ill., 1927.
Some Uses of School Assemblies (Pamphlet), The Lincoln School of Teachers College, 425 W. 123d St., N. Y., 1922.
WAGNER, *Assembly Programs*, A. S. Barnes & Co., 1930.

COFFIN, *Some Uses of Elementary School Assemblies,* Bulletin of the Dept. of Elementary School Principals, Jan., 1930, Vol. IX, No. 2.
GALVIN, E. H., and WALKER, M. E., *Assemblies for Junior and Senior High Schools,* Professional and Technical Press, 420 Lexington Ave., N. Y., 1929.
BENTON, CAROLINE, *A Little Cook Book for A Little Girl,* Page.
KEELOR, KATHERINE, *Working with Electricity,* Macmillan Co., N. Y.
DOBBS, ELLA V., *Our Playhouse,* Rand McNally Co., Chicago.
CRAIG, G. S., *Tentative Course of Study in Elementary Science,* Bureau of Publications, Teachers College, Columbia University, N. Y.
GARRETT, LAURA S., *Study of Animal Families in Schools,* Bulletin Number 2, Bureau of Educational Experiments, N. Y., 144 West 13th St., N. Y.
STEVENS, MARION P., *Primary Equipment;* A Classified List of Primary Furnishings and Apparatus and Materials with Descriptive Notes, Ethical Culture School, 33 Central Park West, New York City.

VISUAL AND AUDITORY INSTRUCTION

DORRIS, *Visual Instruction in the Public School,* Ginn & Co., Boston, 1929.
ELLIS, DON CARLOS, and THORNBOROUGH, LAURA, *Motion Pictures in Education,* The Thomas Y. Crowell Co., N. Y., 1923.
WEBER, JOSEPH J., *Visual Aids in Education,* Valparaiso Univ., Valparaiso, Indiana, 1930 (Mimeographed).
Report of the Advisory Committee on Education by Radio, United States Office of Education, Washington, D. C.
WOOD, BEN D., and FREEMAN, F. N., *Motion Pictures in the Classroom,* The Houghton Mifflin Co., Boston, 1929.

ELEMENTARY SCHOOL TEXT BOOKS

ARITHMETIC

Washburne Individual Arithmetics, The World Book Co., Yonkers-on-the-Hudson, Books 1 to 12. Suitable for individual progress.
EVERLY, L. L., *Oral Drill Books in Arithmetic,* Public School Publishing Co., Bloomington, Ill.
Modern-School Individual Number Cards, (combinations), World Book Co., Yonkers-on-the-Hudson, N. Y.
Economy Remedial Exercise Cards, Scott, Foresman Co., Chicago.

NATURE AND SCIENCE

New-World Science Series, World Book Co., Yonkers-on-the-Hudson, N. Y.
   WASHBURNE, C. W., *Common Science.*
   STOUT, A. B., *Gardening.*
   LOEVENGUTH, *General Science Syllabus.*
   RITCHIE, J. W., *Human Physiology.*
   RITCHIE, J. W., *Sanitation and Physiology.*
   FALL, D., *Science for Beginners.*
   MOSELEY, E. L., *Trees, Stars, and Birds.*
WASHBURNE, CARLETON W., *Common Science,* World Book Co., Yonkers-on-the-Hudson, N. Y.

BIBLIOGRAPHY

SHIRLING, ALBERT E., *Outdoor Adventures,* World Book Co., Yonkers-on-the-Hudson, N. Y., 1928.

ENGLISH

CLARK, M. G., *Language in Use,* Clark Language Series, Public School Publishing Co., Bloomington, Ill.
SMITH, JAMES H. ,and BAGLEY, W. C., *The Mastery Spellers,* D. C. Heath & Co., N. Y., 1929.
Washburne Individual Speller, World Book Co., Yonkers-on-the-Hudson. Suitable for individual progress.
CARPENTER, J. H., and HOBEN, ALICE M., *Fairy Grammar,* E. P. Dutton & Co., Inc., N. Y., 1920.
Ten Books for First Year Reading with Work Books. Books for Grades III to VI, published by Harold Rugg, Teachers College, Columbia University, N. Y.
MILLER, OLIVE B., *The Bookhouse,* The Bookhouse for Children, Publishers, Chicago.
Story and Study Readers, Johnson Publishing Co., N. Y.
HANNA PAUL, and BARRY, MARY ELIZABETH, *Wonder Flights of Long Ago,* D. Appleton & Co., N. Y., 1930.
HOBEN, ALICE M., *Knights, New and Old,* D. Appleton & Co., N. Y., 1929.
TIPPETT, JAMES S., *The Singing Farmer,* World Book Co., Yonkers-on-the-Hudson, N. Y. Provides supplementary reading based on farm and farm animals.
——, *Busy Carpenters,* World Book Co., Yonkers-on-the-Hudson, N. Y. Provides supplementary reading based on carpentry activities.

GEOGRAPHY

JORDAN, D. A., and CATHER, K. D., *High Lights of Geography—North America, Europe,* World Book Co., Yonkers-on-the-Hudson, N. Y. Suitable for geographical reference material.
Children of the World Series, The World Book Co., Yonkers-on-the-Hudson, N. Y.
PRICE, OLIVIA, *The Middle Country,* China.
PRATT-CHADWICK, and LAMPREY, *The Alo Man* (Congo), World Book Co., Yonkers-on-the-Hudson, N. Y., 1927.
CURTIS, EDWARD S., *In the Land of the Headhunters* (Indian Life), The World Book Co., Yonkers-on-the-Hudson, N. Y., 1919.
SALISBURY, ETHEL, *From Panama to Cape Horn* (South America), The World Book Co., Yonkers-on-the-Hudson, N. Y., 1927.
GREGORY, J. W. and BOWMAN, ISAIAH, *Africa,* A Geography Reader, Rand McNally & Co., Chicago, 1928.
McGOVNEY, DUDLEY ODELL, *Stories of Long Ago in the Philippines,* World Book Co., Yonkers-on-the-Hudson, N. Y., 1925.
HUNTINGTON, E., and CUSHING, S. W., *Modern Business Geography,* World Book Co., Yonkers-on-the-Hudson, N. Y. Suitable for geographical reference.

HISTORY AND SOCIAL STUDIES

RUGG, HAROLD, Social Studies Text, each with an appropriate work book, published by Ginn & Co., N. Y., 1930.
An Introduction to American Civilization.

Changing Civilizations in the Modern World.
A History of American Civilization.
A History of American Government and Culture.
SCHECK AND ORTON, *Directed History Study,* World Book Co., Yonkers-on-the-Hudson, N. Y.
CHADSEY, WEINBERG and MILLER, *America in the Making,* D. C. Heath & Co., N. Y., 1927.
WEINBERG, SCOTT and HOLSTON, *The World We Live In,* D. C. Heath & Co., N. Y.
Pioneer Life Series, World Book Co., Yonkers-on-the-Hudson, N. Y.
  MEEKER, *Ox Team Days on the Oregon Trail.*
  WILSON, *The White Indian Boy.*
  STOKES, *Deadwood Gold.*
  MCCONNELL, *Frontier Law.*
  RYDELL, *On Pacific Frontiers.*
SCHWARTZ, JULIA AUGUSTA, *From Then Till Now,* The World Book Co., Yonkers-on-the-Hudson, N. Y., 1930.
In the Days of William the Conqueror, Lothrop, Lee & Shepard, Boston.
In the Days of Alfred the Great, Lothrop, Lee & Shepard Co., Boston.
In the Days of Queen Elizabeth, Lothrop, Lee & Shepard Co., Boston, 1902.
In the Days of Queen Victoria, Lothrop, Lee & Shepard, Boston.

BOOKS OF SPECIAL INTEREST

ADAMS, JOHN, *Modern Developments in Educational Practice,* Harcourt Brace & Co., N. Y.
ANONYMOUS, *A Mother's Letters to a Schoolmaster,* Knopf.
BAGLEY, *Education, Crime and Social Progress,* The Macmillan Co., N. Y., 1930.
BOBBITT, *The Curriculum,* Houghton Mifflin Co., Boston, 1918.
BONSER and MOSSMAN, *Industrial Arts in the Elementary Schools,* The Macmillan Co., N. Y., 1927.
BONSER, *The Elementary School Curriculum,* The Macmillan Co., N. Y., 1921.
BUHLER, CHARLOTTE, *The First Year of Life,* The John Day Co., N. Y.
Bureau of Educational Research, University of Illinois, *Two Illustrations of Curriculum Construction,* by W. S. MONROE, D. A. HINDMAN, and R. S. LUNDIN, Urbana, Ill., 1928.
CHARTERS, *Curriculum Construction,* The Macmillan Co., N. Y., 1923.
COBB, STANWOOD, *The New Leaven,* The John Day Co., N. Y., 1929.
COOK, H. C., *The Play Way,* Frederick A. Stokes Co., N. Y.
Department of Superintendence, N. E. A., Third Yearbook, *Research in Constructing the Elementary School Curriculum,* 1925.
FERRIERE, ADOLPH, *The Activity School,* The John Day Co., N. Y., 1928.
FOX, FLORENCE, *Major Projects in Elementary Schools,* U. S. Bureau of Education, Bulletin 1921, No. 36.
HAMILTON, A. E., *Boyways,* The John Day Co., N. Y.
HARAP, *The Technique of Curriculum Making,* The Macmillan Co., N. Y., 1928.
HENDERSON, *Materials and Methods in the Middle Grades,* Ginn & Co., Boston, 1928.
HILLEGAS, BRIGGS, and others, *The Classroom Teacher,* The Classroom Teacher, Inc., Chicago, 1927.

JOHNSON, H. M., *Children in the Nursery School,* The John Day Co., N. Y., 1928.
JOHNSON, MARIETTA, *Youth in a World of Men,* The John Day Co., N. Y., 1929.
KILPATRICK, W. H., *Education for a Changing Civilization,* The Macmillan Co., N. Y., 1926.
LEWIS, MARY H., *An Adventure with Children,* Macmillan Co., N. Y., 1928.
MATEER, F., *Just Normal Children,* D. Appleton & Co., N. Y., 1929.
MCMURRY, *How to Organize the Curriculum,* The Macmillan Co., N. Y., 1923.
MEARNS, HUGHES, *Creative Power,* Doubleday, Doran & Co., N. Y., 1930.
———, *Creative Youth,* Doubleday, Doran & Co., N. Y., 1925.
MIRICK, G. A., *Progressive Education,* Houghton Mifflin Co., Boston, 1923.
MOORE, A. E., *The Primary School,* Houghton Mifflin Co., Boston, 1925.
MOSSMAN, L. C., *Principles of Teaching and Learning in Elementary Schools,* Houghton Mifflin Co., 1928.
O'SHEA, *The Child, His Nature and His Needs,* A Contribution of the Children's Foundation, N. Y., 1924.
PALMER, A. R., *Progressive Practices in Directing Learning,* The Macmillan Co., N. Y., 1929.
RICH, *Projects in All the Grades,* A. Flanagan Co., Chicago, 1925.
RUGG, H. O. and SHUMAKER, ANN, *The Child-Centered School,* The World Book Co., Yonkers-on-the-Hudson, 1928.
———, *Culture and Education in America,* Harcourt Brace Co., N. Y., 1931.
SMITH, E. R., *Education Moves Ahead,* Little Brown & Co., Boston, 1926.
SMITH, *The Heart of the Curriculum,* Doubleday, Page & Co., Garden City, N. Y. 1924.
STORMZAND, M. J., *Progressive Methods in Teaching,* Houghton Mifflin Co., 1922.
WASHBURNE and STEARNS, *Better Schools,* The John Day Co., N. Y., 1928.
WELLS, *A Project Curriculum,* J. B. Lippincott Co., Philadelphia, 1921.
YEOMANS, E., *Shackled Youth,* Atlantic Monthly Press, Boston, 1921.

SOME STANDARD TEXTS IN EDUCATION

BAGLEY, W. C., *Classroom Management,* The Macmillan Co., N. Y., 1922.
BOBBITT, *The Curriculum,* Houghton Mifflin Co., Boston, 1918.
BURTON, W. H., *The Nature and Direction of Learning,* D. Appleton & Co., 1929.
DEWEY, JOHN, *Interest and Effort,* Houghton Mifflin Co., Boston.
———, *School and Society,* University of Chicago Press, Chicago.
GREENE and JORGENSEN, *The Use and Interpretation of Educational Tests,* Longmans Greene & Co.
HOLLEY, C. E., *The Teacher's Technique,* The Century Co., N. Y., 1922.
KLAPPER, PAUL, *Contemporary Education,* D. Appleton & Co., N. Y., 1929.
MONROE, DEVOSS and KELLEY, *Educational Tests and Measurements,* Houghton Mifflin Co., Boston, 1917.
REED, *Psychology of the Elementary School Subjects,* Ginn & Co., N. Y., 1927.
STRAYER, G. D., *A Brief Course in the Teaching Process,* The Macmillan Co., N. Y., 1922.

THE
JOHN DAY

ARISE FOR IT IS DAY.

COMPANY
INC.